Operatioı ıs and
ıpply Management

Business Management H5

Compiled by Ollie Jones
Leeds Metropolitan University

PEARSON

Harlow, England • London • New York • Boston • San Francisco • Toronto • Sydney • Auckland • Singapore • Hong Kong
Tokyo • Seoul • Taipei • New Delhi • Cape Town • Sao Paulo • Mexico City • Madrid • Amsterdam • Munich • Paris • Milan

Pearson Education Limited
Edinburgh Gate
Harlow
Essex CM20 2JE

And associated companies throughout the world

Visit us on the World Wide Web at:
www.pearson.com/uk

© 2014 Published by Pearson Education Limited

ISBN 978 1 78016 441 0

Printed and bound in Great Britain.

Contents

OPERATIONS AND PROCESSES

Introduction

Operations and process management is about how organizations produce goods and services. Everything you wear, eat, use or read comes to you courtesy of the operations managers who organized its production, as does every bank transaction, hospital visit and hotel stay. The people who produced them may not always be called operations managers, but that is what they really are. Within the operations function of any enterprise, operations managers look after the processes that produce products and services. But managers in other functions, such as Marketing, Sales and Finance, *also* manage processes. These processes often supply internal 'customers' with services such as marketing plans, sales forecasts, budgets, and so on. In fact

parts of all organizations are made up of processes. That is what this book is about – the tasks, issues and decisions that are necessary to manage processes effectively, both within the operations function and in other parts of the business where effective process management is equally important. This is an introductory chapter, so we will examine some of the basic principles of operations and process management. The model that is developed to explain the subject is shown in Figure 1.1.

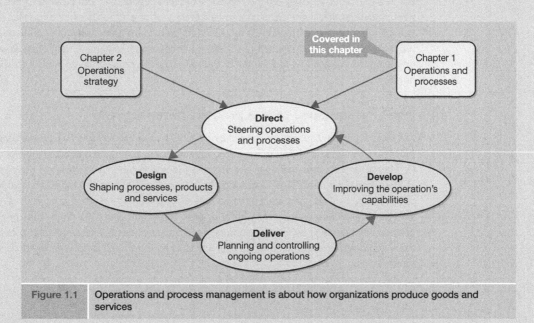

| Figure 1.1 | Operations and process management is about how organizations produce goods and services |

Executive summary

VIDEO
further detail

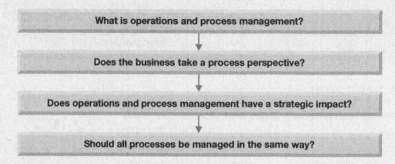

What is operations and process management?

Does the business take a process perspective?

Does operations and process management have a strategic impact?

Should all processes be managed in the same way?

Decision logic chain for operations and processes

Each chapter is structured around a set of diagnostic questions. These questions suggest what you should ask in order to gain an understanding of the important issues of a topic, and as a result, improve your decision making. An executive summary, addressing these questions, is provided below.

What is operations and process management?

The operations function is the part of the organization that produces products or services. Every organization has an operations function because every organization produces some mixture of products and services. 'Operations' is not always called by that name, but whatever its name, it is always concerned with managing the core purpose of the business – producing some mix of products and services. Processes also produce products and services, but on a smaller scale. They are the component parts of operations. But other functions also have processes that need managing. In fact *every* part of *any* business is concerned with managing processes. All managers have something to learn from studying operations and process management, because the subject encompasses the management of all types of operation, no matter in what sector or industry, and all processes, no matter in which function.

Does the business take a process perspective?

A 'process perspective' means understanding businesses in terms of all their individual processes. It is only one way of modelling organizations, but it is a particularly useful one. Operations and process management uses the process perspective to analyze businesses at three levels: the operations function of the business, the higher and more strategic level of the supply network, and a lower, more operational, level of individual processes. Within the business, processes are only what they are defined as being. The boundaries of each process can be drawn as thought appropriate. Sometimes this involves radically reshaping the way processes are organized, for example to form end-to-end processes that fulfil customer needs.

Does operations and process management have a strategic impact?

Operations and process management can make or break a business. When they are well managed, operations and processes can contribute to the strategic impact of the business in four ways: cost, revenue, investment and capabilities. Because the operations function has responsibility for much of a business's cost base, its first imperative is to keep costs under control. But also, through the way it provides service and quality, it should be looking to enhance the business's ability to generate revenue. Also, because operations are often the source of much investment, it should be aiming to get the best possible return on that investment. Finally, the operations function should be laying down the capabilities that will form the long-term basis for future competitiveness.

Should all processes be managed in the same way?

Not necessarily. Processes differ, particularly in what are known as the four Vs: volume, variety, variation and visibility. High volume processes can exploit economies of scale and be systematized. High variety processes require enough inbuilt flexibility to cope with the wide variety of activities expected of them. High variation processes must be able to change their output levels to cope with highly variable and/or unpredictable levels of demand. High visibility processes add value while the customer is 'present' in some way and therefore must be able to manage customers' perceptions of their activities. Generally high volume together with low variety, variation and visibility facilitate low cost processes, while low volume together with high levels of variety, variation and visibility all increase process costs. Yet in spite of these differences, operations managers use a common set of decisions and activities to manage them. These activities can be clustered under four groupings: directing the overall strategy of the operation, designing the operation's products, services and processes, planning and controlling process delivery, and developing process performance.

What is operations and process management?

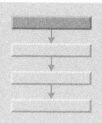

Operations and process management is the activity of managing the resources and processes that produce products and services. The core body of knowledge for the subject comes from 'operations management', which examines how the 'operations function' of a business produces products and services for external customers. We also use the shorter terms 'the operation' or 'operations' interchangeably with the 'operations function'. In some organizations an operations manager could be called by some other name, for example a 'fleet manager' in a logistics company, an 'administrative manager' in a hospital, or a 'store manager' in a supermarket.

All businesses have 'operations', because all businesses produce products, services, or some mixture of both. If you think that you don't have an operations function, you are wrong. If you think that your operations function is not important, you are also wrong. Look at the six businesses illustrated in Figure 1.2. There are two financial service companies, two manufacturing companies and two hotels. All of them have *operations functions* that produce the things that their customers are willing to pay for. Hotels produce accommodation services, financial services invest, store, move or sell us money and investment opportunities, and manufacturing businesses physically change the shape and the nature of materials to produce products. These businesses are from different sectors (banking, hospitality, manufacturing, etc.), but the main differences between their operations activities are not necessarily what one expects. There are often bigger differences *within* economic sectors than *between* them. All the three operations in the left-hand column of the figure provide value-for-money products and services and compete largely on cost. The three in the right-hand column provide more 'up-market' products and services that are more expensive to produce and compete on some combination of high specification and customization. The implication of this is important. It means that the surface appearance of a business and its economic sector are less important to the way its operations should be managed than its intrinsic characteristics, such as the volume of its output, the variety of different products and services it needs to produce, and, above all, how it is trying to compete in its market.

> **Operations principle**
> All organizations have 'operations' that produce some mix of products and services.

> **Operations principle**
> The economic sector of an operation is less important in determining how it should be managed than its intrinsic characteristics.

Operations *and process* management

Within the operations shown in Figure 1.2, resources such as people, computer systems, buildings and equipment will be organized into several individual 'processes'. A 'process' is an arrangement of resources that transforms inputs into outputs that satisfy (internal or external) customer needs. So, amongst other processes, banking operations contain account management processes, hotel operations contain room cleaning

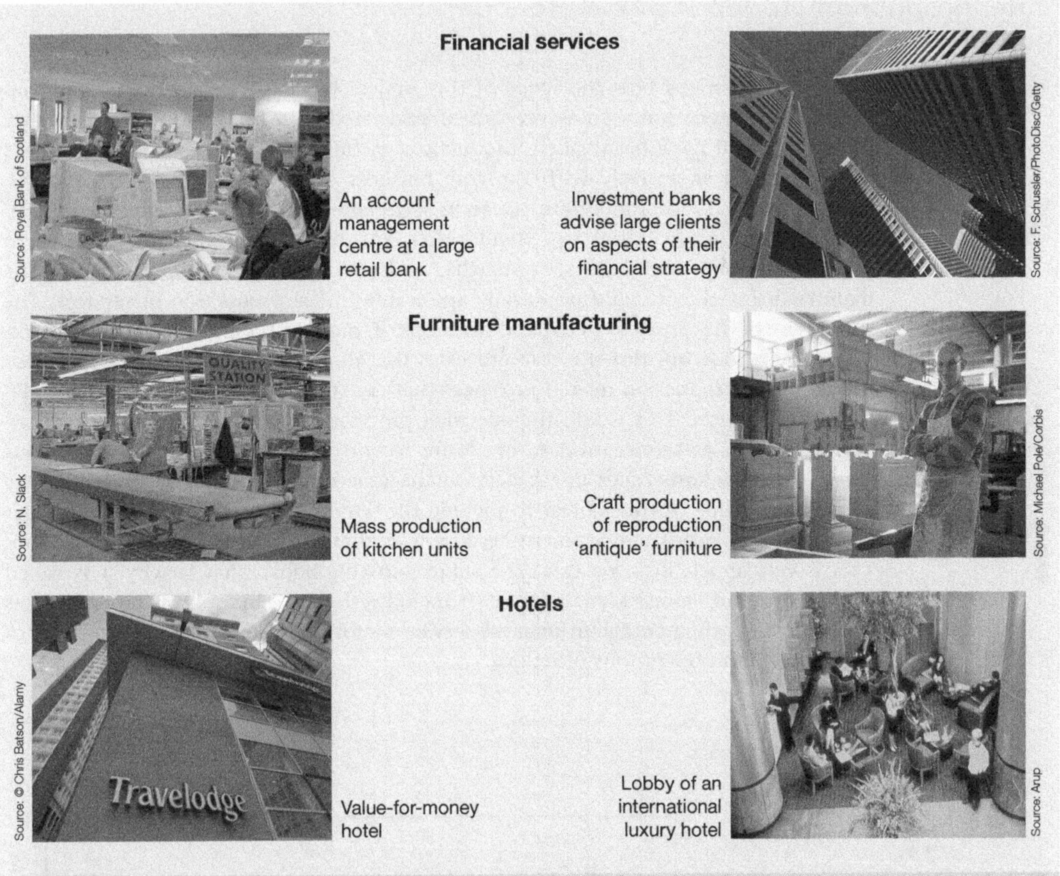

Financial services

An account management centre at a large retail bank

Investment banks advise large clients on aspects of their financial strategy

Furniture manufacturing

Mass production of kitchen units

Craft production of reproduction 'antique' furniture

Hotels

Value-for-money hotel

Lobby of an international luxury hotel

Source: Royal Bank of Scotland
Source: F. Schussler/PhotoDisc/Getty
Source: N. Slack
Source: Michael Pole/Corbis
Source: © Chris Batson/Alamy
Source: Arup

| Figure 1.2 | All types of business have 'operations' because all businesses produce some mix of products and services. And the differences in the operations within a category of business are often greater than the differences between businesses |

processes, furniture manufacturing operations contain assembly processes, and so on. The difference between *operations* and *processes* is one of scale, and therefore complexity. Both transform inputs into outputs, but processes are the smaller version. They are the component parts of operations, so the total operations function is made up of individual processes. But, within any business, the production of products and services is not confined to the operations function. For example, the marketing function 'produces' marketing plans and sales forecasts, the accounting function 'produces' budgets, the human resources function 'produces' development and recruitment plans, and so on. In fact *every* part of *any* business is concerned with managing processes. And operations and process management is the term we use to encompass the management of all types of operation, no matter in what sector or industry, and all processes, no matter in which function of the business. The general truth is that processes are everywhere, and all types of manager have something to learn from studying operations and process management.

From 'production', to 'operations', to 'operations and process' management

Figure 1.3 illustrates how the scope of this subject has expanded. Originally, operations management was seen as very much associated with the manufacturing sector. In fact it would have been called 'production' or 'manufacturing' management, and was concerned exclusively with the core business of producing physical products. Starting in the 1970s and 1980s, the term *operations management* became more common. It was used to reflect two trends. First, and most importantly, it was used to imply that many of the ideas, approaches and techniques traditionally used in the manufacturing sector could be equally applicable in the production of services. The second use of the term was to expand the scope of 'production' in manufacturing companies to include not just the core processes that directly produce products, but also the non-core production-related processes that contribute to the production and delivery of products. This would include such processes as purchasing, physical distribution, after-sales service, and so on. More recently the term *operations and process management* (or sometimes just process management) has been used to denote the shift in the scope of the subject to include the whole organization. It is a far wider term than operations management because it applies to all parts of the organization. This is very much how we treat the subject in this book. That is why it is called 'Operations and *Process* Management'. It includes the examination of the operations function in both manufacturing and service sectors and also the management of processes in non-operations functions.

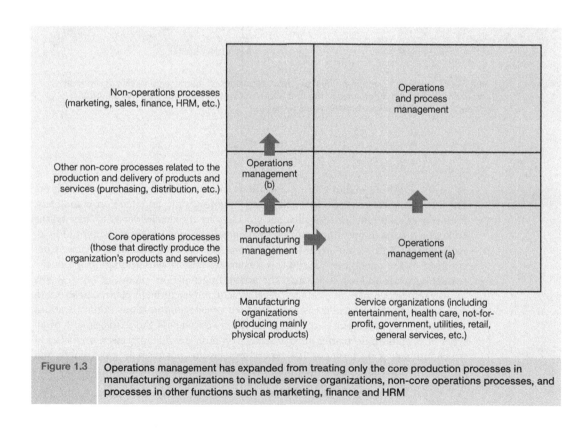

| Figure 1.3 | Operations management has expanded from treating only the core production processes in manufacturing organizations to include service organizations, non-core operations processes, and processes in other functions such as marketing, finance and HRM |

Towards the beginning of all chapters we present two examples of individual businesses, or types of business, that illustrate the topic being examined in the chapter. Here we look at two businesses – one service company and one manufacturing company – which have succeeded partly because of their creative approach to operations and process management.

IKEA[1]

Love it or hate it, IKEA is the most successful furniture retailer ever. With 276 stores in 36 countries, most of them in Europe, the USA, Canada, Asia and Australia, they have managed to develop their own special way of selling furniture. Their stores' layout means customers often spend two hours in the store – far longer than in rival furniture retailers. IKEA's philosophy goes back to the original

Source: Vario Images GmbH & Co./Alamy

business, started in the 1950s in Sweden by Ingvar Kamprad. He built a showroom on the outskirts of Stockholm where land was cheap and simply set out the furniture as it would be in a domestic setting. Also, instead of moving the furniture from the warehouse to the showroom area, he asked customers to pickup the furniture from the warehouse themselves – still the basis of IKEA's process today.

Source: Jim Lai/AFP/Getty

The stores are all designed to facilitate the smooth flow of customers, from parking, moving through the store itself, to ordering and picking up goods. At the entrance to each store large notice-boards provide advice to shoppers who have not used the store before. There is a supervised children's play area, a small cinema, a parent and baby room and toilets. Parents can leave their children in the supervised play area for a time and are recalled via the loudspeaker system if the child has any problems. IKEA 'allows customers to make up their minds in their own time' but 'information points' have staff who can help. All furniture carries a ticket with a code number which indicates its location in the warehouse. (For larger items customers go to the information desks for assistance.) There is also an area where smaller items are displayed and can be picked directly. Customers then pass through the warehouse where they collect the items viewed in the showroom. Finally, customers pay at the checkouts, where a ramped conveyor belt moves purchases up to the checkout staff. The exit area has service points and a loading area that allows customers to bring their cars from the car park and load their purchases.

But success brings its own problems and some customers became increasingly frustrated with overcrowding and long waiting times. In response IKEA in the UK launched a £150,000,000 programme in 2006 to 'design out' the bottlenecks. The changes include:

- clearly marked in-store short cuts allowing customers who want to visit just one area to avoid having to go through all the preceding areas
- express checkout tills for customers with a bag only rather than a trolley
- extra 'help staff' at key points to assist customers
- redesign of the car parks, making them easier to navigate
- dropping the ban on taking trolleys out to the car parks for loading (originally implemented to stop vehicles being damaged)
- a new warehouse system to stop popular product lines running out during the day
- more children's play areas.

IKEA spokeswoman Nicki Craddock said: *'We know people love our products but hate our shopping experience. We are being told that by customers every day, so we can't afford not to make changes. We realized a lot of people took offence at being herded like sheep on the long route around stores. Now if you know what you are looking for and just want to get in, grab it and get out, you can.'*

Example Operations at Virgin Atlantic[2]

The airline business is particularly difficult to get right. Few businesses can cause more customer frustration and few businesses can lose their owners so much money. This is because running an airline, and also running the infrastructure on which the airlines depend, is a hugely complex business, where the difference between success and failure really is how you manage your operations on a day-by-day basis. In this difficult business environment one of the most successful airlines, and one whose reputation has grown because of the way it manages its operations, is Virgin Atlantic. Part of Sir Richard Branson's Virgin group, Virgin Atlantic Airways was founded in 1984 and is owned 51 per cent by the Virgin Group and 49 per cent by Singapore Airlines. Now, the airline flies over 5,000,000 passengers each year to 30 destinations worldwide with a fleet of 38 aircraft and almost 10,000 employees.

In many ways, Virgin Atlantic can be seen as being representative of the whole Virgin story – a small newcomer taking on the giant and complacent establishment while introducing better services and lower costs for passengers, yet also building a reputation for quality and innovative service development. The company's mission statement is 'to grow a profitable airline, that people love to fly and where people love to work', and a commitment to service excellence that is reflected in the many awards it has won.

Virgin Atlantic's reputation includes a history of service innovation. It spent £100,000,000 installing its revolutionary new Upper Class suite that provides the longest and most comfortable flat bed and seat in airline history. It was also the first airline to offer business class passengers individual TVs back in 1989. It now has one of the most advanced in-flight entertainment systems of any airline with over 300 hours of video content, 14 channels of audio, over 50 CDs, audio books, and computer games on demand. The new Upper Class wing recently launched at London's Heathrow airport has a dedicated security channel exclusively for the use of Virgin Atlantic customers, enabling business passengers to speed through the terminal, moving from limousine to lounge in minutes.

Virgin Atlantic emphasizes the practical steps it is taking to make its business as sustainable as possible, using the slogan 'we recycle exhaustively, especially our profits'. This refers to the pledge given by the company's chairman, Sir Richard Branson, to invest profits over the next 10 years from the Virgin transport companies into projects to tackle climate change. *'We must rapidly wean ourselves off our dependence on coal and fossil fuels,'* Sir Richard said. *'The funds will be invested in schemes to develop new renewable energy technologies, through an investment unit called Virgin Fuels.'* Friends of the Earth welcomed Sir Richard's announcement, but the environmental pressure group also warned that the continued rapid growth in air travel could not be maintained 'without causing climatic disaster'.

What do these two examples have in common?

All the operations managers in IKEA and Virgin Atlantic will be concerned with the same basic task – managing the processes that produce their products and services. And many, if not most, of the managers in each company who are called by some other title will also be concerned with managing their own processes that contribute to the success of their business. Although there will be differences between each company's operations and processes, such as the type of services they provide, the resources they use, and so on, the managers in each company will be making the same *type* of decisions, even if *what* they actually decide is different. The fact that both companies are successful because of their innovative and effective operations also implies further commonality. First, it means that they both understand the importance of taking a 'process perspective' in understanding their supply networks, running their operations, and managing all their individual processes. Without this they could not have sustained their strategic impact in the face of stiff market competition. Second, both businesses will expect their operations to make a contribution to their overall competitive strategy. And third, in achieving a strategic impact, both will have come to understand the importance of managing *all* their individual processes throughout the business so that they too can all contribute to the business's success.

Does the business take a process perspective?

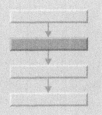

If a business takes a process perspective, it understands that all parts of the business can be seen as processes, and that all processes can be managed using operations management principles. But it is also important to understand that a process perspective is not the only way of describing businesses, or any type of organization. One could represent an organization as a conventional 'organizational structure' that shows the reporting relationships between various departments or groups of resources. But even a little experience in any organization shows that rarely, if ever, does this fully represent the organization. Alternatively one could describe an organization through the way it makes decisions – how it balances conflicting criteria, weighs up risks, decides on actions and learns from its mistakes. Or one could describe the organization's culture – its shared values, ideology, pattern of thinking and day-to-day rituals, or its power relationships – how it is governed, seeks consensus (or at least reconciliation), and so on. Or one can represent the organization as a collection of processes, interconnecting and (hopefully) all contributing to fulfilling its strategic aims. This is the perspective that we emphasize throughout this book. As we define it here, the process perspective analyzes businesses as a collection of interrelated processes. Many of these processes will be within the operations function, and will contribute directly to the production of its products and services. Other processes will be in the other functions of the business, but will still need managing using similar principles to those within the operations function. None of these individual perspectives gives a total picture of real organizations, but nor are they necessarily mutually exclusive. A process perspective does not preclude understanding the influence of power relationships on how processes work, and so on. Each perspective adds something to our ability to understand and therefore more effectively manage a business.

> **Operations principle**
> There are many valid approaches to describing organizations. The process perspective is a particularly important one.

We use the process perspective here, not because it is the only useful and informative way of understanding businesses, but because it is the perspective that directly links the way we manage resources in a business with its strategic impact. Without effective process management, the best strategic plan can never become reality. The most appealing promises made to clients or customers will never be fulfilled. Also the process perspective has traditionally been undervalued. The subject of operations and process management has only recently come to be seen as universally applicable and, more importantly, universally valuable.

So, operations and process management is relevant to all parts of the business

If processes exist everywhere in the organization, operations and process management will be a common responsibility of all managers irrespective of which function they are

in. Each function will have its 'technical' knowledge, of course. In Marketing this includes the market expertise needed for designing and shaping marketing plans; in Finance it includes the technical knowledge of financial reporting conventions. Yet each will also have an *operations* role that entails using its processes to produce plans, policies, reports and services. For example, the marketing function has processes with inputs of market information,

staff, computers, and so on. Its staff transform the information into outputs such as marketing plans, advertising campaigns and sales force organizations. In this sense all functions are operations with their own collection of processes.

The implications of this are very important. Because every manager in all parts of an organization is, to some extent, an operations manager, they should all want to give good service to their customers, and they will all want to do this efficiently. So, operations management must be relevant for all functions, units and groups within the organization. And the concepts, approaches and techniques of operations management can help to improve any process in any part of the organization.

The 'input–transformation–output' model

Central to understanding the processes perspective is the idea that all processes transform *inputs* into *outputs*. Figure 1.4 shows the *general transformation process model* that is used to describe the nature of processes. Put simply, processes take in a set of input resources, some of which are transformed into outputs of products and/or services and some of which do the transforming.

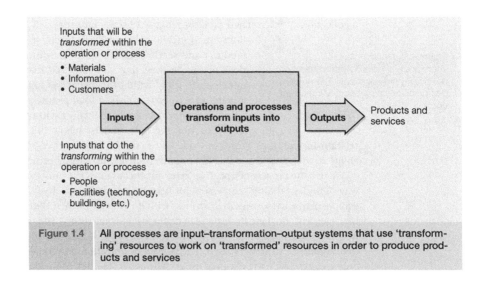

Figure 1.4 All processes are input–transformation–output systems that use 'transforming' resources to work on 'transformed' resources in order to produce products and services

Process inputs

Transformed resource inputs are the resources that are changed in some way within a process. They are usually materials, information or customers. For example, one process in a bank prints statements of accounts for its customers. In doing so, it is processing materials. In the bank's branches, customers are processed by giving them advice regarding their financial affairs, cashing their cheques, etc. However, behind the scenes, most of the bank's processes are concerned with processing information about its customers' financial affairs. In fact, for the bank's operations function as a whole, its information transforming processes are probably the most important. As customers, we may be unhappy with badly printed statements and we may even be unhappy if we are not treated appropriately in the bank. But if the bank makes errors in our financial transactions, we suffer in a far more fundamental way.

There are two types of *transforming* resource that form the 'building blocks' of all processes. They are *facilities* – the buildings, equipment, plant and process technology of the operation – and *people* – who operate, maintain, plan and manage the operation.

The exact nature of both facilities and people will differ between processes. In a five-star hotel, the facilities consist mainly of buildings, furniture and fittings. In a nuclear-powered aircraft carrier, the facilities are the nuclear generator, turbines and sophisticated electronic detection equipment. Although one operation is relatively 'low-technology' and the other 'high-technology', their processes all require effective, well-maintained facilities. People also differ between processes. Most staff employed in a domestic appliance assembly process may not need a very high level of technical skill, whereas most staff employed by an accounting firm in an audit process are highly skilled in their own particular 'technical' skill (accounting). Yet although skills vary, all staff have a contribution to make to the effectiveness of their operation. An assembly worker who consistently misassembles refrigerators will dissatisfy customers and increase costs just as surely as an accountant who cannot add up.

Process outputs

All processes produce products and services, and although products and services are different, the distinction can be subtle. Perhaps the most obvious difference is in their respective tangibility. Products are usually tangible (you can physically touch a television set or a newspaper) whereas services are usually intangible (you cannot touch consultancy advice or a haircut, although you may be able to see or feel the results). Also, services may have a shorter stored life. Products can usually be stored for a time – some food products for only a few days, and some buildings for hundreds of years. But the life of a service is often much shorter. For example, the service of 'accommodation in a hotel room for tonight' will 'perish' if it is not sold before tonight – accommodation in the same room tomorrow is a different service.

The three levels of analysis

Operations and process management uses the process perspective to analyze businesses at three levels. The most obvious level is that of the business itself, or more specifically the operations function of the business. The other functions of the business could also be treated at this level, but that would be beyond the scope of this book. And, while analyzing

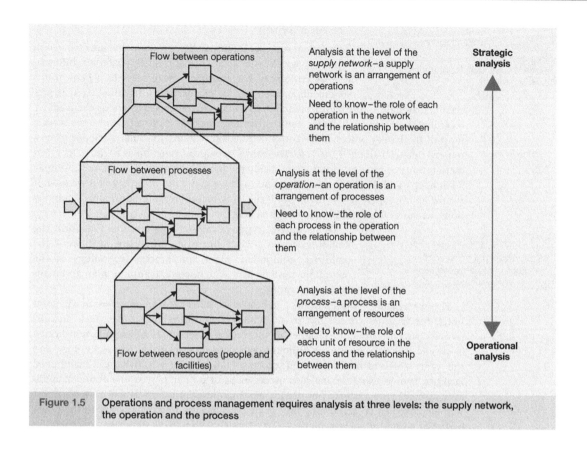

Analysis at the level of the *supply network*–a supply network is an arrangement of operations

Need to know–the role of each operation in the network and the relationship between them

Strategic analysis

Analysis at the level of the *operation*–an operation is an arrangement of processes

Need to know–the role of each process in the operation and the relationship between them

Analysis at the level of the *process*–a process is an arrangement of resources

Need to know–the role of each unit of resource in the process and the relationship between them

Operational analysis

Figure 1.5 | Operations and process management requires analysis at three levels: the supply network, the operation and the process

---

Operations principle
A process perspective can be used at three levels: the level of the operation itself, the level of the supply network and the level of individual processes.

the business at the level of the operation is important, for a more comprehensive assessment we also need to analyze the contribution of operations and process management at a higher and more strategic level (the level of its supply network) and at a lower, more operational level (the level of the individual processes). These three levels of operations analysis are shown in Figure 1.5.

The process perspective at the level of the operation

The operations part of a business is itself an input–transformation–output system, which transforms various inputs to produce (usually) a range of different products and services. Table 1.1 shows some operations described in terms of their main inputs, the purpose of their operations, and their outputs. Note how some of the inputs to the operation are transformed in some way while other inputs do the transforming. For example, an airline's aircraft, pilots, air crew and ground crew are brought into the operation in order to act on passengers and cargo and change (transform) their location. Note also how in some operations customers themselves are inputs. (The airline, department store and police department are all like this.) This illustrates an important distinction between operations whose customers receive their outputs without seeing inside the operation, and those whose customers are inputs to the operation and therefore have some visibility of the operation's processes. Managing high-visibility operations where the customer is inside the operation

12

Table 1.1	Some operations described in terms of their inputs, purpose and outputs		
Type of operation	What are the operation's inputs?*	What does the operation do?	What are the operation's outputs?
Airline	Aircraft Pilots and air crew Ground crew *Passengers* *Cargo*	Move passengers and freight around the world	Transported passengers and freight
Department store	*Goods for sale* Staff sales Computerized registers *Customers*	Display goods Give sales advice Sell goods	Customers and goods 'assembled' together
Police department	Police officers Computer systems *Information* *Public (law-abiding and criminal)*	Prevent crime Solve crime Apprehend criminals	Lawful society Public with feeling of security
Frozen food manufacturer	*Fresh food* Operators Food-processing equipment Freezers	Food preparation Freeze	Frozen food

*Input resources that are transformed are printed in *italics*.

usually involves a different set of requirements and skills from those whose customers never see inside the operation. (We will discuss this issue of visibility later in this chapter.)

Most operations produce both products and services

Some operations produce just products and others just services, but most operations produce a mixture of the two. Figure 1.6 shows a number of operations positioned in a spectrum from almost 'pure' goods producers to almost 'pure' service producers. Crude oil producers are concerned almost exclusively with the product that comes from their oil wells. So are aluminium smelters, but they might also produce some services such as technical advice. To an even greater extent, machine tool manufacturers produce services such as technical advice and applications engineering services as well as products. The services produced by restaurants are an essential part of what the customer is paying for. They both manufacture food and provide service. A computer systems services company may produce software 'products', but more so, it is providing an advice and customization service to its customers. A management consultancy, although producing reports and documents, would see itself largely as a service provider. Finally, some pure services do not produce products at all. A psychotherapy clinic, for example, provides therapeutic treatment for its customers without any physical product.

> **Operations principle**
> Most operations produce a mixture of tangible products and intangible services.

Services and products are merging

Increasingly the distinction between services and products is both difficult to define and not particularly useful. Even the official statistics compiled by governments have difficulty in separating products and services. Software sold on a disk is classified as a product.

13

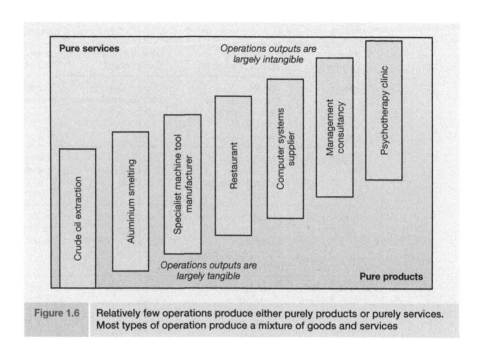

| Figure 1.6 | Relatively few operations produce either purely products or purely services. Most types of operation produce a mixture of goods and services |

The same software sold over the Internet is a service. Some authorities see the essential purpose of all businesses, and therefore all operations, as being to 'serve customers'. Therefore, they argue, all operations are service providers who may (or may not) produce products as a means of serving their customers. Our approach in this book is close to this. We treat operations and process management as being important for all organizations. Whether they see themselves as manufacturers or service providers is very much a secondary issue.

FURTHER EXAMPLE

The process perspective at the level of the supply network

Any operation can be viewed as part of a greater network of operations. It will have operations that supply it with the products and services it needs to make its own products and services. And unless it deals directly with the end consumer, it will supply customers who themselves may go on to supply their own customers. Moreover, any operation could have several suppliers and/or several customers and may be in competition with other operations producing similar services to those it produces itself. This collection of operations is called the supply network.

There are three important issues to understand about any operation's supply network. First, it can be complex. Operations may have a large number of customers and suppliers who themselves have large numbers of customers and suppliers. Also, the relationships between operations in the supply network can be subtle. One operation may be in direct competition with another in some markets while at the same time acting as collaborators or suppliers to each other in others. Second, theoretically the boundaries of any operation's supply chain can be very wide indeed. They could go back to the operation that digs raw material out of the ground and go forward to the ultimate reuse and/or disposal of a product. Sometimes it is necessary to do this (for example, when considering the environmental sustainability of products), but generally some kind of boundary to the network needs to be set so that more attention can be given to the most immediate operations in the network. Third, supply networks are always changing. Not only do operations sometimes lose customers and win others, or change their suppliers, they also may acquire operations that once were their customers or suppliers, or sell parts of their business, so converting them into customers or suppliers.

Thinking about operations management in a supply network context is a particularly important issue for most businesses. The overarching question for any operations manager is 'Does my operation make a contribution to the supply network as a whole?'. In other words, are we a good customer to our suppliers in the sense that the long-term cost of supply to us is reduced because we are easy to do business with? Are we good suppliers to our customers in the sense that, because of our understanding of the supply network as a whole, we understand their needs and have developed the capability to satisfy them? Because of the importance of the supply network perspective, we deal with it twice more in this book: at a strategic level in Chapter 3 where we discuss the overall design of the supply network, and at a more operational level in Chapter 7 where we examine the role of the supply chain in the delivery of products and services.

The process perspective at the level of the individual process

Because processes are smaller versions of operations, they have customers and suppliers in the same way as whole operations. So we can view any operation as a network of individual processes that interact with each other, with each process being, at the same time, an internal supplier and an internal customer for other processes. This 'internal customer' concept provides a model to analyze the internal activities of an operation. If the whole operation is not working as it should, we may be able to trace the problem back along this internal network of customers and suppliers. It can also be a useful reminder to all parts of the operation that, by treating their internal customers with the same degree of care that they exercise on their external customers, the effectiveness of the whole operation can be improved.

Many of the examples used in our treatment of operations and process management are 'operations processes' in that they are part of the operations function. But some are

Table 1.2	Some examples of processes in non-operations functions		
Organizational function	Some of its processes	Outputs from its process	Customer(s) for its outputs
Marketing and sales	Planning process Forecasting process	Marketing plans Sales forecasts	Senior management Sales staff, planners, operations
	Order taking process	Confirmed orders	Operations, finance
Finance and accounting	Budgeting process Capital approval processes Invoicing processes	Budget Capital request evaluations Invoices	Everyone Senior management, requestees External customers
Human resources management	Payroll processes Recruitment processes Training processes	Salary statements New hires Trained employees	Employees All other processes All other processes
Information technology	Systems review process Help desk process System implementation project processes	System evaluation Advice Implemented working systems and aftercare	All other processes All other processes All other processes

'non-operations processes' and are part of some other function. And it is worth emphasizing again that these processes also need managing, using the same principles. Table 1.2 illustrates just some of the processes that are contained within some of the more common non-operations functions, the outputs from these processes and their 'customers'.

'End-to-end' business processes

There is one particularly important thing to understand about processes – we can define them in any way we want. The boundaries between processes, the activities that they perform, and the resources that they use are all there because they have been designed in that way. It is common in organizations to find processes defined by the type of activity they engage in, for example invoicing processes, product design processes, sales processes, warehousing processes, assembly processes, painting processes, etc. This can be convenient because it groups similar resources together. But it is only one way of drawing the boundaries between processes. Theoretically, in large organizations there must be almost an infinite number of ways that activities and resources could be collected together as distinct processes. One way of redefining the boundaries and responsibilities of processes is to consider the 'end-to-end' set of activities that satisfies defined customer needs. Think about the various ways in which a business satisfies its customers. Many different activities and resources will probably contribute to 'producing' each of its products and services. Some authorities recommend grouping the activities and resources together in an end-to-end manner to satisfy each defined customer need. This approach is closely identified with the 'business process engineering' (or re-engineering) movement (examined in Chapter 13). It calls for a radical rethink of process design that will probably involve taking activities and resources out of different functions and placing them together to meet customer needs. Remember, though, that designing processes around end-to-end customer needs is only one way (although often the sensible one) of designing processes.

> **Operations principle**
> Processes are defined by how the organization chooses to draw process boundaries.

FURTHER EXAMPLE

The Programme and Video Division (PVD)

A broadcasting company has several divisions including various television and radio channels (entertainment and news), a 'general services' division that includes a specialist design workshop, and the 'Programme and Video Division' (PVD) that makes programmes and videos for a number of clients including the television and radio channels that are part of the same company. The original ideas for these programmes and videos usually come from the clients who commission them, although PVD itself does share in the creative input. The business is described at the three levels of analysis in Figure 1.7.

At the level of the operation
The division produces products in the form of tapes, discs and media files, but its real 'product' is the creativity and 'artistry' captured in the programmes. *'We provide a service,'* says the division's boss, *'that interprets the client's needs (and sometimes their ideas), and transforms them into appealing and appropriate shows. We can do this because of the skills, experience and creativity of our staff, and our state-of-the-art technology.'*

At the level of the supply network
The division has positioned itself to specialize in certain types of product, including children's programmes, wildlife programmes and music videos. *'We did this so that we could develop a high level of expertise in a few relatively high margin areas. It also reduces our dependence on our own broadcasting channels. Having specialized in this way we are better positioned to partner and do*

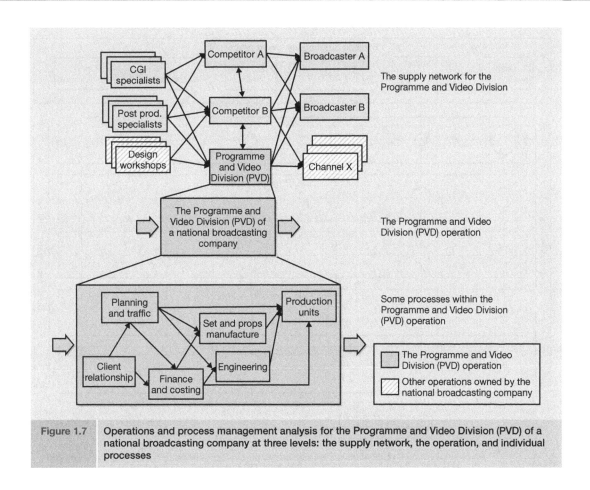

Figure 1.7 | Operations and process management analysis for the Programme and Video Division (PVD) of a national broadcasting company at three levels: the supply network, the operation, and individual processes

work for other programme makers who are our competitors in some other markets. Specialization has also allowed us to outsource some activities such as computer graphic imaging (CGI) and post-production that are no longer worth keeping in-house. However, our design workshop became so successful that they were "spun out" as a division in their own right and now work for other companies as well as ourselves.'

At the level of individual processes

Many smaller processes contribute directly or indirectly to the production of programmes and videos, including the following:

- The planning and traffic department that acts as the operations management for the whole operation, drawing up schedules, allocating resources and 'project managing' each job through to completion
- Workshops that manufacture some of the sets, scenery and props for the productions
- Client liaison staff who liaise with potential customers, test out programme ideas and give information and advice to programme makers
- An engineering department that cares for, modifies and designs technical equipment
- Production units that organize and shoot the programmes and videos
- The finance and costing department that estimates the likely cost of future projects, controls operational budgets, pays bills and invoices customers.

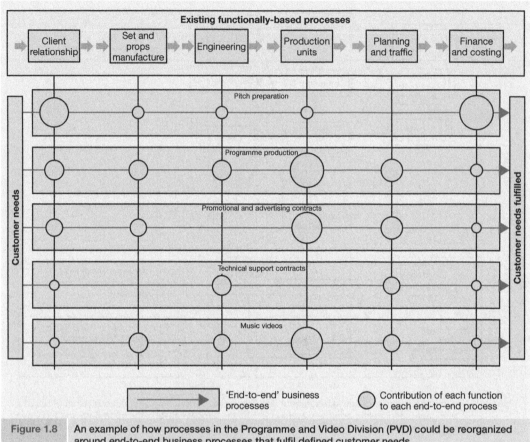

Figure 1.8 An example of how processes in the Programme and Video Division (PVD) could be reorganized around end-to-end business processes that fulfil defined customer needs

Creating end-to-end processes

PVD produces various products and services that fulfil customer needs. Each of these, to different extents, involves several of the existing departments within the company. For example, preparing a 'pitch' (a sales presentation that includes estimates of the time and cost involved in potential projects) needs contributions mainly from Client Relations and the Finance and Costing departments, but also needs smaller contributions from other departments. Figure 1.8 illustrates the contribution of each department to each product or service. (No particular sequence is implied by Figure 1.8.) The contributions of each department may not all occur in the same order. Currently, all the division's processes are clustered into conventional departments defined by the type of activity they perform: engineering, client relationship, etc. A radical redesign of the operation could involve regrouping activities and resources into five 'business' processes that fulfil each of the five defined customer needs. This is shown diagrammatically by the dotted lines in Figure 1.8. It would involve the physical movement of resources (people and facilities) out of the current functional processes into the new end-to-end business processes. This is an example of how processes can be designed in ways that do not necessarily reflect conventional functional groupings.

Does operations and process management have a strategic impact?

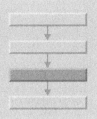

One of the biggest mistakes a business can make is to confuse 'operations' with 'operational'. Operational is the opposite of strategic; it means detailed, localized, short-term, day-to-day. Operations are the resources that produce products and services.[3] Operations can be treated at an operational *and a strategic* level. We shall examine some views of operations strategy in the next chapter. For now, we treat a fundamental question for any operation – does the way we manage operations and processes have a strategic impact? If a business does not fully appreciate the strategic impact that effective operations and process management can have, at the very least it is missing an opportunity. The IKEA and Virgin Atlantic examples earlier in this chapter are just two of many businesses that have harnessed their operations to create strategic impact.

Operations and process management can make or break a business. Although for most businesses, the operations function represents the bulk of its assets and the majority of its people, the true value of the operation is more than 'bulk'. It can 'make' the business in the sense that it gives the ability to compete through both the short-term ability to respond to customers and the long-term capabilities that will keep it ahead of its competitors. But if an operations function cannot produce its products and services effectively, it could 'break' the business by handicapping its performance no matter how it positions and sells itself in its markets.

Cost, revenue, investment and capability

The strategic importance of operations and process management is being increasingly recognized. It attracts far more attention than it did a few years ago and, according to some reports, accounts for the largest share of all the money spent by businesses on consultancy advice.[4] Partly this may be because the area has been neglected in the past. But it also denotes an acceptance that it can have both short-term and long-term impact. This can be seen in the impact that operations and process management can have on the costs, revenues, investment and capabilities of businesses.

- It can reduce the **costs** of producing products and services by being efficient. The more productive the operation is at transforming inputs into outputs, the lower will be the cost of producing a unit of output. Cost is never totally unimportant for any business, but generally the higher the cost of a product or service when compared with the price it commands in the market, the more important cost reduction will be as an operations objective. Even so, cost reduction is almost always treated as an important contribution that operations can make to the success of any business.
- It can increase **revenue** by increasing customer satisfaction through quality, service and innovation. Existing customers are more likely to be retained and new customers are more likely to be attracted to products and services if they are error-free and appropriately designed, if the operation is fast and responsive in meeting their needs and keeping its delivery promises, and if the operation can be flexible, both in customizing its products and services and in introducing new ones. It is operations that directly

influence the quality, speed, dependability and flexibility of the business, all of which have a major impact on a company's ability to maximize its revenue.

- It can ensure **effective investment** (called *capital employed)* to produce its products and services. Eventually all businesses in the commercial world are judged by the return that they produce for their investors. This is a function of profit (the difference between costs and revenues) and the amount of money invested in the business's operations resources. We have already established that effective and efficient operations can reduce costs and increase revenue, but what is sometimes overlooked is their role in reducing the investment required per unit of output. Operations and process management does this by increasing the effective capacity of the operation and by being innovative in how it uses its physical resources.

> **Operations principle**
> All operations should be expected to contribute to their business by controlling costs, increasing revenue, making investment more effective and growing long-term capabilities.

- It can **build capabilities** that will form the basis for *future* innovation by building a solid base of operations skills and knowledge within the business. Every time an operation produces a product or a service, it has the opportunity to accumulate knowledge about how that product or service is best produced. This accumulation of knowledge should be used as a basis for learning and improvement. If so, in the long term, capabilities can be built that will allow the operation to respond to future market challenges. Conversely, if an operations function is simply seen as the mechanical and routine fulfilment of customer requests, then it is difficult to build the knowledge base that will allow future innovation.

FURTHER EXAMPLE

Example **The Programme and Video Division (PVD) continued**

The PVD, described earlier, should be able to identify all four ways in which its operations and processes can have a strategic impact. The division is expected to generate reasonable returns by controlling its costs and being able to command relatively high fees. *'Sure, we need to keep our costs down. We always review our budgets for bought-in materials and services. Just as important, we measure the efficiency of all our processes, and we expect annual improvements in process efficiency to compensate for any increases in input costs.* (Reducing costs) *Our services are in demand by customers because we are good to work with,'* says the division's Managing Director. *'We have the technical resources to do a really great job and we always give good service. Projects are completed on time and within budget. More importantly, our clients know that we can work with them to ensure a high level of programme creativity. That is why we can command reasonably high prices.'* (Increasing revenue) The division also has to justify its annual spend on equipment to its main board. *'We try and keep up to date with the new technology that can really make an impact on our programme making, but we always have to demonstrate how it will improve profitability.* (Effective investment) *We also try to adapt new technology and integrate it into our creative processes in some way so that gives us some kind of advantage over our competitors.'* (Build capabilities)

Operations management in not-for-profit organizations

Terms such as *competitive advantage, markets* and *business* that are used in this book are usually associated with companies in the for-profit sector. Yet operations management is also relevant to organizations whose purpose is not primarily to earn profits. Managing operations in an animal welfare charity, hospital, research organization or government department is essentially the same as in commercial organizations. However, the strategic objectives of not-for-profit organizations may be more complex and involve a mixture of political, economic, social and/or environmental objectives. Consequently, there may be a greater chance of operations decisions being made under conditions of conflicting objectives. So, for example, it is the operations staff in a children's welfare department who have to face the conflict between the cost of providing extra social workers and the risk of a child not receiving adequate protection.

FURTHER EXAMPLE

Should all processes be managed in the same way?

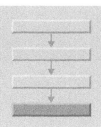

All processes differ in some way, so, to some extent, all processes need to be managed differently. Some of the differences between processes are 'technical' in the sense that different products and services require different skills and technologies to produce them. However, processes also differ in terms of the nature of demand for their products or services. Four characteristics of demand in particular have a significant effect on how processes need to be managed:

> **Operations principle**
> The way in which processes need to be managed is influenced by volume, variety, variation and visibility.

- The volume of the products and services produced
- The variety of the different products and services produced
- The variation in the demand for products and services
- The degree of visibility that customers have of the production of products and services.

The 'four Vs' of processes

Volume

Processes with a high volume of output will have a high degree of repeatability, and because tasks are repeated frequently it often makes sense for staff to specialize in the tasks they perform. This allows the systemization of activities, where standard procedures may be codified and set down in a manual with instructions on how each part of the job should be performed. Also, because tasks are systemized and repeated, it is often worth developing specialized technology that gives higher processing efficiencies. By contrast, low-volume processes with less repetition cannot specialize to the same degree. Staff are likely to perform a wide range of tasks, and while this may be more rewarding, it is less open to systemization. Nor is it likely that efficient, high-throughput technology could be used. The implications of this are that high-volume processes have more opportunities to produce products or services at low unit cost. So, for example, the volume and standardization of large fast-food restaurant chains such as McDonald's or KFC enables them to produce with greater efficiency than a small, local cafeteria or diner.

Variety

Processes that produce a high variety of products and services must engage in a wide range of different activities, changing relatively frequently between each activity. They must also contain a wide range of skills and technology sufficiently 'general purpose' to cope with the range of activities and sufficiently flexible to change between them. A high level of variety may also imply a relatively wide range of inputs to the process and the additional complexity of matching customer requirements to appropriate products or services. So, high-variety processes are invariably more complex and costly than low-variety ones. For example, a taxi company is usually prepared to pick up and drive customers almost anywhere (at a price); they may even take you by the route of your choice. There are an infinite number of potential routes (products) that it offers. But its cost per kilometre travelled will be higher than for a less customized form of transport such as a bus service.

Variation

Processes are generally easier to manage when they only have to cope with predictably constant demand. Resources can be geared to a level that is just capable of meeting demand. All activities can be planned in advance. By contrast, when demand is variable and/or unpredictable, resources will have to be adjusted over time. Worse still, when demand is unpredictable, extra resources will have to be designed into the process to provide a 'capacity cushion' that can absorb unexpected demand. So, for example, processes that manufacture high-fashion garments will have to cope with the general seasonality of the garment market together with the uncertainty of whether particular styles may or may not prove popular. Operations that make conventional business suits are likely to have less fluctuation in demand over time, and be less prone to unexpected fluctuations. Because processes with lower variation do not need any extra safety capacity and can be planned in advance, they generally have lower costs than those with higher variation.

Visibility

Process visibility is a slightly more difficult concept to envisage. It indicates how much of the processes are 'experienced' directly by customers, or how much the process is 'exposed' to its customers. Generally processes that act directly on customers (such as retail or health-care processes) will have more of their activities visible to their customers than those that act on materials and information. However, even material and information-transforming processes may provide a degree of visibility to the customers. For example, parcel distribution operations provide Internet-based 'track and trace' facilities to enable their customers to have visibility of where their packages are at any time. Low-visibility processes, if they communicate with their customers at all, do so using less immediate channels such as the telephone or the Internet. Much of the process can be more 'factory-like'. The time lag between customer request and response could be measured in days rather than the near-immediate response expected from high-visibility processes. This lag allows the activities in a low-visibility process to be performed when it is convenient to the operation, so achieving high utilization. Also, because the customer interface needs managing, staff in high-visibility processes need customer contact skills that shape the customer's perception of process performance. For all these reasons high-visibility processes tend to have higher costs than low-visibility processes.

Many operations have both high- and low-visibility processes. This serves to emphasize the difference that the degree of visibility makes. For example, in an airport some of its processes are relatively visible to its customers (check-in desks, information desks, restaurants, passport control, security staff, etc.). These staff operate in a high-visibility 'front-office' environment. Other processes in the airport have relatively little, if any, customer visibility (baggage handling, overnight freight operations, loading meals on to the aircraft, cleaning, etc.). We rarely see these processes but they perform the vital but low-visibility tasks in the 'back-office' part of the operation.

The implications of the four Vs of processes

FURTHER EXAMPLE

All four dimensions have implications for processing costs. Put simply, high volume, low variety, low variation and low visibility all help to keep processing costs down. Conversely, low volume, high variety, high variation and high customer contact generally carry some kind of cost penalty for the process. This is why the volume dimension is drawn with its 'low' end at the left, unlike the other dimensions, to keep all the 'low cost' implications on the right. Figure 1.9 summarizes the implications of such positioning.

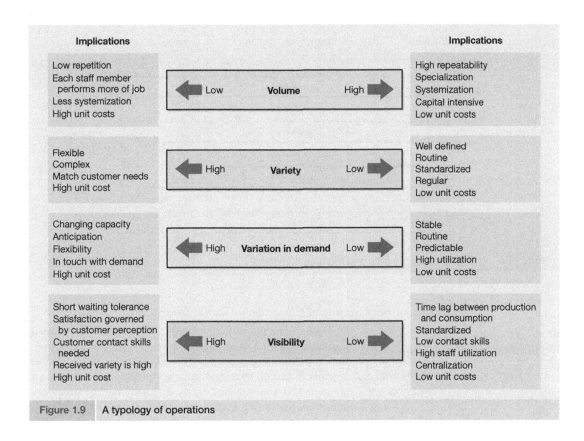

Figure 1.9 A typology of operations

Charting processes using the four Vs

In almost any operation, processes can be identified that have different positions on the four dimensions, and which therefore have different objectives and will need managing in different ways. To a large extent the position of a process on the four dimensions is determined by the demand of the market it is serving. However, most processes have some discretion in moving themselves on the dimensions. Look at the different positions on the visibility dimension that retail banks have adopted. At one time, using branch tellers was the only way customers could contact a bank. Now access to the bank's services could be through (in decreasing order of visibility) a personal banker who visits your home or office, a conversation with a branch manager, the teller at the window, telephone contact through a call centre, Internet banking services or an ATM cash machine. These other processes offer services that have been developed by banks to serve different market needs.

Figure 1.10 illustrates the different positions on the four Vs for some retail banking processes. Note that the personal banking/advice service is positioned at the high-cost end of the four Vs. For this reason such services are often offered only to relatively wealthy customers that represent high profit opportunities for the bank. Note also that the more recent developments in retail banking such as call centres, Internet banking and ATMs all represent a shift towards the low-cost end of the four Vs. New processes that exploit new technologies can often have a profound impact on the implications of each dimension. For example, Internet banking, when compared with an ATM cash machine, offers a far higher variety of options for customers, but because the process is automated through its information technology, the cost of offering this variety is less than at a conventional branch or even a call centre.

PRACTICE NOTE

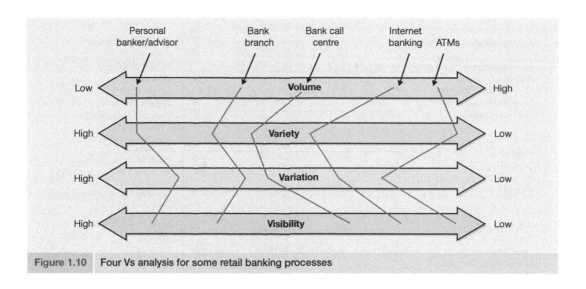

| Figure 1.10 | Four Vs analysis for some retail banking processes |

A model of operations and process management

Operations principle
Operations management activities can be grouped into four broad categories: directing the overall strategy of the operation, designing the operation's products, services and processes, planning and controlling delivery and developing process performance.

Managing operations and processes involves a whole range of separate decisions that will determine their overall purpose, structure and operating practices. These decisions can be grouped together in various ways. Look at other books on operations management and you will find many different ways of structuring operations decisions and therefore the subject as a whole. Here we have chosen to classify activities into four broad groups, relating to four broad activities. Although there are some overlaps between these four categories, they more or less follow a sequence that corresponds to the life cycle of operations and processes.

- **Directing** the overall strategy of the operation. A general understanding of operations and processes and their strategic purpose, together with an appreciation of how strategic purpose is translated into reality (direct), is a prerequisite to the detailed design of operations and process.
- **Designing** the operation's products, services and processes. Design is the activity of determining the physical form, shape and composition of operations and processes together with the products and services that they produce.
- Planning and control process **delivery**. After being designed, the delivery of products and services from suppliers and through the total operation to customers must be planned and controlled.
- **Developing** process performance. Increasingly it is recognized that operations and process managers cannot simply routinely deliver products and services in the same way that they have always done. They have a responsibility to develop the capabilities of their processes to improve process performance.

We can now combine two ideas to develop the model of operations and process management that will be used throughout this book. The first is the idea that *operations* and the *processes* that make up both the operations and other business functions are transformation systems that take in inputs and use process resources to transform them into outputs. The second idea is that the resources both in an organization's operations as a

24

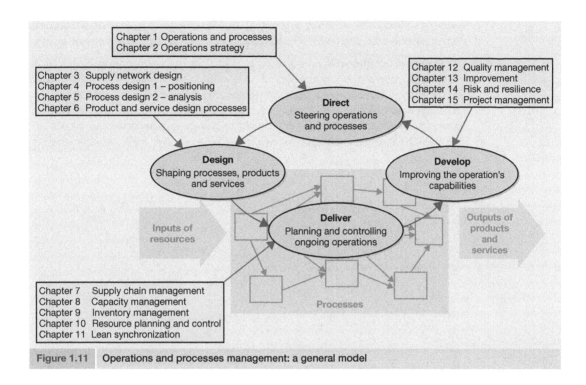

| Figure 1.11 | Operations and processes management: a general model |

whole and in its individual processes need to be managed in terms of how they are *directed*, how they are *designed*, how *delivery* is planned and controlled, and how they are *developed* and improved. Figure 1.11 shows how these two ideas go together. This book will use this model to examine the more important decisions that should be of interest to all managers of operations and processes.

Critical commentary

Each chapter contains a short critical commentary on the main ideas covered in the chapter. Its purpose is not to undermine the issues discussed in the chapter, but to emphasize that, although we present a relatively orthodox view of operations, there are other perspectives.

■ The central idea in this introductory chapter is that all organizations have operations (and other functions) that have processes that produce products and services, and that all these processes are essentially similar. However, some believe that by even trying to characterize organizations in this way (perhaps even by calling them 'processes') one loses or distorts their nature and depersonalizes or takes the 'humanity' out of the way in which we think of the organization. This point is often raised in not-for-profit organizations, especially by 'professional' staff. For example the head of one European 'Medical Association' (a doctors' Trade Union) criticized hospital authorities for expecting a 'sausage factory service based on productivity targets'. No matter how similar they appear on paper, it is argued, a hospital can never be viewed in the same way as a factory. Even in commercial businesses, professionals, such as creative staff, often express discomfort at their expertise being described as a 'process'.

■ To some extent these criticisms of taking such a process perspective are valid. How we describe organizations does say much about our underlying assumptions of what an 'organization' is and how it is supposed to work. Notwithstanding the point we made earlier about how a purely process view can misleadingly imply that organizations are neat and controllable with unambiguous boundaries and lines of accountability, a process perspective can risk depicting the messy reality of organizations in a naive manner. Yet, in our view it is a risk well worth taking.

Summary checklist

DOWNLOADABLE

This checklist comprises questions that can be usefully applied to any type of operations and reflect the major diagnostic questions used within the chapter.

- ☐ Is the operations function of the business clearly defined?
- ☐ Do operations managers realize that they are operations managers even if they are called by some other title?
- ☐ Do the non-operations functions within the business realize that they manage processes?
- ☐ Does everyone understand the inputs, activities and outputs of the processes of which they are part?
- ☐ Is the balance between products and services produced by the operations function well understood?
- ☐ Are future changes that may occur in the balance between products and services produced by the operation understood?
- ☐ What contribution is operations making towards reducing the cost of products and services?
- ☐ What contribution is operations making towards increasing the revenue from products and services?
- ☐ What contribution is operations making towards better use of capital employed?
- ☐ How is operations developing its capability for future innovation?
- ☐ Does the operation understand its position in the overall supply network?
- ☐ Does the operation contribute to the overall supply network?
- ☐ Are the individual processes that comprise the operations function defined and understood?
- ☐ Are individual processes aware of the internal customer and supplier concept?
- ☐ Do they use the internal customer and supplier concept to increase their contribution to the business as a whole?
- ☐ Do they use the ideas and principles of operations management to improve the performance of their processes?
- ☐ Has the concept of end-to-end business processes been examined and considered?
- ☐ Are the differences (in terms of volume, variety, variation and visibility) between processes understood?
- ☐ Are the volume, variety, variation and visibility characteristics of processes reflected in the way they are managed?

AAF Rotterdam

'Our growth over the last two or three years has just been amazing. We have clients all over Europe and although many of the jobs we are now doing are more challenging they are far more interesting. We are also now making a good operating profit, even if almost all of it is being swallowed up to fund our growth. Our biggest problem is now adapting ourselves in a way that is appropriate for a larger company. We aren't just a group of friends having a good time any more; we need to become a professional business.' The speaker was Marco Van Hopen, one of the three directors of AAF, a theatrical services company, based just outside Rotterdam in The Netherlands. He had founded the company with two friends in 1999 when they decided to make a business out of their interest in theatrical and stage design. 'It's the combination of skill and adrenalin that I like,' said Marco. 'Because most events are live there is no chance for a second take; all the equipment must work first time, on time, and every time. Also, there has recently been a dramatic increase in the sophistication of the technology we use, such as programmable automated lighting units.'

Source: Martin Leeuwner, betsy@wedolife.com

Background

From the original three founders of the company, AAF had now grown to employ 16 full-time employees together with over 20 freelance crew, who were hired as and when necessary. In the previous year the company's revenue had been slightly over €3,000,000 and its operating profit slightly under €200,000. It was located on an industrial estate that provided good access to the main European road network. The majority of the company's 2000 square metre building was devoted to a combined storage area and workshop. Also within the site were the administrative and technical offices and a design studio.

The company had started by hiring and selling stage equipment (mainly lighting, sound and staging equipment) to clients that ranged from small local theatrical groups through to very large production and conference companies. Then it had moved into offering 'production services' that included designing, constructing and installing entire sets, particularly for conferences but also for shows and theatrical events. The majority of the company's 'production services' clients were production companies that contracted AAF as a 'second-tier' supplier on behalf of the main client, that was usually a corporation putting on its own event (for example, a sales conference). The events organized for the main client could be anywhere in the world, although AAF confined itself to European locations. As Marco Van Hopen says, 'We have succeeded in differentiating ourselves through offering a complete "design, build and install" service that is creative, dependable and sufficiently flexible to incorporate last-minute changes. The key skill is to articulate client requirements and translate these into a workable set design. This means working closely with clients. It also requires a sound technical understanding of equipment capabilities. Most important, every project is different, that's what makes it so exciting.'

Although both parts of the business were growing, it was the production services business that was growing particularly quickly. In the previous year around 60 per cent of the company's revenue had come from hiring and selling equipment, with the remainder coming from production services. However, production services were far more profitable. 'The large production jobs may be 40 per cent of our revenue but last year they accounted for almost 80 per cent of our profits. Some people ask me why we don't focus on production services, but we will never get out of hiring and sales. Partly this is because we have over €1,000,000 invested in the equipment, partly it is because it provides us with a steady and relatively predictable stream of income, but mostly it is because we need access to the latest equipment in order to win production services contracts. However, in the near future our own production services work could be the biggest "customer" for our hire and sales business.' (Van Hopen)

The workshop and store

The combined workshop and storage area was seen as the heart of the company's operations. Equipment was stored on high-level racks in predetermined locations. A team of eight technicians prepared hire equipment for customers and delivered it to customer sites (about 80 per cent of all orders were delivered, the rest being collected from the AAF site by customers themselves). About 30 per cent of customers, usually the smaller ones, also required the equipment to be installed. The technicians also checked the equipment on return from the customer and carried out any repairs or maintenance that was required. As the equipment had become more sophisticated, the job of preparing, installing and maintaining hire equipment had also become far more technically demanding. These technicians used the workshop area, adjacent to the storage area, to calibrate equipment, pre-program lighting sequences and carry out any repairs. The workshop, which had recently been re-equipped with new wood- and metal-working equipment, was also used to construct the sets used for production services' clients. Two employees worked almost full-time on this, but equipment technicians could also be used for set construction if it was required. If workshop facilities were needed by both equipment hire and production services at the same time, usually production services were given priority, an arrangement that was not always to the liking of the equipment hire technicians.

Design studio

The design studio used computer-aided design equipment and simulations that could predict the effects of different lighting configurations. Although Marco Van Hopen was involved in the design process for many jobs, the company now also employed one full-time and one part-time designer: 'We often bring clients to the design studio to test various ideas on them using our simulation and projection facilities. It is a great way to get clients to visualize the set design and "bring them into" the design process.'

Administrative and crew offices

The administration office received orders from hire and sales customers as well as providing the first point of contact for production services' clients. Three full-time employees organized the company's operations, sched-uled work for the workshop and crew, sent out invoices and generally managed the business. In addition two part-time account assistants were employed to do cost estimates for the more complex 'production services' jobs. Adjacent to the administrative office was the 'crew office', an area for the production crew to plan the logistics required to ensure efficient installation of sets. 'The crew office is the nerve centre of all the project management that goes into a good service. It is a focal point for designers, workshop people and crew to come together.' (Van Hopen)

Problems

Although excited by the recent growth of the company and its future prospects, Van Hopen was also concerned that the company should be able to improve its profitability: 'There's no point in growing and doing exciting things if we can't also make money out of it. I realize that, by its nature, growth is expensive. However, I think maybe that we have let our costs slip out of control. We need to be able to get more out of what we already have, and the best way to do this is to get ourselves organized. The main problem is that our activities are getting less predictable. The hire and sales business is basically routine, and although some of our clients can be late in placing their orders, it is largely predictable. Not only do we have a wide range of equipment, we also have excellent relationships with other sound and lighting companies, so that, if we can only partially fulfil a customer's order, we can hire any other equipment we need from our competitors. This may reduce our profits slightly, but we keep the client happy. The irony is that we don't seem to be able to achieve similar levels of flexibility within our own company. This is important now that production services are growing quickly. We have fewer production services contracts (48 last year, compared with almost 3000 hire contracts) but they are complex and you cannot always predict exactly what you will need to complete them. We have succeeded in growing the production services business partly because of the quality of our designs where we put a lot of time and effort into working closely with the client before we submit a final design, but also because we have built up a reputation for dependability. Clients trust us to be totally reliable. This means that sometimes our crews have to be flexible and sometimes work through the night in order to get things ready on time. But we are paying for this flexibility in terms of excessive hours worked. What we perhaps should consider is improving the agility with which we move people out of the store and workshop area and on to fulfilling production services contracts when necessary. I don't know how it would work yet, I just feel that by working together more we could increase our ability to take on more work without increasing our cost base.'

QUESTIONS

1 Do you think Marco Van Hopen understands the importance of operations to his business?

2 What contribution does he seem to expect from his operations?

3 Sketch out how you see the supply network for AAF and AAF's position within it.

4 What are the major processes within AAF, and how do they relate to each other?

5 Evaluate Van Hopen's idea of increasing the flexibility with which the different parts of the company work with each other.

Active case study   EleXon Computers

ACTIVE CASE

Since its inception 17 years ago, EleXon computers has grown and diversified from a small unit assembling and selling computers primarily within the UK into a much larger international company serving a much wider and more diverse market. Despite its growth, the underlying organization of the company has not changed. The inadequacy of existent systems and processes has become increasingly obvious and increasingly a source of tension within and between departments.

● How would you re-organize the operations and processes to satisfy their differing perspectives and demands?

Please refer to the Active case on the CD accompanying this book to listen to the frustrations of each department.

Applying the principles

HINTS

Some of these exercises can be answered by reading the chapter. Others will require some general knowledge of business activity and some might require an element of investigation. All have hints on how they can be answered on the CD accompanying this book.

1 Quentin Cakes makes about 20,000 cakes per year in two sizes, both based on the same recipe. Sales peak at Christmas time when demand is about 50 per cent higher than in the quieter summer period. The customers (the stores that stock the company's products) order their cakes in advance through a simple Internet-based ordering system. Knowing that there is some surplus capacity, one of the customers has approached the company with two potential new orders.

(a) The *Custom Cake* option – this would involve making cakes in different sizes where consumers could specify a message or greeting to be 'iced' on top of the cake. The consumer would give the inscription to the store which would e-mail it through to the factory. The customer thought that demand would be around 1000 cakes per year, mostly at celebration times such as St Valentine's Day and Christmas.

(b) The *Individual Cake* option – this option involves Quentin Cakes introducing a new line of very small cakes intended for individual consumption. Demand for this individual-sized cake was forecast to be around 4000 per year, with demand likely to be more evenly distributed throughout the year than its existing products.

The total revenue from both options is likely to be roughly the same and the company has the capacity to adopt only one of the two ideas. But which one should it be?

2   Described as having *'revolutionized the concept of sandwich making and eating'*, Prêt A Manger opened its first shop in the mid-1980s, in London. Now it has over 130 shops in the UK, New York, Hong Kong and Tokyo. The company says that its secret is to focus continually on quality, in all its activities. *'Many food retailers focus on extending the shelf life of their food, but that's of no interest to us. We maintain our edge by selling food that simply can't be beaten for freshness. At the end of the day, we give whatever we haven't sold to charity to help feed those who would otherwise go hungry.'* The first Prêt A Manger shop had its own kitchen where fresh ingredients were delivered first thing every morning, and food was prepared throughout the day. Every Prêt shop since has followed this model. The team members serving on the tills at lunchtime will have been making sandwiches in the kitchen that morning. The company rejected the idea of a huge centralized sandwich factory even though it could significantly reduce costs. Prêt also owns and manages all its shops directly so that it can ensure consistently high standards. *'We are determined never to forget that our hardworking people make all the difference. They are our heart and soul. When they care, our business is sound. If they cease to care, our business goes down the drain. We work hard at building great teams. We take our reward schemes and career opportunities very seriously. We don't work nights (generally), we wear jeans, we party!'*

- Do you think Prêt A Manger fully understands the importance of its operations management?
- What evidence is there for this?
- What kind of operations management activities at Prêt A Manger might come under the four headings of direct, design, deliver and develop?

3   Visit a furniture store (other than IKEA). Observe how the shop operates – for example, where customers go, how staff interact with them, how big it is, how the shop has chosen to use its space, what variety of products it offers, and so on. Talk with the staff and managers if you can. Think about how the shop that you have visited is different from IKEA. Then consider the question:

- What implications do the differences between IKEA and the shop you visited have for their operations management?

4   Write down five services that you have 'consumed' in the last week. Try to make these as varied as possible. Examples could include public transport, a bank, any shop or supermarket, attendance at an education course, a cinema, a restaurant, etc. For each of these services, ask yourself the following questions.

- Did the service meet your expectations? If so, what did the management of the service have to do well in order to satisfy your expectations? If not, where did they fail? Why might they have failed?
- If you were in charge of managing the delivery of these services, what would you do to improve the service?
- If they wanted to, how could the service be delivered at a lower cost so that the service could reduce its prices?
- How do you think that the service copes when something goes wrong (such as a piece of technology breaking down)?
- Which other organizations might supply the service with products and services? (In other words, they are your 'supplier', but who are *their* suppliers?)
- How do you think the service copes with fluctuation of demand over the day, week, month or year?

These questions are just some of the issues which the operations managers in these services have to deal with. Think about the other issues they will have to manage in order to deliver the service effectively.

5   Find a copy of a financial newspaper (*Financial Times, The Wall Street Journal, The Economist,* etc.) and identify one company that is described in the paper that day.

- What do you think would be the main operations issues for that company?

Notes on chapter

1 'Ikea plans to end "stressful shopping"' (2006), *London Evening Standard*, 24 April.
2 Source: Virgin Atlantic website.
3 Slack, N. and Lewis, M.A. (2002) *Operations Strategy,* Financial Times Prentice Hall, Harlow, UK.
4 Source: *The Economist,* 22 March 1997.

Taking it further

Chase, R.B., Aquilano, N.J. and Jacobs, F.R. (2001) *Production and Operations Management: Manufacturing and services* (9th edn), Unwin/McGraw-Hill. There are many good general textbooks on operations management. This was one of the first and is still one of the best, though written very much for an American audience.

Hammer, M. and Stanton, S. (1999) *How Process Enterprises Really Work,* Harvard Business Review, November–December Hammer is one of the gurus of process design. This paper is typical of his approach.

Heizer, J. and Render, B. (1999) *Operations Management* (5th edn), Prentice Hall, New Jersey. Another good US-authored general text on the subject.

Johnston, R., Chambers, S., Harland, C., Harrison, A. and Slack, N. (2003) *Cases in Operations Management* (3rd edn), Financial Times Prentice Hall, Harlow, UK. Many great examples of real operations management issues. Not surprisingly, based around a similar structure as this book.

Johnston, R. and Clark, E. (2005) *Service Operations Management,* Financial Times Prentice Hall, Harlow, UK. What can we say! A great treatment of service operations from the same stable as this textbook.

Keen, P.G.W. (1997) *The Process Edge: Creating value where it counts,* Harvard Business School Press. Operations management as 'process' management.

Slack, N. and Lewis, M. (eds) (2005) *The Blackwell Encyclopedic Dictionary of Operations Management* (2nd edn), Blackwell Business, Oxford. For those who like technical descriptions and definitions.

Useful websites

www.opsman.org Definitions, links and opinions on operations and process management.

www.iomnet.org The Institute of Operations Management site. One of the main professional bodies for the subject.

www.poms.org A US academic society for production and operations management. Academic, but some useful material, including a link to an encyclopaedia of operations management terms.

www.sussex.ac.uk/users/dt31/TOMI One of the longest-established portals for the subject. Useful for academics and students alike.

www.ft.com Useful for researching topics and companies.

FURTHER RESOURCES

For further resources including examples, animated diagrams, self-test questions, Excel spreadsheets, active case studies and video materials please explore the CD accompanying this book.

Supply network management

Key questions

➤ Why should an organization take a supply network perspective?

➤ What is involved in managing supply networks?

➤ What is involved in designing a supply network?

➤ What are the types of relationships between operations in supply networks?

➤ What is the 'natural' dynamic of a supply network?

➤ How can supply networks be improved?

Introduction

No operation exists in isolation. Every operation is part of a larger and interconnected *supply network*. These networks not only include suppliers and customers, but also suppliers' suppliers and customers' customers, and so on. As operations outsource many of their activities, the way they manage the supply of services and products is hugely important. At a strategic level, operations managers are involved in 'designing' the shape of their network and determining what to do and what to buy. At a more operational level, operations managers must consider the type of relationships they wish to develop with suppliers, understand the dynamics of their network, and improve their supply networks in order to ultimately satisfy end customers. Figure 7.1 shows where this chapter fits into the overall operations model.

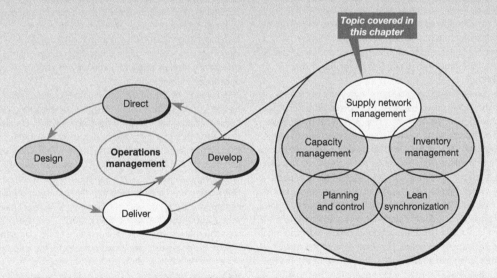

Figure 7.1 This chapter examines supply network management

Check and improve your understanding of this chapter using self-assessment questions and a personalized study plan, audio and video downloads, and an eBook – all at www.myomlab.com.

Operations in practice Dell: no operating model lasts forever[1]

When he was a student at the University of Texas at Austin, Michael Dell's sideline of buying unused stock of PCs from local dealers, adding components, and re-selling the now higher-specification machines to local businesses was so successful that he quit university and founded a computer company which was to revolutionize the industry's supply network management. His fledgling company was just too small to make its own components. Better, he figured to learn how to manage a network of committed specialist component manufacturers and take the best of what was available in the market. Dell says that his commitment to outsourcing was always done for the most positive of reasons. *'We focus on how we can coordinate our activities to create the most value for customers'*. Yet Dell still faced a cost disadvantage against its far bigger competitors, so they decided to sell its computers direct to its customers, bypassing retailers. This allowed the company to cut out the retailer's (often considerable) margin, which in turn allowed Dell to offer lower prices. Dell also realized that cutting out the link in the supply network between them and the customer also provided them with significant learning opportunities to get to know their customers' needs far more intimately. Most importantly it allowed Dell to learn how to run its supply chain so that products could move through the supply chain to the end-customer in a fast and efficient manner, reducing Dell's level of inventory and giving Dell a significant cost advantage.

However, what is right at one time may become a liability later on. Two decades later Dell's growth started to slow down. The irony of this is that, what had been one of the company's main advantages, its direct sales model using the Internet and its market power to squeeze price reductions from suppliers, were starting to be seen as disadvantages. Although the market had changed, Dell's operating model had not. Some commentators questioned Dell's size. How could a $56 billion company remain lean, sharp, and alert? Other commentators pointed out that Dell's rivals had also now learnt to run efficient supply networks. However, one of the main factors was seen as the shift in the nature of the market itself. Sales of PCs to business users had become largely a commodity business with wafer-thin margins, and this part of the market was growing slowly

Source: Corbis/Gianni Giansanti/Sygma

compared to the sale of computers to individuals. Selling computers to individuals provided slightly better margins than the corporate market, but they increasingly wanted up-to-date computers with a high design value, and most significantly, they wanted to see, touch and feel the products before buying them. This was clearly a problem for a company like Dell which had spent 20 years investing in its telephone- and later, internet-based sales channels. What all commentators agreed on was that in the fast-moving and cut-throat computer business, where market requirements could change overnight, operations resources must constantly develop appropriate new capabilities.

However, Michael Dell said it could regain its spot as the world's number one PC maker by switching its focus to consumers and the developing world. He also conceded that the company had missed out on the boom in supplying computers to home users – who make up just 15% of its revenues – because it was focused on supplying businesses. *'Let's say you wanted to buy a Dell computer in a store nine months ago – you'd have searched a long time and not found one. Now we have over 10,000 stores that sell our products.'* He rejected the idea that design was not important to his company, though he accepted that it had not been a top priority when all the focus was on business customers. *'As we've gone to the consumer we've been paying quite a bit more attention to design, fashion, colors, textures and materials.'*

The supply network perspective

Supply network

Supply side
First-tier suppliers
Second-tier suppliers
Demand side

A **supply network** perspective means setting an operation in the context of all the customers and suppliers that interact with it. Materials, parts, information, ideas and people may all flow through the supply network. On its **supply side**, an operation has its suppliers of materials, information or services. These are often called **first-tier suppliers**. These suppliers themselves have their own **second-tier suppliers** who in turn could also have suppliers, and so on. On the **demand side** the operation has customers. These customers might not be the final consumers of the operation's services or products; they might have their own set of customers. 'First-tier' customers are the main customer group for the operation, who in turn supply 'second-tier' customers.

Figure 7.2 illustrates the simplified supply network for two operations. First is a plastic homeware (kitchen bowls, food containers, etc.) manufacturer. Note that on the demand side the homeware manufacturer supplies some of its basic products to wholesalers which supply retail outlets. However, it also supplies some retailers directly with 'made-to-order' products. The second example, an enclosed shopping mall, also has suppliers and customers that themselves have their own suppliers and customers. Along with the flow of services and products in the network, each link in the network will feed back orders and information to its suppliers. It is a two-way process with goods flowing one way and information flowing the other.

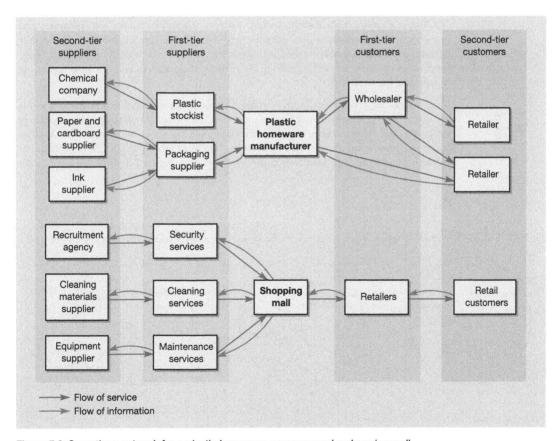

Figure 7.2 Operations network for a plastic homeware company and a shopping mall

Why consider the whole supply network?

There are a number of important reasons for taking a supply network perspective:

It helps an understanding of competitiveness. Immediate customers and immediate suppliers, quite understandably, are the main concern to competitively minded companies. Yet sometimes they need to look beyond these immediate contacts to understand why customers and suppliers act as they do. If it wants to understand its ultimate customers' needs at the end of the network, an operation can and should rely on the intermediate links in the network between itself and its end customers.

Downstream
Upstream

It helps identify significant links in the network. The key to understanding supply networks lies in identifying the parts of the network which contribute to those performance objectives valued by end-customers. Any analysis of networks must start, therefore, by understanding the **downstream** end of the network. After this, the **upstream** parts of the network which contribute most to end-customer service will need to be identified. For example, the important end-customers for domestic plumbing appliances are the installers and service companies that deal directly with domestic consumers. They are supplied by 'stock holders' which must have all parts in stock and deliver them fast. Suppliers of parts to the stock holders can best contribute to their end-customers' competitiveness partly by offering a short delivery lead time but mainly through dependable delivery. The key players in this example are the stock holders. The best way of winning end-customer business in this case is to give the stock holder prompt delivery which helps keep costs down while providing high availability of parts.

It helps focus on long-term issues. There are times when circumstances render parts of a supply network weaker than its adjacent links. A major machine breakdown, for example, or a labour dispute might disrupt a whole network. Should its immediate customers and suppliers exploit the weakness to enhance their own competitive position, or should they tolerate the problems, and hope the customer or supplier will eventually recover? A long-term supply-network view would be to weigh the relative advantages to be gained from assisting or replacing the weak link.

It helps focus on cost. Typically the volume and value of purchased goods and services is increasing as organizations concentrate on their 'core tasks'. *Purchasing has a significant impact on total organizational costs*, thus increasing the impact on an operation's costs. The higher the proportion of procurement costs in relation to total costs, the more profitability can be improved through reduction in procurement costs. Figure 7.3 illustrates this.

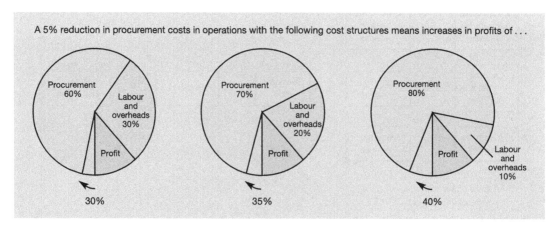

Figure 7.3 Impact of reduced procurement costs on total costs and profit

Designing and managing supply networks

A supply network is all the operations linked together to provide services and products through to the end-customers

A supply chain is a strand of linked operations

Designing and managing **supply networks** is a holistic approach to managing the inter-connection of organizations that combine to produce value to the ultimate consumer in the form of services and products. Within supply networks, there can be many hundreds of strands of linked operations, commonly referred to as **supply chains**. An analogy often used to describe supply chains is that of the 'pipeline'. Just as liquids flow through a pipeline, so services and products flow down a supply chain. Long pipelines will, of course, contain more liquid than short ones, so the time taken for liquid to flow all the way through a long pipeline will be longer.

Some of the terms used in supply network management are not universally applied. Furthermore, some of the concepts behind the terminology overlap in the sense that they refer to common parts of the total supply network (Figure 7.4). *Supply network management* (also called supply chain management) coordinates all the operations on the supply side and the demand side. *Purchasing and supply management* deals with the operation's interface with its supply markets. *Physical distribution management* may mean supplying immediate customers, while *logistics* is an extension that often refers to materials and information flow down through a distribution channel, to the retail store or consumers (increasingly common because of the growth of internet-based retailing). The term *third-party logistics* (TPL) indicates outsourcing to a specialist logistics company. *Materials management* is a more limited term and refers to the flow of materials and information only through the immediate supply network.

Performance objectives of supply networks

The key objective in managing supply networks is the satisfaction of the end-customer. All parts of the network must consider the final customer, no matter how far an individual operation is from them. When customers decide to make a purchase, they trigger action across the whole network. All the businesses in the supply network pass on portions of

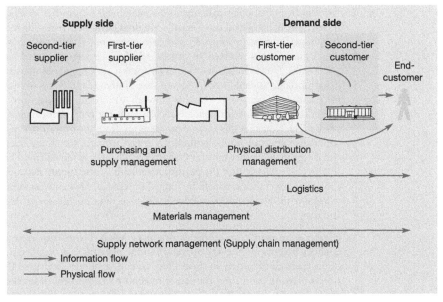

Figure 7.4 Some of the terms used to describe the management of different parts of the supply network

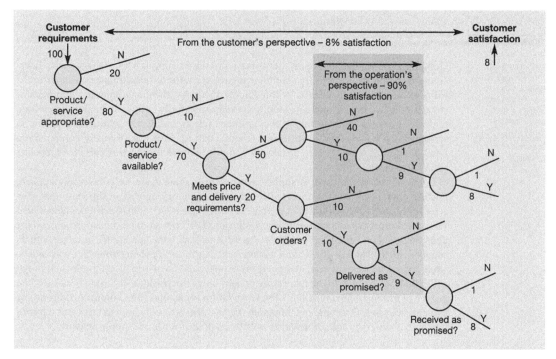

Figure 7.5 Taking a customer perspective of supply network performance can lead to very different conclusions

that end-customer's money to each other, each retaining a margin for the value it has added. Each operation in the network should be satisfying its own customer, but also making sure that eventually the end-customer is satisfied.

For a demonstration of how end-customer perceptions of supply satisfaction can be very different from that of a single operation, examine the customer 'decision tree' in Figure 7.5. It charts the hypothetical progress of a hundred customers requiring service from a business. Supply performance, as seen by the core operation, is represented by the shaded part of the diagram. It has received 20 orders, 18 of which were delivered as promised (on time, and in full). However, of the original customers who requested the service, 20 found it was inappropriate, 10 could not be served due to unavailability, 50 were not satisfied with the price and/or delivery requirements (though 10 did still place an order). So what seems a 90 per cent supply performance is in fact an 8 per cent performance from the customer's perspective. Note that this is just one operation from the operation's perspective. Include the cumulative effect of similar reductions in performance for all the operations in a network, and the probability that the end-customer is adequately served could become remote.

The point here is that the performance both of the supply network as a whole, and its constituent operations, should be judged in terms of how end-customer needs are satisfied, in terms of the five operations performance objectives: quality, speed, dependability, flexibility and cost.

Quality – the quality of a service or product when it reaches the customer is a function of the quality performance of every operation in the network that supplied it. Errors in each stage of the chain can multiply in their effect on end-customer service, so if each of 7 stages in a supply network has a 1 per cent error rate, only 93.2 per cent of services or products will be of good quality on reaching the end-customer. This is why, only by every stage taking some responsibility for its own *and its suppliers'* performance, can a supply network achieve high end-customer quality.

Speed has two meanings in a supply network context. The first is how fast customers can be served. However, fast customer response can be achieved simply by over-resourcing or over-stocking within the network. For example, an accounting firm may be able to respond quickly to customer demand by having a large number of accountants on standby waiting for demand that may (or may not) occur. An alternative perspective on speed is the time taken for services and products to move through the network. So, for example, products that move quickly across a supply network will spend little time as inventory, which in turn reduces inventory-related costs in the network.

Dependability – like speed, one can almost guarantee 'on-time' delivery by keeping excessive resources, such as inventory, within the network. However, dependability of throughput time is a much more desirable aim because it reduces uncertainty. If individual operations do not deliver as promised, there will be a tendency for customers to over-order, or order early, in order to provide some kind of insurance against late delivery. This is why delivery dependability is often measured as 'on time, in full' in supply networks.

Flexibility – in a supply network context, flexibility is usually taken to mean the ability to cope with changes and disturbances. Very often this is referred to as agility. The concept of agility includes previously discussed issues such as focusing on the end-customer and ensuring fast throughput and responsiveness to customer needs. But, in addition, agile supply networks are sufficiently flexible to cope with changes, either in the nature of customer demand or in the supply capabilities of operations within the network.

Cost – in addition to the costs incurred within each operation, the supply network as a whole incurs additional costs that derive from operations doing business with each other. These may include such things as the costs of finding appropriate suppliers, setting up contractual agreements, monitoring supply performance, transporting products between operations, holding inventories, and so on. Many developments in supply network management, such as partnership agreements or reducing the number of suppliers, are attempts to minimize transaction costs.

Short case
Ford Motors' team value management[2]

Source: Getty Images/Getty Images News

Purchasing managers are a vital link between an operation and its suppliers. They work best when teamed up with mainstream operations managers who know what the operation really needs, especially if, between them, they take a role that challenges previous assumptions. That is the basis behind Ford Motor Company's 'team value management' (TVM) approach. Reputedly, it all started when Ford's Head of Global Purchasing, David Thursfield, discovered that a roof rack designed for one of Ford's smaller cars was made of plastic-coated aluminium and capable of bearing a 100 kg load. This prompted the questions, *'Why is this rack covered in plastic? Why would anyone want to put 100 kg on the roof of a car that small?'* He found that no one had ever questioned the original specification. When Ford switched to using steel roof racks capable of bearing a smaller weight, they halved the cost. *'It is important'*, he says, *'to check whether the company is getting the best price for parts and raw material that provide the appropriate level of performance without being too expensive.'* The savings in a large company such as Ford can be huge. Often in multinationals, each part of the business makes sourcing and design decisions independently and does not exploit opportunities for cross-usage of components. The TVM approach is designed to bring together engineering and purchasing staff and identify where cost can be taken out of purchased parts and where there is opportunity for parts commonality (see Chapter 4) between different models. When a company's global purchasing budget is $75bn like Ford's, the potential for cost savings is significant.

Supply network design

Taking a supply network perspective is useful because it prompts a number of important design decisions. These combine to determine how a supply network can operate and its ability to deliver value to customers. These decisions include:

1 Who should do what in the network? How many steps should there be in the network? What is the role of customers, suppliers, complementors and competitors? This is called the network shape decision.
2 How much of the network should the operation own? This is called the do-or-buy, outsourcing or vertical integration decision.
3 How should supply networks be configured when operations compete in different ways in different markets? This is called the supply network matching decision.

The network shape decision

Supply base reduction

Reconfiguring a supply network sometimes involves parts of the operation being merged – not necessarily in the sense of a change of ownership of any parts of an operation, but rather in the way responsibility is allocated for carrying out activities. The most common example of network reconfiguration has come through the many companies that have recently reduced the number of direct suppliers. The complexity of dealing with many thousands of suppliers may both be expensive for an operation and (sometimes more important) prevent the operation from developing a close relationship with a supplier. It is not easy to be close to so many different suppliers.

Disintermediation

Disintermediation

Another trend in some supply networks is that of companies within a network bypassing customers or suppliers to make contact directly with customers' customers or suppliers' suppliers. 'Cutting out the middlemen' in this way is called **disintermediation**. An obvious example of this is the way the Internet has allowed some suppliers to 'disintermediate' traditional retailers in supplying services and products to consumers. So, for example, many services in the travel industry that used to be sold through retail outlets (travel agents) are now also available direct from the suppliers. The option of purchasing the individual components of a vacation through the websites of the airline, hotel, car hire company, etc., is now easier for consumers. Of course, they may still wish to purchase an 'assembled' product from retail travel agents which can have the advantage of convenience.

Co-opetition

One approach to thinking about supply networks sees any business as being surrounded by four types of players: suppliers, customers, competitors and complementors. Complementors enable one's services or products to be valued more by customers because they can also have the complementor's products or services, as opposed to when they have yours alone. Competitors are the opposite: they make customers value your service or product less when they can have their product or service, rather than yours alone. Competitors can also be complementors and vice versa. For example, adjacent restaurants may see themselves as competitors for customers' business. A customer standing outside and wanting a meal will choose between the two of them. Yet, in another way they are complementors. Would that customer have come to this part of town unless there was more than one restaurant to choose from? Restaurants, theatres, art galleries and tourist attractions generally, all cluster together in a form of cooperation to increase the total size of their joint market. It is important to distinguish between the way companies cooperate in increasing the total size of a market and the way in which they then compete for a share of that market. In the long term it creates value for the total network to find ways of increasing value for suppliers and well as customers. All the players in the supply network, whether they are customers, suppliers, competitors or complementors, can be both friends and enemies at different times. The term used to capture this idea is '**co-opetition**'.[3]

The do-or-buy decision

No single business does everything that is required to deliver its services and products. Bakers do not grow wheat or even mill it into flour. Banks do not usually do their own credit checking: they retain the services of specialist agencies that have the information systems and expertise to do it better. Although most companies have always outsourced some of their activities, a larger proportion of direct activities are now being bought from suppliers. In addition, many indirect processes are also being outsourced, often referred to as '**business process outsourcing**' (BPO). Financial service companies in particular are starting to outsource some of their more routine back-office processes. In a similar way many processes within the human resource function, from payroll services through to more complex training and development processes, are being outsourced to specialist companies. The processes may still be physically located where they were before, but the staff and technology are managed by the outsourcing service provider. The reason for doing this is often primarily to reduce cost. However, there can also be significant gains in the quality and flexibility of service offered. Deciding what to do itself in-house and what to outsource is often called the 'do or buy' decision, when individual components or activities are being considered, or the 'vertical integration decision' when it is the ownership of whole operations that is being decided. Vertical integration can be defined in terms of three factors.[4]

1 *The direction of vertical integration.* Should an operation expand by buying one of its suppliers or by buying one of its customers? The strategy of expanding on the supply side of the network is sometimes called 'backward' or 'upstream' vertical integration, and expanding on the demand side is sometimes called 'forward' or 'downstream' vertical integration.

2 *The extent of vertical integration.* How far should an operation take the extent of its vertical integration? Some organizations deliberately choose not to integrate far, if at all, from their original part of the network. Alternatively, some organizations choose to become very vertically integrated.

3 *The balance among stages.* How exclusive should the relationship be between operations? A totally balanced network relationship is one where an operation produces only for the next stage in the network and totally satisfies its requirements. Less than full balance allows each operation to sell its output to other companies or to buy in some of its supplies from other companies.

Making the do-or-buy decision

Whether it is referred to as the do-or-buy, vertical integration or the outsourcing decision, the choice facing operations is rarely simple. Organizations in different circumstances with different objectives are likely to take different decisions. Yet the question itself is relatively simple, even if the decision itself is not: 'Does in-house or outsourced supply in a particular set of circumstances give the appropriate performance objectives that it requires to compete more effectively in its markets?' For example, if the main performance objectives for an operation are dependable delivery and meeting short-term changes in customers' delivery requirements, the key question should be: 'How does in-house or outsourcing give better dependability and delivery flexibility performance?' Table 7.1 summarizes some arguments for in-house supply and outsourcing in terms of each performance objective.

Although the effect of outsourcing on the operation's performance objective is important, there are other factors that companies take into account when deciding if outsourcing an activity is a sensible option. If an activity has long-term **strategic importance** to a company,

Table 7.1 How in-house and outsourced supply may affect an operation's performance objectives

Performance objective	'Do it yourself' in-house supply	'Buy it in' outsourced supply
Quality	The origins of any quality problems are usually easier to trace in-house and improvement can be more immediate but there can be some risk of complacency.	Supplier may have specialized knowledge and more experience, also may be motivated through market pressures, but communication more difficult.
Speed	Can mean synchronized schedules which speeds throughput of materials and information, but if the operation has external customers, internal customers may be low-priority.	Speed of response can be built into the supply contract where commercial pressures will encourage good performance, but there may be significant transport/delivery delays.
Dependability	Easier communications can help dependability, but, if the operation also has external customers, internal customers may be low priority.	Late-delivery penalties in the supply contract can encourage good delivery performance, but organizational barriers may inhibit in communication.
Flexibility	Closeness to real business needs can alert the in-house operation to required changes, but the ability to respond may be limited by the scale and scope of internal operations.	Outsourced suppliers may be larger with wider capabilities and have more ability to respond to changes, but may have to balance conflicting needs of different customers.
Cost	In-house operations do not have to make the margin required by outside suppliers so the business can capture the profits which would otherwise be given to the supplier, but relatively low volumes may mean that it is difficult to gain economies of scale or the benefits of process innovation.	Probably the main reason why outsourcing is so popular. Outsourced companies can achieve economies of scale and they are motivated to reduce their own costs because it directly impacts on their profits, but costs of communication and coordination with supplier need to be taken into account.

it is unlikely to outsource it. For example, a retailer might choose to keep the design and development of its website in-house even though specialists could perform the activity at less cost because it plans to move into web-based retailing at some point in the future. Nor would a company usually outsource an activity where it had specialized skills or knowledge. For example, a company making laser printers may have built up specialized knowledge in the production of sophisticated laser drives. This capability may allow it to introduce product or process innovations in the future. It would be foolish to 'give away' such capability. After these two more strategic factors have been considered, the company's operations performance can be taken into account. Obviously if its operations performance is already superior to any potential supplier, it would be unlikely to outsource the activity. Even if its performance was currently below that of potential suppliers, it may not outsource the activity if it feels that it could significantly improve its performance. Figure 7.6 illustrates this decision logic.

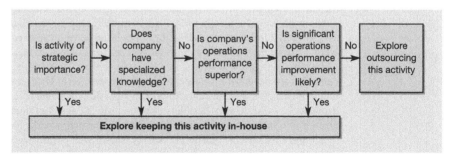

Figure 7.6 The decision logic of outsourcing

Short case
Behind the brand names[5]

The market for notebook computers is a fast-evolving and competitive one. Yet few who buy these products know that the majority of the world's notebooks are made by a small number of Taiwanese and Korean manufacturers. Taiwanese firms alone make around 60 per cent of all notebooks in the world, including most of Dell, Compaq and Apple machines. In a market with unremitting technological innovation and fierce price competition, it makes sense to outsource production to companies that can achieve the economies that come with high-volume manufacture as well as develop the expertise which enables new designs to be put into production without the usual cost overruns and delays. However, the big brand names are keen to defend their products' performance. Dell, for example, admits that a major driver of its outsourcing policy is the requirement to keep costs at a competitive level, but says that it can ensure product quality and performance through

Source: Rex Features

its relationship with its suppliers. *'The production lines are set up by Dell and managed by Dell'*, says Tony Bonadero, Director of Product Marketing for Dell's laptop range. Dell also imposes strict quality control and manages the overall design of the product.

Supply network alignment

An important question for supply managers to consider is 'How should supply networks be configured when operations compete in different ways in different markets?' One answer, proposed by Professor Marshall Fisher of Wharton Business School, is to organize the supply network serving those individual markets in different ways.[6] He points out that many companies have seemingly similar products which, in fact, compete in different ways. Shoe manufacturers may produce classics which change little over the years, as well as fashions which last only one or two seasons. Chocolate manufacturers have stable lines which have been sold for 50 years, but also create 'specials' associated with an event or film release, maybe selling only for a few months. Demand for the former products will be relatively stable and predictable, but demand for the latter will be far more uncertain. Also, the profit margin commanded by the innovative product will probably be higher than that of the more functional product. However, the price (and therefore the margin) of the innovative product may drop rapidly once it has become unfashionable in the market.

Efficient supply networks

Responsive supply networks

The supply network policies which are seen to be appropriate for functional services and products and innovative services and products are termed by Fisher **efficient supply network** policies and **responsive supply network** policies, respectively. Efficient supply network policies include keeping inventories low, especially in the downstream parts of the network, so as to maintain fast throughput and reduce the amount of working capital tied up in the inventory. What inventory there is in the network is concentrated mainly in the manufacturing operation, where it can keep utilization high and therefore manufacturing costs low. Information must flow quickly up and down the chain from retail outlets back up to the manufacturer so that schedules can be given the maximum amount of time to adjust efficiently. The network is then managed to make sure that products flow as quickly as possible down the chain to replenish what few stocks are kept in the network. By contrast, responsive supply policies stress high service levels and responsive supply to the end-customer. The inventory in the network will be deployed as closely as possible to the customer. In this way, the network can still supply even when dramatic changes occur in customer demand. Fast throughput from the upstream parts of the network will still be needed to replenish downstream stocks. But

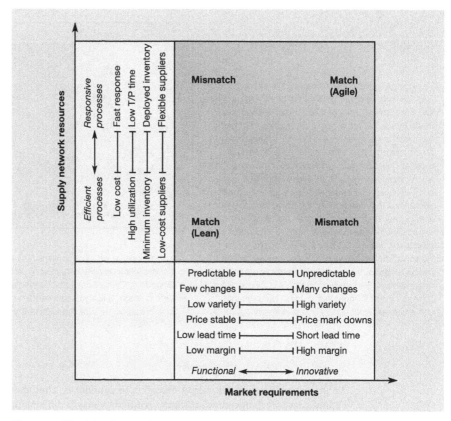

Figure 7.7 Matching the supply network resources with market requirements

Source: Adapted from Fisher, M.C. (1997) What is the right supply chain for your product? *Harvard Business Review*, March–April, 105–16.

those downstream stocks are needed to ensure high levels of availability to end-customers. Figure 7.7 illustrates how the different supply network policies match the different market requirements implied by functional and innovative products.

Types of relationships in supply networks

One of the key issues within a supply network is how relationships with suppliers and customers should be managed. The behaviour of the supply network as a whole is, after all, made up of the relationships which are formed between individual pairs of operations. It is important, therefore, to have some framework which helps us to understand the different ways in which supply relationships can be developed.

Business or consumer relationships?

Business to business
Business to consumer

We can distinguish between relationships that are the final link in the supply network, involving the ultimate consumer, and those involving two commercial businesses (Figure 7.8). So, **business-to-business** (B2B) relationships are by far the most common in a supply network context. **Business-to-consumer** (B2C) relationships include both 'bricks and mortar' retailers

44

	Relationship – to . . .	
	Business	**Consumer (Peer)**
Business	**B2B** *Relationship* • Most common, all but the last link in the supply network *E-commerce examples* • Electronic marketplaces • e.g. b2b Index	**B2C** *Relationship* • Retail operations • Comparison web sites *E-commerce examples* • Online retailers • e.g. Amazon.com
Consumer (Peer)	**C2B** *Relationship* • Consumers offer, business responds *E-commerce examples* • Usually focused on specialist area • e.g. Google Adsense	**C2C (P2P)** *Relationship* • Originally one of the driving forces behind the modern Internet (ARPANET) *E-commerce examples* • File sharing networks (legal and illegal) • e.g. Napster, Gnutella

(left axis label: Relationship – from . . .)

Figure 7.8 The business–consumer relationship matrix

Consumer to business

Customer to customer

and online retailers. **Consumer-to-business** (C2B) relationships involve consumers posting their needs on the web (sometimes stating the price they are willing to pay), and companies then deciding whether to offer. **Customer-to-customer** (C2C) or peer-to-peer (P2P) relationships include the online exchange and auction services and file-sharing services. In this chapter we deal almost exclusively with B2B relationships.

Types of business-to-business relationship

A convenient way of categorizing supply relationships is to examine the extent and nature of what a company chooses to buy in from suppliers. Two dimensions are particularly important – *what* the company chooses to outsource, and *who* it chooses to supply it. In terms of what is outsourced, a key question is, 'how many activities are outsourced?' from doing everything in-house at one extreme, to outsourcing everything at the other extreme. In terms of who is chosen to supply products and services, two questions are important, 'how many suppliers will be used by the operation?' and 'how close are the relationships?' Figure 7.9 illustrates this way of characterizing relationships. It also identifies some of the more common types of relationship and shows some of the trends in how supply relationships have moved.

Traditional market supply relationships

Short-term transactional relationships

The very opposite of performing an operation in-house is to purchase services and products from outside in a 'pure' market fashion, often seeking the 'best' supplier every time it is necessary to purchase. Each transaction effectively becomes a separate decision. The **relationship** between buyer and seller, therefore, can be very short-term. Once the services or products are delivered and payment is made, there may be no further trading between the parties. Short-term relationships may be used on a trial basis when new companies are being considered as more regular suppliers. Also, many purchases which are made by operations are

45

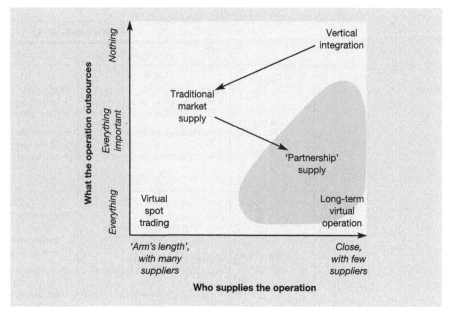

Figure 7.9 **Types of supply chain relationship**

one-off or very irregular. The advantages of traditional market supplier relationships are usually seen as follows:

● They maintain competition between alternative suppliers. This promotes a constant drive between suppliers to provide best value.
● A supplier specializing in a small number of services or products, but supplying them to many customers, can gain natural economies of scale. This enables the supplier to offer the products and services at a lower price than would be obtained if customers performed the activities themselves.
● There is inherent flexibility in outsourced supplies. If demand changes, customers can simply change the number and type of suppliers. This is a far faster and simpler alternative to having to redirect internal activities.
● Innovations can be exploited no matter where they originate. Specialist suppliers are more likely to come up with innovative products and services which can be bought in faster and cheaper than would be the case if the company were itself trying to innovate.
● They help operations to concentrate on their core activities. One business cannot be good at everything. It is sensible therefore to concentrate on the important activities and outsource the rest.

There are, however, disadvantages in buying in a totally 'free market' manner:

● There may be supply uncertainties. Once an order has been placed, it is difficult to maintain control over how that order is fulfilled. This is a particular problem if the buyer is small relative to the supplier, so lacks power to influence their behaviour.
● Choosing who to buy from takes time and effort. Gathering sufficient information and making decisions continually are, in themselves, activities which need to be resourced.
● There are strategic risks in subcontracting activities to other businesses. An over-reliance on outsourcing can 'hollow out' the company, leaving it with few internal capabilities to exploit in its markets.
● Short-term, price-oriented types of relationship can have a downside in terms of ongoing support and reliability. This may mean that a short-term 'least-cost' purchase decision will lead to long-term high cost.

Short case
Northern Foods wins a slice of the in-flight meals business[7]

The companies that provide airline catering services are in a tough business. Meals must be of a quality that is appropriate for the class and type of flight, yet the airlines that are their customers are always looking to keep costs as low as possible, menus must change frequently and the airlines must respond promptly to customer feedback. If this were not enough, forecasting passenger numbers is difficult. Catering suppliers are advised of the likely numbers of passengers for each flight several days in advance, but the actual minimum number of passengers for each class is only fixed six hours before take-off. Also, flight arrivals are sometimes delayed, putting pressure on everyone to reduce the turnaround time, and upsetting work schedules. Even when a flight lands on time no more than 40 minutes are allowed before the flight is ready for take-off again, so complete preparation and a well-ordered sequence of working is essential. It is a specialized business, and in order to maintain a fast, responsive and agile service, airline caterers have traditionally produced food on, or near, airport sites using their own chefs and staff to cook and tray-set meals. The catering companies' suppliers are also usually airline specialists who themselves are located near the caterers so that they can offer very short response times.

The companies that provide catering services may also provide related services. For example, LSG Sky Chefs (a subsidiary of Deutsche Lufthansa AG) is a provider of tailor-made in-flight services for all types of airlines around the world. Their main areas of service are Airline Catering, In-flight Equipment and Logistics and In-flight Management. They are also large, employing 30,000 people at 200 customer service centres in 49 countries. In 2007 they produced 418 million meals for more than 300 airlines, representing more than 30 per cent of the global airline catering market.

The airline sector has over recent years suffered a series of shocks including 9/11, oil price volatility, financial

Specialized companies have developed that prepare food in specialized factories, often for several airlines.

Source: Virgin Atlantic

crises and world recession. This has meant that airlines are reviewing their catering supply solutions. In December 2008 Gate Gourmet, the world's largest independent provider of airline catering lost the contract to supply British Airways' short-haul flights out of Heathrow to new entrants into the airline catering market, a consortium of Northern Foods, a leading food producer, whose normal business is supplying retailers with own-label and branded food, and DHL, a subsidiary of Deutsche Post and the market-leading international express and logistics company. DHL is already a large supplier to 'airside' caterers at Heathrow and already has its own premises at the airport. Northern Foods will make the food at its existing factories and deliver it to DHL, which will assemble onto airline catering trays and transfer them onto aircraft. The new contract is the first time that Northern Foods, whose biggest customer is Marks and Spencer, the UK retail chain, has developed new business outside its normal supermarket customer base.

'Partnership' supply relationships

Partnership relationships **Partnership relationships** in supply networks are sometimes seen as a compromise between vertical integration on the one hand (owning the resources which supply you) and pure market relationships on the other (having only a transactional relationship with those who supply you). Although to some extent this is true, partnership relationships are not only a simple mixture of vertical integration and market trading, although they do attempt to achieve some of the closeness and coordination efficiencies of vertical integration, but at the same time attempt to achieve a relationship that has a constant incentive to improve. Partnership relationships are defined as: *'relatively enduring inter-firm cooperative agreements, involving flows and linkages that use resources and/or governance structures from autonomous organizations, for the joint accomplishment of individual goals linked to the corporate mission of each* *sponsoring firm'.*[8] What this means is that suppliers and customers are expected to cooperate, even to the extent of sharing skills and resources, to achieve joint benefits beyond those they could have achieved by acting alone. At the heart of the concept of partnership lies the issue of the *closeness* of the relationship. Partnerships are close relationships, the degree of which is influenced by a number of factors:

- *Sharing success.* An attitude of shared success means that both partners work together in order to increase the total amount of joint benefit they receive, rather than manoeuvring to maximize their own individual contribution.
- *Long-term expectations.* Partnership relationships imply relatively long-term commitments, but not necessarily permanent ones.
- *Multiple points of contact.* Communication between partners is not only through formal channels, but may take place between many individuals in both organizations.
- *Joint learning.* Partners in a relationship are committed to learn from each other's experience and perceptions of the other operations in the chain.
- *Few relationships.* Although partnership relationships do not necessarily imply single sourcing by customers, they do imply a commitment on the part of both parties to limit the number of customers or suppliers with whom they do business. It is difficult to maintain close relationships with many different trading partners.
- *Joint coordination of activities.* As there are fewer relationships, it becomes possible jointly to coordinate activities such as the flow of materials or service, payment, and so on.
- *Information transparency.* An open and efficient information exchange is seen as a key element in partnerships because it helps to build confidence between the partners.
- *Joint problem-solving.* Although partnerships do not always run smoothly, jointly approaching problems can increase closeness over time.
- *Trust.* This is probably the key element in partnership relationships. In this context, trust means the willingness of one party to relate to the other on the understanding that the relationship will be beneficial to both, even though that cannot be guaranteed. Trust is widely held to be both the key issue in successful partnerships, but also, by far, the most difficult element to develop and maintain.

Virtual operations

Virtual operation

An extreme form of outsourcing operational activities is that of the **virtual operation**. Virtual operations do relatively little themselves, but rely on a network of suppliers that can provide services and products on demand. A network may be formed for only one project and then disbanded once that project ends. For example, some software and Internet companies are virtual in the sense that they buy in all the services needed for a particular development. This may include not only the specific software development skills but also such things as project management, testing, applications prototyping, marketing, physical production, and so on. Much of the Hollywood film industry also operates in this way. A production company may buy and develop an idea for a movie, but it is created, edited and distributed by a loose network of agents, actors, technicians, studios and distribution companies. The advantage of virtual operations is their flexibility and the fact that the risks of investing in production facilities are far lower than in a conventional operation. However, without any solid base of resources, a company may find it difficult to hold onto and develop a unique core of technical expertise. The resources used by virtual companies will almost certainly be available to competitors. In effect, the core competence of a virtual operation lies in the way it is able to manage its supply network.

Selecting suppliers

Choosing appropriate suppliers should involve trading off alternative attributes. Rarely are potential suppliers so clearly superior to their competitors that the decision is self-evident.

Table 7.2 Factors for rating alternative suppliers

Short-term ability to supply	Longer-term ability to supply
Range of services or products provided	Potential for innovation
Quality of services or products	Ease of doing business
Responsiveness	Willingness to share risk
Dependability of supply	Long-term commitment to supply
Delivery and volume flexibility	Ability to transfer knowledge as well as products and services
Total cost of being supplied	Technical capability
Ability to supply in the required quantity	Operations capability Financial capability Managerial capability

Most businesses find it best to adopt some kind of supplier 'scoring' or assessment procedure. This should be capable of rating alternative suppliers in terms of factors such as those in Table 7.2.

Supplier selection

Selecting suppliers should involve evaluating the relative importance of all these factors. So, for example, a business might choose a supplier that, although more expensive than alternative suppliers, has an excellent reputation for on-time delivery, or because the high level of supply dependability allows the business to hold lower stock levels. Other trade-offs may be more difficult to calculate. For example, a potential supplier may have high levels of technical capability, but may be financially weak, with a small but finite risk of going out of business. Other suppliers may have little track record of supplying the products or services required, but show the managerial talent and energy for potential customers to view developing a supply relationship as an investment in future capability.

Worked example

A hotel chain has decided to change its supplier of cleaning supplies because its current supplier has become unreliable in its delivery performance. The two alternative suppliers that it is considering have been evaluated, on a 1–10 scale, against the criteria shown in Table 7.3. That also shows the relative importance of each criterion, also on a 1–10 scale. Based on this evaluation, Supplier B has the superior overall score.

Table 7.3 Weighted supplier selection criteria for the hotel chain

Factor	Weight	Supplier A score	Supplier B score
Cost performance	10	8 (8 × 10 = 80)	5 (5 × 10 = 50)
Quality record	10	7 (7 × 10 = 70)	9 (9 × 10 = 90)
Delivery speed promised	7	5 (5 × 7 = 35)	5 (5 × 7 = 35)
Delivery speed achieved	7	4 (4 × 7 = 28)	8 (8 × 7 = 56)
Dependability record	8	6 (6 × 8 = 48)	8 (8 × 8 = 64)
Range provided	5	8 (8 × 5 = 40)	5 (5 × 5 = 25)
Innovation capability	4	6 (6 × 4 = 24)	9 (9 × 4 = 36)
Total weighted score		325	356

An important decision facing most purchasing managers is whether to source each individual product or service from one or more than one supplier, known, respectively, as **single-sourcing** and **multi-sourcing**. Some of the advantages and disadvantages of single- and multi-sourcing are shown in Table 7.4.

Single-sourcing
Multi-sourcing

Table 7.4 Advantages and disadvantages of single- and multi-sourcing

	Single-sourcing	*Multi-sourcing*
Advantages	• Potentially better quality because more supplier quality assurance possibilities • Strong relationships which are more durable • Greater dependency encourages more commitment and effort • Better communication • Easier to cooperate on new innovation • More scale economies • Higher confidentiality	• Purchaser can drive price down by competitive tendering • Reduces dependency on individual suppliers • Can switch sources in case of supply failure • Wide sources of knowledge and expertise to tap
Disadvantages	• More vulnerable to disruption if a failure to supply occurs • Individual supplier more affected by volume fluctuations • Supplier might exert upward pressure on prices if no alternative supplier is available	• Difficult to encourage commitment by supplier • Less easy to develop effective SQA • More effort needed to communicate • Suppliers less likely to invest in new processes • More difficult to obtain scale economies

It may seem as though companies that multi-source do so exclusively for their own short-term benefit. However, this is not always the case: multi-sourcing can bring benefits to both supplier and purchaser in the long term. For example, Robert Bosch GmbH, the German automotive components business, required that subcontractors do no more than 20 per cent of their total business with them. This was to prevent suppliers becoming too dependent and allow volumes to be fluctuated without pushing the supplier into bankruptcy. However, there has been a trend for purchasing functions to reduce the number of companies supplying any one part or service.

Dual sourcing
Parallel sourcing

Dual sourcing or **parallel sourcing** is often seen as a way to balance the relative merits of single and multi-sourcing. This involves using two suppliers for similar goods or services. Whilst dual suppliers are usually required to cooperate, an element of competition may also be encouraged by adjusting the percentage of the contract awarded to each supplier based on previous performance.

Global sourcing

Global sourcing

One of the major developments of recent years has been the expansion in the proportion of services and products which businesses source from outside their home country; this is called **global sourcing**. Traditionally, even companies that exported their goods and services all over the world (that is, they were international on their demand side) still sourced the majority of their supplies locally. There are a number of factors promoting global sourcing:

- The formation of trading blocs in different parts of the world has lowered tariff barriers, at least within those blocs. For example, the single market developments within the European Union (EU), the North American Free Trade Agreement (NAFTA) and the South American Trade Group (MERCOSUR) have all made it easier to trade internationally within the regions.
- Transportation infrastructures are considerably more sophisticated and cheaper than they once were. Super-efficient port operations in Rotterdam and Singapore, for example, integrated road–rail systems, jointly developed autoroute systems, and cheaper air freight have all reduced some of the cost barriers to international trade.
- Perhaps most significantly, far tougher world competition has forced companies to look to reducing their total costs. Given that in many industries bought-in items are the largest single part of operations costs, an obvious strategy is to source from wherever is cheapest.

There are, of course, challenges to global sourcing. Suppliers that are further away need to transport their products across long distances. The risks of delays and hold-ups can be far greater than when sourcing locally. Also, negotiating with suppliers whose native language is different from one's own makes communication more difficult and can lead to misunderstandings over contract terms. Therefore global sourcing decisions require businesses to balance cost, performance, service and risk factors, not all of which are obvious. These factors are important in global sourcing because of non-price or 'hidden' cost factors such as cross-border freight and handling fees, complex inventory stocking and handling requirements, more complex administrative, documentation and regulatory requirements, and increased operational risk caused by geopolitical factors.

Supply network dynamics

The bullwhip effect

The 'bullwhip effect' is used to describe how a small disturbance at the downstream end of a supply network causes increasingly large disturbances, errors, inaccuracies and volatility as it works its way upstream. Its main cause is an understandable desire by the different links in the supply network to manage their production rates and inventory levels sensibly. To demonstrate this, examine the production rate and stock levels for the supply network shown in Table 7.5. This is a four-stage supply network where the focal operation is served by three tiers of suppliers. The demand from the market has been running at a rate of 100 items per period, but in period 2 demand reduces to 95 items. All stages in the supply chain work on the principle that they will keep in stock one period's demand (a simplification but not a gross one). The 'stock' column shows the starting stock at the beginning, and the finish stock at the end, of the period. At the beginning of period 2, the focal operation has

Table 7.5 Fluctuations of production levels along supply chain in response to small change in end-customer demand

Period	Third-tier supplier		Second-tier supplier		First-tier supplier		Focal operation		Demand
	Prodn.	Stock	Prodn.	Stock	Prodn.	Stock	Prodn.	Stock	
1	100	100 100	100	100 100	100	100 100	100	100 100	100
2	20	100 60	60	100 80	80	100 90	90	100 95	95
3	180	60 120	120	80 100	100	90 95	95	95 95	95
4	60	120 90	90	100 95	95	95 95	95	95 95	95
5	100	90 95	95	95 95	95	95 95	95	95 95	95
6	95	95 95	95	95 95	95	95 95	95	95 95	95

(Note all operations keep one period's inventory.)

100 units in stock. Demand in period 2 is 95 and the operation must produce enough to finish up at the end of the period with 95 in stock (this being the new demand rate). To do this, it need only manufacture 90 items; these, together with 5 items taken out of the starting stock, will supply demand and leave a finished stock of 95 items. Note, however, that a change in demand of only 5 items has produced a fluctuation of 10 items in the operation's production rate.

Now carry this same logic through to the first-tier supplier. At the beginning of period 2, the second-tier supplier has 100 items in stock. The demand which it has to supply in period 2 is derived from the production rate of the focal operation. This has dropped down to 90 in period 2. The first-tier supplier therefore has to produce enough to supply the demand of 90 and leave one month's demand (now 90 items) as its finished stock. A production rate of 80 items per month will achieve this. It will therefore start period 3 with an opening stock of 90 items, but the demand from its customers has now risen to 95 items. It therefore has to produce sufficient to fulfil this demand of 95 items and leave 95 items in stock. To do this, it must produce 100 items in period 3. This logic can be extended right back to the third-tier supplier. The further back up the supply chain an operation is placed, the more drastic are the fluctuations caused by the relatively small change in demand from the final customer. The decision of how much to produce each month is governed by the following relationship:

$$\text{Total available for sale in any period} = \text{Total required in the same period}$$
$$\text{Starting stock} + \text{Production rate} = \text{Demand} + \text{Closing stock}$$
$$\text{Starting stock} + \text{Production rate} = 2 \times \text{Demand (because closing stock must be equal to demand)}$$
$$\text{Production rate} = 2 \times \text{Demand} - \text{Starting stock}$$

Causes of the bullwhip effect

Whenever two operations in a supply network arrange for one to provide services or products to the other, there is the potential for misunderstanding and miscommunication. This may be caused simply by not being sufficiently clear about what a customer expects or what a supplier is capable of delivering. Other causes of the bullwhip effect include errors in forecasting, long or variable lead times, order batching, volatility in demand caused by price fluctuations or promotions, panic ordering (shortage gaming), and the perceived risk of other's bounded rationality within a supply network. Figure 7.10 shows the bullwhip effect in a typical supply network, with relatively small fluctuations in the market causing increasing volatility further back in the network.

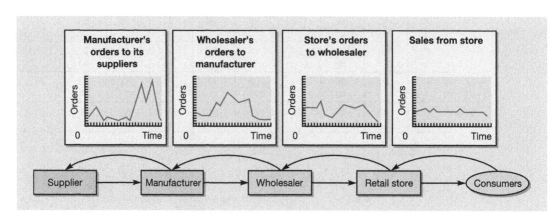

Figure 7.10 Typical supply chain dynamics

Improving supply networks

Increasingly important for operations managers are attempts to improve performance of supply networks. These are usually attempts to either coordinate activities throughout the network or to better understand the complexity of supply processes.

Operational efficiency

Operational efficiency helps improve supply network performance

'**Operational efficiency**' means the efforts that each operation in the network can make to reduce its own complexity, reduce the cost of doing business with other operations and increase throughput time. The cumulative effect of these individual activities is to simplify the whole **network**. For example, imagine a network of operations whose performance level is relatively poor: quality defects are frequent, the lead time to order products and services is long, and delivery is unreliable and so on. The behaviour of the network would be a continual sequence of errors and effort wasted in replanning to compensate for the errors. Poor quality would mean extra and unplanned orders being placed, and unreliable delivery and slow delivery lead times would mean high safety stocks. Just as important, most operations managers' time would be spent coping with the inefficiency. By contrast, a network whose operations had high levels of operations performance would be more predictable and have faster throughput, both of which would help to minimize supply chain fluctuations.

Supply network time compression

One of the most important approaches to improving the operational efficiency of supply networks is known as **time compression**. This means speeding up the flow of materials and information through the network. The bullwhip effect we observed in Table 7.5 and Figure 7.10 was due partly to the slowness of information moving back up the chain. Figure 7.11 illustrates the advantages of time compression in terms of its overall impact on profitability.[9]

The use of e-business to improve supply networks

New information technology applications combined with internet-based e-business have transformed supply networks. Without appropriate information, supply managers cannot make the decisions that coordinate activities and flows through the network. To some extent, they are 'driving blind' and have to rely on the most obvious of mismatches between the activities of different stages in the network (such as excess inventory) to inform their decisions. Conversely, with accurate and 'near real-time' information, integration is possible and can benefit the network and, eventually, the end-customer. Just as importantly, the collection, analysis and distribution of information using e-business technologies is far less expensive to arrange than previous, less automated methods. Table 7.6 summarizes some of the effects of

Table 7.6 Some effects of e-business on supply chain management practice

	Market/sales information flow	Product/service flow	Cash flow
Supply-chain-related activities	Understanding customers' needs Designing appropriate services/products Demand forecasting	Purchasing Inventory management Throughput / waiting times Distribution	Supplier payments Customer invoicing Customer receipts
Beneficial effects of e-business practices	Better customer relationship management Monitoring real-time demand On-line customization Ability to coordinate output with demand	Lower purchasing administration costs Better purchasing deals Reduced bullwhip effect Reduced inventory More efficient distribution	Faster movement of cash Automated cash movement Integration of financial information with sales and operations activities

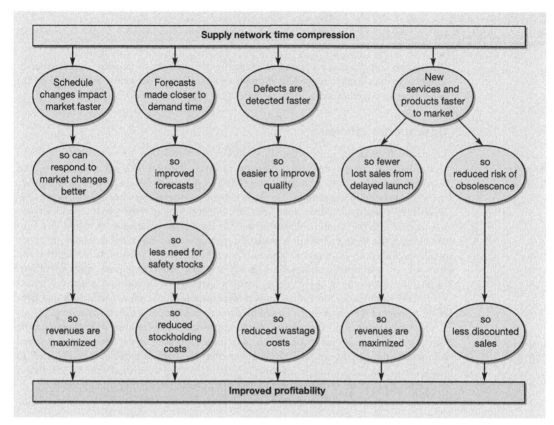

Figure 7.11 Supply network time compression can both reduce costs and increase revenues
Source: Based on Towill

e-business on three important aspects of supply network management – business and market information flow, product and service flow, and the cash flow.

E-procurement

E-procurement

E-procurement is the generic term used to describe the use of electronic methods in every stage of the purchasing process from identification of requirement through to payment, and potentially to contract management.[10] For some years, electronic means have been used by businesses to confirm purchased orders and ensure payment to suppliers. The rapid development of the Internet, however, opened up the potential for far more fundamental changes in purchasing behaviour. Partly this was as the result of supplier information made available through the Internet. By making it easier to search for alternative suppliers, the Internet has changed the economies of the search process and offers the potential for wider searches. It also changed the economies of scale in purchasing. For example, purchasers requiring relatively low volumes find it easier to group together in order to create orders of sufficient size to warrant lower prices. However, whilst the cost savings from purchased goods and services may be the most visible advantage of e-procurement, some managers say that it is just the tip of the iceberg. It can also be far more efficient because purchasing staff are no longer chasing purchase orders and performing routine administrative tasks. Much of the advantage and time savings comes from the decreased need to re-enter information, from streamlining the interaction with suppliers and from having a central repository for data with everything contained in one system. Purchasing staff can negotiate with vendors faster and more effectively. Online auctions can compress negotiations from months to one or two hours, or even minutes.

E-procurement has grown largely because of the development over the last ten years of electronic marketplaces (also sometimes called infomediaries or cybermediaries). These intermediaries allow buyers and sellers in a B2B context to exchange information about prices and offerings. They can be categorized as consortium, private or third party.

- A private e-marketplace is where buyers or sellers conduct business in the market only with their partners and suppliers by previous arrangement.
- The consortium e-marketplace is where several large businesses combine to create an e-marketplace controlled by the consortium.
- A third-party e-marketplace is where an independent party creates an unbiased, market-driven e-marketplace for buyers and sellers in an industry.

The Internet is an important source of purchasing information, even if the purchase itself is made using more traditional methods. Also, even though many businesses have gained advantages by using e-procurement, it does not mean that everything should be bought electronically. When businesses purchase very large amounts of strategically important products or services, they will negotiate multimillion-euro deals, which involve months of discussion, arranging for deliveries up to a year ahead. In such environments, e-procurement may add little value.

Logistics and the Internet

In supply networks dealing with physical assets, transportation is required. Internet communications in this area of supply management have had two major effects. The first is to make information more readily available along the **distribution chain**. This means that the transport companies, warehouses, suppliers and customers that make up the network can share knowledge of where things are at any given time. This allows the operations within the network to coordinate their activities more readily, with potentially significant cost savings. For example, an important issue for transportation companies is **back-loading**. When the company is contracted to transport goods from A to B, its vehicles may have to return from B to A empty. Back-loading means finding a potential customer that wants their goods transported from B to A in the right time frame. Companies which can fill their vehicles on both the outward and return journeys will have significantly lower costs per distance travelled than those whose vehicles are empty for half the total journey.

The second impact of the Internet on logistics has been in the 'business to consumer' part of the supply network. While the last few years have seen an increase in the number of goods bought by consumers online, most goods still have to be physically transported to the customer. Often early e-retailers ran into major problems in the **order fulfilment** task of actually supplying their customers. Partly this was because many traditional warehouse and distribution operations were not designed for e-commerce fulfilment. Supplying a conventional retail operation requires relatively large vehicles to move relatively large quantities of goods from warehouses to shops. Distributing to individual customers requires a large number of smaller deliveries.

Information-sharing

One of the reasons for the fluctuations in output described in the bullwhip example earlier was that each operation in the network reacted to the orders placed by its immediate customer. None of the operations had an overview of what was happening throughout the chain. If information had been available and **shared throughout the chain**, it is unlikely that such wild fluctuations would have occurred. It is sensible therefore to try to transmit information throughout the chain so that all the operations can monitor true demand, free of these distortions. An obvious improvement is to make information on end-customer demand

Distribution chain

Back-loading

Order fulfilment

Information sharing helps improve supply chain performance

Short case
TDG serving the whole supply chain[11]

TDG are specialists in providing *third-party* logistics services to the growing number of manufacturers and retailers that choose not to do their own distribution. Instead they outsource to companies like TDG, which have operations spread across 250 sites that cover the UK, Ireland, France, Spain, Poland and Holland, employ 8,000 people and use 1,600 vehicles.

'There are a number of different types of company *providing distribution services'*, says David Garman, Chief Executive Officer of TDG, *'each with different propositions for the market. At the simplest level, there are the "haulage" and "storage" businesses. These companies either move goods around or they store them in warehouses. Clients plan what has to be done and it is done to order. One level up from the haulage or storage operations are the physical distribution companies, who bring haulage and storage together. These companies collect clients' products, put them into storage facilities and deliver them to the end-customer as and when required. After that there are the companies who offer contract logistics. As a contract logistics service provider, you are likely to be dealing with the more sophisticated clients who are looking for better quality facilities and management and the capability to deal with more complex operations. One level further up is the market for supply chain management services. To do this you have to be able to manage supply chains from end to end, or at least some significant part of the whole chain. Doing this requires a much greater degree of* analytical and modelling capability, business process reengineering and consultancy skills.'

TDG, along with other prominent logistics companies, describes itself as a 'lead logistics provider'. This means that they can provide the consultancy-led, analytical and strategic services integrated with a sound base of practical experience in running successful 'on-the-road' operations. *'In 1999 TDG was a UK distribution company'*, says David Garman, *'now we are a European contract logistics provider with a vision to becoming a full supply chain management company. Providing such services requires sophisticated operations capability, especially in terms of information technology and management dynamism. Because our sites are physically dispersed with our vehicles at any time spread around the motorways of Europe, IT is fundamental to this industry. It gives you visibility of your operation. We need the best operations managers, supported by the best IT.'*

available to upstream operations. Electronic point-of-sale (EPOS) systems used by many retailers attempt to do this. Sales data from checkouts or cash registers are consolidated and transmitted to the warehouses, transportation companies and supplier manufacturing operations that form their supply network. Similarly, electronic data interchange (EDI) helps to share information (see the short case on Seven-Eleven Japan). EDI can also affect the economic order quantities shipped between operations in the supply chain.

Channel alignment

Channel alignment focuses on harmonizing the network

Channel alignment means the adjustment of scheduling, material movements, stock levels, pricing and other sales strategies so as to bring all the operations in the network into line with each other. This goes beyond the provision of information. It means that the systems and methods of planning and control decision-making are harmonized through the network. For example, even when using the same information, differences in forecasing methods or purchasing practices can lead to fluctuations in orders between operations in the chain. One way of avoiding this is to allow an upstream supplier to manage the inventories of its downstream customer. This is known as **vendor-managed inventory** (VMI). So, for example, a packaging supplier could take responsibility for the stocks of packaging materials held by a food manufacturing customer. In turn, the food manufacturer takes responsibility for the stocks of its products which are held in its customer's, the supermarket's warehouses.

Vendor-managed inventory

Short case
Seven-Eleven Japan's agile supply chain[12]

Seven-Eleven Japan (SEJ) is Japan's largest and most successful retailer. The average amount of stock in an SEJ store is between 7 and 8.4 days of demand, a remarkably fast stock turnover for any retailer. Industry analysts see SEJ's agile supply management as being the driving force behind its success. It is an agility that is supported by a fully integrated information system that provides visibility of the whole supply network and ensures fast replenishment of goods in its stores customized exactly to the needs of individual stores. As a customer comes to the checkout counter the assistant first keys in the customer's gender and approximate age and then scans the bar codes of the purchased goods. This sales data is transmitted to the Seven-Eleven headquarters through its own high-speed lines. Simultaneously, the store's own computer system records and analyzes the information so that store managers and headquarters have immediate point-of-sale information. This allows both store managers and headquarters to, hour by hour, analyze sales trends, any stock-outs, types of customer buying certain products, and so on. The headquarter's computer aggregates all this data by region, product and time so that all parts of the supply network, from suppliers through to the stores, have the information by the next morning. Every Monday, the company chairman and top executives review all performance information for the previous week and develop plans for the up-coming week. These plans are presented on Tuesday morning to SEJ's 'operations field counsellors' each of which is responsible for facilitating performance improvement in around eight stores. On Tuesday afternoon the field counsellors for each region meet to decide how they will implement the overall plans

Source: Getty Images

for their region. On Tuesday night the counsellors fly back to their regions and by next morning are visiting their stores to deliver the messages developed at headquarters which will help the stores implement their plans. SEJ's physical distribution is also organized on an agile basis. The distribution company maintains radio communications with all drivers and SEJ's headquarters keeps track of all delivery activities. Delivery times and routes are planned in great detail and published in the form of a delivery time-table. On average each delivery takes only one and a half minutes at each store, and drivers are expected to make their deliveries within ten minutes of scheduled time. If a delivery is late by more than thirty minutes the distribution company has to pay the store a fine equivalent to the gross profit on the goods being delivered. The agility of the whole supply system also allows SEJ headquarters and the distribution company to respond to disruptions. For example, on the day of the Kobe earthquake, SEJ used 7 helicopters and 125 motor cycles to rush through a delivery of 64,000 rice balls to earthquake victims.

The SCOR model

The Supply Chain Operations Reference model (SCOR) is a broad, but highly structured and systematic, framework for improving supply networks. The framework uses a methodology, diagnostic and benchmarking tools that are increasingly widely accepted for evaluating and comparing supply activities and their performance. Just as important, the SCOR model allows its users to improve, and communicate management practices within and between all interested parties in their supply network by using a standard language and a set of structured definitions. Companies that have used the model include BP, AstraZeneca, Shell, SAP AG, Siemens AG and Bayer. Claimed benefits from using the SCOR model include improved process understanding and performance, improved supply network performance, increased customer satisfaction and retention, a decrease in required capital, better profitability and return on investment, and increased productivity. The model uses three individual techniques turned into an integrated approach. These are:

- Business process modelling.
- Benchmarking performance.
- Best practice analysis.

Business process modelling

SCOR does not represent organizations or functions, but rather processes. Each basic 'link' in the supply network is made up of five types of process, each process being a 'supplier–customer' relationship, see Figure 7.12.

- 'Source' is the procurement, delivery, receipt and transfer of raw material items, sub-assemblies, and/or services.
- 'Make' is the transformation process of adding value to products and services through mixing operations processes.
- 'Deliver' processes perform all customer-facing order management and fulfilment activities including outbound logistics.
- 'Plan' processes manage each of these customer–supplier links and balance the activity of the supply network. They are the supply and demand reconciliation process, which includes prioritization when needed.
- 'Return' processes look after the reverse logistics flow of moving material back from end-customers upstream in the supply chain because of product defects, post-delivery customer support, or recycling (end-of-life reverse supply).

All these processes are modelled at increasingly detailed levels from level 1 through to level 3.

Benchmarking performance

Performance metrics in the SCOR model are also structured by level. Level 1 metrics are the yardsticks by which an organization can measure how successful it is in achieving its desired positioning within the competitive environment, as measured by the performance of a particular supply chain. These level 1 metrics are the key performance indicators (KPIs) of the chain and are created from lower-level diagnostic metrics (called level 2 and level 3 metrics) which are calculated on the performance of lower-level processes.

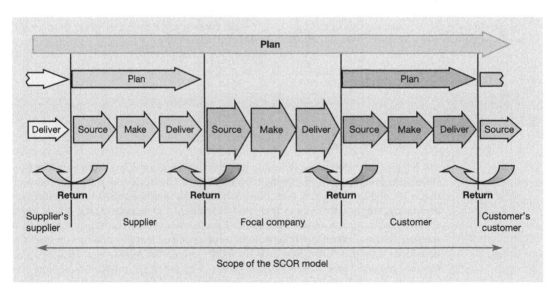

Figure 7.12 Matching the operations resources in the supply network with market requirements

Best practice analysis

Best practice analysis follows the benchmarking activity that should have measured the performance of the supply network processes and identified the main performance gaps. Best practice analysis identifies the activities that need to be performed to close the gaps. The definition of a 'best practice' in the SCOR model is one that:

- Is current – neither untested (emerging) nor outdated.
- Is structured – it has clearly defined goals, scope and processes.
- Is proven – there has been some clearly demonstrated success.
- Is repeatable – it has been demonstrated to be effective in various contexts.
- Has an unambiguous method – the practice can be connected to business processes, operations strategy, technology, supply relationships, and information or knowledge management systems.
- Has a positive impact on results – operations improvement can be linked to KPIs.

The SCOR roadmap

The SCOR model can be implemented by using a five-phase project 'roadmap'. Within this roadmap lies a collection of tools and techniques that both help to implement and support the SCOR framework. In fact many of these tools are commonly used management decision tools such as Pareto charts, cause–effect diagrams, maps of material flow and brainstorming.

Phase 1: Discover – Involves supply-network definition and prioritization where a 'Project Charter' sets the scope for the project. This identifies logic groupings of supply network within the scope of the project. The priorities, based on a weighted rating method, determine which supply network should be dealt with first. This phase also identifies the resources that are required, identified and secured through business process owners or actors.

Phase 2: Analyse – Using data from benchmarking and competitive analysis, the appropriate level of performance metrics are identified; that will define the strategic requirements of each supply network.

Phase 3: Material flow design – In this phase the project teams have their first go at creating a common understanding of how processes can be developed. The current state of processes is identified and an initial analysis attempts to see where there are opportunities for improvement.

Phase 4: Work and information flow design – The project teams collect and analyse the work involved in all relevant processes (plan, source, make, deliver and return) and map the productivity and yield of all transactions.

Phase 5: Implementation planning – This is the final and preparation phase for communicating the findings of the project. Its purpose is to transfer the knowledge of the SCOR team(s) to individual implementation or deployment teams.

Summary answers to key questions

Check and improve your understanding of this chapter using self-assessment questions and a personalized study plan, audio and video downloads, and an eBook – all at **www.myomlab.com.**

➤ Why should an organization take a supply network perspective?

■ The main advantage is that it helps any operation to understand how it can compete effectively within the network. This is because a supply network approach requires operations managers to think about their suppliers and their customers *as operations*. It can also help to identify particularly significant links within the network and hence identify long-term strategic changes which will affect the operation.

➤ What is involved in managing supply networks?

■ Managing supply networks involves understanding and influencing the various linkages between upstream and downstream operations with the objective of delivering better performance to the end-customer.

■ Key activities include designing the supply network, determining the type of supply relationships, understanding supply dynamics and improving supply networks.

➤ What is involved in designing a supply network?

■ Deciding the 'shape' of the supply network: This may involve reducing the number of suppliers to the operation so as to develop closer relationships, bypassing or disintermediating operations in the network, and co-opetition.

■ Deciding what to do and what to buy: This concerns the nature of the ownership of the operations within a supply network. The direction of vertical integration refers to whether an organization wants to own operations on its supply side or demand side (backwards or forwards integration). The extent of vertical integration relates to whether an organization wants to own a wide span of the supply network. The balance of integration refers to whether operations can trade with only their vertically integrated partners or with organizations as well.

■ Deciding how to align supply and demand in the network: Marshall Fisher distinguishes between functional markets and innovative markets. He argues that functional markets, which are relatively predictable, require efficient supply networks, whereas innovative markets, which are less predictable, require responsive supply networks.

➤ What are the types of relationship between operations in supply networks?

■ Supply networks are made up of individual pairs of buyer–supplier relationships. Business-to-business (B2B) relationships are of the most interest to operations managers. They can be characterized on two dimensions – what is outsourced to a supplier, and the number and closeness of the relationships.

■ Traditional market supplier relationships are where a purchaser chooses suppliers on an individual periodic basis. No long-term relationship is usually implied by such 'transactional' relationships, but it makes it difficult to build internal capabilities.

■ Partnership supplier relationships involve customers forming long-term relationships with suppliers. In return for the stability of demand, suppliers are expected to commit to high levels of service. True partnerships are difficult to sustain and rely heavily on the degree of trust which is allowed to build up between partners.

- Virtual operations are an extreme form of outsourcing where an operation does relatively little itself and subcontracts almost all its activities.
- Selecting suppliers involves deciding whether to source from one (single), two (dual or parallel) or many (multi) suppliers. One must then consider the relative merits of alternative suppliers.

➤ What is the 'natural' dynamic of a supply network?

- Supply networks exhibit a dynamic behaviour known as the 'bullwhip' effect. This shows how small changes at the demand end of a supply chain are progressively amplified for operations further back in the network.
- Common causes of the bullwhip effect include errors in forecasting, long and variable lead-times, order batching, demand volatility, panic ordering, and bounded rationality.

➤ How can supply networks be improved?

- To reduce the 'bullwhip' effect, operations can adopt some mixture of coordination strategies:
  - operational efficiency: this means eliminating sources of inefficiency or ineffectiveness in the network; of particular importance is 'time compression', which attempts to increase the throughput speed of the operations in the network;
  - e-business: new IT applications have transformed supply networks, enabling improvements in flows of services, information, and products;
  - information-sharing: the efficient distribution of information throughout the chain can reduce demand fluctuations along the chain by linking all operations to the source of demand;
  - channel alignment: this means adopting the same or similar decision-making processes throughout the chain to coordinate how and when decisions are made.
- The Supply Chain Operations Reference model (SCOR) is a highly structured framework for supply network improvement using business process modelling, benchmarking and best practice analysis in an integrated approach.

Learning exercises

These problems and applications will help to improve your analysis of operations. You can find more practice problems as well as worked examples and guided solutions on MyOMLab at www.myomlab.com.

1. Visit sites on the Internet that offer (legal) downloadable music using MP3 or other compression formats. Consider the music business supply network, **(a)** for the recordings of a well-known popular music artist, and **(b)** for a less well-known (or even largely unknown) artist struggling to gain recognition. How might the transmission of music over the Internet affect each of these artists' sales? What implications does electronic music transmission have for record shops?

2. 'Look, why should we waste our time dealing with suppliers who can merely deliver good product, on time, and in full? There are any number of suppliers who can do that. What we are interested in is developing a set of suppliers who will be able to supply us with suitable components for the generation of products that comes after the next products we launch. It's the underlying capability of suppliers that we are really interested in.'

   (a) Devise a set of criteria that this manager could use to evaluate alternative suppliers.
   (b) Suggest ways in which she could determine how to weight each criterion.

3 The example of the bullwhip effect shown in Table 7.5 shows how a simple 5 per cent reduction in demand at the end of the supply network causes fluctuations that increase in severity the further back an operation is placed in the chain.

(a) Using the same logic and the same rules (i.e. all operations keep one period's inventory), what would the effect on the chain be if demand fluctuated period by period between 100 and 95? That is, period 1 has a demand of 100, period 2 has a demand of 95, period 3 a demand of 100, period 4 a demand of 95, and so on?

(b) What happens if all operations in the supply network decided to keep only half of the period's demand as inventory?

4 Visit a C2C auction site (for example eBay) and analyse the function of the site in terms of the way it facilitates transactions. What does such a site have to get right to be successful?

Want to know more?

Carmel, E. and Tjia, P. (2005) *Offshoring Information Technology: Sourcing and Outsourcing to a Global Workforce*, Cambridge University Press, Cambridge. An academic book on outsourcing.

Chopra, S. and Meindl, P. (2001) *Supply Chain Management: Strategy, Planning and Operations*, Prentice Hall, Upper Saddle River, NJ. A good textbook that covers both strategic and operations issues.

Fisher, M.L. (1997) What is the right supply chain for your product?, *Harvard Business Review*, vol. 75, no. 2. A particularly influential article that explores the issue of how supply networks are not all the same.

Harrison, A. and van Hoek, R. (2002) *Logistics Management and Strategy*, Financial Times Prentice Hall, Harlow. A short but readable book that explains many of the modern ideas in supply network management including lean supply networks and agile supply networks.

Vashistha, A. and Vashistha, A. (2006) *The Offshore Nation: Strategies for Success in Global Outsourcing and Offshoring*, McGraw-Hill Higher Education. A topical book on outsourcing.

Useful websites

www.cio.com/topic/3207/supply_chain_management Site of CIO's Supply Chain Management Research Center. Topics include procurement and fulfilment, with case studies.

www.gsb.stanford.edu/scforum/ Stanford University's supply chain forum. Interesting debate.

www.rfidc.com/ Site of the RFID Centre that contains RFID demonstrations and articles to download.

www.spychips.com/ Vehemently anti-RFID site. If you want to understand the nature of some activists' concern over RFID, this site provides the arguments.

www.cips.org/ The Chartered Institute of Purchasing and Supply (CIPS) is an international organization, serving the purchasing and supply profession and dedicated to promoting best practice. Some good links.

www.opsman.org Lots of useful stuff.

Now that you have finished reading this chapter, why not visit MyOMLab at www.myomlab.com where you'll find more learning resources to help you make the most of your studies and get a better grade.

Process design

Key questions

➤ What is process design?
➤ How do volume and variety affect process design?
➤ How are processes designed in detail?
➤ What are the human implications for process design?

Introduction

Say you are a 'designer' and most people will assume that you are someone who is concerned with how a product looks. However, the design activity is much broader than that and while there is no universally recognized definition of 'design'. We take it to mean 'the process by which some functional requirement of people is satisfied through the shaping or configuration of the resources and/or activities that compose a service, a product, or the transformation process that creates and delivers them'. All operations managers are designers. When they purchase or rearrange the position of a piece of equipment, or when they change the way of working within a process, it is a design decision because it affects the physical shape and nature of their processes. This chapter examines the design of processes. Figure 5.1 shows where this chapter fits within the overall model of operations management.

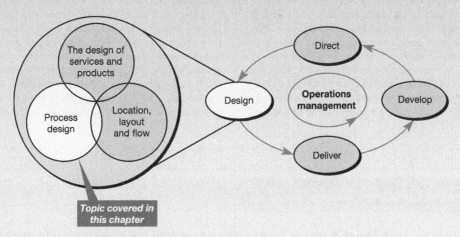

Figure 5.1 This chapter examines process design

Check and improve your understanding of this chapter using self-assessment questions and a personalized study plan, audio and video downloads, and an eBook – all at **www.myomlab.com**.

Operations in practice   Fast-food drive-throughs[1]

The quick-service restaurant (QSR) industry reckons that the very first drive-through dates back to 1928 when Royce Hailey first promoted the drive-through service at his Pig Stand restaurant in Los Angeles. Customers would simply drive by the back door of the restaurant where the chef would come out and deliver the restaurant's famous 'Barbequed Pig' sandwiches. Today, drive-through processes are slicker and faster. They are also more common. In 1975, McDonald's did not have any drive-throughs, but now more than 90 per cent of its US restaurants incorporate a drive-through process. In fact 80 per cent of recent fast-food growth has come through the growing number of drive-throughs. Says one industry specialist, *'There are a growing number of customers for whom fast-food is not fast enough. They want to cut waiting time to the very minimum without even getting out of their car. Meeting their needs depends on how smooth we can get the process.'*

The competition to design the fastest and most reliable drive-through process is fierce. Starbucks' drive-throughs have strategically placed cameras at the order boards so that servers can recognize regular customers and start making their order even before it's placed. Burger King has experimented with sophisticated sound systems, simpler menu boards and see-through food bags to ensure greater accuracy (no point in being fast if you don't deliver what the customer ordered). These details matter. McDonald's reckon that their sales increase one per cent for every six seconds saved at a drive-through, while a single Burger King restaurant calculated that its takings increased by 15,000 dollars a year each time it reduced queuing time by one second.

Source: Getty Images

Menu items must be easy to read and understand. Designing 'combo meals' (burger, fries and a cola), for example, saves time at the ordering stage. Perhaps the most remarkable experiment in making drive-through process times slicker is being carried out by McDonald's in the USA. On California's central coast 150 miles from Los Angeles, a call centre takes orders remotely from 40 McDonald's outlets around the country. The orders are then sent back to the restaurants through the Internet and the food is assembled only a few metres from where the order was placed. It may only save a few seconds on each order, but that can add up to extra sales at busy times of the day. However, not everyone is thrilled by the boom in drive-throughs. People living in the vicinity may complain of the extra traffic they attract and the unhealthy image of fast food combined with a process that does not even make customers get out of their car, is, for some, a step too far.

What is process design?

Design happens before creation

To 'design' is to conceive the looks, arrangement, and workings of something *before it is created*. In that sense it is a conceptual exercise. Yet it is one which must deliver a solution that will work in practice. Design is also an activity that can be approached at different levels of detail. One may envisage the general shape and intention of something before getting down to defining its details. This is certainly true for process design. At the start of the process design activity it is important to understand the design objectives, especially at first, when the overall shape and nature of the process is being decided. The most common way of doing this is by positioning it according to its volume and variety characteristics. Eventually the details of the process must be analysed to ensure that it fulfils its objectives effectively. Yet, it is often only through getting to grips with the detail of a design that the feasibility of its overall shape can be assessed. Don't think of this as a simple sequential process. There may be aspects concerned with the objectives or the broad positioning of the process that will need to be modified following its more detailed analysis.

What objectives should process design have?

The whole point of process design is to make sure that the performance of the process is appropriate for whatever it is trying to achieve. For example, if an operation competed primarily on its ability to respond quickly to customer requests, its processes would need to be designed to give fast throughput times. This would minimize the time between customers requesting a service or product and their receiving it. Similarly, if an operation competed on low price, cost-related objectives would dominate its process design. Some kind of logic should link what the operation as a whole is attempting to achieve and the **performance objectives** of its individual processes. This is illustrated in Table 5.1.

Process design should reflect process objectives

Operations performance objectives translate directly to process design objectives as shown in Table 5.1. As processes are managed at a very operational level, process design also needs to consider a more 'micro' and detailed set of objectives. These are largely concerned with flow through the process. When whatever are being 'processed' enter a process, they will progress through a series of activities where they are 'transformed' in some way. Between these activities they may dwell for some time in inventories, waiting to be transformed by the next activity. This means that the time that a unit spends in the process (its throughput time) will be longer than the sum of all the transforming activities that it passes through. Also the resources that perform the processes activities may not be used all the time because not all units will necessarily require the same activities and the capacity of each resource may not match the demand placed upon it. So neither the units moving through the process, nor the resources performing the activities may be fully utilized.

Table 5.1 The impact of strategic performance objectives on process design objectives and performance

Operations performance objective	Typical process design objectives	Some benefits of good process design
Quality	• Provide appropriate resources, capable of achieving the services or product specification • Error-free processing	• Products and services produced 'on-specification' • Less recycling and wasted effort within the process
Speed	• Minimum throughput time • Output rate appropriate for demand	• Short customer waiting time • Low in-process inventory
Dependability	• Provide dependable process resources • Reliable process output timing and volume	• On-time deliveries of products and services • Less disruption, confusion and rescheduling within the process
Flexibility	• Provide resources with an appropriate range of capabilities • Change easily between processing states (what, how, or how much is being processed)	• Ability to process a wide range of products and services • Low cost/fast product and service change • Low cost/fast volume and timing changes • Ability to cope with unexpected events (e.g. supply or a processing failure)

Cost	• Appropriate capacity to meet demand
	• Eliminate process waste in terms of
	  – excess capacity
	  – excess process capability
	  – in-process delays
	  – in-process errors
	  – inappropriate process inputs
		• Low processing costs
		• Low resource costs (capital costs)
		• Low delay and inventory costs (working capital costs)

Because of this the way that units leave the process is unlikely to be exactly the same as the way they arrive at the process. It is common for more 'micro' performance flow objectives to be used that describe process flow performance. For example:

Throughput rate

- **Throughput rate** (or flow rate) is the rate at which units emerge from the process, i.e. the number of units passing through the process per unit of time.

Throughput time

- **Throughput time** is the average elapsed time taken for inputs to move through the process and become outputs.

Work in process

- The number of units in the process (also called the '**work in process**' or in-process inventory), as an average over a period of time.

Utilization

- The **utilization** of process resources is the proportion of available time that the resources within the process are performing useful work.

Environmentally sensitive design

With the issues of environmental protection becoming more important, both process and service/product designers have to take account of 'green' issues. In many developed countries, legislation has already provided some basic standards which restrict the use of toxic materials, limit discharges to air and water, and protect employees and the public from immediate and long-term harm. Interest has focused on some fundamental issues:

Short case
Ecologically smart[2]

Source: Getty Images

When Daimler-Chrysler started to examine the feasibility of the Smart town car, the challenge was not just to examine the economic feasibility of the product but also to build in environmental sensitivity to the design of the product and the process that was to make it. This is why environmental protection is now a fundamental part of all production activities in its 'Smartville' plant at Hambach near France's border with Germany. The product itself is designed on environmentally compatible principles. Even before assembly starts, the product's disassembly must be considered. In fact the modular construction of the Smart car helps to guarantee economical dismantling at the end of its life. This also helps with the recycling of materials. Over 85 per cent of the Smart's components are recyclable and recycled material is used in its initial construction. For example, the Smart's instrument panel comprises 12 per cent recycled plastic material. Similarly, production processes are designed to be ecologically sustainable. The plant's environmentally friendly painting technique allows less paint to be used while maintaining a high quality of protection. It also involves no solvent emission and no hazardous waste, as well as the recycling of surplus material. It is not only the use of new technology that contributes to the plant's ecological credentials. Ensuring a smooth and efficient movement of materials within the plant also saves time, effort and, above all, energy. So, traffic flow outside and through the building has been optimized, buildings are made accessible to suppliers delivering to the plant, and conveyor systems are designed to be loaded equally in both directions so as to avoid empty runs. The company even claims that the buildings themselves are a model for ecological compatibility. No construction materials contain formaldehyde or CFCs and the outside of the buildings are lined with 'TRESPA', a raw material made from European timber that is quick to regenerate.

- *The sources of inputs* to a service or product. (Will they damage rainforests? Will they use up scarce minerals? Will they exploit the poor or use child labour?)
- *Quantities and sources of energy* consumed in the process. (Do plastic beverage bottles use more energy than glass ones? Should waste heat be recovered and used in fish farming?)
- *The amounts and type of waste material* that are created in the processes. (Can this waste be recycled efficiently, or must it be burnt or buried in landfill sites? Will the waste have a long-term impact on the environment as it decomposes and escapes?)
- *The life of the product itself.* It is argued that if a product has a useful life of, say, twenty years, it will consume fewer resources than one that only lasts five years, which must therefore be replaced four times in the same period. However, the long-life product may require more initial inputs, and may prove to be inefficient in the latter part of its use, when the latest products use less energy or maintenance to run.
- *The end-of-life of the product.* (Will the redundant product be difficult to dispose of in an environmentally friendly way? Could it be recycled or used as a source of energy? Could it still be useful in third-world conditions? Could it be used to benefit the environment, such as old cars being used to make artificial reefs for sea life?)

Designers are faced with complex trade-offs between these factors, although it is not always easy to obtain all the information that is needed to make the 'best' choices. For example, it is relatively straightforward to design a long-life product, using strong material, over-designed components, ample corrosion protection, and so on. However, its production might use more materials and energy and it could create more waste on disposal. To help make more rational decisions in the design activity, some industries are experimenting with **life cycle analysis**. This technique analyses all the production inputs, the life-cycle use of the product and its final disposal, in terms of total energy used (and more recently, of all the emitted wastes such as carbon dioxide, sulphurous and nitrous gases, organic solvents, solid waste, etc.). The inputs and wastes are evaluated at *every* stage in its creation, beginning with the extraction or farming of the basic raw materials. The short case 'Ecologically smart' demonstrates that it is possible to include ecological considerations in all aspects of product and process design.

(margin note: Life cycle analysis)

Process types – the volume–variety effect on process design

In Chapter 1 we saw how processes in operations can range from creating a very high volume of products or services (for example, a food canning factory) to a very low volume (for example, major project consulting engineers). Also they can range from producing a very low variety of products or services (for example, in an electricity utility) to a very high variety (as, for example, in an architects' practice). Usually the two dimensions of volume and variety go together. Low-volume operations processes often have a high variety of services and products, and high-volume operations processes often have a narrow variety of services and products. Thus there is a continuum from low volume and high variety through to high volume and low variety, on which we can position operations. Different operations, even those in the same operation, may adopt different types of processes. In a medical service, compare the approach taken during mass medical treatments, such as large-scale immunization programmes, with that taken for a transplant operation where the treatment is designed specifically to meet the needs of one person. These differences go well beyond their differing technologies or the processing requirements of their products or services. They are explained by the fact that no one type of process design is best for all types of operation in all circumstances. The differences are because of the different **volume–variety positions** of the operations.

(margin note: Volume–variety positions)

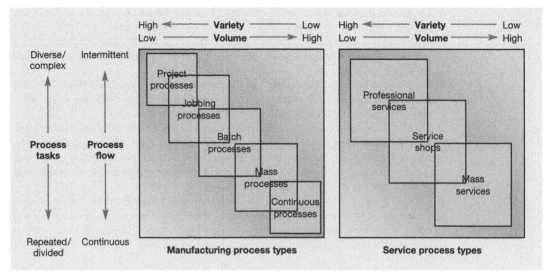

Figure 5.2 Different process types imply different volume–variety characteristics for the process

Process types

Process types

The position of a process on the volume–variety continuum shapes its overall design and the general approach to managing its activities. These 'general approaches' to designing and managing processes are called **process types**. Different terms are sometimes used to identify process types depending on whether they are predominantly manufacturing or service processes, and there is some variation in the terms used. For example, it is not uncommon to find the 'manufacturing' terms used in service industries. Figure 5.2 illustrates how these 'process types' are used to describe different positions on the volume–variety spectrum.

Project processes

Project processes

Project processes are those which deal with discrete, usually highly customized products. Often the timescale of making the product or service is relatively long, as is the interval between the completion of each product or service. So low volume and high variety are characteristics of project processes. The activities involved in making the product can be ill-defined and uncertain, sometimes changing during the production process itself. Examples of project processes include shipbuilding, most construction companies, movie production companies, large fabrication operations such as those manufacturing turbo generators, and installing a computer system. The essence of project processes is that each job has a well-defined start and finish, the time interval between starting

The major construction site shown in this picture is a project process. Each 'product' (project) is different and poses different challenges to those running the process (civil engineers).

different jobs is relatively long and the transforming resources which make the product will probably have been organized especially for each product. The process map for project processes will almost certainly be complex. This is partly because each unit of output is so large with many activities occurring at the same time and partly because the activities in such processes often involve significant discretion to act according to professional judgement.

68

Jobbing processes

Jobbing processes

Jobbing processes also deal with very high variety and low volumes. Whereas in project processes each product has resources devoted more or less exclusively to it, in jobbing processes each product has to share the operation's resources with many others. The resources of the operation will process a series of products but, although all the products will require the same kind of attention, each will differ in its exact needs. Examples of jobbing processes include many precision engineers such as specialist tool-makers, furniture restorers, bespoke tailors, and the printer who produces tickets for the local social event. Jobbing processes produce more and usually smaller items than project processes but, like project processes, the degree of repetition

This craftsperson is using general purpose wood-cutting technology to make a product for an individual customer. The next product he makes will be different (although it may be similar), possibly for a different customer.

is low. Many jobs will probably be 'one-offs'. Again, any process map for a jobbing process could be relatively complex for similar reasons to project processes. However, jobbing processes usually produce physically smaller products and, although sometimes involving considerable skill, such processes often involve fewer unpredictable circumstances.

Batch processes

Batch processes

Batch processes can often look like jobbing processes, but batch does not have quite the degree of variety associated with jobbing. As the name implies, each time batch processes produce a product they produce more than one. So each part of the operation has periods when it is repeating itself, at least while the 'batch' is being processed. The size of the batch could be just two or three, in which case the batch process will differ little from jobbing, especially if each batch is a totally novel product. Conversely, if the batches are large, and especially if the products are familiar to the

In this kitchen, food is being prepared in batches. All batches go through the same sequence (preparation, cooking, storing), but each batch is a different dish.

operation, batch processes can be fairly repetitive. Because of this, the batch type of process can be found over a wide range of volume and variety levels. Examples of batch processes include machine tool manufacturing, the production of some special gourmet frozen foods, and the manufacture of most of the component parts which go into mass-produced assemblies such as automobiles.

Mass processes

Mass processes

Mass processes are those which produce goods in high volume and relatively narrow variety – narrow, that is, in terms of the fundamentals of the product design. An automobile plant, for example, might produce several thousand variants of car if every option of engine size, colour, extra equipment, etc. is taken into account. Yet essentially it is a mass operation because the different variants of its product do not affect

This automobile plant is everyone's idea of a mass process. Each product is almost (but not quite) the same, and is made in large quantities.

the basic process of production. The activities in the automobile plant, like all mass operations, are essentially repetitive and largely predictable. Examples of mass processes include the automobile plant, a television factory, most food processes and DVD production. Several variants of a product could be produced on a mass process such as an assembly line, but the process itself is unaffected. The equipment used at each stage of the process can be designed to handle several different types of components loaded into the assembly equipment. So, provided the sequence of components in the equipment is synchronized with the sequence of models moving through the process, the process seems to be almost totally repetitive.

Continuous processes

Continuous processes

Continuous processes are one step beyond mass processes insomuch as they operate at even higher volume and often have even lower variety. They also usually operate for longer periods of time. Sometimes they are literally continuous in that their products are inseparable, being produced in an endless flow. Continuous processes are often associated with relatively inflexible, capital-intensive technologies with highly predictable flow. Examples of continuous processes include petrochemical refineries, electricity utilities, steel making and some paper making. There are often few elements of discretion in this type of process and although products may be stored during the process, the predominant characteristic of most continuous

This continuous water treatment process almost never stops (it only stops for maintenance) and performs a narrow range of tasks (filters impurities). Often we only notice the process if it goes wrong!

processes is of smooth flow from one part of the process to another. Inspections are likely to form part of the process, although the control applied as a consequence of those inspections is often automatic rather than requiring human discretion.

Professional services

Professional services

Professional services are defined as high-contact organizations where customers spend a considerable time in the service process. Such services provide high levels of customization, the service process being highly adaptable in order to meet individual customer needs. A great deal of staff time is spent in the front office and contact staff are given considerable discretion in servicing customers. Professional services tend to be people-based rather than equipment-based, with emphasis placed on the process (how the service is delivered) rather than the 'product' (what is delivered). Professional services include management consultants, lawyers' practices, architects, doctors' surgeries, auditors, health and safety inspectors and some computer field service operations. A typical example would be OEE, a consultancy that sells the problem-solving

Here consultants are preparing to start a consultancy assignment. They are discussing how they might approach the various stages of the assignment, from understanding the real nature of the problem through to the implementation of their recommended solutions. This is a process map, although a very high level one. It guides the nature and sequence of the consultants' activities.

expertise of its skilled staff to tackle clients' problems. Typically, the problem will first be discussed with clients and the boundaries of the project defined. Each 'product' is different, and a high proportion of work takes place at the client's premises, with frequent contact between consultants and the client.

Service shops

Service shops

Service shops are characterized by levels of customer contact, customization, volumes of customers and staff discretion, which position them between the extremes of professional and mass services (see next paragraph). Service is provided via mixes of front- and back-office activities. Service shops include banks, high-street shops, holiday tour operators, car rental companies, schools, most restaurants, hotels and travel agents. For example, an equipment hire and sales organization may have a range of products displayed in front-office outlets, while back-office operations look after purchasing and administration. The front-office staff have some technical training and can advise customers dur-ing the process of selling the product. Essentially the customer is buying a fairly standardized product but will be influenced by the process of the sale which is customized to the customer's individual needs.

The health club shown in the picture has front-office staff who can give advice on exercise programmes and other treatments. To maintain a dependable service the staff need to follow defined processes every day.

Source: Getty Images

Mass services

Mass services

Mass services have many customer transac-tions, involving limited contact time and little customization. Such services may be equipment-based and 'product'-oriented, with most value added in the back office and relatively little judgement applied by front-office staff. Staff are likely to have a closely defined division of labour and to follow set procedures. Mass services include supermarkets, a national rail network, an airport, telecommunications ser-vices and libraries. For example, rail services such as SNCF in France all move a large num-ber of passengers with a variety of rolling stock on an immense infrastructure of railways.

This is an account management centre for a large retail bank. It deals with thousands of customer requests every day. Although each customer request is different, they are all of the same type – involving customers' accounts.

Source: © Royal Bank of Scotland Group plc

Passengers pick a journey from the range offered. One of the most common types of mass service is the call centres used by almost all companies that deal directly with consumers. Coping with a very high volume of enquiries requires some kind of structuring of the process of communicating with customers. This is often achieved by using a carefully designed enquiry process (sometimes known as a 'script').

Critical commentary

Although the idea of process types is useful insomuch as it reinforces the, sometimes important, distinctions between different types of process, it is in many ways simplistic. In reality there is no clear boundary between process types. For example, a specialist camera retailer would normally be categorized as a service shop, yet it also will give, sometimes very specialized, technical advice to customers. It is not a professional service like a consultancy of course, but it does have elements of a professional service process within its design. This is why the volume and variety characteristics of a process are sometimes seen as being a more realistic way of describing processes. The product–process matrix described next adopts this approach.

The product–process matrix

Making comparisons between different processes along a spectrum which goes, for example, from shipbuilding at one extreme to electricity generation at the other has limited value. No one grumbles that yachts are so much more expensive than electricity. The real point is that because the different process types overlap, organizations often have a choice of what type of process to employ. This choice will have consequences to the operation, especially in terms of its cost and flexibility. The classic representation of how cost and flexibility vary with process choice is the **product–process matrix** that comes from Professors Hayes and Wheelwright of Harvard University.[3] They represent process choices on a matrix with the volume–variety as one dimension, and process types as the other (our matrix has been updated to incorporate both product and service operations). Figure 5.3 shows their matrix adapted to fit with the terminology used here. Most operations stick to **the 'natural' diagonal** of the matrix, and few, if any, are found in the extreme corners of the matrix. However, because there is some overlap between the various process types, operations might be positioned slightly off the diagonal.

The diagonal of the matrix shown in Figure 5.3 represents a 'natural' lowest cost position for an operation. Operations which are on the right of the 'natural' diagonal have processes which would normally be associated with lower volumes and higher variety. This means that their processes are likely to be more flexible than seems to be warranted by their actual volume–variety position. Put another way, they are not taking advantage of their ability to standardize their processes. Therefore, their costs are likely to be higher than they would be with a process that was closer to the diagonal. Conversely, operations that are on the left of the diagonal have adopted processes which would normally be used in a higher-volume and lower-variety situation. Their processes will therefore be 'over-standardized' and probably too inflexible for their volume–variety position. This lack of flexibility can also lead to high costs because the process will not be able to change from one activity to another as efficiently as a more flexible process.

Marginal notes: Product–process matrix · The 'natural' diagonal

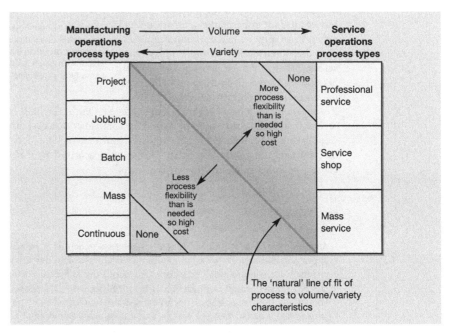

Figure 5.3 Deviating from the 'natural' diagonal on the product–process matrix has consequences for cost and flexibility

Source: Based on Hayes and Wheelwright[4]

Detailed process design

After the overall design of a process has been determined, its individual activities must be configured. At its simplest this detailed design of a process involves identifying all the individual activities that are needed to fulfil the objectives of the process and deciding on the sequence in which these activities are to be performed and who is going to do them. There will, of course, be some constraints on this. Some activities must be carried out before others and some activities can only be done by certain people or machines. Nevertheless, for a process of any reasonable size, the number of alternative process designs is usually large. This means that process design is often done using some simple visual approach such as **process mapping**.

Process mapping

Process mapping

Process mapping simply involves describing processes in terms of how the activities within the process relate to each other. There are many techniques which can be used for *process mapping* (or **process blueprinting**, or **process analysis**, as it is sometimes called). However, all the techniques identify the different *types of* activity that take place during the process and show the flow of materials or people or information through the process.

Process blueprinting
Process analysis

Process mapping symbols

Process mapping symbols are used to classify different types of activity. And although there is no universal set of symbols used all over the world for any type of process, there are some that are commonly used. Most of these derive either from the early days of 'scientific' management around a century ago or, more recently, from information system flowcharting. Figure 5.4 shows the symbols we shall use here.

Process mapping symbols

These symbols can be arranged in order, and in series or in parallel, to describe any process. For example, the retail catering operation of a large campus university has a number of outlets around the campus selling sandwiches. Most of these outlets sell 'standard' sandwiches that are made in the university's central kitchens and transported to each outlet every day. However, one of these outlets is different; it is a kiosk that makes more expensive

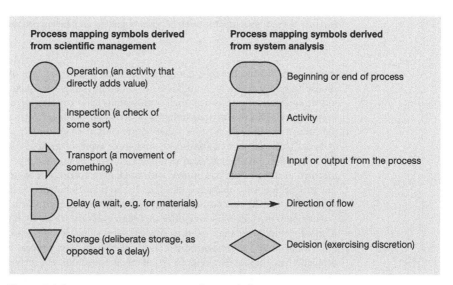

Figure 5.4 Some common process mapping symbols

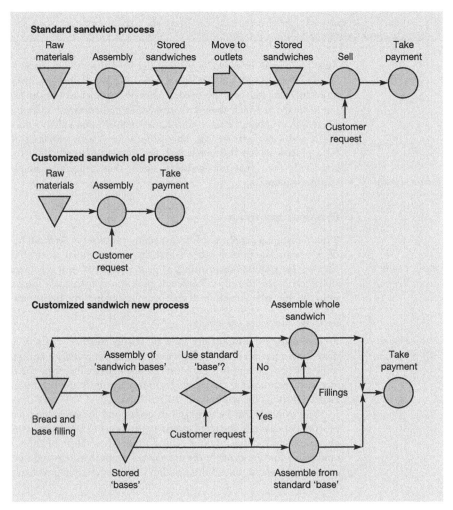

Figure 5.5 Process maps for three sandwich making and selling processes

'customized' sandwiches to order. Customers can specify the type of bread they want and choose from a very wide combination of different fillings. As queues for this customized service are becoming excessive, the catering manager is considering redesigning the process to speed it up. This new process design is based on the findings from a recent student study of the current process which proved that 95 per cent of all customers ordered only two types of bread (soft roll and Italian bread) and three types of protein filling (cheese, ham and chicken). Therefore the six 'sandwich bases' (2 types of bread × 3 protein fillings) could be prepared in advance and customized with salad, mayonnaise, etc. as customers ordered them. The process maps for making and selling the standard sandwiches, the current customized sandwiches and the new customized process are shown in Figure 5.5.

Note how the introduction of some degree of discretion in the new process makes it more complex to map at this detailed level. This is one reason why processes are often mapped at a more aggregated level, called **high-level process mapping**, before more detailed maps are drawn. Figure 5.6 illustrates this for the new customized sandwich operation. At the highest level the process can be drawn simply as an input–transformation–output process with sandwich materials and customers as its input resources and satisfied

High-level process mapping

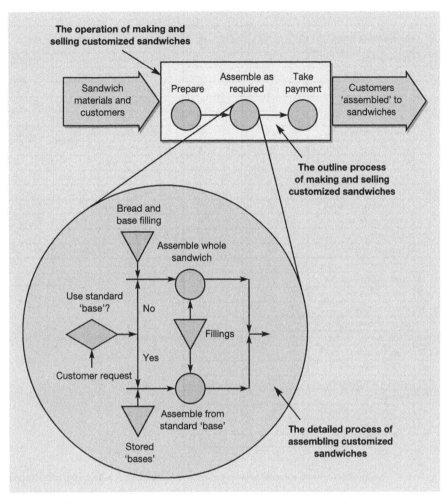

Figure 5.6 The new customized sandwich process mapped at three levels

customers with 'assembled' sandwiches as outputs. No details of how inputs are transformed into outputs are included. At a slightly lower, or more detailed level, what is sometimes called an **outline process map** (or chart) identifies the sequence of activities but only in a general way. So the activity of finding out what type of sandwich a customer wants, deciding if it can be assembled from a sandwich 'base' and then assembling it to meet the customer's request, is all contained in the general activity 'assemble as required'. At the more detailed level, all the activities are shown (we have shown the activities within 'assemble as required').

Outline process map

Using process maps to improve processes

One significant advantage of mapping processes is that each activity can be systematically challenged in an attempt to improve the process. For example, Figure 5.7 shows the flow process chart which Intel Corporation, the computer chip company, drew to describe its method of processing expense reports (claims forms). It also shows the process chart for the same process after critically examining and improving the process. The new process cut the number

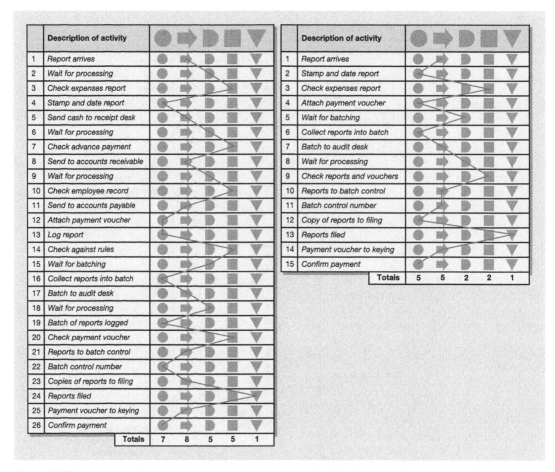

Figure 5.7 Flow process charts for processing expense reports at Intel before and after improving the process

of activities from 26 down to 15. The accounts payable's activities were combined with the cash-receipt's activities of checking employees' past expense accounts (activities 8, 10 and 11) which also eliminated activities 5 and 7. After consideration, it was decided to eliminate the activity of checking items against company rules, because it seemed '*more trouble than it was worth*'. Also, logging the batches was deemed unnecessary. All this combination and elimination of activities had the effect of removing several 'delays' from the process. The end-result was a much-simplified process which reduced the staff time needed to do the job by 28 per cent and considerably speeded up the whole process.

Throughput, cycle time and work-in-process

The new customized sandwich process has one indisputable advantage over the old process: it is faster in the sense that customers spend less time in the process. The additional benefit this brings is a reduction in cost per customer served (because more customers can be served without increasing resources). Note, however, that the total amount of work needed to make and sell a sandwich has not reduced. All the new process has done is to move some of the work to a less busy time. So the **work content** (the total amount of work required to produce a unit of output) has not changed but customer **throughput time** (the time for a unit to move through the process) has improved.

Work content
Throughput time

76

For example, suppose that the time to assemble and sell a sandwich (the work content) using the old process was two minutes and that two people were staffing the process during the busy period. Each person could serve a customer every two minutes, therefore every two minutes two customers were being served, so on average a customer is emerging from the process every minute. This is called the **cycle time** of the process, the average time between units of output emerging from the process. When customers join the queue in the process they become **work-in-process** (or work-in-progress) sometimes written as WIP. If the queue is ten people long (including that customer) when the customer joins it, he or she will have to wait ten minutes to emerge from the process. Put more succinctly:

Cycle time

Work-in-process

$$\text{Throughput time} = \text{Work-in-process} \times \text{Cycle time}$$

In this case,

$$10 \text{ minutes wait} = 10 \text{ people in the system} \times 1 \text{ minute per person}$$

Worked example

Suppose the regional back-office operation of a large bank is designing an operation which will process its mortgage applications. The number of applications to be processed is 160 per week and the time available to process the applications is 40 hours per week.

$$\text{Cycle time for the process} = \frac{\text{time available}}{\text{number to be processed}} = \frac{40}{160} = \frac{1}{4} \text{ hour}$$

$$= 15 \text{ minutes}$$

So the bank's layout must be capable of processing a completed application once every 15 minutes.

Little's law

Little's law

This mathematical relationship (throughput time = work-in-process × cycle time) is called **Little's law**. It is simple but very useful, and it works for any stable process. For example, suppose it is decided that, when the new process is introduced, the average number of customers in the process should be limited to around ten and the maximum time a customer is in the process should be on average four minutes. If the time to assemble and sell a sandwich (from customer request to the customer leaving the process) in the new process has reduced to 1.2 minutes, how many staff should be serving?

Putting this into Little's law:

$$\text{Throughput time} = 4 \text{ minutes}$$

and

$$\text{Work-in-progress, WIP} = 10$$

So, since

$$\text{Throughput time} = \text{WIP} \times \text{Cycle time}$$

$$\text{Cycle time} = \frac{\text{Throughput time}}{\text{WIP}}$$

$$\text{Cycle time for the process} = \frac{4}{10} = 0.4 \text{ minute}$$

That is, a customer should emerge from the process every 0.4 minute, on average.

Given that an individual can be served in 1.2 minutes,

$$\text{Number of servers required} = \frac{1.2}{0.4} = 3$$

In other words, three servers would serve three customers in 1.2 minutes. Or one customer in 0.4 minute.

Worked example

Mike was totally confident in his judgement, *'You'll never get them back in time'*, he said. *'They aren't just wasting time, the process won't allow them to all have their coffee and get back for 11 o'clock.'* Looking outside the lecture theatre, Mike and his colleague Silvia were watching the 20 business people who were attending the seminar queuing to be served coffee and biscuits. The time was 10.45 and Silvia knew that unless they were all back in the lecture theatre at 11 o'clock there was no hope of finishing his presentation before lunch. *'I'm not sure why you're so pessimistic'*, said Silvia. *'They seem to be interested in what I have to say and I think they will want to get back to hear how operations management will change their lives.'* Mike shook his head. *'I'm not questioning their motivation'*, he said, *'I'm questioning the ability of the process out there to get through them all in time. I have been timing how long it takes to serve the coffee and biscuits. Each coffee is being made fresh and the time between the server asking each customer what they want and them walking away with their coffee and biscuits is taking 48 seconds. Remember that, according to Little's law, throughput equals work-in-process multiplied by cycle time. If the work-in-process is the 20 managers in the queue and cycle time is 48 seconds, the total throughput time is going to be 20 multiplied by 0.8 minute which equals 16 minutes. Add to that sufficient time for the last person to drink their coffee and you must expect a total throughput time of a bit over 20 minutes. You just haven't allowed long enough for the process.'* Silvia was impressed. *'Err . . . what did you say that law was called again?'* *'Little's law'*, said Mike.

Worked example

Every year it was the same. All the workstations in the building had to be renovated (tested, new software installed, etc.) and there was only one week in which to do it. The one week fell in the middle of the August vacation period when the renovation process would cause minimum disruption to normal working. Last year the company's 500 workstations had all been renovated within one working week (40 hours). Each renovation last year took on average 2 hours and 25 technicians had completed the process within the week. This year there would be 530 workstations to renovate but the company's IT support unit had devised a faster testing and renovation routine that would only take on average $1^{1}/_{2}$ hours instead of 2 hours. How many technicians will be needed this year to complete the renovation processes within the week?

Last year:

$$\text{Work-in-progress (WIP)} = 500 \text{ workstations}$$
$$\text{Time available } (T_{t}) = 40 \text{ hours}$$
$$\text{Average time to renovate} = 2 \text{ hours}$$
$$\text{Therefore throughput rate } (T_{r}) = {}^{1}/_{2} \text{ hour per technician}$$
$$= 0.5N$$

where $N = $ Number of technicians

$\rightarrow$

Little's law:
$$\text{WIP} = T_t \times T_r$$
$$500 = 40 \times 0.5N$$
$$N = \frac{500}{40 \times 0.5}$$
$$= 25 \text{ technicians}$$

This year:
$$\text{Work-in-progress (WIP)} = 530 \text{ workstations}$$
$$\text{Time available} = 40 \text{ hours}$$
$$\text{Average time to renovate} = 1.5 \text{ hours}$$
$$\text{Throughput rate } (T_r) = 1/1.5 \text{ per technician}$$
$$= 0.67N$$

where
$$N = \text{Number of technicians}$$

Little's law:
$$\text{WIP} = T_t \times T_r$$
$$530 = 40 \times 0.67N$$
$$N = \frac{530}{40 \times 0.67}$$
$$= 19.88 \text{ technicians}$$
$$\approx 20 \text{ technicians}$$

Balancing and bottlenecks

Balancing

One of the most important design decisions in layout is that of **balancing**. Perfect balancing would mean that work content is allocated equally to each stage in the process. This is nearly always impossible to achieve in practice and some imbalance in the work allocation results. Inevitably this will increase the effective cycle time of the process. If it becomes greater than the required cycle time, it may be necessary to devote extra resources, in the shape of a further stage, to compensate for the imbalance. The effectiveness of the balancing activity is

Balancing loss

measured by **balancing loss**. This is the time wasted through the unequal allocation of work as a percentage of the total time invested in processing the product or service. The longest

Bottleneck

stage in the process is called a '**bottleneck**'. It will govern the flow of items through the whole process.

Worked example

In Figure 5.8 the work allocations in a four-stage process are illustrated. The total amount of time invested in creating each service or product is four times the cycle time because, for every unit produced, all four stages have been working for the cycle time. When the work is equally allocated between the stages, the total time invested in each service or product is $4 \times 2.5 = 10$ minutes. However, when work is unequally allocated, as illustrated, the time invested is $3.0 \times 4 = 12$ minutes, i.e. 2.0 minutes of time, 16.67 per cent of the total, is wasted.

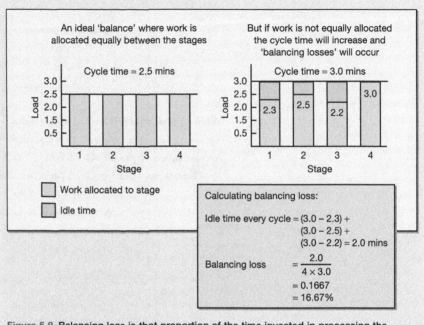

An ideal 'balance' where work is allocated equally between the stages

Cycle time = 2.5 mins

But if work is not equally allocated the cycle time will increase and 'balancing losses' will occur

Cycle time = 3.0 mins

Work allocated to stage

Idle time

Calculating balancing loss:

Idle time every cycle $= (3.0 - 2.3) +$
$(3.0 - 2.5) +$
$(3.0 - 2.2) = 2.0$ mins

$$\text{Balancing loss} = \frac{2.0}{4 \times 3.0}$$
$$= 0.1667$$
$$= 16.67\%$$

Figure 5.8 Balancing loss is that proportion of the time invested in processing the product or service which is not used productively

'Long thin' on 'short fat' processes

Return to the mortgage-processing process in the earlier worked example. It requires four stages working on the task to maintain a cycle time of one processed application every 15 minutes. The conventional arrangement of the four stages would be to lay them out in one line, each stage having 15 minutes' worth of work. However, nominally, the same output rate could also be achieved by arranging the four stages as two shorter lines, each of two stages with 30 minutes' worth of work each. Alternatively, following this logic to its ultimate conclusion, the stages could be arranged as four parallel stages, each responsible for the whole work content. Figure 5.9 shows these options.

This may be a simplified example, but it represents a genuine issue. Should the process be arranged as a single **long thin** line, as several **short fat** parallel lines, or somewhere in between? (Note that 'long' refers to the number of stages and 'fat' to the amount of work allocated to each stage.) In any particular situation there are usually technical constraints which limit either how 'long and thin' or how 'short and fat' the process can be, but there is usually a range of possible options within which a choice needs to be made.

The advantages of long thin processes include:

- *Controlled flow of materials or customers* – which is easy to manage.
- *Simple materials handling* – especially if a product being manufactured is heavy, large or difficult to move.
- *Lower capital requirements*. If a specialist piece of equipment is needed for one element in the job, only one piece of equipment would need to be purchased; on short fat arrangements every stage would need one.
- *More efficient operation*. If each stage is only performing a small part of the total job, the person at the stage will have a higher proportion of direct productive work as opposed to the non-productive parts of the job, such as picking up tools and materials.

Long thin
Short fat

80

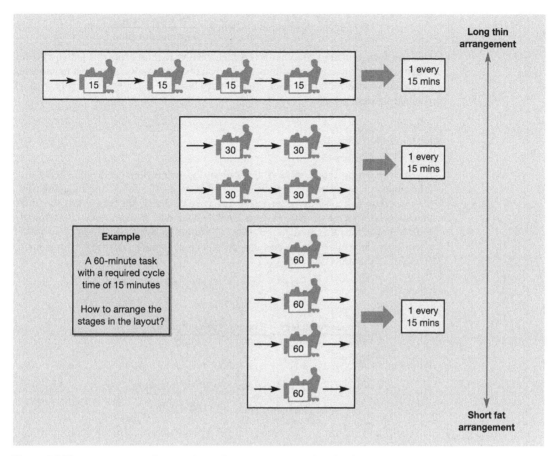

Figure 5.9 The arrangement of stages in product layout can be described on a spectrum from 'long thin' to 'short fat'

The advantages of the short fat processes include:

- *Higher mix flexibility*. If the layout needs to process several types of product or service, each stage or line could specialize in different types.
- *Higher volume flexibility*. As volume varies, stages can simply be closed down or started up as required; long thin processes would need rebalancing each time the cycle time changed.
- *Higher robustness*. If one stage breaks down or ceases operation in some way, the other parallel stages are unaffected; a long thin process would cease operating completely.
- *Less monotonous work*. In the mortgage example, the staff in the short fat arrangement are repeating their tasks only every hour; in the long thin arrangement it is every 15 minutes.

Throughput efficiency

This idea that the throughput time of a process is different from the work content of whatever it is processing has important implications. What it means is that for significant amounts of time no useful work is being done to the materials, information or customers that are progressing through the process. In the case of the simple example of the sandwich process described earlier, customer throughput time is restricted to 4 minutes, but the work content of the task (serving the customer) is only 1.2 minutes. So, the item being processed (the customer) is only being 'worked on' for 1.2/4 = 30 per cent of its time. This is called the **Throughput efficiency** **throughput efficiency** of the process.

81

$$\text{Percentage throughput efficiency} = \frac{\text{Work content}}{\text{Throughput time}} \times 100$$

In this case the throughput efficiency is very high, relative to most processes, perhaps because the 'items' being processed are customers who react badly to waiting. In most material and information transforming processes, throughput efficiency is far lower, usually in single percentage figures.

Worked example

A vehicle licensing centre receives application documents, keys in details, checks the information provided on the application, classifies the application according to the type of licence required, confirms payment and then issues and mails the licence. It is currently processing an average of 5,000 licences every 8-hour day. A recent spot check found 15,000 applications that were 'in progress' or waiting to be processed. The sum of all activities that are required to process an application is 25 minutes. What is the throughput efficiency of the process?

$$\text{Work-in-progress} = 15{,}000 \text{ applications}$$

$$\text{Cycle time} =$$

$$\frac{\text{Time producing}}{\text{Number produced}} = \frac{8 \text{ hours}}{5{,}000} = \frac{480 \text{ minutes}}{5{,}000} = 0.096 \text{ minute}$$

From Little's law,

$$\text{Throughput time} = \text{WIP} \times \text{Cycle time}$$

$$\text{Throughput time} = 15{,}000 \times 0.096$$

$$= 1{,}440 \text{ minutes}$$

$$\text{Throughput efficiency} = \frac{\text{Work content}}{\text{Throughput time}} = \frac{25}{1{,}440} = 1.74 \text{ per cent}$$

Although the process is achieving a throughput time of 24 hours (which seems reasonable for this kind of process) the applications are only being worked on for 1.74 per cent of the time they are in the process.

Value-added throughput efficiency

The approach to calculating throughput efficiency that is described above assumes that all the 'work content' is actually needed. Yet we have already seen from the Intel expense report example that changing a process can significantly reduce the time that is needed to complete the task. Therefore, work content is actually dependent upon the methods and technology used to perform the task. It may be also that individual elements of a task may not be considered 'value-added'. In the Intel expense report example the new method eliminated some steps because they were 'not worth it', that is, they were not seen as adding value. So, **value-added throughput efficiency** restricts the concept of work content to only those tasks that are actually adding value to whatever is being processed. This often eliminates activities such as movement, delays and some inspections.

Value-added throughput efficiency

For example, if in the licensing worked example, of the 25 minutes of work content only 20 minutes were actually adding value, then

$$\text{Value-added throughput efficiency} = \frac{20}{1{,}440} = 1.39 \text{ per cent}$$

Workflow[5]

When the transformed resource in a process is information (or documents containing information), and when information technology is used to move, store and manage the information, process design is sometimes called 'workflow' or 'workflow management'. It is defined as 'the automation of procedures where documents, information or tasks are passed between participants according to a defined set of rules to achieve, or contribute to, an overall business goal'. Although workflow may be managed manually, it is almost always managed using an IT system. More specifically, workflow is concerned with the following:

- analysis, modelling, definition and subsequent operational implementation of business processes;
- the technology that supports the processes;
- the procedural (decision) rules that move information or documents through processes;
- defining the process in terms of the sequence of work activities, the human skills needed to perform each activity and the appropriate IT resources.

The effects of process variability

So far in our treatment of process design we have assumed that there is no significant variability either in the demand to which the process is expected to respond or in the time taken for the process to perform its various activities. Clearly, this is not the case in reality. So, it is important to take account of variability in process design.

Process variability

There are many reasons why **variability** occurs in processes. These can include: the late or early arrival of material, information or customers, a temporary malfunction or breakdown of process technology within a stage of the process, the recycling of 'mis-processed' materials, information or customers to an earlier stage in the process, and variation in the requirements of items being processed. All these sources of variation interact with each other, but result in two fundamental types of variability.

- Variability in the demand for processing at an individual stage within the process, usually expressed in terms of variation in the inter-arrival times of units to be processed.
- Variation in the time taken to perform the activities (i.e. process a unit) at each stage.

To understand the effect of arrival variability on process performance, it is first useful to examine what happens to process performance in a very simple process as arrival time changes under conditions of no variability. For example, the simple process shown in Figure 5.10 is composed of one stage that performs exactly 10 minutes of work. Units arrive at the process at a constant and predictable rate. If the arrival rate is one unit every 30 minutes, then the process will be utilized for only 33.33% of the time, and the units will never have to wait to be processed. This is shown as point A on Figure 5.10. If the arrival rate increases to one arrival every 20 minutes, the utilization increases to 50%, and again the units will not have to wait to be processed. This is point B on Figure 5.10. If the arrival rate increases to one arrival every 10 minutes, the process is now fully utilized, but, because a unit arrives just as the previous one has finished being processed, no unit has to wait. This is point C on Figure 5.10. However, if the arrival rate ever exceeded one unit every 10 minutes, the waiting line in front of the process activity would build up indefinitely, as is shown as point D in Figure 5.10. So, in a perfectly constant and predictable world, the relationship between process waiting time and utilization is a rectangular function as shown by the red dotted line in Figure 5.10.

The relationship between average waiting time and process utilization is a particularly important one

However, when arrival and process times are variable, then sometimes the process will have units waiting to be processed, while at other times the process will be idle, waiting for units to arrive. Therefore the process will have both a 'non-zero' average queue and be under-utilized in the same period. So, a more realistic point is that shown as point X in Figure 5.10. If the average arrival time were to be changed with the same variability, the blue line in Figure 5.10 would show **the relationship between average waiting time and process utilization**. As the process moves closer to 100% utilization the higher the average waiting time will become. To put it another way, the only way to guarantee very low waiting times for the units is to suffer low process utilization.

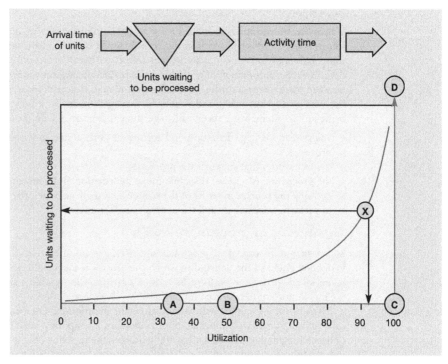

Figure 5.10 The relationship between process utilization and number of units waiting to be processed for constant, and variable, arrival and process times

The greater the variability in the process, the more the waiting time utilization deviates from the simple rectangular function of the 'no variability' conditions that was shown in Figure 5.10. A set of curves for a typical process is shown in Figure 5.11(a). This phenomenon has important implications for the design of processes. In effect it presents three options to process designers wishing to improve the waiting time or utilization performance of their processes, as shown in Figure 5.11(b):

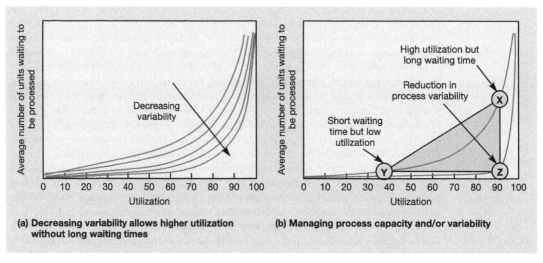

Figure 5.11 The relationship between process utilization and number of units waiting to be processed for variable arrival and activity times

- accept long average waiting times and achieve high utilization (point X);
- accept low utilization and achieve short average waiting times (point Y); or
- reduce the variability in arrival times, activity times, or both, and achieve higher utilization and short waiting times (point Z).

To analyse processes with both inter-arrival and activity time variability, queuing or 'waiting line' analysis can be used (see Chapter 8). However, do not dismiss the relationship shown in Figures 5.10 and 5.11 as some minor technical phenomenon. It is far more than this. It identifies an important choice in process design that could have strategic implications. Which is more important to a business, fast throughput time or high utilization of its resources? The only way to have both of these simultaneously is to reduce variability in its processes, which may itself require strategic decisions such as limiting the degree of customization of products or services, or imposing stricter limits on how products or services can be delivered to customers, and so on. It also demonstrates an important point concerned with the day-to-day management of processes – the only way to absolutely guarantee a hundred per cent utilization of resources is to accept an infinite amount of work-in-progress and/or waiting time.

Short case
Heathrow delays caused by capacity utilization[6]

Source: Alamy Images

It may be the busiest international airport in the world, but it is unlikely to win any prizes for being the most loved. Long delays, overcrowding and a shortage of capacity has meant that Heathrow is often a cause of frustration to harassed passengers. Yet to the airlines it is an attractive hub. Its size and location give it powerful 'network effects'. This means that it can match incoming passengers with outgoing flights to hundreds of different cities. Actually it is its attractiveness to the airlines that is one of its main problems. Heathrow's runways are in such demand that they are almost always operating at, or close to, their maximum capacity. In fact, its runways operate at 99% of capacity. This compares with about 70% at most other large airports. This means that the slightest variability (bad weather or an unscheduled landing such as a plane having to turn back with engine

trouble) causes delays, which in turn cause more delays. (See Figure 5.11 for the theoretical explanation of this effect.) The result is that 33% of all flights at Heathrow are delayed by at least 15 minutes. This is poor when compared with other large European airports such as Amsterdam and Frankfurt, which have 21% and 24% of flights delayed respectively.

Human implications for process design

Although we are here dealing with the human implications of process design as the last topic of this chapter, this does not mean that it should be seen as secondary, or unimportant in any way. On the contrary, it is regarded by many as by far the dominant issue of process design. However, there is a whole other field of study – organizational behaviour – that specialises in these issues. Yet, it is included in this chapter in recognition that operations managers are, in practice, the ones who have a significant influence on how people's reactions to their jobs are accommodated in the design of processes.

Task allocation – the division of labour

Division of labour

The idea of the **division of labour** – dividing the total task down into smaller parts, was first formalized as a concept by the economist Adam Smith in his *Wealth of Nations* in 1746.

Perhaps the epitome of the division of labour is the assembly line, where products move along a single path and are built up by operators continually repeating a single task. This is the predominant model of job design in most mass-produced products and in some mass-produced services (fast food, for example). There are some *real advantages* in division of labour:

- *It promotes faster learning.* It is obviously easier to learn how to do a relatively short and simple task than a long and complex one.
- *Automation becomes easier.* Dividing a total task into small parts raises the possibility of automating some of those small tasks.
- *Reduced non-productive work.* This is probably the most important benefit of division of labour. In large, complex tasks the proportion of time spent picking up tools and materials, putting them down again and generally finding, positioning and searching can be very high indeed (called non-productive elements of work). But in shorter, divided, tasks non-productive work can be considerably reduced, which would be very significant to the costs of the operation.

There are also serious drawbacks to highly divided jobs:

- *Monotony.* The shorter the task, the more often operators will need to repeat it. Repeating the same task, for example every 30 seconds, eight hours a day and five days a week, can hardly be called a fulfilling job. As well as any ethical objections, there are other, more obviously practical objections. These include the increased likelihood of absenteeism and staff turnover and the increased likelihood of error.
- *Physical injury.* The continued repetition of a very narrow range of movements can, in extreme cases, lead to physical injury. The over-use of some parts of the body (especially the arms, hands and wrists) can result in pain and a reduction in physical capability. This is sometimes called repetitive strain injury (RSI).
- *Low flexibility.* Dividing a task up into many small parts often gives the job design a rigidity which is difficult to change under changing circumstances.
- *Poor robustness.* Highly divided jobs imply customers, materials or information passing between several stages. If one of these stages is not working correctly, for example because some equipment is faulty, the whole operation is affected.

Scientific management

Scientific management

Related to the division of labour are the ideas of 'scientific' management. The term **scientific management** became established in 1911 with the publication of the book of the same name by Fredrick Taylor (this whole approach to job design is sometimes referred to, pejoratively, as

Taylorism

Taylorism). In this work he identified what he saw as the basic tenets of scientific management:[7]

- All aspects of work should be investigated on a scientific basis to establish the laws, rules and formulae governing the best methods of working.
- Such an investigative approach to the study of work is necessary to establish what constitutes a 'fair day's work'.
- Workers should be selected, trained and developed methodically to perform their tasks.
- Managers should act as the planners of the work (analysing jobs and standardizing the best method of doing the job) while workers should be responsible for carrying out the jobs to the standards laid down.
- Cooperation should be achieved between management and workers based on the 'maximum prosperity' of both.

The important thing to remember about scientific management is that it is not 'scientific' as such, although it certainly does take an 'investigative' approach to improving operations. Perhaps a better term for it would be 'systematic management'. It gave birth to two separate, but related,

Method study
Work measurement
Work study

fields of study, **method study**, which determines the methods and activities to be included in jobs, and **work measurement**, which is concerned with measuring the time that should be taken for performing jobs. Together, these two fields are often referred to as **work study**.

Critical commentary

Even in 1915, criticisms of the scientific management approach were being voiced.[8] In a submission to the United States Commission on Industrial Relations, scientific management is described as:

- being in 'spirit and essence a cunningly devised speeding up and sweating system';
- intensifying the 'modern tendency towards specialization of the work and the task';
- condemning 'the worker to a monotonous routine';
- putting 'into the hands of employers an immense mass of information and methods that may be used unscrupulously to the detriment of workers';
- tending to 'transfer to the management all the traditional knowledge, the judgement and skills of workers';
- greatly intensifying 'unnecessary managerial dictation and discipline';
- tending to 'emphasize quantity of product at the expense of quality'.

Designing the human interface – ergonomic workplace design

Ergonomics is the side note: **Ergonomics**

Ergonomics is concerned primarily with the physiological aspects of job design. Physiology is about the way the body functions. It involves two aspects: firstly, how a person interfaces with his or her immediate working area; secondly, how people react to environmental conditions. Ergonomics is sometimes referred to as **human factors engineering** or just 'human factors'. Both aspects are linked by two common ideas:

side note: **Human factors engineering**

- There must be a fit between people and the jobs they do. To achieve this fit there are only two alternatives. Either the job can be made to fit the people who are doing it, or, alternatively, the people can be made (or perhaps less radically, recruited) to fit the job. Ergonomics addresses the former alternative.
- It is important to take a 'scientific' approach to job design, for example collecting data to indicate how people react under different job design conditions and trying to find the best set of conditions for comfort and performance.

We will explain further some of the aspects of ergonomics in Chapter 6.

Job commitment – behavioural approaches to job design

Processes which are designed purely on division of labour, scientific management or even purely ergonomic principles can alienate the people performing them. Process design should also take into account the desire of individuals to fulfil their needs for self-esteem and personal development. This is where motivation theory and its contribution to the **behavioural approach** to process design is important. This achieves two important objectives. Firstly, it provides jobs which have an intrinsically higher quality of working life – an ethically desirable end in itself. Secondly, because of the higher levels of motivation it engenders, it is instrumental in achieving better performance for the operation, in terms of both the quality and the quantity of output.[9] This approach to job design involves two conceptual steps: firstly, exploring how the various characteristics of the job affect people's motivation; secondly, exploring how individuals' motivation towards the job affects their performance at that job.

side note: **Behavioural approach**

Some of the job characteristics that are held to have a positive effect on job satisfaction are as follows.

Job rotation

side note: **Job rotation**

If increasing the number of related tasks in the job is constrained in some way, for example by the technology of the process, one approach may be to encourage **job rotation**. This means moving individuals periodically between different sets of tasks to provide some variety in their activities. When successful, job rotation can increase skill flexibility and make a small contribution to reducing monotony. However, it is not viewed as universally beneficial either by management (because it can disrupt the smooth flow of work) or by the people performing the jobs (because it can interfere with their rhythm of work).

Job enlargement

Job enlargement

The most obvious method of achieving at least some of the objectives of behavioural job design is by allocating a larger number of tasks to individuals. If these extra tasks are broadly of the same type as those in the original job, the change is called **job enlargement**. This may not involve more demanding or fulfilling tasks, but it may provide a more complete and therefore slightly more meaningful job. If nothing else, people performing an enlarged job will not repeat themselves as often, which could make the job less monotonous.

Job enrichment

Job enrichment

Job enrichment, not only means increasing the number of tasks, but also allocating extra tasks which involve more decision making, greater autonomy and greater control over the job. For example, the extra tasks could include maintenance, planning and control, or monitoring quality levels. The effect is both to reduce repetition in the job and to increase autonomy and personal development. So, in the assembly-line example, each operator, as well as being allocated a job which is twice as long as that previously performed could also be allocated responsibility for carrying out routine maintenance and such tasks as record-keeping and managing the supply of materials.

Empowerment

Empowerment

Empowerment is usually taken to mean more than simple autonomy. Whereas autonomy means giving staff the *ability* to change how they do their jobs, empowerment means giving staff the *authority* to make changes to the job itself, as well as how it is performed. This can be designed into jobs to different degrees.[10] At a minimum, staff could be asked to contribute their suggestions for how the operation might be improved. Going further, staff could be empowered to redesign their jobs. Further still, staff could be included in the strategic direction and performance of the whole organization. The *benefits* of empowerment are generally seen as providing fast responses to customer needs, employees who feel better about their jobs and who will interact with customers with more enthusiasm, promoting 'word-of-mouth' advertising and customer retention. However, there are *costs* associated with empowerment, including higher selection and training costs, perceived inequity of service and the possibility of poor decisions being made by employees.

Team-working

Team-based work organization

A development in job design which is closely linked to the empowerment concept is that of **team-based work organization** (sometimes called self-managed work teams). This is where staff, often with overlapping skills, collectively perform a defined task and have a high degree of discretion over how they actually perform the task. The team would typically control such things as task allocation between members, scheduling work, quality measurement and improvement, and sometimes the hiring of staff. To some extent most work has always been a group-based activity. The concept of teamwork, however, is more prescriptive and assumes a shared set of

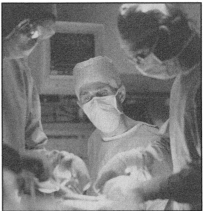

Source: Getty Images

objectives and responsibilities. Groups are described as teams when the virtues of working together are being emphasized, such as the ability to make use of the various skills within the team. Teams may also be used to compensate for other organizational changes such as the move towards flatter organizational structures. When organizations have fewer managerial levels, each manager will have a wider span of activities to control. Teams which are capable of autonomous decision-making have a clear advantage in these circumstances.

Summary answers to key questions

 *Check and improve your understanding of this chapter using self-assessment questions and a personalized study plan, audio and video downloads, and an eBook – all at www.myomlab.com.*

➤ What is process design?

- Process design is the activity which shapes the physical form and purpose of the processes that create and deliver services and products.

- The overall purpose of process design is to meet the needs of customers through achieving appropriate levels of quality, speed, dependability, flexibility and cost.

- The design activity must also take account of environmental issues. These include examination of the source and suitability of materials, the sources and quantities of energy consumed, the amount and type of waste material, the life of the product itself, and the end-of-life state of the product.

➤ How do volume and variety affect process design?

- The overall nature of any process is strongly influenced by the volume and variety of what it has to process.

- The concept of process types summarizes how volume and variety affect overall process design.

- In manufacturing, these process types are (in order of increasing volume and decreasing variety) project, jobbing, batch, mass and continuous processes. In service operations, the terms often used (again in order of increasing volume and decreasing variety) are professional services, service shops and mass services.

➤ How are processes designed in detail?

- Processes are designed initially by breaking them down into their individual activities. Often common symbols are used to represent types of activity. The sequence of activities in a process is then indicated by the sequence of symbols representing activities. This is called 'process mapping'. Alternative process designs can be compared using process maps and improved processes considered in terms of their operations performance objectives.

- Process performance in terms of throughput time, work-in-progress, and cycle time are related by a formula known as Little's law: throughput time equals work-in-progress multiplied by cycle time.

- Variability has a significant effect on the performance of processes, particularly the relationship between waiting time and utilization.

➤ What are the human implications for process design?

- There are many ideas (and a whole field of study – organizational behaviour) that should be taken into account when designing processes. These include the division of labour, ergonomics and more behavioural approaches such as job rotation, job enlargement, job enrichment, empowerment and team-working.

Learning exercises

These problems and applications will help to improve your analysis of operations. You can find more practice problems as well as worked examples and guided solutions on MyOMLab at www.myomlab.com.

1 Read again the description of fast-food drive-through processes at the beginning of this chapter. (a) Draw a process map that reflects the types of process described. (b) What advantage do you think is given to McDonald's through its decision to establish a call centre for remote order-taking for some of its outlets?

2 A regional government office that deals with passport applications is designing a process that will check applications and issue the documents. The number of applications to be processed is 1,600 per week and the time available to process the applications is 40 hours per week. What is the required cycle time for the process?

3 For the passport office, described above, the total work content of all the activities that make up the total task of checking, processing and issuing a passport is, on average, 30 minutes. How many people will be needed to meet demand?

4 The same passport office has a 'clear desk' policy that means that all desks must be clear of work by the end of the day. How many applications should be loaded onto the process in the morning in order to ensure that every one is completed and desks are clear by the end of the day? (Assume a 7.5-hour (450-minute) working day.)

Want to know more?

Chopra, S., Anupindi, R., Deshmukh, S.D., Van Mieghem, J.A. and Zemel, E. (2006) *Managing Business Process Flows*, Prentice-Hall, Englewood Cliffs, NJ. An excellent, although mathematical, approach to process design in general.

Hammer, M. (1990) Reengineering work: don't automate, obliterate, *Harvard Business Review*, July–August. This is the paper that launched the whole idea of business processes and process management in general to a wider managerial audience. Slightly dated but worth reading.

Hopp, W.J. and Spearman, M.L. (2001) *Factory Physics*, 2nd edn, McGraw-Hill, New York. Very technical so don't bother with it if you aren't prepared to get into the maths. However, there is some fascinating analysis, especially concerning Little's law.

Smith, H. and Fingar, P. (2003) *Business Process Management: The Third Wave*, Meghan-Kiffer Press, Tampa, Fl. A popular book on process management from a business process re-engineering perspective.

Useful websites

www.bpmi.org Site of the Business Process Management Initiative. Some good resources including papers and articles.

www.bptrends.com News site for trends in business process management generally. Some interesting articles.

www.bls.gov/oes/ US Department of Labor employment statistics.

www.fedee.com Federation of European Employers guide to employment and job trends in Europe.

www.iienet.org The Global Association of Productivity and Efficiency Professionals site. This is an important professional body for process design and related topics.

www.opsman.org Lots of useful stuff.

www.waria.com A Workflow and Reengineering Association web site. Some useful topics.

Now that you have finished reading this chapter, why not visit MyOMLab at www.myomlab.com where you'll find more learning resources to help you make the most of your studies and get a better grade.

Capacity management

Key questions

- ➤ What is capacity management?
- ➤ How are demand and capacity measured?
- ➤ What are the alternative ways of coping with demand fluctuation?
- ➤ How can operations manage their capacity level?
- ➤ How can queuing theory be used to plan capacity?

Introduction

Providing the capability to satisfy current and future demand is a fundamental responsibility of operations management. Get the balance between capacity and demand right and the operation can satisfy its customers cost-effectively. Get it wrong and it will fail to satisfy demand, and have excessive costs. Capacity management is also sometimes referred to as *aggregate planning*. This is because, at this level, demand and capacity calculations are usually performed on an aggregated basis which does not discriminate between the different services and products that an operation might offer. The essence of the task is to reconcile, at a general and aggregated level, the supply of capacity with the level of demand which it must satisfy. Figure 8.1 shows where this chapter fits into the overall operations model.

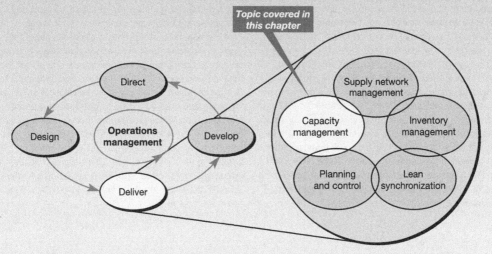

Figure 8.1 This chapter examines capacity management

Check and improve your understanding of this chapter using self-assessment questions and a personalized study plan, audio and video downloads, and an eBook – all at www.myomlab.com.

Operations in practice The London Eye

The British Airways London Eye is the world's largest observation wheel and one of the UK's most spectacular tourist attractions. The 32 passenger capsules each hold 25 people. The wheel rotates continuously, so entry requires customers to step into the capsules which are moving at 0.26 metres per second, which is a quarter of normal walking speed. One complete 360 degree rotation takes 30 minutes, at the end of which the doors open and passengers disembark. Boarding and disembarkation are separated on the specially designed platform which is built out over the river. The attraction has a 'timed admissions booking system' (TABS) for both individual and group bookings. This allocates requests for 'flights' on the basis of half-hour time slots. At the time of writing, the BA London Eye is open every day except Christmas Day. Admission is from 10.00 am to 9.30 pm in the summer, from the beginning of April to mid-September. For the rest of the year, the winter season, admission begins at 10.00 am, and last admissions are for the 5.30 to 6.00 pm slot.

When opened, in 2000, the London Eye was known as the Millennium Wheel. At that time, British Airways was the main sponsor. Today, the London Eye is operated by the London Eye Company Limited of the Merlin Entertainment group. It has become an iconic landmark and a symbol of modern Britain. The London Eye is the UK's most popular paid-for visitor attraction, visited by over 3.5 million people a year enjoying the 40 kilometres view in all directions (weather permitting!). In addition to the spectacular views, the Eye offers many other possibilities. Since opening, 433 weddings and civil partnerships have been celebrated 'on board'. New Year's Eve fireworks displays are also a regular feature. For a fee, private capsules can be hired for up to 25 guests, with the option of food, champagne, or even a 'Mulled Wine and Mince Pies Capsule' in the Christmas period. Partnerships with local hotels, river cruise companies and restaurants also allow the Eye to offer 'package deals'.

Source: British Airways London Eye

To 'fly' on the Eye, customers must first buy their (timed) tickets in the Ticket Hall then queue to board the wheel itself. And because The Eye is extremely popular (especially in summer) queues can last up to four hours although, on a wet and cold winter's day, demand (and therefore queues) can be far lower. Fast Track tickets (at a premium price) will avoid the queues. However, the best way for customers to avoid queues at busy times is to book tickets online, but this means risking poor weather the day of your 'flight'. Groups of customers hiring a private capsule are asked for one member of the group to check-in at a priority check-in desk 15 minutes before their scheduled flight time. Once the whole group is ready, the 'capsule host' escorts the group through the Fast Track entrance bypassing most of the queue. There are also special arrangements for other 'special' ticket holders such as schools' bookings, disabled tickets, flexi tickets, flexi fast-track and so on.

What is capacity management?

The most common use of the word capacity is in the static, physical sense of the fixed *volume* of a container, or the space in a building. This meaning of the word is also sometimes used by operations managers. For example, a pharmaceutical manufacturer may invest in new 1,000-litre capacity reactor vessels, a property company purchases a 500-vehicle capacity city-centre car park, and a 'multiplex' cinema is built with 10 screens and a total capacity of 2,500 seats. Although these capacity measures describe the **scale** of these operations, they do not reflect the processing capacities of these investments. To do this we must incorporate a **time** dimension appropriate to the use of assets. So the pharmaceutical company will be concerned with the level of output that can be achieved using the 1,000-litre reactor vessel. If a batch of standard products can be produced every hour, the planned processing capacity could be as high as 24,000 litres per day. If the reaction takes four hours, and two hours are used for cleaning between batches, the vessel may only produce 4,000 litres per day. Similarly, the car park may be fully occupied by office workers during the working day, 'processing' only 500 cars per day. Alternatively, it may be used for shoppers staying on average only one hour, and theatre-goers occupying spaces for three hours in the evening. The processing capacity would then be up to 5,000 cars per day. Thus the definition of the capacity of an operation is the **maximum level of value-added activity over a period of time** that the process can achieve under normal operating conditions.

Capacity considers scale and time dimensions

Capacity is the maximum level of activity over a time period

Capacity constraints

Many organizations operate at below their maximum processing capacity, either because there is insufficient demand to completely 'fill' their capacity, or as a deliberate policy, so that the operation can respond quickly to extra demand. Often organizations find themselves with some parts of their operation operating below their capacity while other parts are at their capacity 'ceiling'. It is the parts of the operation that are operating at their capacity ceiling which are the **capacity constraint** for the whole operation. For example, a retail superstore might offer a gift-wrapping service which at normal times can cope with all requests for its services without delaying customers unduly. At Christmas, however, the demand for gift wrapping might increase proportionally far more than the overall increase in custom for the store as a whole. Unless extra resources are provided to increase the capacity of this micro-operation, it could constrain the capacity of the whole store.

Capacity constraint

Managing capacity

Capacity management is the task of setting the effective capacity of the operation so that it can respond to the demands placed upon it. This usually means deciding how the operation should react to fluctuations in demand. Long-term changes in demand and the alternative capacity strategies for dealing with the changes is usually concerned with introducing (or deleting) major increments of capacity. We called this task **long-term capacity strategy**. In this chapter we are treating the shorter timescale where capacity decisions are being made largely within the constraints of the capacity limits set by the operation's long-term capacity strategy.

Long-term capacity strategy

Medium- and short-term capacity

Having established long-term capacity, operations managers must decide how to adjust the capacity of the operation in the **medium term**. This usually involves an assessment of the demand forecasts over a period of 2–18 months ahead, during which time planned output can be varied, for example, by changing the number of hours the equipment is used. In practice, however, few forecasts are accurate, and most operations also need to respond to changes in

Medium-term capacity management

Short-term capacity management

demand which occur over a shorter timescale. Hotels and restaurants have unexpected and apparently random changes in demand from night to night, but also know from experience that certain days are on average busier than others. So operations managers also have to make **short-term capacity** adjustments, which enable them to flex output for a short period, either on a predicted basis (for example, bank checkouts are always busy at lunchtimes) or at short notice (for example, a sunny day at a theme park).

Aggregate demand and capacity

Aggregate capacity management

The important characteristic of capacity management, as we are treating it here, is that it is concerned with setting capacity levels over the medium and short terms in **aggregated** terms. This means making broad capacity decisions without concern for all of the detail of the individual services and products offered. This may mean some degree of approximation, especially if the mix of offerings varies significantly (as we shall see later in this chapter). Nevertheless, as a first step in capacity management, aggregation is necessary. For example, a hotel might think of demand and capacity in terms of 'room nights per month', which ignores the number of guests in each room and their individual requirements, but is a good first approximation. A woollen knitwear factory might measure demand and capacity in the number of garments it is capable of making per month, ignoring size, colour or style variations. Aluminium producers could use tonnes per month, ignoring types of alloy, gauge and batch size variation. The ultimate aggregation measure is money. For example, retail stores, which sell an exceptionally wide variety of services and products, use revenue per month, ignoring variation in spend, number of items bought, the gross margin of each item and the number of items per customer transaction. If all this seems very approximate, remember that most operations have sufficient experience of dealing with aggregated data to find it useful.

The objectives of capacity management

The decisions taken by operations managers in devising their capacity plans will affect several different aspects of performance:

- *Quality* of services or products might be affected by a capacity plan which involves large fluctuations in capacity levels, by hiring temporary staff for example. The disruption to the routine working of the operation could increase the probability of errors.
- *Speed* of response to customer demand could be enhanced, either by the build-up of inventories or by the deliberate provision of surplus capacity to avoid queuing.
- *Dependability* of supply will also be affected by how close demand levels are to capacity. The closer demand gets to the operation's capacity ceiling, the less able it is to cope with any unexpected disruptions.
- *Flexibility*, especially volume flexibility, will be enhanced by surplus capacity, which allows the operation to respond to any unexpected increase in demand.
- *Costs* will be affected by the balance between capacity and demand. Capacity levels in excess of demand could mean under-utilization of capacity and therefore high unit cost.
- *Revenues* will also be affected by the balance between capacity and demand, but in the opposite way. Capacity levels equal to or higher than demand at any point in time will ensure that all demand is satisfied and no revenue lost.
- *Working capital* will be affected if an operation decides to build up finished goods inventory prior to demand. This might allow demand to be satisfied, but the organization will have to fund the inventory until it can be sold.

The steps of capacity management

The sequence of capacity management decisions which need to be taken by operations managers is illustrated in Figure 8.2. Typically, operations managers are faced with a forecast of demand which is unlikely to be either certain or constant. They will also have some idea of their own ability to meet this demand. Nevertheless, before any further decisions are

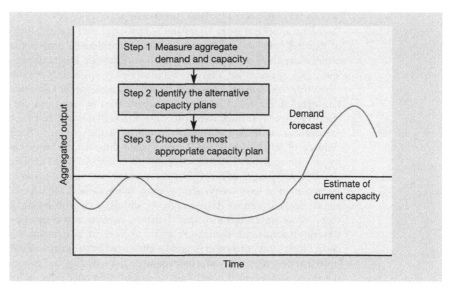

Figure 8.2 **The steps in capacity management**

taken, they must have quantitative data on both capacity and demand. So the first step will be to measure the aggregate demand and capacity levels for the planning period. The second step will be to identify the alternative capacity plans which could be adopted in response to the demand fluctuations. The third step will be to choose the most appropriate capacity plan for their circumstances.

Measuring demand and capacity

Forecasting demand fluctuations

Forecasting is a key input to capacity management

Although **demand forecasting** is usually the responsibility of the sales and/or marketing functions, it is a very important input into capacity management decisions, and is therefore of interest to operations managers. After all, without an estimate of future demand it is not possible to plan effectively for future events, only to react to them. It is therefore important to understand the basis and rationale for these demand forecasts. As far as capacity management is concerned, there are three requirements from a demand forecast.

It is expressed in terms which are useful for capacity management
If forecasts are expressed only in money terms and give no indication of the demands that will be placed on an operation's capacity, they will need to be translated into realistic expectations of demand, expressed in the same units as the capacity (for example, operatives required, space needed, machine hours per year, etc.).

It is as accurate as possible
In capacity management, the accuracy of a forecast is important because, whereas demand can change instantaneously, there is a lag between deciding to change capacity and the change taking effect. Thus, many operations managers are faced with a dilemma. In order to attempt to meet demand, they must often decide output in advance, based on a forecast which might change before the demand occurs, or worse, prove not to reflect actual demand at all.

It gives an indication of relative uncertainty

Decisions to operate extra hours and recruit extra staff are usually based on forecast levels of demand, which could in practice differ considerably from actual demand, leading to unnecessary costs or unsatisfactory customer service. For example, a forecast of demand levels in a supermarket may show initially slow business that builds up to a lunchtime rush. After this, demand slows, only to build up again for the early evening rush, and it finally falls again at the end of trading. The supermarket manager can use this forecast to adjust checkout capacity throughout the day. But although this may be an accurate average demand forecast, no single day will exactly conform to this pattern. Of equal importance is an estimate of how much actual demand could differ from the average. This can be found by examining demand statistics to build up a distribution of demand at each point in the day. The importance of this is that the manager now has an understanding of when it will be important to have reserve staff, perhaps filling shelves, but on call to staff the checkouts should demand warrant it. Generally, the advantage of probabilistic forecasts such as this is that it allows operations managers to make a judgement between possible plans that would virtually guarantee the operation's ability to meet actual demand, and plans that minimize costs. Ideally, this judgement should be influenced by the nature of the way the business wins orders: price-sensitive markets may require a risk-avoiding cost minimization plan that does not always satisfy peak demand, whereas markets that value responsiveness and service quality may justify a more generous provision of operational capacity.

Seasonality of demand

In many organizations, capacity management is concerned largely with coping with seasonal demand fluctuations. Almost all services and products have some **demand seasonality** and some also have **supply seasonality**, usually where the inputs are seasonal agricultural products – for example, in processing frozen vegetables. These fluctuations in demand or supply may be reasonably forecastable, but some are usually also affected by unexpected variations in the weather and by changing economic conditions. Figure 8.3 gives some examples of seasonality, and the short case 'Operating while the sun shines' discusses the sometimes unexpected link between weather conditions and demand levels.

Consider the four different types of operation described previously: a city hotel, a wool knitwear factory, a supermarket and an aluminium producer. Their demand patterns are shown in Figure 8.4. The city hotel and the woollen knitwear business both have seasonal

Demand seasonality
Supply seasonality

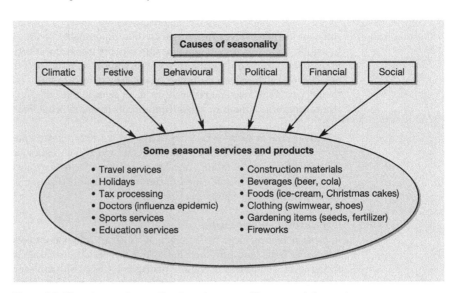

Figure 8.3 Many types of operation have to cope with seasonal demand

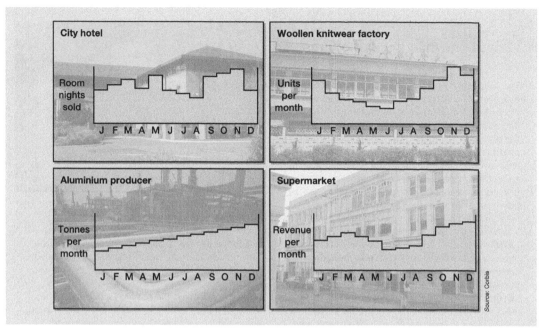

Figure 8.4 Aggregate demand fluctuations for four organizations

sales demand patterns, but for different reasons: the woollen knitwear business because of climatic patterns (cold winters, warm summers) and the hotel because of demand from business people, who take vacations from work at Christmas and in the summer. The retail supermarket is a little less seasonal, but is affected by pre-vacation peaks and reduced sales during vacation periods. The aluminium producer shows virtually no seasonality, but is showing a steady growth in sales over the forecast period.

Weekly and daily demand fluctuations

Seasonality of demand occurs over a year, but similar predictable variations in demand can also occur for some services and products on a shorter cycle. The daily and weekly demand patterns of a supermarket will fluctuate, with some degree of predictability. Demand might be low in the morning, higher in the afternoon, with peaks at lunchtime and after work in the evening. Demand might be low on Monday and Tuesday, build up during the latter part of the week and reach a peak on Friday and Saturday. Banks, public offices, telephone sales organizations and electricity utilities all have weekly and daily, or even hourly, demand patterns which require capacity adjustment. The extent to which an operation will have to cope with very short-term demand fluctuations is partly determined by how long its customers are prepared to wait for their services. An operation whose customers are incapable of, or unwilling to, wait will have to plan for very short-term demand fluctuations. Emergency services, for example, will need to understand the hourly variation in the demand for their services and plan capacity accordingly.

Measuring capacity

The main problem with measuring capacity is the complexity of most operations. Only when the operation is highly standardized and repetitive is capacity easy to define unambiguously. A government office, for example, may have the capacity to print and post 500,000 tax forms

Short case
Operating while the sun shines[1]

The sales of many operations are profoundly affected by the weather. Sunglasses, sunscreen, waterproof clothing and ice cream are all obvious examples. Yet the range of operations interested in weather forecasting has expanded significantly. Energy utilities, soft drink producers and retailers are all keen to purchase the latest weather forecasts. But so are operations such as banking call centres and mobile phone operators. It would appear that the demand for telephone banking falls dramatically when the sun shines, as does the use of mobile phones. A motorway catering group was surprised to find that their sales of hot meals fell predictably by €110,000 per day for each degree temperature rise above 20 °C. Similarly, insurance companies have found it wise to sell their offerings when the weather is poor and likely customers are trapped indoors rather than relaxing outside in the sun, refusing to worry about the future. In the not-for-profit sector, new understanding is being developed on the link between various illnesses and temperature. Here temperature is often used as a predictor of demand. So, for example, coronary thrombosis cases peak two days after a drop in temperature, for strokes the delay is around five days, while deaths from respiratory infections peak twelve days from a temperature drop. Knowing this, hospital managers can plan for changes in their demand.

Because of this, meteorological services around the world now sell increasingly sophisticated forecasts to a wide range of companies. In the UK, the Meteorological Office offers an internet-based service for its customers.

Source: Alamy/Medical-on-line

It is also used to help insurance specialists price insurance policies to provide compensation against weather-related risk. Complex financial products called 'weather derivates' are now available to compensate for weather-related uncertainty. So, for example, an energy company could buy a financial option before winter where the seller pays the company a guaranteed sum of money if the temperature rises above a certain level. If the weather is mild and energy sales are low, the company gets compensation. If the weather is cold, the company loses the premium it has paid to the seller but makes up for it by selling more power at higher prices. However, as meteorologists point out, it is up to the individual businesses to use the information wisely. Only they have the experience to assess the full impact of weather on their operation. So, for example, supermarkets know that a rise in temperature will impact on the sales of cottage cheese, whereas, unaccountably, the sales of cottage cheese with pineapple chunks are not affected!

per week. A fast ride at a theme park might be designed to process batches of 60 people every three minutes – a capacity to convey 1,200 people per hour. In each case, an **output** **capacity measure** is the most appropriate measure because the output from the operation does not vary in its nature. For many operations, however, the definition of capacity is not so obvious. When a much wider range of outputs places varying demands on the process, for instance, output measures of capacity are less useful. Here **input capacity measures** are frequently used to define capacity. Almost every type of operation could use a mixture of both input and output measures, but in practice, most choose to use one or the other (see Table 8.1).

Output capacity measure

Input capacity measures

Capacity depends on activity mix

The hospital measures its capacity in terms of its resources, partly because there is not a clear relationship between the number of beds it has and the number of patients it treats. If all its patients required relatively minor treatment with only short stays in hospital, it could treat many people per week. Alternatively, if most of its patients required long periods of observation or recuperation, it could treat far fewer. Output depends on the mix of activities in which the hospital is engaged and, because most hospitals perform many different types of activities, output is difficult to predict. Certainly it is difficult to compare directly the capacity of hospitals which have very different activities.

Table 8.1 Input and output capacity measures for different operations

Operation	Input measure of capacity	Output measure of capacity
Hospital	**Beds available**	Number of patients treated per week
Theatre	**Number of seats**	Number of customers entertained per week
University	**Number of students**	Students graduated per year
Retail store	**Sales floor area**	Number of items sold per day
Airline	**Number of seats available on the sector**	Number of passengers per week
Air-conditioner plant	Machine hours available	**Number of units per week**
Electricity company	Generator size	**Megawatts of electricity generated**
Brewery	Volume of fermentation tanks	**Litres per week**

Note: The most commonly used measure is shown in bold.

Worked example

Suppose an air-conditioner factory produces three different models of air-conditioner unit: the de luxe, the standard and the economy. The de luxe model can be assembled in 1.5 hours, the standard in 1 hour and the economy in 0.75 hour. The assembly area in the factory has 800 staff hours of assembly time available each week.

If demand for de luxe, standard and economy units is in the ratio 2:3:2, the time needed to assemble $2 + 3 + 2 = 7$ units is:

$$(2 \times 1.5) + (3 \times 1) + (2 \times 0.75) = 7.5 \text{ hours}$$

The number of units produced per week is:

$$\frac{800}{7.5} \times 7 = 746.7 \text{ units}$$

If demand changes to a ratio of de luxe, economy, standard units of 1:2:4, the time needed to assemble $1 + 2 + 4 = 7$ units is:

$$(1 \times 1.5) + (2 \times 1) + (4 \times 0.75) = 6.5 \text{ hours}$$

Now the number of units produced per week is:

$$\frac{800}{6.5} \times 7 = 861.5 \text{ units}$$

Overall equipment effectiveness[2]

Overall equipment effectiveness

The **overall equipment effectiveness** (OEE) measure is an increasingly popular method of judging the effectiveness of operations equipment. It is based on three aspects of performance:

- *the time* that equipment is available to operate;
- *the quality* of the product or service it creates;
- *the speed,* or throughput rate, of the equipment.

Overall equipment effectiveness is calculated by multiplying an availability rate by a performance (or speed) rate multiplied by a quality rate. Some of the reduction in available capacity of a piece of equipment (or any process) is caused by time losses such as set-up and changeover losses (when the equipment or process is being prepared for its next activity), and breakdown failures when the machine is being repaired. Some capacity is lost through speed losses such as when equipment is idling (for example when it is temporarily waiting for work from another process) and when equipment is being run below its optimum work rate.

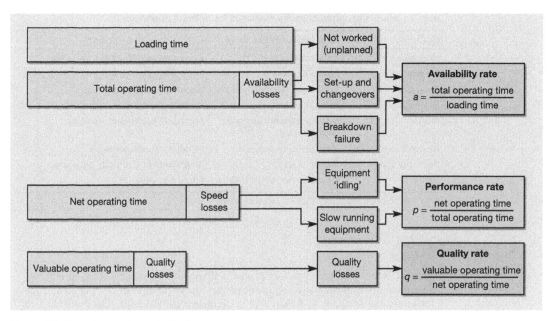

Figure 8.5 Operating equipment effectiveness

Finally, not everything processed by a piece of equipment will be error-free. So some capacity is lost through quality losses (see Figure 8.5).

Taking the notation in Figure 8.5,

$$OEE = a \times p \times q$$

For equipment to operate effectively, it needs to achieve high levels of performance against all three of these dimensions. Viewed in isolation, these individual metrics are important indicators of performance, but they do not give a complete picture of *overall* effectiveness. This can only be understood by looking at the combined effect of the three measures, calculated by multiplying the three individual metrics together. All these losses to the OEE performance can be expressed in terms of units of time – the design cycle time to deliver one unit. In effect, this means that an OEE represents the valuable operating time as a percentage of the design capacity.

> ### Worked example
>
> In a typical 7-day period, the planning department programmes a particular machine to work for 150 hours – its loading time. Changeovers and set-ups take an average of 10 hours and breakdown failures average 5 hours every 7 days. The time when the machine cannot work because it is waiting for material to be delivered from other parts of the process is 5 hours on average and during the period when the machine is running, it averages 90 per cent of its rated speed. Three per cent of the parts processed by the machine are subsequently found to be defective in some way.
>
> $$\text{Maximum time available} = 7 \times 24 \text{ hours}$$
> $$= 168 \text{ hours}$$
>
> $$\text{Loading time} = 150 \text{ hours}$$
>
> $$\text{Availability losses} = 10 \text{ hours (set-ups)} + 5 \text{ hrs (breakdowns)}$$
> $$= 15 \text{ hours}$$

So, Total operating time = Loading time – Availability
$$= 150 \text{ hours} - 15 \text{ hours}$$
$$= 135 \text{ hours}$$

Speed losses = 5 hours (idling) + ((135 – 5) × 0.1)(10% of remaining time)
$$= 18 \text{ hours}$$

So, Net operating time = Total operating time – Speed losses
$$= 135 - 18$$
$$= 117 \text{ hours}$$

Quality losses = 117 (Net operating time) × 0.03 (Error rate)
$$= 3.51 \text{ hours}$$

So, Valuable operating time = Net operating time – Quality losses
$$= 117 - 3.51$$
$$= 113.49 \text{ hours}$$

Therefore, availability rate $= a = \dfrac{\text{Total operating time}}{\text{Loading time}}$

$$= \frac{135}{150} = 90\%$$

and, performance rate $= p = \dfrac{\text{Net operating time}}{\text{Total operating time}}$

$$= \frac{117}{135} = 86.67$$

and quality rate $= q = \dfrac{\text{Valuable operating time}}{\text{Net operating time}}$

$$= \frac{113.49}{117} = 97\%$$

OEE $(a \times p \times q) = 75.6\%$

The alternative capacity plans

With an understanding of both demand and capacity, the next step is to consider the alternative methods of responding to demand fluctuations. There are three 'pure' options available for coping with such variation:

Level capacity plan
Chase demand plan
Demand management

- Ignore the fluctuations and keep activity levels constant (**level capacity plan**).
- Adjust capacity to reflect the fluctuations in demand (**chase demand plan**).
- Attempt to change demand to fit capacity availability (**demand management**).

In practice, most organizations will use a mixture of all of these 'pure' plans, although often one plan might dominate. The Short case 'Seasonal salads' describes how one operation pursues some of these options.

Level capacity plan

In a level capacity plan, the processing capacity is set at a uniform level throughout the planning period, regardless of the fluctuations in forecast demand. This means that the same

Seasonal salads

Lettuce is an all-year-round ingredient for most salads, but both the harvesting of the crop and its demand are seasonal. Lettuces are perishable and must be kept in cold stores and transported in refrigerated vehicles. Even then the product only stays fresh for a maximum of a week. In most north European countries, demand continues throughout the winter at around half the summer levels, but outdoor crops cannot be grown during the winter months. Glasshouse cultivation is possible but expensive.

One of Europe's largest lettuce growers is G's Fresh Salads. Their supermarket customers require fresh produce to be delivered 364 days a year, but because of the limitations of the English growing season, the company has developed other sources of supply in Europe. It acquired a farm and packhouse in the Murcia region of south-eastern Spain, which provides the bulk of salad crops during the winter, transported daily to the UK by a fleet of refrigerated trucks. Further top-up produce is imported by air from around the world.

Sales forecasts are agreed with the individual supermarkets well in advance, allowing the planting and growing programmes to be matched to the anticipated level of sales. However, the programme is only a rough guide. The supermarkets may change their orders right up to the afternoon of the preceding day. Weather is a dominant factor. First, it determines supply – how well the crop grows and how easy it is to harvest. Second, it influences sales – cold, wet periods during the summer discourage the eating of salads, whereas hot spells boost demand greatly.

The fluctuating nature of the actual sales is the result of a combination of weather-related availability and supermarket demand. These do not always match. When demand is higher than expected, the picking rigs and their crews continue to work into the middle of night, under floodlights. Another capacity problem is the operation's staffing levels. It relies on temporary seasonal harvesting and packing staff to supplement the full-time employees for both the English and Spanish seasons. Since most of the crop is transported to the UK in bulk, a large permanent staff is maintained for packing and distribution in the UK. The majority of the Spanish workforce is temporary, with only a small number retained during the extremely hot summer to grow and harvest other crops such as melons.

The specialist lettuce harvesting machines (the 'rigs') are shipped over to Spain every year at the end of the English season, so that the company can achieve maximum utilization from all this expensive capital equipment. These rigs not only enable very high productivity of the pickers, but also ensure the best possible conditions for quality packing and rapid transportation to the cold stores.

number of staff operate the same processes and should therefore be capable of delivering the same aggregate output in each period. Where non-perishable materials are processed, but not immediately sold, they can be transferred to finished goods inventory in anticipation of sales at a later time. Thus this plan is feasible (but not necessarily desirable) for our examples of the woollen knitwear company and the aluminium producer (see Figure 8.6).

Level capacity plans of this type can achieve the objectives of stable employment patterns, high process utilization, and usually also high productivity with low unit costs. Unfortunately, they can also create considerable inventory which has to be financed and stored. Perhaps the biggest problem, however, is that decisions have to be taken as to what to produce for inventory rather than for immediate sale. Will green woollen sweaters knitted in July still be fashionable in October? Could a particular aluminium alloy in a specific sectional shape still be sold months after it has been produced? Most firms operating this plan, therefore, give priority to only creating inventory where future sales are relatively certain and unlikely to be affected by changes in fashion or design. Clearly, such plans are not suitable for 'perishable' products, such as foods and some pharmaceuticals, for products where fashion changes rapidly and unpredictably (for example, popular music CDs, fashion garments), or for customized products.

A level capacity plan could also be used by the hotel and supermarket, although this would not be the usual approach of such organizations, because it usually results in a waste of staff

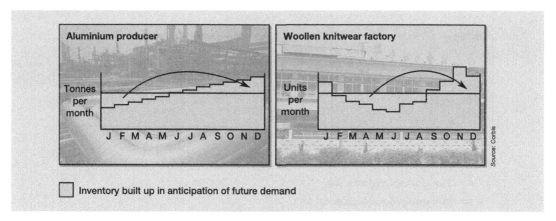

Figure 8.6 Level capacity plans which use anticipation inventory to supply future demand

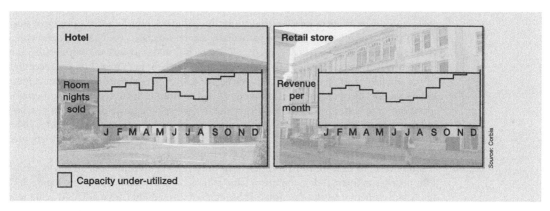

Figure 8.7 Level capacity plans with under-utilization of capacity

resources, reflected in low productivity. Because service cannot be stored as inventory, a level capacity plan would involve running the operation at a uniformly high level of capacity availability. The hotel would employ sufficient staff to service all the rooms, to run a full restaurant, and to staff the reception even in months when demand was expected to be well below capacity. Similarly, the supermarket would plan to staff all the checkouts, warehousing operations, and so on, even in quiet periods (see Figure 8.7).

Low utilization can make level capacity plans prohibitively expensive in many service operations, but may be considered appropriate where the opportunity costs of individual lost sales are very high. For example, in the high-margin retailing of jewellery and in (real) estate agents. It is also possible to set the capacity somewhat below the forecast peak demand level in order to reduce the degree of under-utilization. However, in the periods where demand is expected to exceed planned capacity, customer service may deteriorate. Customers may have to queue for long periods or may be 'processed' faster and less sensitively. While this is obviously far from ideal, the benefits to the organization of stability and productivity may outweigh the disadvantages of upsetting some customers.

Chase demand plan

The opposite of a level capacity plan is one which attempts to match capacity closely to the varying levels of forecast demand. This is much more difficult to achieve than a level capacity plan, as different numbers of staff, different working hours, and even different amounts of equipment may be necessary in each period. For this reason, pure chase demand plans are

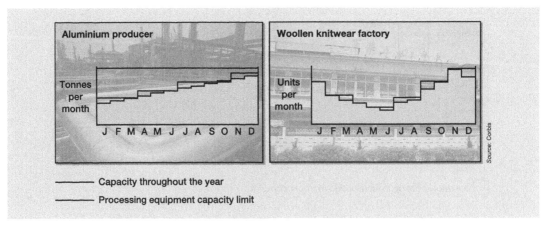

Figure 8.8 Chase demand capacity plans with changes in capacity which reflect changes in demand

unlikely to appeal to operations which manufacture standard, non-perishable products. Also, where manufacturing operations are particularly capital-intensive, the chase demand policy would require a level of physical capacity, all of which would only be used occasionally. It is for this reason that such a plan is less likely to be appropriate for the aluminium producer than for the woollen garment manufacturer (see Figure 8.8). A pure chase demand plan is more usually adopted by operations which cannot store their output, such as customer-processing operations or operations with perishable products. It avoids the wasteful provision of excess staff that occurs with a level capacity plan, and yet should satisfy customer demand throughout the planned period. Where output can be stored, the chase demand policy might be adopted in order to minimize or eliminate finished goods inventory.

Sometimes it is difficult to achieve very large variations in capacity from period to period. If the changes in forecast demand are as large as those in the hotel example (see Figure 8.9), significantly different levels of staffing will be required throughout the year. This would mean employing part-time and temporary staff, requiring permanent employees to work longer hours, or even bringing in contract labour. The operations managers will then have the difficult task of ensuring that quality standards and safety procedures are still adhered to, and that the customer service levels are maintained.

Methods of adjusting capacity

The chase demand approach requires that capacity is adjusted by some means. There are a number of different methods for achieving this, although they may not all be feasible for all types of operation. Some of these methods are now discussed.

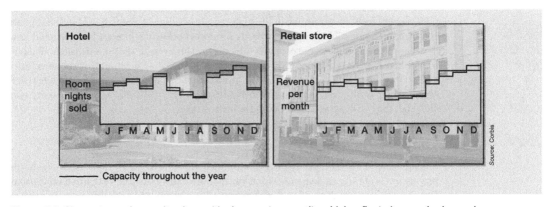

Figure 8.9 Chase demand capacity plans with changes in capacity which reflect changes in demand

Overtime and idle time

Often the quickest and most convenient method of adjusting capacity is by varying the number of productive hours worked by the staff in the operation. When demand is higher than nominal capacity, **overtime** is worked, and when demand is lower than nominal capacity the amount of time spent by staff on productive work can be reduced. In the latter case, it may be possible for staff to engage in some other activity such as cleaning or maintenance. This method is only useful if the timing of the extra productive capacity matches that of the demand. For example, there is little to be gained in asking a retail operation's staff to work extra hours in the evening if all the extra demand is occurring during their normal working period. The costs associated with this method are either the extra payment which is normally necessary to secure the agreement of staff to work overtime, or in the case of **idle time**, the costs of paying staff who are not engaged in direct productive work. Further, there might be costs associated with the fixed costs of keeping the operation heated, lit and secure over the extra period staff are working. There is also a limit to the amount of extra working time which any workforce can deliver before productivity levels decrease. **Annualized hours** approaches, as described below in the Short case 'Working by the year', are one way of flexing working hours without excessive extra costs.

Varying the size of the workforce

If capacity is largely governed by workforce size, one way to adjust it is to adjust the size of the workforce. This is done by hiring extra staff during periods of high demand and laying them off as demand falls, or **hire and fire**. However, there are cost and ethical implications to be taken into account before adopting such a method. The costs of hiring extra staff include those associated with recruitment, as well as the costs of low productivity while new staff go through the learning curve. The costs of lay-off may include possible severance payments, but might also include the loss of morale in the operation and loss of goodwill in the local labour market. At a micro-operation level, one method of coping with peaks in demand in one area of an operation is to build sufficient flexibility into job design and job demarcation so that staff can transfer across from less busy parts of the operation. For example, the French hotel chain Novotel has trained some of its kitchen staff to escort customers from the reception area up to their rooms. The peak times for registering new customers coincide with the least busy times in the kitchen and restaurant areas.

Using part-time staff

A variation on the previous strategy is to recruit **part-time staff**, that is, for less than the normal working day. This method is extensively used in service operations such as supermarkets and fast-food restaurants but is also used by some manufacturers to staff an evening shift after the normal working day. However, if the fixed costs of employment for each employee, irrespective of how long he or she works, are high then using this method may not be worthwhile.

Subcontracting

In periods of high demand, an operation might buy capacity from other organizations, called **subcontracting**. This might enable the operation to meet its own demand without the extra expense of investing in capacity which will not be needed after the peak in demand has passed. Again, there are costs associated with this method. The most obvious one is that subcontracting can be very expensive. The subcontractor will also want to make sufficient margin out of the business. A subcontractor may not be as motivated to deliver on time or to the desired levels of quality. Finally, there is the risk that the subcontractors might decide to enter the same market themselves.

Manage demand plan

The most obvious mechanism of **demand management** is to **change demand** through price. Although this is probably the most widely applied approach in demand management, it is more common for services than for products. For example, some city hotels offer low-cost

(Margin notes: Overtime, Idle time, Annualized hours, Hire and fire, Part-time staff, Subcontracting, Demand management, Change demand)

Critical commentary

To many, the idea of fluctuating the workforce to match demand, either by using part-time staff or by hiring and firing, is more than just controversial. It is regarded as unethical. It is any business's responsibility, they argue, to engage in a set of activities which are capable of sustaining employment at a steady level. Hiring and firing merely for seasonal fluctuations, which can be predicted in advance, is treating human beings in a totally unacceptable manner. Even hiring people on a short-term contract, in practice, leads to them being offered poorer conditions of service and leads to a state of permanent anxiety as to whether they will keep their jobs. On a more practical note, it is pointed out that, in an increasingly global business world where companies may have sites in different countries, those countries that allow hiring and firing are more likely to have their plants 'downsized' than those where legislation makes this difficult.

'city break' vacation packages in the months when fewer business visitors are expected. Skiing and camping holidays are cheapest at the beginning and end of the season and are particularly expensive during school vacations. Discounts are given by photo-processing firms during winter periods, but never around summer holidays. Ice cream is 'on offer' in many supermarkets during the winter. The objective is invariably to stimulate off-peak demand and to constrain peak demand, in order to smooth demand as much as possible. Organizations can also attempt to increase demand in low periods by appropriate advertising. For example, turkey growers in the UK and the USA make vigorous attempts to promote their products at times other than Christmas and Thanksgiving.

Short case
Working by the year[3]

One method of fluctuating capacity as demand varies throughout the year without many of the costs associated with overtime or hiring temporary staff is called the Annual Hours Work Plan. This involves staff contracting to work a set number of hours per year rather than a set number of hours per week. The advantage of this is that the amount of staff time available to an organization can be varied throughout the year to reflect the real state of demand. Annual hours plans can also be useful when supply varies throughout the year. For example, a UK cheese factory of Express Foods, like all cheese factories, must cope with processing very different quantities of milk at different times of the year. In spring and during early summer, cows produce large quantities of milk, but in late summer and autumn the supply of milk slows to a trickle. Before the introduction of annualized hours, the factory had relied on overtime and

hiring temporary workers during the busy season. Now the staff are contracted to work a set number of hours a year with rotas agreed more than a year in advance and after consultation with the union. This means that at the end of July staff broadly know what days and hours they will be working up to September of the following year. If an emergency should arise, the company can call in people from a group of 'super crew' who work more flexible hours in return for higher pay but can do any job in the factory.

However, not all experiments with annualized hours have been as successful as that at Express Foods. In cases where demand is very unpredictable, staff can be asked to come in to work at very short notice. This can cause considerable disruption to social and family life. For example, at one news-broadcasting company, the scheme caused problems. Journalists and camera crew who went to cover a foreign crisis found that they had worked so many hours they were asked to take the whole of one month off to compensate. Since they had no holiday plans, many would have preferred to work.

Alternative offerings

Alternative offerings

Sometimes, a more radical approach is required to fill periods of low demand such as developing offerings which can be delivered using existing processes, but have different demand patterns throughout the year (see the Short case 'Getting the message' for an example of this approach). Most universities fill their accommodation and lecture theatres with conferences and company meetings during vacations. Ski resorts provide organized mountain activity holidays in the summer. Some garden tractor companies in the US now make snow movers in the autumn and winter. The apparent benefits of filling capacity in this way must be weighted against the risks of damaging the core service or product, and the operation must be fully capable of serving both markets. Some universities have been criticized for providing sub-standard, badly decorated accommodation which met the needs of impecunious undergraduates, but which failed to impress executives at a trade conference.

Mixed plans

Each of the three 'pure' plans is applied only where its advantages strongly outweigh its disadvantages. For many organizations, however, these 'pure' approaches do not match their required combination of competitive and operational objectives. Most operations managers are required simultaneously to reduce costs and inventory, to minimize capital investment, and yet to provide a responsive and customer-oriented approach at all times. For this reason, most choose to follow a mixture of the three approaches. This can be best illustrated by the woollen knitwear company example (see Figure 8.10). Here some of the peak demand has been brought forward by the company offering discounts to selected retail customers (manage demand plan). Capacity has also been adjusted at two points in the year to reflect the broad changes in demand (chase demand plan). Yet the adjustment in capacity is not sufficient to totally avoid the build-up of inventories (level capacity plan).

Yield management

In operations which have relatively fixed capacities, such as airlines and hotels, it is important to use the capacity of the operation for generating revenue to its full potential. One approach used by such operations is called **yield management**.[4] This is really a collection of methods, some of which we have already discussed, which can be used to ensure that an operation maximizes its potential to generate profit. Yield management is especially useful where:

- capacity is relatively fixed;
- the market can be fairly clearly segmented;
- the service cannot be stored in any way;

Yield management

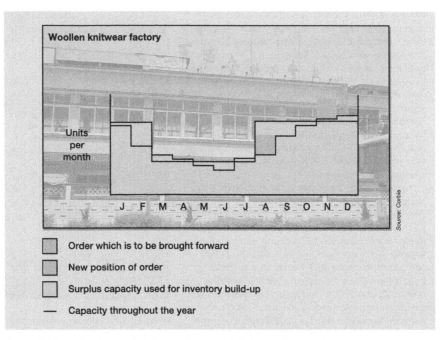

Figure 8.10 A mixed capacity plan for the woollen knitwear factory

- the services are sold in advance;
- the marginal cost of making a sale is relatively low.

Airlines, for example, fit all these criteria. They adopt a collection of methods to try to maximize the yield (i.e. profit) from their capacity. These include the following:

- *Over-booking capacity.* Not every passenger who has booked a place on a flight will actually show up for the flight. If the airline did not fill this seat it would lose the revenue from it. Because of this, airlines regularly book more passengers onto flights than the capacity of the aircraft can cope with. If they over-book by the exact number of passengers who fail to show up, they have maximized their revenue under the circumstances. Of course, if more passengers show up than they expect, the airline will have a number of upset passengers to deal with (although they may be able to offer financial inducements for the passengers to take another flight). If they fail to over-book sufficiently, they will have empty seats. By studying past data on flight demand, airlines try to balance the risks of over-booking and under-booking.
- *Price discounting.* At quiet times, when demand is unlikely to fill capacity, airlines will also sell heavily discounted tickets to agents who themselves take the risk of finding customers for them. In effect, this is using the price mechanism to affect demand.
- *Varying service types.* Discounting and other methods of affecting demand are also adjusted depending on the demand for particular types of service. For example, the relative demand for first-, business- and economy-class seats varies throughout the year. There is no point discounting tickets in a class for which demand will be high. Yield management also tries to adjust the availability of the different classes of seat to reflect their demand. They will also vary the number of seats available in each class by upgrading or even changing the configuration of airline seats.

Short case
Getting the message[5]

Companies which traditionally operate in seasonal markets can demonstrate some considerable ingenuity in their attempts to develop counter-seasonal products. One of the most successful industries in this respect has been the greetings card industry. Mother's Day, Father's Day, Halloween, Valentine's Day and other occasions have all been promoted as times to send (and buy) appropriately designed cards. Now, having run out of occasions to promote, greetings card manufacturers have moved on to 'non-occasion' cards, which can be sent at any time. These have the considerable advantage of being less seasonal, thus making the companies' seasonality less marked.

Hallmark Cards, the market leader in North America, has been the pioneer in developing non-occasion cards. Their cards include those intended to be sent from a parent to a child with messages such as 'Would a hug help?', 'Sorry I made you feel bad' and 'You're perfectly wonderful – it's your room that's a mess'. Other cards deal with more serious adult themes such as friendship ('You're more than a friend, you're just like family') or even alcoholism ('This is hard to say, but I think you're a much neater person when you're not drinking'). Now Hallmark Cards has founded a 'loyalty marketing group' that 'helps companies communicate with their customers at an emotional level'. It promotes the use of greetings cards for corporate use, to show that customers and employees are valued. Whatever else these products may be, they are not seasonal!

Source: Press Association Images

Choosing a capacity management approach

Before an operation can decide which of the capacity plans to adopt, it must be aware of the consequences of adopting each plan in its own set of circumstances. Two methods are particularly useful in helping to assess the consequences of adopting particular capacity plans:

Cumulative representations

Queuing theory

● **cumulative representations** of demand and capacity;
● **queuing theory**.

Cumulative representations

Figure 8.11 shows the forecast aggregated demand for a chocolate factory which makes confectionery products. Demand for its products in the shops is greatest at Christmas. To meet this demand and allow time for the products to work their way through the distribution system, the factory must supply a demand which peaks in September, as shown. One method of assessing whether a particular level of capacity can satisfy the demand would be to calculate the degree of over-capacity below the graph which represents the capacity levels (areas A and C) and the degree of under-capacity above the graph (area B). If the total over-capacity is greater than the total under-capacity for a particular level of capacity, then that capacity could be regarded as adequate to satisfy demand fully, the assumption being that inventory has been accumulated in the periods of over-capacity. However, there are two problems with this approach. The first is that each month shown in Figure 8.11 may not have the same amount of productive time. Some months (August, for example) may contain vacation periods which reduce the availability of capacity. The second problem is that a capacity level which seems adequate may only be able to supply products *after* the demand for them has occurred. For example, if the period of under-capacity occurred at the beginning of the year, no inventory could have accumulated to meet demand. A far superior way of assessing capacity plans is first to plot demand on a *cumulative* basis. This is shown as the blue line in Figure 8.12.

The cumulative representation of demand immediately reveals more information. First, it shows that although total demand peaks in September, because of the restricted number of available productive days, the peak demand per productive day occurs a month earlier in August. Second, it shows that the fluctuation in demand over the year is even greater than it seemed. The ratio of monthly peak demand to monthly lowest demand is 6.5:1, but the ratio of peak to lowest demand per productive day is 10:1. Demand per productive day is more relevant to operations managers, because productive days represent the time element of capacity.

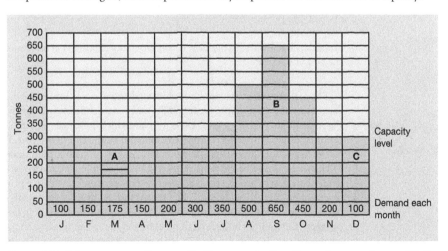

Figure 8.11 If the over-capacity areas (A+C) are greater than the under-capacity area (B), the capacity level seems adequate to meet demand. This may not necessarily be the case, however

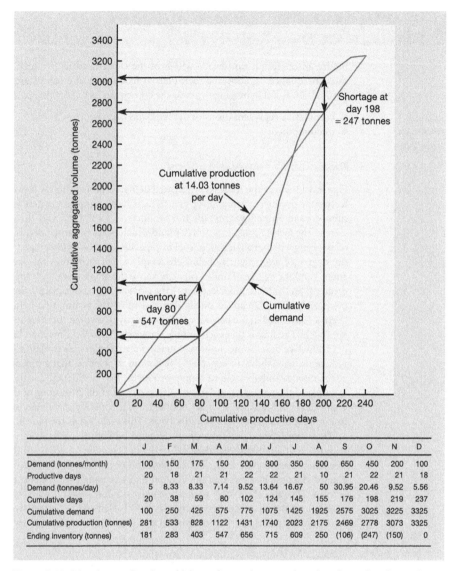

	J	F	M	A	M	J	J	A	S	O	N	D
Demand (tonnes/month)	100	150	175	150	200	300	350	500	650	450	200	100
Productive days	20	18	21	21	22	22	21	10	21	22	21	18
Demand (tonnes/day)	5	8.33	8.33	7.14	9.52	13.64	16.67	50	30.95	20.46	9.52	5.56
Cumulative days	20	38	59	80	102	124	145	155	176	198	219	237
Cumulative demand	100	250	425	575	775	1075	1425	1925	2575	3025	3225	3325
Cumulative production (tonnes)	281	533	828	1122	1431	1740	2023	2175	2469	2778	3073	3325
Ending inventory (tonnes)	181	283	403	547	656	715	609	250	(106)	(247)	(150)	0

Figure 8.12 A level capacity plan which produces shortages in spite of meeting demand at the end of the year

The most useful consequence of plotting demand on a cumulative basis is that, by plotting capacity on the same graph, the feasibility and consequences of a capacity plan can be assessed. Figure 8.12 also shows a level capacity plan which produces at a rate of 14.03 tonnes per productive day. This meets cumulative demand by the end of the year. It would also pass our earlier test of total over-capacity being the same as or greater than under-capacity.

However, if one of the aims of the plan is to supply demand when it occurs, the plan is inadequate. Up to around day 168, the line representing cumulative production is above that representing cumulative demand. This means that at any time during this period, more product has been produced by the factory than has been demanded from it. In fact the vertical distance between the two lines is the level of inventory at that point in time. So by day 80, 1,122 tonnes have been produced but only 575 tonnes have been demanded. The surplus of production above demand, or inventory, is therefore 547 tonnes. When the cumulative demand line lies above the cumulative production line, the reverse is true. The vertical distance between the two lines now indicates the shortage, or lack of supply. So by day 198, 3,025 tonnes have been demanded but only 2,778 tonnes produced. The shortage is therefore 247 tonnes.

For any capacity plan to meet demand as it occurs, its cumulative production line must always lie above the cumulative demand line. This makes it a straightforward task to judge the adequacy of a plan, simply by looking at its cumulative representation. An impression of the inventory implications can also be gained from a cumulative representation by judging the area between the cumulative production and demand curves. This represents the amount of inventory carried over the period. Figure 8.13 illustrates an adequate level capacity plan for the chocolate manufacturer, together with the costs of carrying inventory. It is assumed that

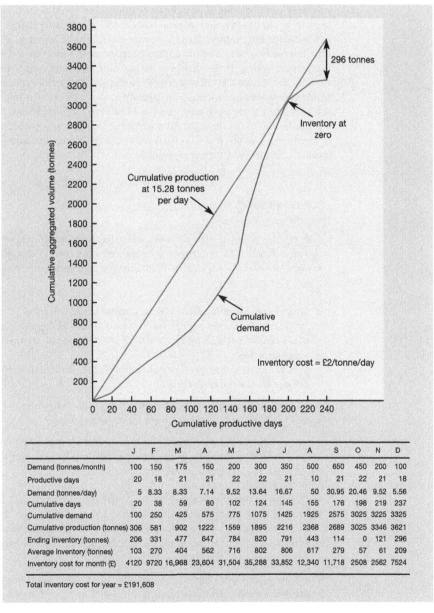

	J	F	M	A	M	J	J	A	S	O	N	D
Demand (tonnes/month)	100	150	175	150	200	300	350	500	650	450	200	100
Productive days	20	18	21	21	22	22	21	10	21	22	21	18
Demand (tonnes/day)	5	8.33	8.33	7.14	9.52	13.64	16.67	50	30.95	20.46	9.52	5.56
Cumulative days	20	38	59	80	102	124	145	155	176	198	219	237
Cumulative demand	100	250	425	575	775	1075	1425	1925	2575	3025	3225	3325
Cumulative production (tonnes)	306	581	902	1222	1559	1895	2216	2368	2689	3025	3346	3621
Ending inventory (tonnes)	206	331	477	647	784	820	791	443	114	0	121	296
Average inventory (tonnes)	103	270	404	562	716	802	806	617	279	57	61	209
Inventory cost for month (£)	4120	9720	16,968	23,604	31,504	35,288	33,852	12,340	11,718	2508	2562	7524

Total inventory cost for year = £191,608

Figure 8.13 A level capacity plan which meets demand at all times during the year

111

inventory costs £2 per tonne per day to keep in storage. The average inventory each month is taken to be the average of the beginning- and end-of-month inventory levels, and the inventory-carrying cost each month is the product of the average inventory, the inventory cost per day per tonne and the number of days in the month.

Comparing plans on a cumulative basis

Chase demand plans can also be illustrated on a cumulative representation. Rather than the cumulative production line having a constant gradient, it would have a varying gradient representing the output rate at any point in time. If a pure demand chase plan was adopted, the cumulative production line would match the cumulative demand line. The gap between the two lines would be zero and hence inventory would be zero. Although this would eliminate inventory-carrying costs, as we discussed earlier, there would be costs associated with changing capacity levels. Usually, the marginal cost of making a capacity change increases with the size of the change. For example, if the chocolate manufacturer wishes to increase capacity by 5 per cent, this can be achieved by requesting its staff to work overtime – a simple, fast and relatively inexpensive option. If the change is 15 per cent, overtime cannot provide sufficient extra capacity and temporary staff will need to be employed – a more expensive solution which also would take more time. Increases in capacity of above 15 per cent might only be achieved by subcontracting some work out. This would be even more expensive. The cost of the change will also be affected by the point from which the change is being made, as well as the direction of the change. Usually, it is less expensive to change capacity towards what is regarded as the 'normal' capacity level than away from it.

Worked example

Suppose the chocolate manufacturer, which has been operating the level capacity plan as shown in Figure 8.13, is unhappy with the inventory costs of this approach. It decides to explore two alternative plans, both involving some degree of demand chasing.

Plan 1

- Organize and staff the factory for a 'normal' capacity level of 8.7 tonnes per day.
- Produce at 8.7 tonnes per day for the first 124 days of the year, then increase capacity to 29 tonnes per day by heavy use of overtime, hiring temporary staff and some subcontracting.
- Produce at 29 tonnes per day until day 194, then reduce capacity back to 8.7 tonnes per day for the rest of the year.

The costs of changing capacity by such a large amount (the ratio of peak to normal capacity is 3.33:1) are calculated by the company as being:

Cost of changing from 8.7 tonnes/day to 29 tonnes/day = £110,000
Cost of changing from 29 tonnes/day to 8.7 tonnes/day = £60,000

Plan 2

- Organize and staff the factory for a 'normal' capacity level of 12.4 tonnes per day.
- Produce at 12.4 tonnes per day for the first 150 days of the year, then increase capacity to 29 tonnes per day by overtime and hiring some temporary staff.
- Produce at 29 tonnes/day until day 190, then reduce capacity back to 12.4 tonnes per day for the rest of the year.

The costs of changing capacity in this plan are smaller because the degree of change is smaller (a peak to normal capacity ratio of 2.34:1), and they are calculated by the company as being:

Cost of changing from 12.4 tonnes/day to 29 tonnes/day = £35,000
Cost of changing from 29 tonnes/day to 12.4 tonnes/day = £15,000

Figure 8.14 illustrates both plans on a cumulative basis. Plan 1, which envisaged two drastic changes in capacity, has high capacity change costs but, because its production levels are close to demand levels, it has low inventory carrying costs. Plan 2 sacrifices some of the inventory cost advantage of Plan 1 but saves more in terms of capacity change costs.

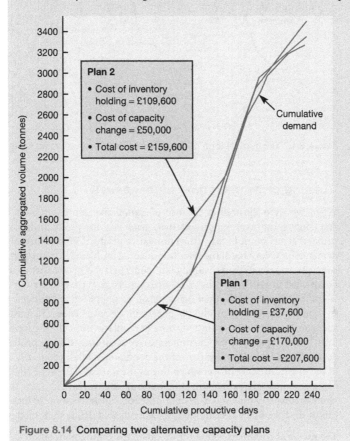

Figure 8.14 Comparing two alternative capacity plans

Capacity planning as a queuing problem

Cumulative representations of capacity plans are useful where the operation has the ability to store its finished goods as inventory. However, for operations where it is not possible to produce products and services *before* demand for them has occurred, a cumulative representation would tell us relatively little. The cumulative 'production' could never be above the cumulative demand line. At best, it could show when an operation failed to meets its demand. So the vertical gap between the cumulative demand and production lines would indicate the amount of demand unsatisfied. Some of this demand would look elsewhere to be satisfied, but some would wait. This is why, for operations which, by their nature, cannot store their output, such as most service operations, capacity planning and control is best considered using waiting or **queuing theory**.

Queuing theory

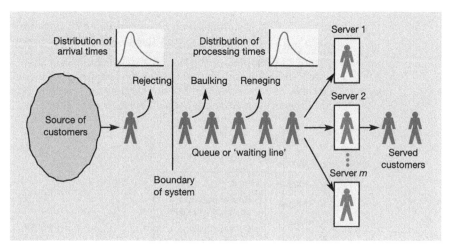

Figure 8.15 The general form of the capacity decision in queuing systems

Queuing or 'waiting line' management

When we were illustrating the use of cumulative representations for capacity planning and control, our assumption was that, generally, any production plan should aim to meet demand at any point in time (the cumulative production line must be above the cumulative demand line). Looking at the issue as a queuing problem (in many parts of the world queuing concepts are referred to as 'waiting line' concepts) accepts that, while sometime demand may be satisfied instantly, at other times customers may have to wait. This is particularly true when the arrival of individual demands on an operation are difficult to predict, or the time to produce a service or product is uncertain, or both. These circumstances make providing adequate capacity at all points in time particularly difficult. Figure 8.15 shows the general form of this capacity issue. Customers arrive according to some probability distribution and wait to be processed (unless part of the operation is idle); when they have reached the front of the queue, they are processed by one of the n parallel 'servers' (their processing time also being described by a probability distribution), after which they leave the operation. There are many examples of this kind of system. Table 8.2 illustrates some of these. All of these examples can be described by a common set of elements that define their queuing behaviour.

Calling population

The source of customers – sometimes called the **calling population** – is the source of supply of customers. In queue management 'customers' are not always human. 'Customers' could for example be trucks arriving at a weighbridge, orders arriving to be processed or machines waiting to be serviced, etc. The source of customers for queuing system can be either *finite*

Table 8.2 Examples of operations which have parallel processors

Operation	Arrivals	Processing capacity
Bank	Customers	Tellers
Supermarket	Shoppers	Checkouts
Hospital clinic	Patients	Doctors
Graphic artist	Commissions	Artists
Custom cake decorators	Orders	Cake decorators
Ambulance service	Emergencies	Ambulances with crews
Telephone switchboard	Calls	Telephonists
Maintenance department	Breakdowns	Maintenance staff

or *infinite*. A finite source has a known number of possible customers. For example, if one maintenance person serves four assembly lines, the number of customers for the maintenance person is known, i.e. four. There will be a certain probability that one of the assembly lines will break down and need repairing. However, if one line really does break down the probability of another line needing repair is reduced because there are now only three lines to break down. So, with a finite source of customers the probability of a customer arriving depends on the number of customers already being serviced. By contrast, an infinite customer source assumes that there is a large number of potential customers so that it is always possible for another customer to arrive no matter how many are being serviced. Most queuing systems that deal with outside markets have infinite, or 'close-to-infinite', customer sources.

Balancing capacity and demand

The dilemma in managing the capacity of a queuing system is how many servers to have available at any point in time in order to avoid unacceptably long queuing times or unacceptably low utilization of the servers. Because of the probabilistic arrival and processing times, only rarely will the arrival of customers match the ability of the operation to cope with them. Sometimes, if several customers arrive in quick succession and require longer-than-average processing times, queues will build up in front of the operation. At other times, when customers arrive less frequently than average and also require shorter-than-average processing times, some of the servers in the system will be idle. So even when the average capacity (processing capability) of the operation matches the average demand (arrival rate) on the system, both queues and idle time will occur.

If the operation has too few servers (that is, capacity is set at too low a level), queues will build up to a level where customers become dissatisfied with the time they are having to wait, although the utilization level of the servers will be high. If too many servers are in place (that is, capacity is set at too high a level), the time which customers can expect to wait will not be long but the utilization of the servers will be low. This is why the capacity management problem for this type of operation is often presented as a trade-off between customer waiting time and system utilization. What is certainly important in making capacity decisions is being able to predict both of these factors for a given operation.

Variability in demand or supply

Variability reduces effective capacity

The variability, either in demand or capacity, as discussed above, will reduce the ability of an operation to process its inputs. That is, it will **reduce its effective capacity**. This effect was explained in Chapter 5 when the consequences of variability in individual processes were discussed. As a reminder, the greater the variability in arrival time or activity time at a process the more the process will suffer both high throughput times and reduced utilization. This principle holds true for whole operations, and because long throughput times mean that queues will build up in the operation, high variability also affects inventory levels. This is illustrated in Figure 8.16. The implication of this is that the greater the variability, the more extra capacity will need to be provided to compensate for the reduced utilization of available capacity. Therefore, operations with high levels of variability will tend to set their base level of capacity relatively high in order to provide this extra capacity.

Customer perceptions of queuing

If the 'customers' waiting in a queue are real human customers, an important aspect of how they judge the service they receive from a queuing system is how they perceive the time spent queuing. It is well known that if you are told that you'll be waiting in a queue for fifteen minutes and you are actually serviced in ten minutes, your perception of the queuing experience will be more positive than if you were told that you would be waiting five minutes but the queue actually took ten minutes. Because of this, the management of queuing systems

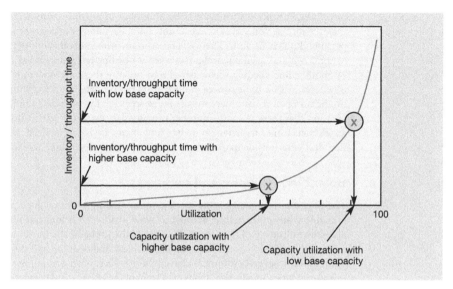

Figure 8.16 The effect of variability on the utilization of capacity

usually involves attempting to manage customers' perceptions and expectations in some way (see the Short case on Madame Tussaud's for an example of this). There are a number of principles that influence how customers perceive waiting times:[6]

Short case
Managing queues at Madame Tussaud's, Amsterdam

A short holiday in Amsterdam would not be complete without a visit to Madame Tussaud's, located on four upper floors of the city's most prominent department store in Dam Square. With 600,000 visitors each year, this is one of the most popular tourist attractions in Amsterdam. On busy days in the summer, the centre can just manage to handle 5,000 visitors. On a wet day in January, however, there may only be 300 visitors throughout the whole day. The centre is open for admission, seven days a week, from 10.00 am to 5.30 pm. In the streets outside, orderly queues of expectant tourists snake along the pavement, looking in at the displays in the store windows. In this public open space, Tussaud's can do little to entertain the visitors, but entrepreneurial buskers and street artists are quick to capitalize on a captive market. On reaching the entrance lobby, individuals, families and groups purchase their admission tickets. The lobby is in the shape of a large horseshoe, with the ticket sales booth in the centre. On winter days or at quiet spells, there will only be one sales assistant, but on busier days, visitors can pay at either side of the ticket booth, to speed up the process. Having paid, the visitors assemble in the

Source: Madame Tussaud's

lobby outside the two lifts. While waiting in this area, a photographer wanders around offering to take photos of the visitors standing next to life-sized wax figures of famous people. They may also be entertained by living look-alikes of famous personalities who act as guides to groups of visitors in batches of around 25 customers (the capacity of each of the two lifts which takes visitors up to the facility). The lifts arrive every four minutes and customers simultaneously disembark, forming one group of about 50 customers, who stay together throughout the session.

- Time spent idle is perceived as longer than time spent occupied.
- The wait before a service starts is perceived as more tedious than a wait within the process.
- Anxiety and/or uncertainty heightens the perception that time spent waiting is long.
- A wait of unknown duration is perceived as more tedious than a wait of known duration.
- An unexplained wait is perceived as more tedious than a wait that is explained.
- The higher the value of the service for the customer, the longer the waiting tolerance.
- Waiting on one's own is more tedious than waiting in a group (unless you really don't like the others in the group).

Summary answers to key questions

Check and improve your understanding of this chapter using self-assessment questions and a personalized study plan, audio and video downloads, and an eBook – all at www.myomlab.com.

➤ What is capacity management?

- It is the way operations organize the level of value-added activity which they can achieve under normal operating conditions over a period of time.
- It is usual to distinguish between long-, medium- and short-term capacity decisions. Medium- and short-term capacity management, where the capacity level of the organization is adjusted within the fixed limits which are set by long-term capacity decisions, is sometimes called aggregate planning and control.
- Almost all operations have some kind of fluctuation in demand (or seasonality) caused by some combination of climatic, festive, behavioural, political, financial or social factors.

➤ How are demand and capacity measured?

- Either by the availability of its input resources or by the output which is created. Which of these measures is used partly depends on how stable the mix of outputs is. If it is difficult to aggregate the different types of output from an operation, input measures are usually preferred.
- The usage of capacity can be measured by overall equipment effectiveness (OEE).

➤ What are the alternative ways of coping with demand fluctuation?

- Output can be kept level, in effect ignoring demand fluctuations. This will result in under-utilization of capacity where outputs cannot be stored, or the build-up of inventories where output can be stored or queues when they can't be stored.
- Output can chase demand by fluctuating the output level through some combination of over-time, varying the size of the workforce, using part-time staff and subcontracting.
- Demand can be changed, either by influencing the market through such measures as advertising and promotion, or by developing alternative products with a counter-seasonal demand pattern.
- Most operations use a mix of all these three 'pure' strategies.

Capacity Management

> **How can operations manage their capacity level?**

■ Representing demand and output in the form of cumulative representations allows the feasibility of alternative capacity plans to be assessed.

■ In many operations, especially service operations, a queuing approach can be used to explore capacity strategies.

> **How can queuing theory be used to plan capacity?**

■ By considering the capacity decision as a dynamic decision which periodically updates the decisions and assumptions upon which decisions are based.

Learning exercises

These problems and applications will help to improve your analysis of operations. You can find more practice problems as well as worked examples and guided solutions on MyOMLab at www.myomlab.com.

1. A local government office issues hunting licences. Demand for these licences is relatively slow in the first part of the year but then increases after the middle of the year before slowing down again towards the end of the year. The department works a 220-day year on a 5-days-a-week basis. Between working days 0 and 100, demand is 25 per cent of demand during the peak period which lasts between day 100 and day 150. After 150 demand reduces to about 12 per cent of the demand during the peak period. In total, the department processes 10,000 applications per year. The department has 2 permanent members of staff who are capable of processing 15 licence applications per day. If an untrained temporary member of staff can only process 10 licences per day, how many temporary staff should the department recruit between days 100 and 150?

2. In the example above, if a new computer system is installed that allows experienced staff to increase their work rate to 20 applications per day, and untrained staff to 15 applications per day, (a) does the department still need 2 permanent staff, and (b) how many temporary members of staff will be needed between days 100 and 150?

3. A field service organization repairs and maintains printing equipment for a large number of customers. It offers one level of service to all its customers and employs 30 staff. The operation's marketing vice-president has decided that in future the company will offer 3 standards of service, platinum, gold and silver. It is estimated that platinum-service customers will require 50 per cent more time from the company's field service engineers than the current service. The current service is to be called 'the gold service'. The silver service is likely to require about 80 per cent of the time of the gold service. If future demand is estimated to be 20 per cent platinum, 70 per cent gold and 10 per cent silver service, how many staff will be needed to fulfil demand?

4. Look again at the principles which govern customers' perceptions of the queuing experience. For the following operations, apply the principles to minimize the perceived negative effects of queuing.

   (a) A cinema
   (b) A doctor's surgery
   (c) Waiting to board an aircraft.

Want to know more?

Hopp, W.J. and Spearman, M.L. (2000) *Factory Physics*, 2nd edn, McGraw-Hill, New York, NY. Very mathematical indeed, but includes some interesting maths on queuing theory.

Olhager, J., Rudberg, M. and Wikner, J. (2001) Long-term capacity management: linking the perspectives from manufacturing strategy and sales and operations planning, *International Journal of Production Economics*, vol. 69, issue 2, 215–25. Academic article, but interesting.

Vollmann, T., Berry, W., Whybark, D.C. and Jacobs, F.R. (2004) *Manufacturing Planning and Control Systems for Supply Chain Management: The Definitive Guide for Professionals*, McGraw-Hill Higher Education, New York. The latest version of the 'bible' of manufacturing planning and control. It's exhaustive in its coverage of all aspects of planning and control including aggregate planning.

Useful websites

www.bis.gov.uk/employment Website which has developed a framework for employers and employees to promote a skilled and flexible labour market founded on principles of partnership.

www.worksmart.org.uk/index.php This site is from the Trades Union Congress. Its aim is 'to help today's working people get the best out of the world of work'.

www.opsman.org Lots of useful stuff.

www.equalityhumanrights.com This web site aims to provide a resource for legal advisers and representatives who are conducting claims on behalf of applicants in sex discrimination and equal pay cases in England and Wales. This site covers employment-related sex discrimination only.

www.dol.gov/index.htm US Department of Labor's site with information regarding using part-time employees.

www.downtimecentral.com/ Lots of information on operational equipment efficiency (OEE).

Now that you have finished reading this chapter, why not visit MyOMLab at www.myomlab.com where you'll find more learning resources to help you make the most of your studies and get a better grade.

Inventory management

Key questions

➤ What is inventory?

➤ What are the reasons for holding inventory and what are the disadvantages?

➤ How much inventory should an operation hold?

➤ When should an operation replenish its inventory?

➤ How can inventory be managed?

Introduction

Operations managers often have an ambivalent attitude towards inventories. On the one hand, they are costly, sometimes tying up considerable amounts of working capital. They are also risky because items held in stock could deteriorate, become obsolete or just get lost, and, furthermore, they take up valuable space in the operation. This risk is also seen when inventory is in the form of customers who rarely enjoy waiting. On the other hand, inventories provide some security in an uncertain environment that one can deliver items in stock or work on customers in process should demand materialize. This is the dilemma of inventory management: in spite of the cost and the other disadvantages associated with inventories, they do facilitate the smoothing of supply and demand. In fact they only exist because supply and demand are not exactly in harmony with each other. Figure 9.1 shows where this chapter fits into the overall operations model.

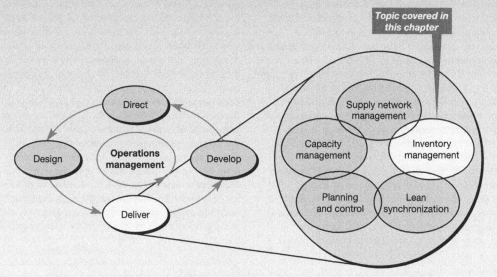

Figure 9.1 This chapter examines inventory management

 Check and improve your understanding of this chapter using self-assessment questions and a personalized study plan, audio and video downloads, and an eBook – all at www.myomlab.com.

Operations in practice The UK's National Blood Service[1]

No inventory manager likes to run out of stock. But for blood services, such as the UK's National Blood Service (NBS) the consequences of running out of stock can be particularly serious. Many people owe their lives to transfusions that were made possible by the efficient management of blood, stocked in a supply network that stretches from donation centres through to hospital blood banks. The NBS supply chain has three main stages:

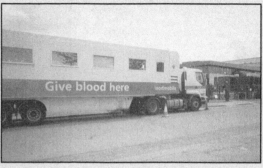

Source: Alamy/Van Hilversum

1 *Collection*, which involves recruiting and retaining blood donors, encouraging them to attend donor sessions (at mobile or fixed locations) and transporting the donated blood to their local blood centre.
2 *Processing*, which breaks blood down into its constituent parts (red cells, platelets and plasma) as well over twenty other blood-based 'products'.
3 *Distribution*, which transports blood from blood centres to hospitals in response to both routine and emergency requests. Of the Service's 200,000 deliveries a year, about 2,500 are emergency deliveries.

Inventory accumulates at all three stages, and in individual hospitals' blood banks. Within the supply chain, around 11.5 per cent of donated red blood cells donated are lost. Much of this is due to losses in processing, but around 5 per cent is not used because it has 'become unavailable', mainly because it has been stored for too long. Part of the Service's inventory control task is to keep this 'time-expired' loss to a minimum. In fact, only small losses occur within the NBS, most blood being lost when it is stored in hospital blood banks that are outside its direct control. However, it does attempt to provide advice and support to hospitals to enable them to use blood efficiently.

Blood components and products need to be stored under a variety of conditions, but will deteriorate over time. This varies depending on the component; platelets have a shelf life of only five days and demand can fluctuate significantly. This makes stock control particularly difficult. Even red blood cells that have a shelf life of 35 days may not be acceptable to hospitals if they are close to their 'use-by date'. Stock accuracy is crucial. Giving a patient the wrong type of blood can be fatal.

At a local level demand can be affected significantly by accidents. For example, one serious accident involving a cyclist used 750 units of blood, which completely exhausted the available supply (miraculously, he survived). Large-scale accidents usually generate a surge of offers from donors wishing to make immediate donations. There is also a more predictable seasonality to the donating of blood, however, with a low period during the summer vacation. Yet there is always an unavoidable tension between maintaining sufficient stocks to provide a very high level of supply dependability to hospitals and minimizing wastage. Unless blood stocks are controlled carefully, they can easily go past the 'use-by date' and be wasted. But avoiding outdated blood products is not the only inventory objective at NBS. It also measures the percentage of requests that it was able to meet in full, the percentage emergency requests delivered within two hours, the percentage of units banked to donors bled, the number of new donors enrolled, and the number of donors waiting longer than 30 minutes before they are able to donate. The traceability of donated blood is also increasingly important. Should any problems with a blood product arise, its source can be traced back to the original donor.

What is inventory?

Inventory

Inventory, or 'stock' as it is more commonly called in some countries, is defined here as the *stored accumulation of resources in a transformation system*. Sometimes the term 'inventory' is also used to describe any capital-transforming resource, such as rooms in a hotel, or cars in a vehicle-hire firm, but we will not use that definition here. Usually the term refers only to *transformed resources*. So a manufacturing company will hold stocks of materials, a tax office will hold stocks of information, and a theme park will hold stocks of customers. Note that when it is customers who are being processed we normally refer to these 'stocks' as 'queues'. This chapter will deal particularly with inventories of materials.

Revisiting operations objectives; the roles of inventory

Inventory can influence all performance objectives

Most of us are accustomed to keeping inventory for use in our personal lives, but often we don't think about it. For example, most families have some stocks of food and drinks, so that they don't have to go out to the shops before every meal. Holding a variety of food ingredients in stock in the kitchen cupboard or freezer gives us the ability to respond quickly (with *speed*) in preparing a meal whenever unexpected guests arrive. It also allows us the *flexibility* to choose a range of menu options without having to go to the time and trouble of purchasing further ingredients. We may purchase some items because we have found something of exceptional *quality*, but intend to save it for a special occasion. Many people buy multiple packs to achieve lower *costs* for a wide range of goods. In general, our inventory planning protects us from critical stock-outs; so this approach gives a level of *dependability* of supplies.

It is, however, entirely possible to manage our inventory differently. For example, some people are short of available cash and/or space, and so cannot 'invest' in large inventories of goods. They may shop locally for much smaller quantities. They forfeit the cost benefits of bulk-buying, but do not have to transport heavy or bulky supplies. They also reduce the risk of forgetting an item in the cupboard and letting it go out of date. Essentially, they purchase against specific known requirements (the next meal). However, they may find that the local shop is temporarily out of stock of a particular item, forcing them, for example, to drink coffee without their usual milk. How we control our own supplies is therefore a matter of choice which can affect their quality (e.g. freshness), availability or speed of response, dependability of supply, flexibility of choice, and cost. It is the same for most organizations. Significant levels of inventory can be held for a range of sensible and pragmatic reasons but it must also be tightly controlled for other equally good reasons.

Why is inventory necessary?

No matter what is being stored as inventory, or where it is positioned in the operation, it will be there because there is a difference in the timing or rate of supply and demand. If the supply of any item occurred exactly when it was demanded, the item would never be stored. A common analogy is the water tank shown in Figure 9.2. If, over time, the rate of supply of water to the tank differs from the rate at which it is demanded, a tank of water (inventory) will be needed if supply is to be maintained. When the rate of supply exceeds the rate of demand, inventory increases; when the rate of demand exceeds the rate of supply, inventory decreases. So if an operation can match supply and demand rates, it will also succeed in reducing its inventory levels.

123

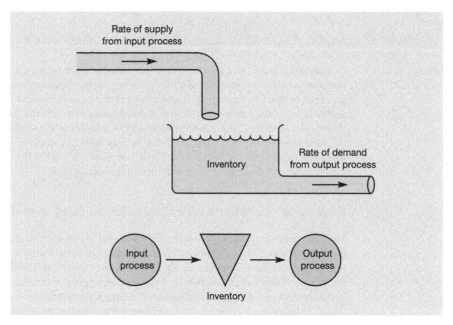

Figure 9.2 Inventory is created to compensate for the differences in timing between supply and demand

Types of inventory

The various reasons for an imbalance between the rates of supply and demand at different points in any supply network lead to the different types of inventory. There are five of these: buffer inventory, cycle inventory, de-coupling inventory, anticipation inventory and pipeline inventory.

Buffer inventory

Buffer inventory
Safety inventory

Buffer inventory is also called **safety inventory**. Its purpose is to compensate for the unexpected fluctuations in supply and demand. For example, a retail operation can never forecast demand perfectly, even when it has a good idea of the most likely demand level. It will order goods from its suppliers such that there is always a certain amount of most items in stock. This minimum level of inventory is there to cover against the possibility that demand will be greater than expected during the time taken to deliver the goods. It can also compensate for the uncertainties in the process of the supply of goods into the store, perhaps because of the unreliability of certain suppliers or transport firms.

Cycle inventory

Cycle inventory

Cycle inventory occurs because one or more stages in the process cannot supply all the items it produces simultaneously. For example, suppose a baker makes three types of bread, each of which is equally popular with its customers. Because of the nature of the mixing and baking process, only one kind of bread can be produced at any time. The baker would have to produce each type of bread in batches as shown in Figure 9.3. The batches must be large enough to satisfy the demand for each kind of bread between the times when each batch is ready for sale. So even when demand is steady and predictable, there will always be some inventory to compensate for the intermittent supply of each type of bread. Cycle inventory only results from the need to produce products in batches, and the amount of it depends on volume decisions which are described in a later section of this chapter.

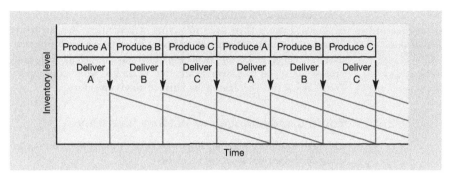

Figure 9.3 **Cycle inventory in a bakery**

De-coupling inventory

De-coupling inventory

Wherever an operation is designed to use a process layout, the transformed resources move intermittently between specialized areas or departments that comprise similar operations. Each of these areas can be scheduled to work relatively independently in order to maximize the local utilization and efficiency of the equipment and staff. As a result, each batch of work-in-progress inventory joins a queue, awaiting its turn in the schedule for the next processing stage. This also allows each operation to be set to the optimum processing speed (cycle time), regardless of the speed of the steps before and after. Thus **de-coupling inventory** creates the opportunity for independent scheduling and processing speeds between process stages.

Anticipation inventory

Anticipation inventory

In Chapter 8 we saw how anticipation inventory can be used to cope with seasonal demand. Rather than trying to make the product (such as chocolate) only when it was needed, it was produced throughout the year ahead of demand and put into inventory until it was needed. **Anticipation inventory** is most commonly used when demand fluctuations are large but relatively predictable. It might also be used when supply variations are significant, such as in the canning or freezing of seasonal foods.

Pipeline inventory

Pipeline inventory

Pipeline inventory exists because material cannot be transported instantaneously between the point of supply and the point of demand. If a retail store orders a consignment of items from one of its suppliers, the supplier will allocate the stock to the retail store in its own warehouse, pack it, load it onto its truck, transport it to its destination, and unload it into the retailer's inventory. From the time that stock is allocated (and therefore it is unavailable to any other customer) to the time it becomes available for the retail store, it is pipeline inventory. Pipeline inventory also exists within processes where the layout is geographically spread out. For example, a large European manufacturer of specialized steel regularly moves cargoes of part-finished materials between its two mills in the UK and Scandinavia using a dedicated vessel that shuttles between the two countries every week. All the thousands of tonnes of material in transit are pipeline inventory.

The position of inventory

Not only are there several reasons for supply–demand imbalance, there could also be several points where such imbalance exists between different stages in the operation. Perhaps the simplest level is the single-stage inventory system, such as a retail store, which will have only one stock of goods to manage. An automotive parts distribution operation will have a central

Raw materials inventory
Components inventory

Work-in-progress
Finished goods inventory

depot and various local distribution points which contain inventories. In many manufacturers of standard items, there are three types of inventory. The **raw material** and **components inventories** (sometimes called input inventories) receive goods from the operation's suppliers; the raw materials and components work their way through the various stages of the production process but spend considerable amounts of time as **work-in-progress** (or work-in-process) (WIP) before finally reaching the **finished goods inventory**.

Some disadvantages of holding inventory

Although inventory plays an important role in many operations performance, there are a number of negative aspects of inventory:

- Inventory ties up money, in the form of working capital, which is therefore unavailable for other uses, such as reducing borrowings or making investment in productive fixed assets.
- Inventory incurs storage costs (leasing space, maintaining appropriate conditions, etc.).
- Inventory may become obsolete as alternatives become available.
- Inventory can be damaged, or deteriorate.
- Inventory could be lost, or be expensive to retrieve, as it gets hidden amongst other inventory.
- Inventory might be hazardous to store (for example flammable solvents, explosives, chemicals and drugs), requiring special facilities and systems for safe handling.
- Inventory uses space that could be used to add value.
- Inventory involves administrative and insurance costs.

Day-to-day inventory decisions

At each point in the inventory system, operations managers need to manage the day-to-day tasks of running the system. Orders will be received from internal or external customers; these will be dispatched and demand will gradually deplete the inventory. Orders will need to be placed for replenishment of the stocks; deliveries will arrive and require storing. In managing the system, operations managers are involved in three major types of decision:

- *How much to order*. Every time a replenishment order is placed, how big should it be (sometimes called the *volume decision*)?
- *When to order*. At what point in time, or at what level of stock, should the replenishment order be placed (sometimes called the *timing decision*)?
- *How to control the system*. What procedures and routines should be installed to help make these decisions? Should different priorities be allocated to different stock items? How should stock information be stored?

The rest of this chapter examines the three key decisions.

The volume decision – how much to order

To illustrate this decision, consider again the example of the food and drinks we keep at our home. In managing this inventory we implicitly make decisions on *order quantity*, which is how much to purchase at one time. In making this decision we are balancing two sets of costs: the costs associated with going out to purchase the food items and the costs associated with holding the stocks. The option of holding very little or no inventory of food and purchasing each item only when it is needed has the advantage that it requires little money since purchases are made only when needed. However, it would involve purchasing provisions several times a day, which is inconvenient. At the very opposite extreme, making one journey to the local superstore every few months and purchasing all the provisions we would need until our next visit reduces the time and costs incurred in making the purchase but requires a very large amount of money each time the trip is made – money which could otherwise be in the bank and earning interest. We might also have to invest in extra cupboard units and a very large freezer. Somewhere between these extremes there will lie an ordering strategy which will minimize the total costs and effort involved in the purchase of food.

Inventory costs

The same principles apply in commercial order-quantity decisions as in the domestic situation. In making a decision on how much to purchase, operations managers must try to identify the costs which will be affected by their decision. Several types of costs are directly associated with order size.

Cost of placing an order

1 *Cost of placing the order*. Every time that an order is placed to replenish stock, a number of transactions are needed which incur costs to the company. These include the clerical tasks of preparing the order and all the documentation associated with it, arranging for the delivery to be made, arranging to pay the supplier for the delivery, and the general costs of keeping all the information which allows us to do this. Also, if we are placing an 'internal order' on part of our own operation, there are still likely to be the same types of transaction concerned with internal administration. In addition, there could also be a 'changeover' cost incurred by the part of the operation which is to supply the items, caused by the need to change from producing one type of item to another.

Price discounts

2 *Price discount costs*. In many industries suppliers offer discounts on the normal purchase price for large quantities; alternatively they might impose extra costs for small orders.

3 *Stock-out costs*. If we misjudge the order-quantity decision and we run out of stock, there will be costs to us incurred by failing to supply our customers. If the customers are external, they may take their business elsewhere; if internal, stock-outs could lead to idle time at the next process, inefficiencies and disatisfaction.

Working capital

4 *Working capital costs*. Soon after we receive a replenishment order, the supplier will demand payment for their goods. Eventually, when (or after) we supply our own customers, we in turn will receive payment. However, there will probably be a lag between paying our suppliers and receiving payment from our customers. During this time we will have to fund the costs of inventory. This is called the *working capital* of inventory. The costs associated with it are the interest we pay the bank for borrowing it, or the opportunity costs of not investing it elsewhere.

Storage costs

5 *Storage costs*. These are the costs associated with physically storing the inventories. Renting, heating and lighting the warehouse, as well as insuring the inventory, can be expensive, especially when special conditions are required such as low temperature or high security.

Obsolescence costs

6 *Obsolescence costs*. When we order large quantities, this usually results in stocked items spending a long time stored in inventory. Then there is a risk that the items might either become obsolete (in the case of a change in fashion, for example) or deteriorate with age (in the case of most foodstuffs, for example).

Operating inefficiencies

7 *Operating inefficiency costs*. According to lean synchronization philosophies, high inventory levels prevent us seeing the full extent of problems within the operation. This argument is fully explored in Chapter 11.

There are two points to be made about this list of costs. The first is that some of the costs will decrease as order size is increased; the first three costs are like this, whereas the other costs generally increase as order size is increased. The second point is that it may not be the same organization that incurs the costs. For example, sometimes suppliers agree to

Consignment stock

hold **consignment stock**. This means that they deliver large quantities of inventory to their customers to store but will only charge for the goods as and when they are used. In the meantime they remain the supplier's property so do not have to be financed by the customer, who does, however, provide storage facilities.

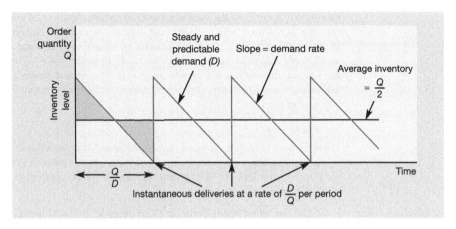

Figure 9.4 Inventory profiles chart the variation in inventory level

Inventory profiles

An inventory profile is a visual representation of the inventory level over time. Figure 9.4 shows a simplified inventory profile for one particular stock item in a retail operation. Every time an order is placed, Q items are ordered. The replenishment order arrives in one batch instantaneously. Demand for the item is then steady and perfectly predictable at a rate of D units per month. When demand has depleted the stock of the items entirely, another order of Q items instantaneously arrives, and so on. Under these circumstances:

The average inventory $= \dfrac{Q}{2}$ (because the two shaded areas in Figure 9.4 are equal)

The time interval between deliveries $= \dfrac{Q}{D}$

The frequency of deliveries = the reciprocal of the time interval $= \dfrac{D}{Q}$

The economic order quantity (EOQ) formula

Economic order quantity The most common approach to deciding how much of any particular item to order when stock needs replenishing is called the **economic order quantity** (EOQ) approach. This approach attempts to find the best balance between the advantages and disadvantages of holding stock. For example, Figure 9.5 shows two alternative order-quantity policies for an item. Plan A, represented by the unbroken line, involves ordering in quantities of 400 at a time. Demand in this case is running at 1,000 units per year. Plan B, represented by the dotted line, uses smaller but more frequent replenishment orders. This time only 100 are ordered at a time, with orders being placed four times as often. However, the average inventory for plan B is one-quarter of that for plan A.

To find out whether either of these plans, or some other plan, minimizes the total cost of stocking the item, we need some further information, namely the total cost of holding one unit in stock for a period of time (C_h) and the total costs of placing an order (C_o). Generally, holding costs are taken into account by including:

- working capital costs
- storage costs
- obsolescence risk costs.

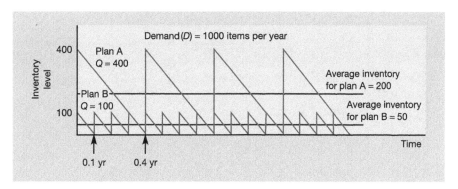

Figure 9.5 Two alternative inventory plans with different order quantities (Q)

Order costs are calculated by taking into account:

- cost of placing the order (including transportation of items from suppliers if relevant);
- price discount costs.

In this case the cost of holding stocks is calculated at £1 per item per year and the cost of placing an order is calculated at £20 per order.

We can now calculate total holding costs and ordering costs for any particular ordering plan as follows:

$$\text{Holding costs} = \text{holding cost/unit} \times \text{average inventory}$$

$$= C_h \times \frac{Q}{2}$$

$$\text{Ordering costs} = \text{ordering cost} \times \text{number of orders per period}$$

$$= C_o \times \frac{D}{Q}$$

$$\text{So, total cost, } C_t = \frac{C_h Q}{2} + \frac{C_o D}{Q}$$

We can now calculate the costs of adopting plans with different order quantities. These are illustrated in Table 9.1. As we would expect with low values of Q, holding costs are low but the costs of placing orders are high because orders have to be placed very frequently. As Q increases, the holding costs increase but the costs of placing orders decrease. Initially

Table 9.1 Costs of adoption of plans with different order quantities

Demand (D) = 1,000 units per year Order costs (C_o) = £20 per order			Holding costs (C_h) = £1 per item per year		
Order quantity (Q)	Holding costs (0.5Q × C_h)	+	Order costs ((D/Q) × C_o)	=	Total costs
50	25		20 × 20 = 400		425
100	50		10 × 20 = 200		250
150	75		6.7 × 20 = 134		209
200	100		5 × 20 = 100		200*
250	125		4 × 20 = 80		205
300	150		3.3 × 20 = 66		216
350	175		2.9 × 20 = 58		233
400	200		2.5 × 20 = 50		250

*Minimum total cost.

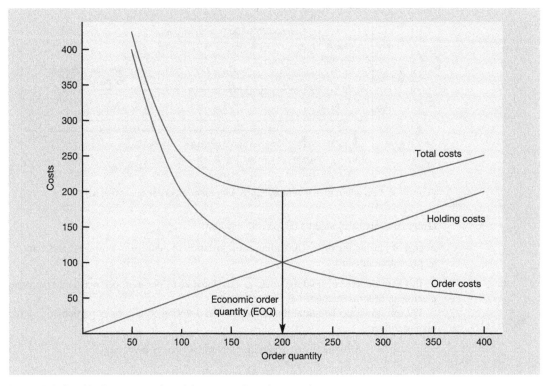

Figure 9.6 Graphical representation of the economic order quantity

the decrease in ordering costs is greater than the increase in holding costs and the total cost falls. After a point, however, the decrease in ordering costs slows, whereas the increase in holding costs remains constant and the total cost starts to increase. In this case the order quantity, Q, which minimizes the sum of holding and order costs, is 200. This 'optimum' order quantity is called the *economic order quantity* (*EOQ*). This is illustrated graphically in Figure 9.6.

A more elegant method of finding the EOQ is to derive its general expression. This can be done using simple differential calculus as follows. From before:

$$\text{Total cost} = \text{holding cost} + \text{order cost}$$

$$C_t = \frac{C_h Q}{2} + \frac{C_o D}{Q}$$

The rate of change of total cost is given by the first differential of C_t with respect to Q:

$$\frac{dC_t}{dQ} = \frac{C_h}{2} - \frac{C_o D}{Q^2}$$

The lowest cost will occur when $dC_t/dQ = 0$, that is:

$$0 = \frac{C_h}{2} - \frac{C_o D}{Q_o^2}$$

where Q_o = the EOQ. Rearranging this expression gives:

$$Q_o = \text{EOQ} = \sqrt{\frac{2C_o D}{C_h}}$$

130

When using the EOQ:

$$\text{Time between orders} = \frac{\text{EOQ}}{D}$$

$$\text{Order frequency} = \frac{D}{\text{EOQ}} \text{ per period}$$

Sensitivity of the EOQ

Examination of the graphical representation of the total cost curve in Figure 9.6 shows that, although there is a single value of Q which minimizes total costs, any relatively small deviation from the EOQ will not increase total costs significantly. In other words, costs will be near-optimum provided a value of Q which is reasonably close to the EOQ is chosen. Put another way, small errors in estimating either holding costs or order costs will not result in a significant deviation from the EOQ. This is a particularly convenient phenomenon because, in practice, both holding and order costs are not easy to estimate accurately.

Worked example

A building materials supplier obtains its bagged cement from a single supplier. Demand is reasonably constant throughout the year, and last year the company sold 2,000 tonnes of this product. It estimates the costs of placing an order at around £25 each time an order is placed, and calculates that the annual cost of holding inventory is 20 per cent of purchase cost. The company purchases the cement at £60 per tonne. How much should the company order at a time?

$$\text{EOQ for cement} = \sqrt{\frac{2C_oD}{C_h}}$$

$$= \sqrt{\frac{2 \times 25 \times 2,000}{0.2 \times 60}}$$

$$= \sqrt{\frac{100,000}{12}}$$

$$= 91.287 \text{ tonnes}$$

After calculating the EOQ the operations manager feels that placing an order for 91.287 tonnes *exactly* seems somewhat over-precise. Why not order a convenient 100 tonnes?

Total cost of ordering plan for Q = 91.287:

$$= \frac{C_hQ}{2} + \frac{C_oD}{Q}$$

$$= \frac{(0.2 \times 60) \times 91.287}{2} + \frac{25 \times 2,000}{91.287}$$

$$= £1,095.454$$

Total cost of ordering plan for Q = 100:

$$= \frac{(0.2 \times 60) \times 100}{2} + \frac{25 \times 2,000}{100}$$

$$= £1,100$$

The extra cost of ordering 100 tonnes at a time is £1,100 − £1,095.45 = £4.55. The operations manager therefore should feel confident in using the more convenient order quantity.

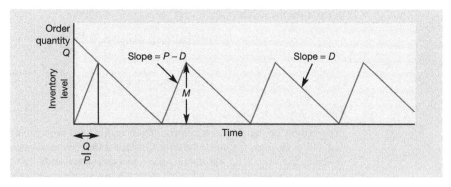

Figure 9.7 Inventory profile for gradual replacement of inventory

Gradual replacement – the economic batch quantity (EBQ) model

Although the simple inventory profile shown in Figure 9.4 made some simplifying assumptions, it is broadly applicable in most situations where each complete replacement order arrives at one point in time. In many cases, however, replenishment occurs over a time period rather than in one lot. A typical example of this is where an internal order is placed for a batch of parts to be produced on a machine. The machine will start to produce the parts and ship them in a more or less continuous stream into inventory, but at the same time demand is continuing to remove parts from the inventory. Provided the rate at which parts are being made and put into the inventory (P) is higher than the rate at which demand is depleting the inventory (D), then the size of the inventory will increase. After the batch has been completed the machine will be reset (to produce some other part), and demand will continue to deplete the inventory level until production of the next batch begins. The resulting profile is shown in Figure 9.7. Such a profile is typical for cycle inventories supplied by batch processes, where items are produced internally and intermittently. For this reason the minimum-cost batch quantity for this profile is called the **economic batch quantity** (EBQ). It is also sometimes known as the economic manufacturing quantity (EMQ), or the production order quantity (POQ). It is derived as follows:

Economic batch quantity

$$\text{Maximum stock level} = M$$

$$\text{Slope of inventory build-up} = P - D$$

Also, as is clear from Figure 9.7:

$$\text{Slope of inventory build-up} = M \div \frac{Q}{P}$$

$$= \frac{MP}{Q}$$

So,

$$\frac{MP}{Q} = P - D$$

$$M = \frac{Q(P - D)}{P}$$

$$\text{Average inventory level} = \frac{M}{2}$$

$$= \frac{Q(P - D)}{2P}$$

132

As before:

$$\text{Total cost} = \text{holding cost} + \text{order cost}$$

$$C_t = \frac{C_h Q(P - D)}{2P} + \frac{C_o D}{Q}$$

$$\frac{dC_t}{dQ} = \frac{C_h(P - D)}{2P} - \frac{C_o D}{Q^2}$$

Again, equating to zero and solving Q gives the minimum-cost order quantity EBQ:

$$\text{EBQ} = \sqrt{\frac{2C_o D}{C_h(1 - (D/P))}}$$

Worked example

The manager of a bottle-filling plant which bottles soft drinks needs to decide how long a 'run' of each type of drink to process. Demand for each type of drink is reasonably constant at 80,000 per month (a month has 160 production hours). The bottling lines fill at a rate of 3,000 bottles per hour, but take an hour to clean and reset between different drinks. The cost (of labour and lost production capacity) of each of these changeovers has been calculated at £100 per hour. Stock-holding costs are counted at £0.1 per bottle per month.

$$D = 80,000 \text{ per month}$$

$$= 500 \text{ per hour}$$

$$\text{EBQ} = \sqrt{\frac{2C_o D}{C_h(1 - (D/P))}}$$

$$= \sqrt{\frac{2 \times 100 \times 80,000}{0.1(1 - (500/3,000))}}$$

$$\text{EBQ} = 13,856$$

The staff who operate the lines have devised a method of reducing the changeover time from 1 hour to 30 minutes. How would that change the EBQ?

$$\text{New } C_o = £50$$

$$\text{New EBQ} = \sqrt{\frac{2 \times 50 \times 80,000}{0.1(1 - (500/3,000))}}$$

$$= 9,798$$

Critical commentary

The approach to determining order quantity which involves optimizing costs of holding stock against costs of ordering stock, typified by the EOQ and EBQ models, has always been subject to criticisms. Originally these concerned the validity of some of the assumptions of the model; more recently they have involved the underlying rationale of the approach itself. The criticisms fall into four broad categories, all of which we shall examine further:

- The assumptions included in the EOQ models are simplistic.
- The real costs of stock in operations are not as assumed in EOQ models.
- The models are really descriptive, and should not be used as prescriptive devices.
- Cost minimization is not an appropriate objective for inventory management.

Responding to the criticisms of EOQ

In order to keep EOQ-type models relatively straightforward, it was necessary to make assumptions. These concerned such things as the stability of demand, the existence of a fixed and identifiable ordering cost, that the cost of stock holding can be expressed by a linear function, shortage costs which were identifiable, and so on. While these assumptions are rarely strictly true, most of them can approximate to reality. Furthermore, the shape of the total cost curve has a relatively flat optimum point which means that small errors will not significantly affect the total cost of a near-optimum order quantity. However, at times the assumptions do pose severe limitations to the models. For example, the assumption of steady demand is untrue for a wide range of inventory problems.

Cost of stock

Other questions surround some of the assumptions made concerning the nature of stock-related costs. For example, placing an order with a supplier as part of a regular and multi-item order might be relatively inexpensive, whereas asking for a special one-off delivery of an item could prove far more costly. Similarly with stock-holding costs – although many companies make a standard percentage charge on the purchase price of stock items, this might not be appropriate. The marginal costs of increasing stock-holding levels might be merely the cost of the working capital involved. On the other hand, it might necessitate the lease of a whole new stock-holding facility such as a warehouse. Operations managers using an EOQ-type approach must check that the decisions implied by the use of the formulae do not exceed the boundaries within which the cost assumptions apply. And it is useful at this stage to examine the effect on an EOQ approach of regarding inventory as being more costly than previously believed. Increasing the slope of the holding cost line increases the level of total costs of *any* order quantity, but more significantly, shifts the minimum cost point substantially to the left, in favour of a lower economic order quantity. In other words, the less willing an operation is to hold stock on the grounds of cost, the more it should move towards smaller, more frequent ordering.

Using EOQ models as prescriptions

Perhaps the most fundamental criticism of the EOQ approach comes from the 'lean' and JIT philosophies. The EOQ tries to optimize order decisions. Implicitly the costs involved are taken as fixed, in the sense that the task of operations managers is to find out what are the true costs rather than to change them in any way. EOQ is essentially a reactive approach. Some critics would argue that it fails to ask the right question. Rather than asking the EOQ question of 'What is the optimum order quantity?', operations managers should really be asking, 'How can I change the operation in some way so as to reduce the overall level of inventory I need to hold?' The EOQ approach may be a reasonable description of stock-holding costs but should not necessarily be taken as a strict prescription over what decisions to take. For example, many organizations have made considerable efforts to reduce the effective cost of placing an order. Often they have done this by working to reduce changeover times on machines. This means that less time is taken changing over from one product to the other, and therefore less operating capacity is lost, which in turn reduces the cost of the changeover. Under these circumstances, the order cost curve in the EOQ formula reduces and, in turn, reduces the effective economic order quantity. Figure 9.8 shows the EOQ formula represented graphically with increased holding costs (*see* the previous discussion) and reduced order costs. The net effect of this is to significantly reduce the value of the EOQ.

Should the cost of inventory be minimized?

Many organizations (such as supermarkets and wholesalers) make the most of their revenue and profits simply by holding and supplying inventory. Because their main investment is in the inventory it is critical that they make a good return on this capital, by ensuring that it has the highest possible 'stock turn' (defined later in this chapter) and/or gross profit

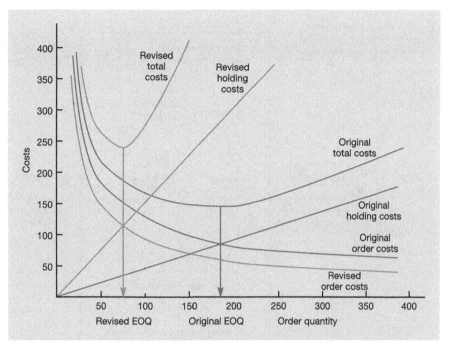

Figure 9.8 If the true costs of stock holding are taken into account, and if the cost of ordering (or changeover) is reduced, the economic order quantity (EOQ) is much smaller

Short case
Howard Smith Paper Group[2]

The Howard Smith Paper Group operates the most advanced warehousing operation within the European paper merchanting sector, delivering over 120,000 tonnes of paper annually. The function of a paper merchant is to provide the link between the paper mills and the printers or converters. This is illustrated in Figure 9.9. It is a sales- and service-driven business, so the role of the operation function is to deliver whatever the salesperson has promised to the customer. Usually, this means precisely the right product at the right time at the right place and in the right quantity. The company's operations are divided into two areas, 'logistics' which combines all warehousing and logistics tasks, and 'supply side' which includes inventory planning, purchasing and merchandizing decisions. Its main stocks are held at the national distribution centre, which was chosen because it is at the centre of the company's main customer location and also because it has good access to motorways. The key to any efficient merchanting operation lies in its ability to do three things well. Firstly, it must efficiently store the desired volume of required inventory. Secondly, it must have a 'goods inward' programme that sources the

Dispatch activity at Howard Smith Paper Group

required volume of desired inventory. Thirdly, it must be able to fulfil customer orders by 'picking' the desired goods fast and accurately from its warehouse. The warehouse is operational 24 hours per day, 5 days per week. A total of 52 staff are employed in the warehouse, including maintenance and cleaning staff. Skill sets are not an issue, since all pickers are trained for all tasks. This facilitates easier capacity management, since pickers can be deployed where most urgently needed. Contract labour is used on occasions, although this is less effective because the staff tend to be less motivated, and have to learn the job.

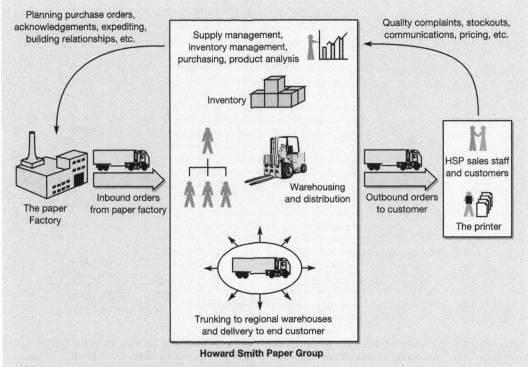

Planning purchase orders, acknowledgements, expediting, building relationships, etc.

Quality complaints, stockouts, communications, pricing, etc.

Supply management, inventory management, purchasing, product analysis

Inventory

Warehousing and distribution

The paper Factory

Inbound orders from paper factory

Outbound orders to customer

HSP sales staff and customers

The printer

Trunking to regional warehouses and delivery to end customer

Howard Smith Paper Group

Figure 9.9 The role of the paper merchant

At the heart of the company's operations is a warehouse known as a 'dark warehouse'. All picking and movement within the dark warehouse is fully automatic and there is no need for any person to enter the high-bay stores and picking area. The important difference with this warehouse operation is that pallets are brought to the pickers. Conventional paper merchants send pickers with handling equipment into the warehouse aisles for stock. A warehouse computer system (WCS) controls the whole operation without the need for human input. It manages pallet location and retrieval, robotic crane missions, automatic conveyors, bar-code label production and scanning, and all picking routines and priorities. It also calculates operator activity and productivity measures, as well as issuing documentation and planning transportation schedules. The fact that all products are identified by a unique bar code means that accuracy is guaranteed. The unique user log-on ensures that any picking errors can be traced back to the name of the picker, to ensure further errors do not occur. The WCS is linked to the company's ERP system such that once the order has been placed by a customer, computers manage the whole process from order placement to order dispatch.

margin. Alternatively, they may also be concerned to maximize the use of space by seeking to maximize the profit earned per square metre. The EOQ model does not address these objectives. Similarly for products that deteriorate or go out of fashion, the EOQ model can result in excess inventory of slower-moving items. In fact, the EOQ model is rarely used in such organizations, and there is more likely to be a system of periodic review (described later) for regular ordering of replenishment inventory. For example, a typical builders' supply merchant might carry around 50,000 different items of stock (SKUs – stock-keeping units). However, most of these cluster into larger families of items such as paints, sanitaryware or metal fixings. Single orders are placed at regular intervals for all the required replenishments in the supplier's range, and these are then delivered together at one time. For example, if such deliveries were made weekly, then on average, the individual item order quantities will be for only one week's usage. Less popular items, or ones with erratic demand patterns, can be individually ordered at the same time, or (when urgent) can be delivered the next day by carrier.

The timing decision – when to place an order

When we assumed that orders arrived instantaneously and demand was steady and predictable, the decision on when to place a replenishment order was self-evident. An order would be placed as soon as the stock level reached zero. This would arrive instantaneously and prevent any stock-out occurring. If replenishment orders do not arrive instantaneously, but have a lag between the order being placed and it arriving in the inventory, we can calculate the timing of a replacement order as shown in Figure 9.10. In this case, the lead time for an order to arrive is two weeks, so the **re-order point** (ROP) is the point at which stock will fall to zero minus the order lead time. Alternatively, we can define the point in terms of the level which the inventory will have reached when a replenishment order needs to be placed. In this case this occurs at a **re-order level** (ROL) of 200 items.

Re-order point

Re-order level

However, this assumes that both the demand and the order lead time are perfectly predictable. In most cases, of course, this is not so. Both demand and the order lead time are likely to vary to produce a profile which looks something like that in Figure 9.11. In these

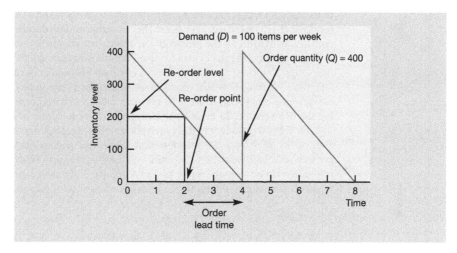

Figure 9.10 Re-order level (ROL) and re-order point (ROP) are derived from the order lead time and demand rate

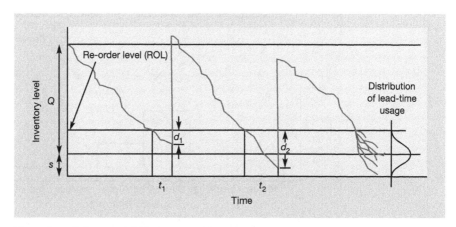

Figure 9.11 Safety stock (s) helps to avoid stock-outs when demand and/or order lead time are uncertain

circumstances it is necessary to make the replenishment order somewhat earlier than would be the case in a purely deterministic situation. This will result in, on average, some stock still being in the inventory when the replenishment order arrives. This is buffer (safety) stock. The earlier the replenishment order is placed, the higher will be the expected level of safety stock (s) when the replenishment order arrives. But because of the variability of both lead time (t) and demand rate (d), there will sometimes be a higher-than-average level of safety stock and sometimes lower. The main consideration in setting safety stock is not so much the average level of stock when a replenishment order arrives but rather the probability that the stock will not have run out before the replenishment order arrives.

Worked example

A company which imports running shoes for sale in its sports shops can never be certain of how long, after placing an order, the delivery will take. Examination of previous orders reveals that out of ten orders: one took one week, two took two weeks, four took three weeks, two took four weeks and one took five weeks. The rate of demand for the shoes also varies between 110 pairs per week and 140 pairs per week. There is a 0.2 probability of the demand rate being either 110 or 140 pairs per week, and a 0.3 chance of demand being either 120 or 130 pairs per week. The company needs to decide when it should place replenishment orders if the probability of a stock-out is to be less than 10 per cent.

Both lead time and the demand rate during the lead time will contribute to the lead-time usage. So the distributions which describe each will need to be combined. Figure 9.12 and Table 9.2 show how this can be done. Taking lead time to be one, two, three, four or five weeks, and demand rate to be 110, 120, 130 or 140 pairs per week, and also assuming the two variables to be independent, the distributions can be combined as shown in Table 9.2. Each element in the matrix shows a possible lead-time usage with the probability of its occurrence. So if the lead time is one week and the demand rate is 110 pairs per week, the actual lead-time usage will be $1 \times 110 = 110$ pairs. Since there is a 0.1 chance of the lead time being one week, and a 0.2 chance of demand rate being 110 pairs per week, the probability of both these events occurring is $0.1 \times 0.2 = 0.02$.

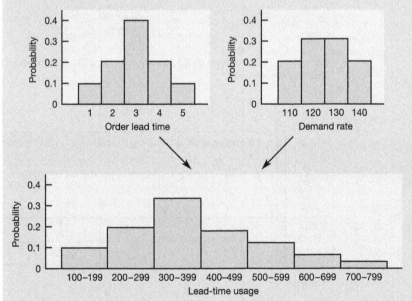

Figure 9.12 The probability distributions for order lead time and demand rate combine to give the lead-time usage distribution

→

Table 9.2 Matrix of lead-time and demand-rate probabilities

			Lead-time probabilities				
			1 0.1	2 0.2	3 0.4	4 0.2	5 0.1
Demand-rate probabilities	110	0.2	110 (0.02)	220 (0.04)	330 (0.08)	440 (0.04)	550 (0.02)
	120	0.3	120 (0.03)	240 (0.06)	360 (0.12)	480 (0.06)	600 (0.03)
	130	0.3	130 (0.03)	260 (0.06)	390 (0.12)	520 (0.06)	650 (0.03)
	140	0.2	140 (0.02)	280 (0.04)	420 (0.08)	560 (0.04)	700 (0.02)

We can now classify the possible lead-time usages into histogram form. For example, summing the probabilities of all the lead-time usages which fall within the range 100–199 (all the first column) gives a combined probability of 0.1. Repeating this for subsequent intervals results in Table 9.3.

Table 9.3 Combined probabilities

Lead-time usage	100–199	200–299	300–399	400–499	500–599	600–699	700–799
Probability	0.1	0.2	0.32	0.18	0.12	0.06	0.02

This shows the probability of each possible range of lead-time usage occurring, but it is the cumulative probabilities that are needed to predict the likelihood of stock-out (see Table 9.4).

Table 9.4 Combined probabilities

Lead-time usage X	100	200	300	400	500	600	700	800
Probability of usage being greater than X	1.0	0.9	0.7	0.38	0.2	0.08	0.02	0

Setting the re-order level at 600 would mean that there is only a 0.08 chance of usage being greater than available inventory during the lead time, i.e. there is a less than 10 per cent chance of a stock-out occurring.

Lead-time usage

The key statistic in calculating how much safety stock to allow is the probability distribution which shows the **lead-time usage**. The lead-time usage distribution is a combination of the distributions which describe lead-time variation and the demand rate during the lead time. If safety stock is set below the lower limit of this distribution then there will be shortages every single replenishment cycle. If safety stock is set above the upper limit of the distribution, there is no chance of stock-outs occurring. Usually, safety stock is set to give a predetermined likelihood that stock-outs will not occur. Figure 9.11 shows that, in this case, the first replenishment order arrived after t_1, resulting in a lead-time usage of d_1. The second replenishment order took longer, t_2, and demand rate was also higher, resulting in a lead-time usage of d_2. The third order cycle shows several possible inventory profiles for different conditions of lead-time usage and demand rate.

Continuous and periodic review

Continuous review

The approach we have described to making the replenishment timing decision is often called the **continuous review** approach. This is because, to make the decision in this way, there must be a process to review the stock level of each item continuously and then place an order when the stock level reaches its re-order level. The virtue of this approach is that, although the timing of orders may be irregular (depending on the variation in demand rate), the order size (Q) is constant and can be set at the optimum economic order quantity. Such continual checking on inventory levels can be time-consuming, especially when there are many stock withdrawals compared with the average level of stock, but in an environment where all inventory records are computerized, this should not be a problem unless the records are inaccurate.

Periodic review

An alternative and far simpler approach, but one which sacrifices the use of a fixed (and therefore possibly optimum) order quantity, is called the **periodic review** approach. Here, rather than ordering at a predetermined re-order level, the periodic approach orders at a fixed and regular time interval. So the stock level of an item could be found, for example, at the end of every month and a replenishment order placed to bring the stock up to a predetermined level. This level is calculated to cover demand between the replenishment order being placed and the following replenishment order arriving. Figure 9.13 illustrates the parameters for the periodic review approach.

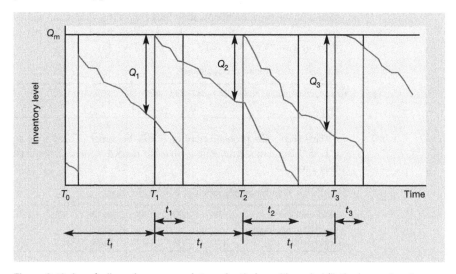

Figure 9.13 A periodic review approach to order timing with probabilistic demand and lead time

At time T_1 in Figure 9.13 the inventory manager would examine the stock level and order sufficient to bring it up to some maximum, Q_m. However, that order of Q_1 items will not arrive until a further time of t_1 has passed, during which demand continues to deplete the stocks. Again, both demand and lead time are uncertain. The Q_1 items will arrive and bring the stock up to some level lower than Q_m (unless there has been no demand during t_1). Demand then continues until T_2, when again an order Q_2 is placed which is the difference between the current stock at T_2 and Q_m. This order arrives after t_2, by which time demand has depleted the stocks further. Thus the replenishment order placed at T_1 must be able to cover for the demand which occurs until T_2 and t_2. Safety stocks will need to be calculated, in a similar manner to before, based on the distribution of usage over this period.

The time interval

The interval between placing orders, t_1, is usually calculated on a deterministic basis, and derived from the EOQ. So, for example, if the demand for an item is 2,000 per year, the cost of placing an order £25, and the cost of holding stock £0.5 per item per year:

$$\text{EOQ} = \sqrt{\frac{2C_oD}{C_h}} = \sqrt{\frac{2 \times 2,000 \times 25}{0.5}} = 447$$

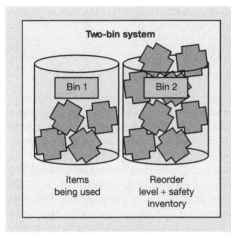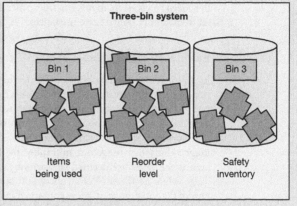

Figure 9.14 The two-bin and three-bin systems of re-ordering

The optimum time interval between orders, t_f, is therefore:

$$t_f = \frac{EOQ}{D} = \frac{447}{2,000} \text{ years}$$

$$= 2.68 \text{ months}$$

It may seem paradoxical to calculate the time interval assuming constant demand when demand is, in fact, uncertain. However, uncertainties in both demand and lead time can be allowed for by setting Q_m to allow for the desired probability of stock-out based on usage during the period t_f + lead time.

Two-bin and three-bin systems

Keeping track of inventory levels is especially important in continuous review approaches to re-ordering. A simple and obvious method of indicating when the re-order point has been reached is necessary, especially if there are a large number of items to be monitored. The two- and three-bin systems illustrated in Figure 9.14 are such methods. The simple **two-bin system** involves storing the re-order point quantity plus the safety inventory quantity in the second bin and using parts from the first bin. When the first bin empties, that is the signal to order the next re-order quantity. Sometimes the safety inventory is stored in a third bin (the **three-bin system**), so it is clear when demand is exceeding that which was expected. Different 'bins' are not always necessary to operate this type of system. For example, a common practice in retail operations is to store the second 'bin' quantity upside-down behind or under the first 'bin' quantity. Orders are then placed when the upside-down items are reached.

Two-bin system

Three-bin system

Inventory analysis and control systems

The models we have described, even the ones which take a probabilistic view of demand and lead time, are still simplified compared with the complexity of real stock management. Coping with many thousands of stocked items, supplied by many hundreds of different suppliers, with possibly tens of thousands of individual customers, makes for a complex and dynamic operations task. In order to control such complexity, operations managers have to do two things. First, they have to discriminate between different stocked items, so that they can apply a degree of control to each item which is appropriate to its importance. Second, they need to invest in an information-processing system which can cope with their particular set of inventory control circumstances.

Inventory priorities – the ABC system

In any inventory which contains more than one stocked item, some items will be more important to the organization than others. Some, for example, might have a very high usage rate, so if they ran out many customers would be disappointed. Other items might be of particularly high value, so excessively high inventory levels would be particularly expensive. One common way of discriminating between different stock items is to rank them by the **usage value** (their usage rate multiplied by their individual value). Items with a particularly high usage value are deemed to warrant the most careful control, whereas those with low usage values need not be controlled quite so rigorously. Generally, a relatively small proportion of the total range of items contained in an inventory will account for a large proportion of the total usage value. This phenomenon is known as the **Pareto law** (after the person who described it), sometimes referred to as the 80/20 rule. It is called this because, typically, 80 per cent of an operation's sales are accounted for by only 20 per cent of all stocked item types. The relationship can be used to classify the different types of items kept in an inventory by their usage value. **ABC inventory control** allows inventory managers to concentrate their efforts on controlling the more significant items of stock.

Usage value

Pareto law

ABC inventory control

Worked example

Table 9.5 shows all the parts stored by an electrical wholesaler. The 20 different items stored vary in terms of both their usage per year and cost per item as shown. However, the wholesaler has ranked the stock items by their usage value per year. The total usage value per year is £5,569,000. From this it is possible to calculate the usage value per year of each item as a percentage of the total usage value, and from that a running cumulative

Table 9.5 Warehouse items ranked by usage value

Stock no.	Usage (items/year)	Cost (£/item)	Usage value (£000/year)	% of total value	Cumulative % of total value
A/703	700	20.00	1,400	25.14	25.14
D/012	450	2.75	1,238	22.23	47.37
A/135	1,000	0.90	900	16.16	63.53
C/732	95	8.50	808	14.51	78.04
C/375	520	0.54	281	5.05	83.09
A/500	73	2.30	168	3.02	86.11
D/111	520	0.22	114	2.05	88.16
D/231	170	0.65	111	1.99	90.15
E/781	250	0.34	85	1.53	91.68
A/138	250	0.30	75	1.34	93.02
D/175	400	0.14	56	1.01	94.03
E/001	80	0.63	50	0.89	94.92
C/150	230	0.21	48	0.86	95.78
F/030	400	0.12	48	0.86	96.64
D/703	500	0.09	45	0.81	97.45
D/535	50	0.88	44	0.79	98.24
C/541	70	0.57	40	0.71	98.95
A/260	50	0.64	32	0.57	99.52
B/141	50	0.32	16	0.28	99.80
D/021	20	0.50	10	0.20	100.00
Total			5,569	100.00	

total of the usage value as shown. The wholesaler can then plot the cumulative percentage of all stocked items against the cumulative percentage of their value. So, for example, the part with stock number A/703 is the highest-value part and accounts for 25.14 per cent of the total inventory value. As a part, however, it is only one-twentieth or 5 per cent of the total number of items stocked. This item together with the next highest value item (D/012) accounts for only 10 per cent of the total number of items stocked, yet accounts for 47.37 per cent of the value of the stock, and so on.

This is shown graphically in Figure 9.15. Here the wholesaler has classified the first four part numbers (20 per cent of the range) as Class A items and will monitor the usage and ordering of these items very closely and frequently. A few improvements in order quantities or safety stocks for these items could bring significant savings. The six next, part numbers C/375 through to A/138 (30 per cent of the range), are to be treated as Class B items with slightly less effort devoted to their control. All other items are classed as Class C items whose stocking policy is reviewed only occasionally.

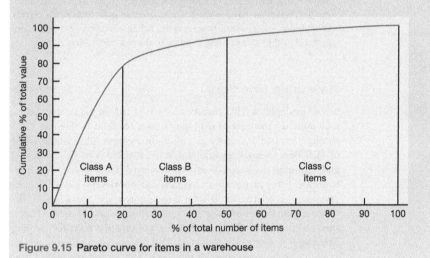

Figure 9.15 Pareto curve for items in a warehouse

- *Class A items* are those 20 per cent or so of high-usage-value items which account for around 80 per cent of the total usage value.
- *Class B items* are those of medium usage value, usually the next 30 per cent of items which often account for around 10 per cent of the total usage value.
- *Class C items* are those low-usage-value items which, although comprising around 50 per cent of the total types of items stocked, probably only account for around 10 per cent of the total usage value of the operation.

Although annual usage and value are the two criteria most commonly used to determine a stock classification system, other criteria might also contribute towards the (higher) classification of an item:

- *Consequence of stock-out.* High priority might be given to those items which would seriously delay or disrupt other operations, or the customers, if they were not in stock.
- *Uncertainty of supply.* Some items, although of low value, might warrant more attention if their supply is erratic or uncertain.
- *High obsolescence or deterioration risk.* Items which could lose their value through obsolescence or deterioration might need extra attention and monitoring.

Some more complex stock classification systems might include these criteria by classifying on an A, B, C basis for each. For example, a part might be classed as A/B/A meaning it is an

A category item by value, a class B item by consequence of stock-out and a class A item by obsolescence risk.

Critical commentary

This approach to inventory classification can sometimes be misleading. Many professional inventory managers point out that the Pareto law is often misquoted. It does not say that 80 per cent of the SKUs (stock-keeping units) account for only 20 per cent inventory value. It accounts for 80 per cent of inventory 'usage' or throughput value, in other words sales value. In fact it is the slow-moving items (the C category items) that often pose the greatest challenge in inventory management. Often these slow-moving items, although only accounting for 20 per cent of sales, require a large part (typically between one-half and two-thirds) of the total investment in stock. This is why slow-moving items are a real problem. Moreover, if errors in forecasting or ordering result in excess stock in 'A class' fast-moving items, it is relatively unimportant in the sense that excess stock can be sold quickly. However, excess stock in a slow-moving C item will be there a long time. According to some inventory managers, it is the A items that can be left to look after themselves, it is the B and even more the C items that need controlling.

Measuring inventory

In our example of ABC classifications we used the monetary value of the annual usage of each item as a measure of inventory usage. Monetary value can also be used to measure the absolute level of inventory at any point in time. This would involve taking the number of each item in stock, multiplying it by its value (usually the cost of purchasing the item) and summing the value of all the individual items stored. This is a useful measure of the investment that an operation has in its inventories but gives no indication of how large that investment is relative to the total throughput of the operation. To do this we must compare the total number of items in stock against their rate of usage. There are two ways of doing this. The first is to calculate the amount of time the inventory would last, subject to normal demand, if it were not replenished. This is sometimes called the number of weeks' (or days', months', years', etc.) *cover* of the stock. The second method is to calculate how often the stock is used up in a period, usually one year. This is called the **stock turn** or turnover of stock and is the reciprocal of the stock-cover figure.

Stock cover
Stock turn

Inventory information systems

Most inventories of any significant size are managed by computerized systems. The many relatively routine calculations involved in stock control lend themselves to computerized support. This is especially so since data capture has been made more convenient through the use of bar-code readers, radio-frequency identification (RFID), and the point-of-sale recording of sales transactions. Many commercial systems of stock control are available, although they tend to share certain common functions.

Updating stock records
Every time a transaction takes place (such as the sale of an item, the movement of an item from a warehouse into a truck, or the delivery of an item into a warehouse) the position, status and possibly value of the stock will have changed. This information must be recorded so that operations managers can determine their current inventory status at any time.

Generating orders
The two major decisions we have described previously, namely how much to order and when to order, can both be made by a computerized stock control system. The first decision,

setting the value of how much to order (Q), is likely to be taken only at relatively infrequent intervals. Originally almost all computer systems automatically calculated order quantities by using the EOQ formulae covered earlier. Now more sophisticated algorithms are used, often using probabilistic data and based on examining the marginal return on investing in stock. The system will hold all the information which goes into the ordering algorithm but might periodically check to see if demand or order lead times, or any of the other parameters, have changed significantly and recalculate Q accordingly. The decision on when to order, on the other hand, is a far more routine affair which computer systems make according to whatever decision rules operations managers have chosen to adopt: either continuous review or periodic review. Furthermore, the systems can automatically generate whatever documentation is required, or even transmit the re-ordering information electronically through an electronic data interchange (EDI) system.

Generating inventory reports

Inventory control systems can generate regular reports of stock value for the different items stored, which can help management monitor its inventory control performance. Similarly, customer service performance, such as the number of stock-outs or the number of incomplete orders, can be regularly monitored. Some reports may be generated on an exception basis. That is, the report is only generated if some performance measure deviates from acceptable limits.

Summary answers to key questions

Check and improve your understanding of this chapter using self-assessment questions and a personalized study plan, audio and video downloads, and an eBook – all at **www.myomlab.com.**

➤ What is inventory?

■ Inventory, or stock, is the stored accumulation of the transformed resources in an operation. Sometimes the words 'stock' and 'inventory' are also used to describe transforming resources, but the terms *stock control* and *inventory control* are nearly always used in connection with transformed resources.

■ Almost all operations keep some kind of inventory, most usually of materials but also of information and customers (customer inventories are normally called 'queues').

➤ What are the reasons for holding inventory and what are the disadvantages?

■ Inventory occurs in operations because the timing of supply and the timing of demand do not always match. Inventories are needed, therefore, to smooth the differences between supply and demand.

■ There are five main reasons for keeping inventory:
  - to cope with random or unexpected interruptions in supply or demand (buffer inventory);
  - to cope with an operation's inability to make all products simultaneously (cycle inventory);
  - to allow different stages of processing to operate at different speeds and with different schedules (de-coupling inventory);
  - to cope with planned fluctuations in supply or demand (anticipation inventory);
  - to cope with transportation delays in the supply network (pipeline inventory).

- There are a number of disadvantages of holding inventory:
  - Inventory is often a major part of working capital, tying up money which could be used more productively elsewhere.
  - If inventory is not used quickly, there is an increasing risk of damage, loss, deterioration, or obsolescence.
  - Inventory invariably takes up space and has to be managed, stored in appropriate conditions, insured and physically handled when transactions occur. It therefore contributes to overhead costs.

➤ How much inventory should an operation hold?

- This depends on balancing the costs associated with holding stocks against the costs associated with placing an order. The main stock-holding costs are usually related to working capital, whereas the main order costs are usually associated with the transactions necessary to generate the information to place an order.
- The best-known approach to determining the amount of inventory to order is the economic order quantity (EOQ) formula. The EOQ formula can be adapted to different types of inventory profile using different stock behaviour assumptions.
- The EOQ approach, however, has been subject to a number of criticisms regarding the true cost of holding stock, the real cost of placing an order, and the use of EOQ models as prescriptive devices.

➤ When should an operation replenish its inventory?

- Partly this depends on the uncertainty of demand. Orders are usually timed to leave a certain level of average safety stock when the order arrives. The level of safety stock is influenced by the variability of both demand and the lead time of supply. These two variables are usually combined into a lead-time usage distribution.
- Using re-order level as a trigger for placing replenishment orders necessitates the continual review of inventory levels. This can be time-consuming and expensive. An alternative approach is to make replenishment orders of varying size but at fixed time periods.

➤ How can inventory be managed?

- The key issue here is how managers discriminate between the levels of control they apply to different stock items. The most common way of doing this is by what is known as the ABC classification of stock. This uses the Pareto principle to distinguish between the different values of, or significance placed on, types of stock.
- Inventory is usually managed through sophisticated computer-based information systems which have a number of functions: the updating of stock records, the generation of orders, the generation of inventory status reports and demand forecasts. These systems critically depend on maintaining accurate inventory records.

Learning exercises

These problems and applications will help to improve your analysis of operations. You can find more practice problems as well as worked examples and guided solutions on MyOMLab at www.myomlab.com.

1 An electronics circuit supplier buys microchips from a large manufacturer. Last year the company supplied 2,000 specialist D/35 chips to customers. The cost of placing an order is $50 and the annual holding cost is estimated to be $2.4 per chip per year. How much should the company order at a time, and what is the total cost of carrying inventory of this product?

2 Supermedicosupplies.com works a 44-week year. If the lead time between placing an order for stethoscopes and receiving them is two weeks, what is the re-order point for the Thunderer stethoscopes?

3 The Super Pea Canning Company produces canned peas. It uses 10,000 litres of green dye per month. Because of the hazardous nature of this product it needs special transport; therefore the cost of placing an order is €2,000. If the storage costs of holding the dye are €5 per litre per month, how much dye should be ordered at a time?

4 In the example above, if the storage costs of keeping the dye reduce to €3 per litre per month, how much will inventory costs reduce?

Want to know more?

DeHoratius, N. and Raman, Ananth (2008) Inventory Record Inaccuracy: An Empirical Analysis, University of Chicago, http://faculty.chicagobooth.edu/nicole.dehoratius/research.

Viale, J.D. (1997) *The Basics of Inventory Management*, Crisp Publications, Menlo Park, CA. Very much 'the basics', but that is exactly what most people need.

Waters, D. (2003) *Inventory Control and Management*, John Wiley and Sons Ltd, Chichester. Conventional but useful coverage of the topic.

Wild, T. (2002) *Best Practice in Inventory Management*, Elsevier Science, Oxford. A straightforward and readable practice-based approach to the subject.

Useful websites

www.inventoryops.com/dictionary.htm A great source for information on inventory management and warehouse operations.

www.apics.org Site of APICS: a US 'educational society for resource managers'.

www.inventorymanagement.com Site of the Centre for Inventory Management. Cases and links.

www.opsman.org Lots of useful stuff.

Now that you have finished reading this chapter, why not visit MyOMLab at www.myomlab.com where you'll find more learning resources to help you make the most of your studies and get a better grade.

Social, environmental and economic performance

Key questions

- ➤ Why is operations performance important in any organization?
- ➤ How should the operations function judge itself?
- ➤ What does top management expect from the operations function?
- ➤ What are the performance objectives of operations and what are the internal and external benefits which derive from excelling in each of them?
- ➤ How do operations performance objectives trade off against each other?

Introduction

Operations are judged by the way they perform. There are many individuals and groups doing the judging and there are many different aspects of performance on which the assessment is being made. Here, we take what is called a 'triple bottom line' approach to understand an operation's total performance. If we want to understand the strategic contribution of the operations function, it is important to understand how we can measure its performance. This chapter examines social, environmental, and economic performance before focusing on how operations can impact on the success of the whole organization. Finally, we examine how performance objectives trade off against each other. Figure 3.1 shows where this chapter fits into the overall operations model.

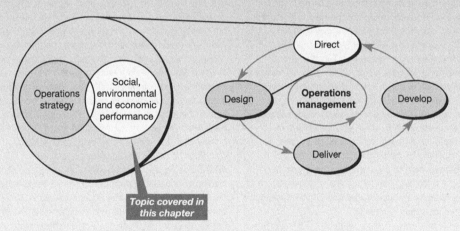

Figure 3.1 This chapter examines social, environmental and economic performance

 *Check and improve your understanding of this chapter using self-assessment questions and a personalized study plan, audio and video downloads, and an eBook – all at www.myomlab.com.*

From Chapter 3 of *Essentials of Operations Management*, 1/e. Nigel Slack, Alistair Brandon-Jones and Robert Johnston. © Nigel Slack, Alistair Brandon-Jones and Robert Johnston 2011. All rights reserved.

Operations in practice A tale of two terminals[1]

On 15 April 2008 British Airways (BA) announced that two of its most senior executives, its director of operations and its director of customer services, would leave the company. They were paying the price for the disastrous opening of British Airways' new Terminal 5 at London's Heathrow airport. The opening of the £4.3bn terminal, said BA's boss, Willie Walsh, with magnificent understatement, 'was not the company's finest hour'. The chaos at the terminal on its opening days made news around the world and was seen by many as one of the most public failures of basic operations management in the modern history of aviation. 'It's a terrible, terrible PR nightmare to have hanging over you', said David Learmount, an aviation expert. 'Somebody who may have been a faithful customer and still not have their luggage after three weeks is not good for their [BA's] image. The one thing that's worse than having a stack of 15,000 bags is adding 5,000 a day to that heap.' According to a BA spokeswoman it needed an extra 400 volunteer staff and courier companies to wade through the backlog of late baggage. So the new terminal that had opened on 27 March could not even cope with BA's full short-haul service until 8 April (two hundred flights in and out of T5 were cancelled in its first three days). This delayed moving its long-haul operations to the new building from Terminal 4 as scheduled on 30 April, which, in turn, disrupted the operations of other airlines, many of which were scheduled to move into Terminal 4 once BA had moved its long-haul flights from there. Sharing the blame with BA was the British Airports Authority (BAA) which was already suffering criticism from passenger groups, airlines and businesses for allegedly poor performance. BAA's non-executive chairman, Sir Nigel Rudd, said he was 'bitterly disappointed' about the opening of the terminal. 'It was clearly a huge embarrassment to the company, me personally, and the board. Nothing can take away that failure. We had all believed genuinely that it would be a great opening, which clearly it wasn't.'

Yet it all should have been so different. T5 took more than six years and around 60,000 workers to build, and it's an impressive building. It is Europe's largest free-standing structure. It was also keenly anticipated by travellers and BA alike. Willie Walsh has said that the terminal 'will completely change his passengers' experience'. He was right, but not in the way he imagined! So what went wrong? As is often the case with major operations failures, it was not one thing, but several interrelated problems (all of which could have been avoided). Press reports initially blamed glitches with the state-of-the-art baggage handling system that consisted

Source: Alamy Images

of 18 km of conveyor belts and was (theoretically) capable of transporting 12,000 bags per hour. Almost inevitably, the baggage handling system experienced problems which had not been exposed in testing. However, BAA, the airport operator, doubted that the main problem was the baggage system itself. The system had worked until it became clogged with bags that were overwhelming BA's handlers loading them onto the aircraft. Partly this may have been because staff were not sufficiently familiar with the new system and its operating processes, but handling staff had also suffered delays getting to their new (and unfamiliar) work areas, negotiating (new) security checks and finding (again, new) car parking spaces. Also, once staff were 'airside' they had problems logging in. The cumulative effect of these problems meant that the airline was unable to get ground handling staff to the correct locations for loading and unloading bags from the aircraft, so baggage could not be loaded onto aircraft fast enough, so baggage backed up, clogging the baggage handling system, which in turn meant closing baggage check-in and baggage drops, leading eventually to baggage check-in being halted.

However, not every airline underestimates the operational complexity of airport processes. During the same year that Terminal 5 at Heathrow was suffering queues, lost bags and bad publicity, Dubai International Airport's Terminal 3 opened quietly with little publicity and fewer problems. Like T5, it is also huge and designed to impress. Its new shimmering facilities are solely dedicated to Emirates Airline. Largely built underground (20 metres beneath the taxiway area) the multi-level environment reduces passenger walking by using 157 elevators, 97 escalators and 82 moving walkways. Its underground baggage handling system is the deepest and the largest of its kind in the world with 90 km of baggage belts handling around 15,000 items →

Source: Rex Features

customer service is under-promise and over-deliver because that way you get their loyalty. BA was telling people that they were getting a glimpse of the future with T5, which created expectation and increased the chances of disappointment. Having watched the development of T5, it was clear that we had to make sure that everyone was on-message. We just had to bang heads together so that people realized what was at stake. We knew the world would be watching and waiting after T5 to see whether T3 was the next big terminal fiasco. We worked very hard to make sure that didn't happen.'

Paul Griffiths was also convinced that Terminal 3 should undergo a phased programme with flights added progressively, rather than a 'big bang' approach where the terminal opened for business on one day. 'We exhaustively tested the terminal systems throughout the summer . . . We continue to make sure we're putting large loads on it, week by week, improving reliability. We put a few flights in bit by bit, in waves rather than a big bang.' Prior to the opening he also said that Dubai Airports would never reveal a single opening date for its new Terminal 3 until all pre-opening test programmes had been completed. 'T3 opened so quietly', said one journalist, 'that passengers would have known that the terminal was new only if they had touched the still-drying paint.'

per hour. Also like T5 it handles about 30 million passengers a year.

A key difference between the two terminals was that Dubai's T3 could observe and learn lessons from the botched opening of Heathrow's Terminal 5. Paul Griffiths, the former head of London's Gatwick Airport, who is now Dubai Airport's chief executive, insisted that his own new terminal should not be publicly shamed in the same way. 'There was a lot of arrogance and hubris around the opening of T5, with all the . . . publicity that BA generated', Mr Griffiths says. 'The first rule of

Operations performance is vital for any organization

Operations management is a 'make or break' activity

It is no exaggeration to view operations management as being able to either 'make or break' any business. This is not just because the operations function is large and, in most businesses, represents the bulk of its assets and the majority of its people, but because the operations function gives the ability to compete by providing customer responsiveness and by developing the capabilities that will keep it ahead of its competitors in the future. For example, operations management principles and the performance of its operations function proved hugely important in the Heathrow T5 and Dubai T3 launches. It was a basic failure to understand the importance of operations processes that (temporarily) damaged British Airways' reputation. It was Dubai's attention to detail and thorough operational preparation that avoided similar problems.

Operations managers face many new challenges as the economic, social, political and technological environment changes. Many of these decisions and challenges seem largely economic in nature. What will be the impact on our costs of adding a new product or service feature? Can we generate an acceptable return if we invest in new technology? Other decisions have more of a 'social' aspect. How do we make sure that all our suppliers treat their staff fairly? Finally, some have an environmental impact. Are we doing enough to reduce our carbon footprint? Furthermore, the 'economic' decisions also have an environmental aspect to them. Will a new product feature make end-of-life recycling more difficult? Will the new technology increase pollution? Similarly the 'social' decisions must be made in the context of their economic consequences. Sure, we want suppliers to treat staff well, but we also need to make a profit. And this is the great dilemma. How do operations managers try to be, simultaneously, economically viable whilst being socially and environmentally responsible?

The triple bottom line

One common term that tries to capture the idea of a broader approach to assessing an organization's performance is the '**triple bottom line**' (TBL, or 3BL), also known as 'people, planet and profit'. Essentially, it is a straightforward idea, simply that organizations should measure themselves not just on the traditional economic profit that they generate for their owners, but also on the impact their operations have on society (broadly, in the sense of communities, and individually, for example in terms of their employees) and the ecological impact on the environment. The influential initiative that has come out of this triple bottom line approach is that of 'sustainability'. A sustainable business is one that creates an acceptable profit for its owners, but minimizes the damage to the environment and enhances the existence of the people with whom it has contact. In other words, it balances economic, environmental and societal interests. This gives the organization its 'license to operate' in society. The assumption underlying the triple bottom line (which is not universally accepted) is that a sustainable business is more likely to remain successful in the long-term than one which focuses on economic goals alone. Only a company that produces a balanced TBL is really accounting for the total cost of running its operations. Figure 3.2 illustrates some of the issues involved in achieving the triple bottom line.

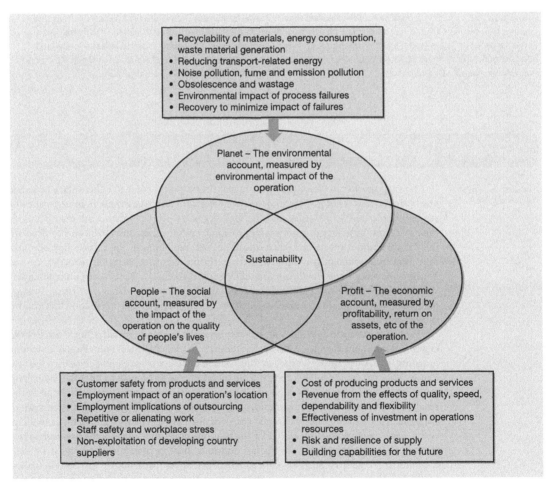

Figure 3.2 Some ways in which operations can impact each element of the triple bottom line

The social bottom line

The fundamental idea behind the social bottom line is not simply that there is a connection between businesses and the society in which they operate (defined broadly) – that is self-evident. Rather it is that businesses should accept that they bear some responsibility for the impact they have on society and balance the external 'societal' consequences of their actions with the more direct internal consequences, such as profit.

Society is made up of organizations, groups and individuals. Each is more than a simple unit of economic exchange. Organizations have responsibility for the general well-being of society beyond short-term economic self-interest. At the level of the individual, this means devising jobs and work patterns which allow individuals to contribute their talents without undue stress. At a group level, it means recognizing and dealing honestly with employee representatives. This principle also extends beyond the boundaries of the organization. Any business has a responsibility to ensure that it does not knowingly disadvantage individuals in its suppliers or trading partners. Businesses are also a part of the larger community, often integrated into the economic and social fabric of an area. Increasingly, organizations are recognizing their responsibility to local communities by helping to promote their economic and social well-being. Of the many issues that affect society at large, arguably the one that has had the most profound effect on the way business has developed over the last few decades has been the globalization of business activity.

Globalization

Globalization

The International Monetary Fund defines globalization as 'the growing economic inter-dependence of countries worldwide through increasing volume and variety of cross-border transactions in goods and services, free international capital flows, and more rapid and widespread diffusion of technology'. It reflects the idea that the world is a smaller place to do business in. Even many medium-sized companies are sourcing and selling their products and services on a global basis. Considerable opportunities have emerged for operations managers to develop both supplier and customer relationships in new parts of the world. All of this is exciting but it also poses many problems. **Globalization** of trade is considered by some to be the root cause of exploitation and corruption in many developing countries. Others see it as the only way of spreading the levels of prosperity enjoyed by developed countries throughout the world.

The ethical globalization movement seeks to reconcile the globalization trend with how it can impact on societies. Typical aims include the following:

- Acknowledging shared responsibilities for addressing global challenges and affirming that our common humanity doesn't stop at national borders.
- Recognizing that all individuals are equal in dignity and have the right to certain entitlements, rather than viewing them as objects of benevolence or charity.
- Embracing the importance of gender and the need for attention to the often different impacts of economic and social policies on women and men.
- Affirming that a world connected by technology and trade must also be connected by shared values, norms of behaviour and systems of accountability.

Corporate social responsibility (CSR)

Corporate social responsibility

Strongly related to the social 'bottom line' (and to some extent the environmental 'bottom line') is that of **corporate social responsibility** (generally known as CSR). According to the UK government's definition, *'CSR is essentially about how business takes account of its economic, social and environmental impacts in the way it operates – maximizing the benefits and minimizing the downsides. . . . Specifically, we see CSR as the voluntary actions that business can take, over and above compliance with minimum legal requirements, to address both its own competitive interests and the interests of wider society.'* A more direct link with the stakeholder concept is to be found in the definition used by Marks and Spencer, the UK-based retailer. *'Corporate Social Responsibility . . . is listening and responding to the needs of a company's stakeholders. This includes the requirements of sustainable development. We believe that building good relationships with employees, suppliers and wider society is the best guarantee of long-term success. This is the backbone of our approach to CSR.'* The issue of how broader social performance objectives can be included in operations management's activities is of increasing importance, from both an ethical and a commercial point of view.

The environmental bottom line

Environmental sustainability (according to the World Bank) means 'ensuring that the overall productivity of accumulated human and physical capital resulting from development actions more than compensates for the direct or indirect loss or degradation of the environment', or (according to the Brundtland Report from the United Nations) it is 'meeting the needs of the present without compromising the ability of future generations to meet their own needs'. Put more directly, it is generally taken to mean the extent to which business activity negatively impacts on the natural environment. It is clearly an important issue, not only because of the obvious impact on the immediate environment of hazardous waste, air and even noise pollution, but also because of the less obvious, but potentially far more damaging issues around global warming.

From the perspective of individual organizations, the challenging issues of dealing with sustainability are connected with the scale of the problem and the general perception of 'green' issues. Firstly, the scale issue is that cause and effect in the environmental sustainability area are judged at different levels. The effects of, and arguments for, environmentally sustainable activities are felt at a global level, while those activities themselves are essentially local. It has been argued that it is difficult to use the concept at a corporate or even at a regional level. Secondly, there is a paradox with sustainability-based decisions. It is that the more the public becomes sensitized to the benefits of firms acting in an environmentally sensitive way, the more those firms are tempted to exaggerate their environmental credentials, the so-called 'greenwashing' effect.

Environmental protection Operations managers cannot avoid responsibility for **environmental protection** generally, or their organization's environmental performance more specifically. It is often operational failures which are at the root of pollution disasters and operations decisions (such as product design) which impact on longer-term environmental issues. The pollution-causing disasters which make the headlines seem to be the result of a whole variety of causes – oil tankers run aground, nuclear waste is misclassified, chemicals leak into a river, or gas clouds drift over industrial towns. But in fact they all have something in common. They were all the result of an operational failure. Somehow operations procedures were inadequate. Less dramatic in the short term, but perhaps more important in the long term, is the environmental impact of products which cannot be recycled and processes which consume large amounts of energy – again, both issues which are part of the operations management's broader responsibilities.

Again, it is important to understand that broad issues such as environmental responsibility are intimately connected with the day-to-day decisions of operations managers. Many of these are concerned with waste. Operations management decisions in product and service design significantly affect the utilization of materials both in the short term and in long-term recyclability. Process design influences the proportion of energy and labour that is wasted as well as materials wastage. Planning and control may affect material wastage (packaging being wasted by mistakes in purchasing, for example), but also affects energy and labour wastage. Improvement, of course, is dedicated largely to reducing wastage. Here environmental responsibility and the conventional concerns of operations management coincide. Reducing waste, in all it forms, may be environmentally sound but it also saves cost for the organization. At other times, decisions can be more difficult. Process technologies may be efficient from the operations point of view but may cause pollution, the economic and social consequences of which are borne by society at large. Such conflicts are usually resolved through regulation and legislation. Not that such mechanisms are always effective – there is evidence that just-in-time principles applied in Japan may have produced significant economic gains for the companies which adopted them, but at the price of an overcrowded and polluted road system.

The economic bottom line

An organization's top management represent the interests of the owners (or trustees, or electorate, etc.) and therefore are the direct custodians of the organization's basic purpose. They also have responsibility for translating the broad objectives of the organization into a more tangible form. Broadly they should expect all their operations managers to contribute to the economic success of the organization by **using its resources effectively**. To do this it must be creative, innovative and energetic in improving its processes, products and services. In more detail, effective operations management can give five types of advantage to the business (see Figure 3.3):

Operations can have a significant impact on economic success

- It can reduce the **costs** of producing services and products.
- It can achieve customer satisfaction through good quality and service (and therefore **revenue** in a for-profit organization).
- It can reduce the **risk** of operational failure, because well designed and well-run operations should be less likely to fail, and if they do they should be able to recover faster and with less disruption (this is called *resilience*).
- It can reduce the amount of **investment** (sometimes called *capital employed*) that is necessary to produce the required type and quantity of products and services by increasing the effective capacity of the operation and by being innovative in how it uses its physical resources.
- It can provide the basis for *future* **innovation** by learning from its experience of operating its processes, so building a solid base of operations skills, knowledge and capability within the business.

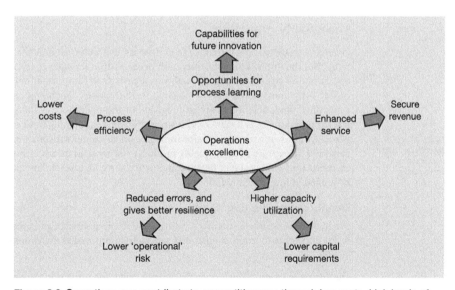

Figure 3.3 Operations can contribute to competitiveness through low costs, high levels of service (securing revenue), lower operational risk, lower capital requirements, and providing the capabilities that determine future innovation

155

The five operations performance objectives

Five basic 'performance objectives'

Broad stakeholder objectives form the backdrop to operations decision-making, and top management's objectives provide a strategic framework, but running operations at an operational day-to-day level requires a more tightly defined set of objectives. These are the **five basic 'performance objectives'** and they apply to all types of operation. Imagine that you are an operations manager in any kind of business – a hospital administrator, for example, or a production manager at a car plant. What kind of things are you likely to want to do in order to satisfy customers and contribute to competitiveness?

Quality

- You would want to do things right; that is, you would not want to make mistakes, and would want to satisfy your customers by providing error-free services and products which are 'fit for their purpose'. This is giving a **quality** advantage.

Speed

- You would want to do things fast, minimizing the time between a customer asking for services or products and the customer receiving them in full, thus increasing the availability of your services and products and giving a **speed** advantage.

Dependability

- You would want to do things on time, so as to keep the delivery promises you have made. If the operation can do this, it is giving a **dependability** advantage.

Flexibility

- You would want to be able to change what you do; that is, being able to vary or adapt the operation's activities to cope with unexpected circumstances or to give customers individual treatment. Being able to change far enough and fast enough to meet customer requirements gives a **flexibility** advantage.

Cost

- You would want to do things cheaply; that is, create and deliver services and products at a cost which enables them to be priced appropriately for the market while still allowing for a return to the organization; or, in a not-for-profit organization, give good value to the taxpayers or whoever is funding the operation. When the organization is managing to do this, it is giving a **cost** advantage.

The next part of this chapter examines these five performance objectives in more detail by looking at what they mean for four different operations: a general hospital, an automobile factory, a city bus company and a supermarket chain.

The quality objective

Quality is consistent conformance to customers' expectations, in other words, 'doing things right', but the things which the operation needs to do right will vary according to the kind of operation. All operations regard quality as a particularly important objective. In some ways quality is the most visible part of what an operation does. Furthermore, it is something that a customer finds relatively easy to judge about the operation. Is the service or product as it is supposed to be? Is it right or is it wrong? There is something fundamental about quality. Because of this, it is clearly **a major influence on customer satisfaction or dissatisfaction**. A customer perception of high-quality products and services means customer satisfaction and therefore the likelihood that the customer will return. Figure 3.4 illustrates how quality could be judged in four operations.

Quality is a major influence on customer satisfaction or dissatisfaction

Quality inside the operation

When quality means consistently creating and delivering services and products to specification, it not only leads to external customer satisfaction, but makes life easier inside the operation as well.

Quality reduces costs. The fewer mistakes made by each process in the operation, the less time will be needed to correct the mistakes and the less confusion and irritation will be spread. For example, if a supermarket's regional warehouse sends the wrong goods to the supermarket, it will mean staff time, and therefore cost, being used to sort out the problem.

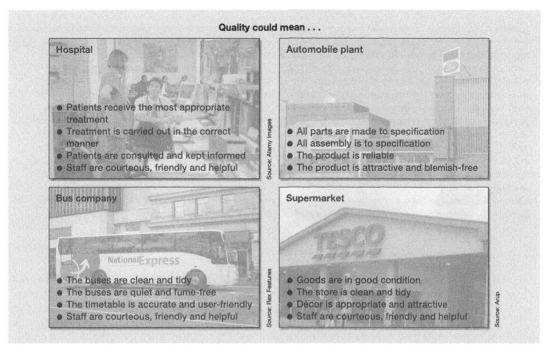

Quality could mean . . .

Hospital
- Patients receive the most appropriate treatment
- Treatment is carried out in the correct manner
- Patients are consulted and kept informed
- Staff are courteous, friendly and helpful

Source: Alamy Images

Automobile plant
- All parts are made to specification
- All assembly is to specification
- The product is reliable
- The product is attractive and blemish-free

Bus company
- The buses are clean and tidy
- The buses are quiet and fume-free
- The timetable is accurate and user-friendly
- Staff are courteous, friendly and helpful

Source: Rex Features

Supermarket
- Goods are in good condition
- The store is clean and tidy
- Décor is appropriate and attractive
- Staff are courteous, friendly and helpful

Source: Arup

Figure 3.4 **Quality means different things in different operations**

Quality increases dependability. Increased costs are not the only consequence of poor quality. At the supermarket, poor quality could also mean that products run out on the shelves, resulting in lost revenue to the operation. Sorting the problem out could also distract the supermarket management from giving attention to the other parts of the supermarket operation. This in turn could result in further mistakes being made. So, quality (like the other performance objectives, as we shall see) has both an external impact which influences customer satisfaction and an internal impact which leads to stable and efficient processes.

Short case
Organically good quality[2]

'Organic farming means taking care and getting all the details right. It is about quality from start to finish. Not only the quality of the meat that we produce but also quality of life and quality of care for the countryside.' Nick Fuge is the farm manager at Lower Hurst Farm located within the Peak District National Park of the UK. He has day-to-day responsibility for the well-being of all the livestock and the operation of the farm on strict organic principles. The 85-hectare farm has been producing high-quality beef for almost 20 years but changed to fully organic production in 1998. Organic farming is a tough regime. No artificial fertilizers, genetically modified feedstuff or growth-promoting agents are used. All beef sold from the farm is home-bred and can be traced back to the animal from which it came.

Source: Alamy Images

'The quality of the herd is most important', says Nick, 'as is animal care. Our customers trust us to ensure that the cattle are organically and humanely reared, and slaughtered in a manner that minimizes any distress. If you want to *understand the difference between conventional and organic farming, look at the way we use veterinary help. Most conventional farmers use veterinarians like an emergency service to put things right when there is a problem with an animal. The amount we pay for veterinary assistance is lower because we try to avoid problems with the animals from the start. We use veterinarians as consultants to help us in preventing problems in the first place.'*

Catherine Pyne runs the butchery and the mail-order meat business. 'After butchering, the cuts of meat are individually vacuum-packed, weighed and then blast-frozen. We worked extensively with the Department of Food and Nutrition at Oxford Brooks University to devise the best way to encapsulate the nutritional, textural and flavoursome characteristics of the meat in its prime state.

So, when you defrost and cook any of our products you will have the same tasty and succulent eating qualities associated with the best fresh meat.' After freezing, the products are packed in boxes, designed and labelled for storage in a home freezer. Customers order by phone or through the Internet for next-day delivery in a special 'mini-deep-freeze' reusable container which maintains the meat in its frozen state. 'It isn't just the quality of our product which has made us a success', says Catherine. 'We give a personal and inclusive level of service to our customers that makes them feel close to us and maintains trust in how we produce and prepare the meat. The team of people we have here is also an important aspect of our business. We are proud of our product and feel that it is vitally important to be personally identified with it.'

The speed objective

Speed means the elapsed time between customers requesting services or products and receiving them. Figure 3.5 illustrates what speed means for the four operations. The main benefit to the operation's (external) customers of speedy delivery of services or products is that the faster they can have the service or product, the more likely they are to buy it, or the more they will pay for it, or the greater the **benefit they receive** (see the short case 'When speed means life or death').

Speed increases value for some customers

Speed inside the operation

Inside the operation, speed is also important. Fast response to external customers is greatly helped by speedy decision-making and speedy movement of materials and information inside the operation. Speed brings other benefits too.

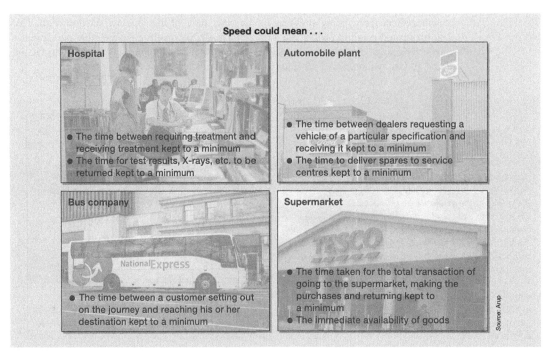

Figure 3.5 Speed means different things in different operations

Speed reduces inventories. Take, for example, the automobile plant. Steel for the vehicle's door panels is delivered to the press shop, pressed into shape, transported to the painting area, coated for colour and protection, and moved to the assembly line where it is fitted to the automobile. This is a simple three-stage process, but in practice material does not flow smoothly from one stage to the next. Firstly, the steel is delivered as part of a far larger batch containing enough steel to make possibly several hundred products. Eventually it is taken to the press area, pressed into shape, and again waits to be transported to the paint area. It then waits to be painted, only to wait once more until it is transported to the assembly line. Yet again, it waits until it is eventually fitted to the automobile. The material's journey time is far longer than the time needed to make and fit the product. It actually spends most of its time waiting as stocks (inventories) of parts and products. The longer items take to move through a process, the more time they will be waiting and the higher inventory will be.

Speed reduces risks. Forecasting tomorrow's events is far less of a risk than forecasting next year's. The further ahead companies forecast, the more likely they are to get it wrong. The faster the throughput time of a process the later forecasting can be left. Consider the automobile plant again. If the total throughput time for the door panel is six weeks, door panels are being processed through their first operation six weeks before they reach their final destination. The quantity of door panels being processed will be determined by the forecasts for demand six weeks ahead. If instead of six weeks, they take only one week to move through the plant, the door panels being processed through their first stage are intended to meet demand only one week ahead. Under these circumstances it is far more likely that the number and type of door panels being processed are the number and type which eventually will be needed.

Source: Alamy Images

Of all the operations which have to respond quickly to customer demand, few have more need of speed than the emergency services. In responding to road accidents especially, every second is critical. The treatment you receive during the first hour after your accident (what is called the 'golden hour') can determine whether you survive and fully recover or not. Making full use of the golden hour means speeding up three elements of the total time to treatment – the time it takes for the emergency services to find out about the accident, the time it takes them to travel to the scene of the accident, and the time it takes to get the casualty to appropriate treatment.

Alerting the emergency services immediately is the idea behind Mercedes-Benz's TeleAid system. As soon as the vehicle's airbag is triggered, an on-board computer reports through the mobile phone network to a control centre (drivers can also trigger the system manually if not too badly hurt), satellite tracking allows the vehicle to be precisely located and the owner identified (if special medication is needed). Getting to the accident quickly is the next hurdle. Often the fastest method is by helicopter. When most rescues are only a couple of minutes' flying time back to the hospital speed can really saves lives.

However, it is not always possible to land a helicopter safely at night (because of possible overhead wires and other hazards) so conventional ambulances will always be needed, both to get paramedics quickly to accident victims and to speed them to hospital. One increasingly common method of ensuring that ambulances arrive quickly at the accident site is to position them, not at hospitals, but close to where accidents are likely to occur. Computer analysis of previous accident data helps to select the ambulance's waiting position, and global positioning systems help controllers to mobilize the nearest unit. At all times a key requirement for fast service is effective communication between all who are involved in each stage of the emergency. Modern communications technology can play an important role in this.

The dependability objective

Dependability means doing things in time for customers to receive their services or products exactly when they are needed, or at least when they were promised. Figure 3.6 illustrates what dependability means in the four operations. Customers might only judge the dependability of an operation after the service or product has been delivered. Initially this may not affect the likelihood that customers will select the service – they have already 'consumed' it. **Over time**, however, dependability can override all other criteria. No matter how cheap or fast a bus service is, if the service is always late (or unpredictably early) or the buses are always full, then potential passengers will be better off calling a taxi.

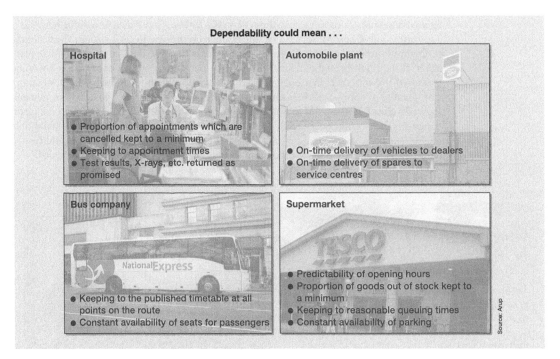

Figure 3.6 Dependability means different things in different operations

Short case
Dabbawalas hit 99.9999% dependability[4]

Mumbai is India's most densely populated city, and every working day its millions of commuters crowd onto packed trains for an often lengthy commute to their workplaces. Going home for lunch is not possible, so many office workers have a cooked meal sent either from their home, or from a caterer. It is Mumbai's 5,000-strong dabbawala collective that provides this service, usually for a monthly fee. The meal is cooked in the morning (by family or

→

caterer), placed in regulation dabbas or tiffin (lunch) boxes and delivered to each individual worker's office at lunch time. After lunch the boxes are collected and returned so that they can be re-sent the next day. 'Dabbawala' means 'one who carries a box', or more colloquially, 'lunch box delivery man'. This is how the service works:

7am–9am The dabbas (boxes) are collected by dabbawalas on bicycles from nearly 200,000 suburban homes or from the dabba makers and taken to railway stations. The dabbas have distinguishing marks on them, using colours and symbols (necessary because many dabbawalas are barely literate). The dabbawala then takes them to a designated sorting place, where he and other collecting dabbawalas sort (and sometimes bundle) the lunch boxes into groups.

9am–11am The grouped boxes are put in the coaches of trains, with markings to identify the destination of the box (usually there is a designated car for the boxes). The markings include the rail station where the boxes are to be unloaded and the building address where the box has to be delivered. This may involve boxes being sorted at intermediary stations, with each single dabba changing hands up to four times.

10am–12midday Dabbas taken into Mumbai using the otherwise under-utilized capacity on commuter trains in the mid-morning.

11am–12midday Arrive downtown Mumbai where dabbas are handed over to **local dabbawalas**, who distribute them to more locations where there is more sorting and loading on to handcarts, bicycles and dabbawalas.

12midday–1pm Dabbas are delivered to appropriate office locations.

2pm Process moves into reverse, after lunch, when the empty boxes are collected from office locations and returned to suburban stations.

6pm Empty dabbas sent back to the respective houses.

The service has a remarkable record of almost flawlessly reliable delivery, even on the days of severe weather such as Mumbai's characteristic monsoons. Dabbawalas all receive the same pay and at both the receiving and the sending ends, are known to the customers personally, so are trusted by customers. Also, they are well accustomed to the local areas they collect from or deliver to, which reduces the chances of errors. Raghunath Medge, the president of the Bombay Tiffin Box Supply Charity Trust, which oversees the dabbawallas, highlights the importance of their hands-on operations management. *'Proper time management is our key to success. We do everything to keep the customer happy and they help in our marketing.'* There is no system of documentation. The success of the operation depends on teamwork and human ingenuity. Such is the dedication and commitment of the barefoot delivery men (there are only a few delivery women) that the complex logistics operation works with only three layers of management. Although the service remains essentially low-tech, with the barefoot delivery men as the prime movers, the dabbawalas now use some modern technology, for example they now allow booking for delivery through SMS and their web site, (www.mydabbawala.com).

Dependability inside the operation

Inside the operation, internal customers will judge each other's performance partly by how reliable the other processes are in delivering material or information on time. Operations where internal dependability is high are more effective than those which are not, for a number of reasons.

Dependability saves time. Take, for example, the maintenance and repair centre for the city bus company. If the centre runs out of some crucial spare parts, the manager of the centre will need to spend time trying to arrange a special delivery of the required parts and the resources allocated to service the buses will not be used as productively as they would have been without this disruption. More seriously, the fleet will be short of buses until they can be repaired and the fleet operations manager will have to spend time rescheduling services. So, entirely due to the one failure of dependability of supply, a significant part of the operation's time has been wasted coping with the disruption.

Dependability saves money. Ineffective use of time will translate into extra cost. The spare parts might cost more to be delivered at short notice and maintenance staff will expect to be paid even when there is not a bus to work on. Nor will the fixed costs of the operation, such as heating and rent, be reduced because the two buses are not being serviced. The rescheduling of buses will probably mean that some routes have inappropriately sized buses and some services could have to be cancelled. This will result in empty bus seats (if too large a bus has to be used) or a loss of revenue (if potential passengers are not transported).

Dependability gives stability. The disruption caused to operations by a lack of dependability goes beyond time and cost. It affects the 'quality' of the operation's time. If everything in an operation is always perfectly dependable, a level of trust will have built up between the different parts of the operation. There will be no 'surprises' and everything will be predictable. Under such circumstances, each part of the operation can concentrate on improving its own area of responsibility without having its attention continually diverted by a lack of dependable service from the other parts.

The flexibility objective

Flexibility means being able to **change** the operation in some way. This may mean changing what the operation does, how it is doing it, or when it is doing it. Specifically, customers will need the operation to change so that it can provide four types of requirement:

- **Service/product flexibility** – the operation's ability to introduce new or modified services and products;

- **mix flexibility** – the operation's ability to create a wide range or mix of services and products;

- **volume flexibility** – the operation's ability to change its level of output or activity to produce different quantities or volumes of services and products over time;

- **delivery flexibility** – the operation's ability to change the timing of the delivery of its services or products.

Figure 3.7 gives examples of what these different types of flexibility mean to the four different operations.

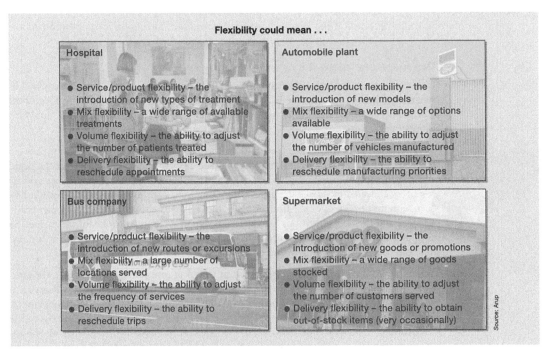

Flexibility could mean . . .

Hospital
- Service/product flexibility – the introduction of new types of treatment
- Mix flexibility – a wide range of available treatments
- Volume flexibility – the ability to adjust the number of patients treated
- Delivery flexibility – the ability to reschedule appointments

Automobile plant
- Service/product flexibility – the introduction of new models
- Mix flexibility – a wide range of options available
- Volume flexibility – the ability to adjust the number of vehicles manufactured
- Delivery flexibility – the ability to reschedule manufacturing priorities

Bus company
- Service/product flexibility – the introduction of new routes or excursions
- Mix flexibility – a large number of locations served
- Volume flexibility – the ability to adjust the frequency of services
- Delivery flexibility – the ability to reschedule trips

Supermarket
- Service/product flexibility – the introduction of new goods or promotions
- Mix flexibility – a wide range of goods stocked
- Volume flexibility – the ability to adjust the number of customers served
- Delivery flexibility – the ability to obtain out-of-stock items (very occasionally)

Source: Arup

Figure 3.7 Flexibility means different things in different operations

Short case
Flexibility and dependability in the newsroom[5]

Television news is big business. Satellite and cable, as well as developments in terrestrial transmission, have all helped to boost the popularity of 24-hour news services. However, news perishes fast. A daily newspaper delivered one day late is practically worthless. This is why broadcasting organizations like the BBC have to ensure that up-to-date news is delivered on time, every time. The BBC's ability to achieve high levels of dependability is made possible by the technology employed in news gathering and editing. At one time news editors would have to schedule a video-taped report to start its countdown five seconds prior to its broadcasting time. With new technology the video can be started from a freeze-frame and will broadcast the instant the command to play is given. The team have faith in the dependability of the process. In addition, technology allows them the flexibility to achieve dependability, even when news stories break just before transmission. In the hours before scheduled transmission, journalists and editors prepare an 'inventory' of news items stored electronically. The presenter will prepare his or her commentary on the autocue and each item will be timed to the second. If the team needs to make a short-term adjustment to the planned schedule, the news studio's technology allows the editors to take broadcasts live from journalists at their locations, on satellite 'takes', directly into the programme. Editors can even type news reports directly onto the autocue for the presenter to read as they are typed – nerve-racking, but it keeps the programme on time.

Mass customization

One of the beneficial external effects of flexibility is the increased ability of operations to do different things for different customers. So, high flexibility gives the ability to create a high variety of services or products. Normally high variety means high cost (see Chapter 1). Furthermore, high-variety operations do not usually produce in high volume. Some companies have developed their flexibility in such a way that products and services are customized for each individual customer. Yet they manage to produce them in a high-volume, mass-production manner which keeps costs down. This approach is called **mass customization**. Sometimes this is achieved through flexibility in design. For example, Dell is one of the largest volume producers of personal computers in the world, yet allows each customer to 'design' (albeit in a limited sense) their own configuration. Sometimes flexible technology is used to achieve the same effect. For example, Paris Miki, an up-market eyewear retailer which has the largest number of eyewear stores in the world, uses its own 'Mikissimes Design System' to capture a digital image of the customer and analyse facial characteristics. Together with a list of customers' personal preferences, the system then recommends a particular design and displays it on the image of the customer's face. In consultation with the optician the customer can adjust shapes and sizes until the final design is chosen. Within the store the frames are assembled from a range of pre-manufactured components and the lenses ground and fitted to the frames. The whole process takes around an hour.

Mass customization

Agility

Agility

Judging operations in terms of their **agility** has become popular. Agility is really a combination of all the five performance objectives, but particularly flexibility and speed. In addition, agility implies that an operation and the supply chain of which it is a part (supply networks are described in Chapter 7) can respond to uncertainty in the market. Agility means responding to market requirements by creating new and existing services and products fast and flexibly.

Flexibility inside the operation

Developing a flexible operation can also have advantages to the internal customers within the operation.

Flexibility speeds up response. Fast service often depends on the operation being flexible. For example, if the hospital has to cope with a sudden influx of patients from a road accident, it clearly needs to deal with injuries quickly. Under such circumstances a flexible hospital which can speedily transfer extra skilled staff and equipment to the Accident and Emergency department will provide the fast service which the patients need.

Flexibility saves time. In many parts of the hospital, staff have to treat a wide variety of complaints. Fractures, cuts or drug overdoses do not come in batches. Each patient is an individual with individual needs. The hospital staff cannot take time to 'get into the routine' of treating a particular complaint; they must have the flexibility to adapt quickly. They must also have sufficiently flexible facilities and equipment so that time is not wasted waiting for equipment to be brought to the patient. The time of the hospital's resources is being saved because they are flexible in 'changing over' from one task to the next.

Flexibility maintains dependability. Internal flexibility can also help to keep the operation on schedule when unexpected events disrupt the operation's plans. For example, if the sudden influx of patients to the hospital requires emergency surgical procedures, routine operations will be disrupted. This is likely to cause distress and considerable inconvenience. A flexible hospital might be able to minimize the disruption by possibly having reserved operating theatres for such an emergency, and being able to bring in medical staff quickly that are 'on call'.

The cost objective

To the companies which compete directly on price, cost will clearly be their major operations objective. The lower the cost of creating and delivering their services and products, the lower can be the price to their customers. Even those companies which do not compete on price will be interested in keeping costs low. Every euro or dollar removed from an operation's

Short case
Everyday low prices at Aldi[6]

Aldi is an international 'limited assortment' supermarket specializing in 'private label', mainly food products. It has carefully focused its service concept and delivery system to attract customers in a highly competitive market. The company believes that its unique approach to operations management make it 'virtually impossible for competitors to match our combination of price and quality'.

Aldi operations challenge the norms of retailing. They are deliberately simple, using basic facilities to keep down overheads. Most stores stock only a limited range of goods (typically around 700 compared with 25,000 to 30,000 stocked by conventional supermarket chains). The private label approach means that the products have been produced according to Aldi quality specifications and are only sold in Aldi stores. Without the high costs of brand marketing and advertising and with Aldi's formidable purchasing power, prices

Source: Alamy Images

can be 30 per cent below their branded equivalents. Other cost-saving practices include open carton displays which eliminate the need for special shelving, no grocery bags to encourage reuse as well as saving costs, and using a 'cart rental' system which requires customers to return the cart to the store to get their coin deposit back.

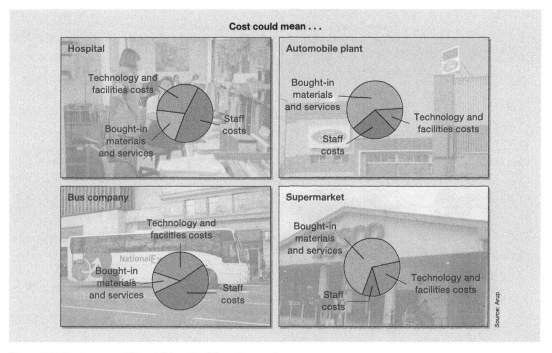

Cost could mean ...

Figure 3.8 Cost means different things in different operations

Source: Arup

Low cost is a universally attractive objective

cost base is a further euro or dollar added to its profits. Not surprisingly, **low cost is a universally attractive objective.** The short-case 'Everyday low prices at Aldi' describes how one retailer keeps its costs down. The ways in which operations management can influence cost will depend largely on where the operation costs are incurred. The operation will spend its money on staff (the money spent on employing people), facilities, technology and equipment (the money spent on buying, caring for, operating and replacing the operation's 'hardware') and materials (the money spent on the 'bought-in' materials consumed or transformed in the operation). Figure 3.8 shows typical cost breakdowns for the hospital, car plant, supermarket and bus company.

Cost reduction through internal effectiveness

Our previous discussion distinguished between the benefits of each performance objective to externally and internally. Each of the various performance objectives has several internal effects, but **all of them affect cost.** So, one important way to improve cost performance is to improve the performance of the other operations objectives (see Figure 3.9).

All performance objectives affect cost

- High-quality operations do not waste time or effort having to re-do things, nor are their internal customers inconvenienced by flawed service.
- Fast operations reduce the level of in-process inventory between and within processes, as well as reducing administrative overheads.
- Dependable operations do not spring any unwelcome surprises on their internal customers. They can be relied on to deliver exactly as planned. This eliminates wasteful disruption and allows the other micro-operations to operate efficiently.
- Flexible operations adapt to changing circumstances quickly and without disrupting the rest of the operation. Flexible micro-operations can also change over between tasks quickly and without wasting time and capacity.

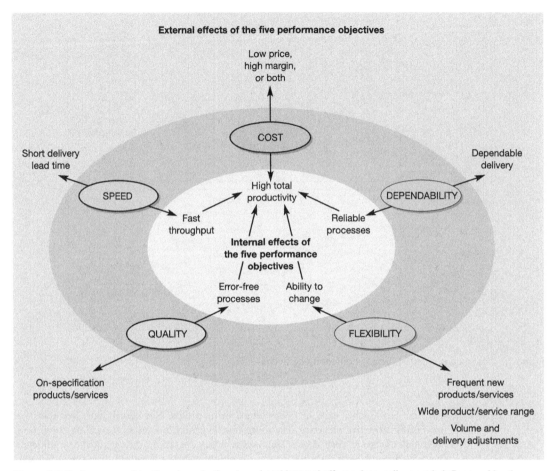

External effects of the five performance objectives

Figure 3.9 **Performance objectives have both external and internal effects. Internally, cost is influenced by the other performance objectives**

The polar representation of performance objectives

A useful way of representing the relative importance of performance objectives for a product or service is shown in Figure 3.10(a). This is called the **polar representation** because the scales which represent the importance of each performance objective have the same origin. A line describes the relative importance of each performance objective. The closer the line is to the centre, the less important is the performance objective to the operation. Two services are shown, a taxi and a bus service. Each essentially provides the same basic service, but with different objectives. The differences between the two services are clearly shown by the diagram. Of course, the polar diagram can be adapted to accommodate any number of different performance objectives. For example, Figure 3.10(b) shows a proposal for using a polar diagram to assess the relative performance of different police forces in the UK.[7] Note that this proposal uses three measures of quality (reassurance, crime reduction and crime detection), one measure of cost (economic efficiency), and one measure of how the police force develops its relationship with 'internal' customers (the criminal justice agencies). Note also that actual performance as well as required performance is marked on the diagram.

166

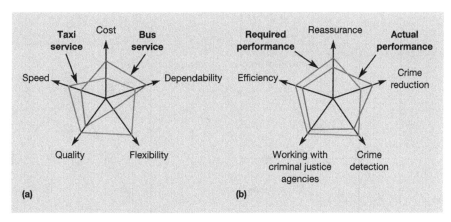

Figure 3.10 Polar representations of (a) the relative importance of performance objectives for a taxi service and a bus service, and (b) a police force targets and performance

Trade-offs between performance objectives

Earlier we examined how improving the performance of one objective inside the operation could also improve other performance objectives. Most notably, better quality, speed, dependability and flexibility can improve cost performance. But externally this is not always the case. In fact there may be a '*trade-off*' between performance objectives. In other words improving the performance of one performance objective might only be achieved by sacrificing the performance of another. So, for example, an operation might wish to improve its cost efficiencies by reducing the variety of products or services that it offers to its customers. '*There is no such thing as a free lunch*' could be taken as a summary of this approach. Probably the best-known summary of the trade-off idea comes from Professor Wickham Skinner, who said:

> '*most managers will readily admit that there are compromises or trade-offs to be made in designing an airplane or truck. In the case of an airplane, trade-offs would involve matters such as cruising speed, take-off and landing distances, initial cost, maintenance, fuel consumption, passenger comfort and cargo or passenger capacity. For instance, no one today can design a 500-passenger plane that can land on an aircraft carrier and also break the sound barrier. Much the same thing is true in [operations]*'.[8]

But there are two views of trade-offs. The first emphasizes 'repositioning' performance objectives by trading off improvements in some objectives for a reduction in performance in others. The other emphasizes increasing the 'effectiveness' of the operation by overcoming trade-offs so that improvements in one or more aspects of performance can be achieved without any reduction in the performance of others. Most businesses at some time or other will adopt both approaches. This is best illustrated through the concept of the '**efficient frontier**' of operations performance.

Trade-offs and the efficient frontier

Figure 3.11(a) shows the relative performance of several companies in the same industry in terms of their cost efficiency and the variety of products or services that they offer to their customers. Presumably all the operations would ideally like to be able to offer very high variety while still having very high levels of cost efficiency. However, the increased complexity that a high variety of product or service offerings brings will generally reduce the operation's ability to operate efficiently. Conversely, one way of improving cost efficiency is to severely

There can be a trade-off between an operation's performance objectives

The efficient frontier

167

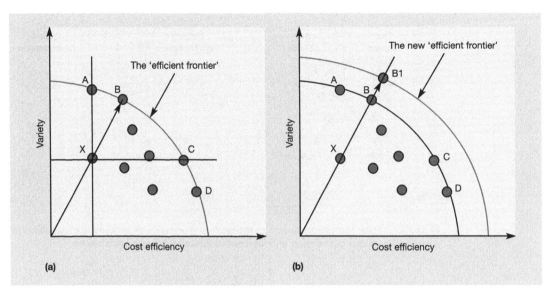

Figure 3.11 The efficient frontier identifies operations with performances that dominate other operations' performance

limit the variety on offer to customers. The spread of results in Figure 3.11(a) is typical of an exercise such as this. Operations A, B, C, D have all chosen a different balance between variety and cost efficiency. However, none is dominated by any other operation in the sense that another operation necessarily has 'superior' performance. Operation X, however, has an inferior performance because operation A is able to offer higher variety at the same level of cost efficiency and operation C offers the same variety but with better cost efficiency. The convex line on which operations A, B, C and D lie is known as the 'efficient frontier'. They may choose to position themselves differently (presumably because of different market strategies) but they cannot be criticized for being ineffective. Of course, any of these operations that lie on the efficient frontier may come to believe that the balance they have chosen between variety and cost efficiency is inappropriate. In these circumstances they may choose to reposition themselves at some other point along the efficient frontier. By contrast, operation X has also chosen to balance variety and cost efficiency in a particular way but is not doing so effectively. Operation B has the same ratio between the two performance objectives but is achieving them more effectively.

However, a strategy that emphasizes increasing effectiveness is not confined to those operations that are dominated, such as operation X. Those with a position on the efficient frontier will generally also want to improve their operations effectiveness by overcoming the trade-off that is implicit in the efficient frontier curve. For example, suppose operation B in Figure 3.11(b) wants to improve both its variety and its cost efficiency simultaneously and move to position B1. It may be able to do this, but only if it adopts operations improvements that extend the efficient frontier. For example, one of the decisions that any supermarket manager has to make is how many checkout positions to open at any time. If too many checkouts are opened then there will be times when the checkout staff do not have any customers to serve and will be idle. The customers, however, will have excellent service in terms of little or no waiting time. Conversely, if too few checkouts are opened, the staff will be working all the time but customers will have to wait in long queues. There seems to be a direct trade-off between staff utilization (and therefore cost) and customer waiting time (speed of service). Yet even the supermarket manager might, for example, allocate a number of 'core' staff to operate the checkouts but also arrange for those other staff who are performing other jobs in the supermarket to be trained and 'on call' should demand suddenly increase. If the manager

168

on duty sees a build-up of customers at the checkouts, these other staff could quickly be used to staff checkouts. By devising a flexible system of staff allocation, the manager can both improve customer service and keep staff utilization high.

This distinction between positioning on the efficient frontier and increasing operations effectiveness by extending the frontier is an important one. Any business must make clear the extent to which it is expecting the operation to reposition itself in terms of its performance objectives and the extent to which it is expecting the operation to improve its effectiveness in several ways simultaneously.

Summary answers to key questions

Check and improve your understanding of this chapter using self-assessment questions and a personalized study plan, audio and video downloads, and an eBook – all at **www.myomlab.com**.

➤ Why is operations performance important in any organization?

■ Operations management can either 'make or break' any business. It is large and, in most businesses, represents the bulk of its assets, but also because the operations function gives the ability to compete by providing the ability to respond to customers and by developing the capabilities that will keep it ahead of its competitors in the future.

➤ How should the operations function judge itself?

■ Operations performance can be judged using the 'triple bottom line' approach. This includes social, environmental and economic performance.

➤ What does top management expect from the operations function?

■ Operations can contribute to the organization as a whole by:
  – achieving customer satisfaction
  – reducing the costs
  – reducing the risk of operational failure
  – reducing the amount of investment
  – providing the basis for future innovation.

➤ What are the performance objectives of operations and what are the internal and external benefits which derive from excelling in each of them?

■ By 'doing things right', operations seek to influence the quality of the company's services and products. Externally, quality is an important aspect of customer satisfaction or dissatisfaction. Internally, quality operations both reduce costs and increase dependability.

■ By 'doing things fast', operations seek to influence the speed with which services and products are delivered. Externally, speed is an important aspect of customer service. Internally, speed both reduces inventories by decreasing internal throughput time and reduces risks by delaying the commitment of resources.

- By 'doing things on time', operations seek to influence the dependability of the delivery of services and products. Externally, dependability is an important aspect of customer service. Internally, dependability within operations increases operational reliability, thus saving the time and money that would otherwise be taken up in solving reliability problems and also giving stability to the operation.

- By 'changing what they do', operations seek to influence the flexibility with which the company creates its offerings. Externally, flexibility can:
  - create new offerings (service/product flexibility);
  - create a wide range or mix of offerings (mix flexibility);
  - create different quantities or volumes of offerings (volume flexibility);
  - create offerings at different times (delivery flexibility).

  Internally, flexibility can help speed up response times, save time wasted in changeovers, and maintain dependability.

- By 'doing things cheaply', operations seek to influence the cost of the company's offerings. Externally, low costs allow organizations to reduce their price in order to gain higher volumes or, alternatively, increase their profitability on existing volume levels. Internally, cost performance is helped by good performance in the other performance objectives.

➤ How do operations performance objectives trade off against each other?

- Trade-offs are the extent to which improvements in one performance objective can be achieved by sacrificing performance in others. The 'efficient frontier' concept is a useful approach to articulating trade-offs and distinguishes between repositioning performance on the efficient frontier and improving performance by overcoming trade-offs.

Learning exercises

These problems and applications will help to improve your analysis of operations. You can find more practice problems as well as worked examples and guided solutions on MyOMLab at www.myomlab.com.

1. The 'forensic science' service of a European country has traditionally been organized to provide separate forensic science laboratories for each police force around the country. In order to save costs, the government has decided to centralize this service in one large central facility close to the country's capital. What do you think are the external advantages and disadvantages of this to the stakeholders of the operation? What do you think are the internal implications to the new centralized operation that will provide this service?

2. *Step 1.* Look again at the figures in the chapter which illustrate the meaning of each performance objective for the four operations. Consider the bus company and the supermarket, and in particular consider their external customers.

    Step 2. Draw the relative required performance for both operations on a polar diagram.

    Step 3. Consider the internal effects of each performance objective. For both operations, identify how quality, speed, dependability and flexibility can help to reduce the cost of producing their services.

3. Visit the websites of two or three large oil companies such as Exxon, Shell, Elf, etc. Examine how they describe their policies towards their customers, suppliers, shareholders, employees and society at large. Identify areas of the company's operations where there may be conflicts between the needs of these different stakeholder groups. Discuss or reflect on how (if at all) such companies try and reconcile these conflicts.

Want to know more?

Bourne, M., Kennerley, M. and Franco, M. (2005) Managing through measures: a study of the impact on performance, *Journal of Manufacturing Technology Management*, vol. 16, issue 4, 373–95. What it says on the tin.

Kaplan, R.S. and Norton, D.P. (2005) The Balanced Scorecard: measures that drive performance, *Harvard Business Review*, Jul/Aug. The latest pronouncements on the Balanced Scorecard approach.

Pine, B.J. (1993) *Mass Customization*, Harvard Business School Press, Boston. The first substantial work on the idea of mass customization. Still a classic.

Savitz, A.W. and Weber, K. (2006) *The Triple Bottom Line: How Today's Best-Run Companies Are Achieving Economic, Social and Environmental Success – and How You Can Too*, Jossey-Bass, San Francisco, CA. An up-to-date treatment of the triple bottom line.

Waddock, S. (2003) Stakeholder performance implications of corporate responsibility, *International Journal of Business Performance Management*, vol. 5, numbers 2–3, 114–24. An introduction to stakeholder analysis.

Useful websites

www.aomonline.org General strategy site of the American Academy of Management.

www.cranfield.ac.uk/som Look for the 'Best factory awards' link. Manufacturing, but interesting.

www.opsman.org Lots of useful stuff.

www.worldbank.org Global issues. Useful for international operations strategy research.

www.weforum.org Global issues, including some operations strategy ones.

www.ft.com Great for industry and company examples.

Now that you have finished reading this chapter, why not visit MyOMLab at www.myomlab.com where you'll find more learning resources to help you make the most of your studies and get a better grade.

CHAPTER 10

Fundamentals of the Theory of Constraints

Chapter Outline

Introduction—In recent years a rather unique and interesting approach to visualizing and managing an operation has emerged. Originally developed by Eliyahu M. Goldratt in his book *The Goal,* this **Theory of Constraints** (also sometimes called constraint management) has allowed many people to successfully rethink their approaches to improving and managing their production processes.

Opinions about the Theory of Constraints differ. Some think that the Theory of Constraints (TOC) is a good way to implement or improve process capability while using other control systems such as JIT or MRP, while others believe that TOC is a "stand-alone" approach completely unique and separate from other techniques. In this context, it is suggested that TOC can provide approaches to design, manage, schedule, and improve virtually any production system. Still others believe it can be either just a process improvement approach or a complete system approach, depending on the extent of the implementation taken. It may not, in the opinion of this third group, be the most appropriate approach for certain business environments, while it may prove highly effective for other business environments. Chapter 12 will address the issue of linkages between business environment and appropriate planning and control system design more completely. The intent of this chapter is merely to explain the fundamental concepts of the Theory of Constraints itself.

10.1 FUNDAMENTAL PRINCIPLES OF THE THEORY OF CONSTRAINTS

The fundamental concept behind the Theory of Constraints (as it impacts planning and control) is that every operation producing a product or service is primarily a series of linked processes. Each process has a specific capacity to produce the given defined output for the operation, and that in virtually every case there is one process that limits or constrains the throughput from the entire operation. Consider the diagram in Figure 10.1.

The analogy often used is, as the diagram illustrates, that production flowing through operational processes is like liquid flowing through a pipeline. Each process has a certain defined capacity, illustrated in the analogy by the diameter of the associated pipe. In the diagram shown, process "E" has the largest capacity to process production, while operation "C" has the least amount of capacity. Since operation "C" is the constraint on the entire process, it will limit the amount of output from the process, regardless of the capacity of the remaining processes. Improving any of the other operations (increasing the size of the pipe in that section) will not improve the total amount of liquid coming out of the system of pipes.

A **constraint,** in its most general form, is anything that limits the firm from meeting its goal. For most firms, that goal is to make money, which manifests itself by increasing throughput—as measured by sales, not just production.

As a numerical example, consider the operation producing product A in Figure 10.2. It should be clear from this simple example that the total operation is constrained by process 3 at 4 per hour. No matter how much efficiency you have in the other processes and how many process improvements are made in processes 1, 2, and 4, you will never be able to exceed the overall operational output of 4 per hour unless you address the constraints of process 3. Increased efficiency and utilization in processes 1 and 2 will, in fact, only in-

FIGURE 10.1 The Linked Process Pipe Analogy

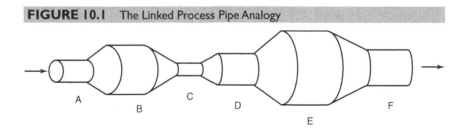

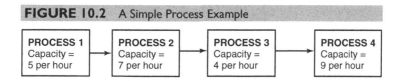

FIGURE 10.2 A Simple Process Example

| PROCESS 1 Capacity = 5 per hour | PROCESS 2 Capacity = 7 per hour | PROCESS 3 Capacity = 4 per hour | PROCESS 4 Capacity = 9 per hour |

crease inventory—not sales. That issue is one of the key points of TOC—the major measure for any operation should be on the throughput of the organization, or, in other words, the contribution to sales. Any other measures of process efficiency, utilization, or other commonly used operational measures have little relevance to the overall effectiveness of the entire system.

This approach has implications far beyond how the process is viewed. Even accounting systems are impacted. For example, many accounting systems allocate overhead costs to products based on direct labor hours of production. Such systems may give the impression that producing more product will help to "pay" for the overhead costs. Unfortunately, if the extra product produced is not linked to actual sales, the result is only more costly inventory and an overall negative impact on the business. TOC principles make the point that only sales should be counted as operational throughput. Another accounting implication is the labor cost itself. Most traditional accounting systems view direct labor as a variable cost. TOC principles, on the other hand, contend that in the short run all operational costs except direct material are largely fixed and should, therefore, be "lumped" together into an overall operational expense. One of the key points made by this example is that *products do not really have a profit—companies do.* This point helps to view the operation more as a system rather than as a set of largely independent functions. Such a view is a critical part of managing by TOC principles.

10.2 UNDERSTANDING AND MANAGING THE CONSTRAINTS

There are several fundamental guidelines developed for understanding the TOC principles and how to manage a constraining process. Some of the more noteworthy guidelines include:

- *A system optimal performance is NOT the sum of local optima.* Any system that is performing as well as possible usually implies that not more than one part of the system is performing at an optimal level. If all parts of the system are performing optimally, the system as a whole will probably not be performing optimally. In other words, it is virtually impossible to obtain a perfect system balance. Even if the system was designed to be perfectly balanced, normal variations in performance will inevitably cause some degree of imbalance.

- *Systems are like chains.* Each system will have a "weakest link" (a constraint) that will limit the performance of the whole system.
- *Knowing what to change requires a complete understanding of the system and the system goal.* Often in TOC, the system goal is to make money through sales, not production. Production completed without a sale (making and storing inventory) does not contribute to the goal of the company until it does become a sale. This is one of the major reasons that Goldratt gave the title "The Goal" to his first book on TOC, where he essentially introduced the concepts to the world.
- *Most undesirable system effects are caused by a few core problems.* This is a common theme in many other systems. For example, the well-known cause-and-effect ("fishbone") diagram from Total Quality Management (TQM) makes the same point. Overall, solving a symptom of a problem will often do little good. If the core problem remains, the symptom (or another one associated with it) will likely reappear very soon. True long-term relief from the undesirable effect will occur only if the core problem is identified and corrected.
- *Core problems are almost never obvious.* They tend to show themselves as a series of undesirable effects, most of which are really symptoms of the underlying problems.
- *Eliminating the undesirable effects provides a false sense of security.* Working on "problems" (often really symptoms) without finding the root cause tends to provide short-lived improvements. On the other hand, eliminating a core problem generally eliminates all of the undesirable effects associated with it.
- *System constraints can be either physical constraints or policy constraints.* Policy constraints are generally more difficult to find and eliminate, but the elimination of a policy constraint generally provides a more pronounced system improvement. The differences between those two types of constraints are discussed more fully later in the chapter.
- *Ideas are not solutions.* Generating ideas can be beneficial, but only if there is follow-through to develop the idea into a solution and then implement it completely.
- *The focus should be on balancing flow through the shop.* The key is throughput that end up as sales, not on throughput that may end up as inventory. As discussed earlier, some accounting systems promote high production rates even if the sales are lower. The systems recognize that adding value to the product will "pay" for the overhead, in that the system allocates overhead to the product as value is added. These systems essentially fool managers into thinking they are helping the company, when in fact they may be doing nothing more than adding extra expense in the form of inventory.

- *Utilization of a nonbottleneck is determined by constraints in the system.* Nonbottleneck operations do not restrict system output. Those resources should, therefore, be managed in such a way as to provide maximum support for constraint resources. Efficiency and utilization for these resources are not deemed that important for the good of the entire system, only their support for the system.

- *Utilization of an operation is not the same as activation.* In the TOC concept, an operation is considered activated only when it is providing benefit for the entire system to give more output. The operation may be utilized, or producing material not needed until some time in the future, but that does not necessarily help the entire system.

- *An hour lost at a constraint operation is an hour lost to throughput for the entire process.* For example, in Figure 10.2, if a quarter hour is lost to just process 3, then the entire operation will be able to produce only three units that hour, regardless of how well the other processes can perform. It is for this reason that the major focus of managing and scheduling an operation is on the constraint.

- *An hour lost at a nonconstraint is a mirage, in the fact that it will not impact total throughput.* It represents instead excess capacity. For example, in Figure 10.2 if there is a loss of time to produce one unit at process 2 it will mean that process 2 can only produce 6 units per hour, but the overall operation will still only have a throughput of 4 per hour, based on the capability of process 3.

- *Transfer batches do not have to be the same size as process batches, and often should not be.* Process batches for constraints should be of a size that maximize the effective utilization of the process (minimize downtime). Process batches at nonconstraints are not so critical. Transfer batches (the amount of material moved, may often be smaller to maximize throughput and minimize process inventories.

- *A schedule should be determined by using all the operational constraints.* In many operations schedules are set sequentially. TOC argues that all constraint areas should be considered at the same time when making a schedule. The theory also argues that lead times are a result of the schedule and should not be determined before the scheduling process.

10.3 IMPROVING THE PROCESS USING TOC PRINCIPLES

If a TOC approach is deemed appropriate to help improve a business system, there is a five-step process that is recommended to help improve the performance of the business. Those five steps are summarized below:

1. *Identify the constraint.* This implies the need to examine the entire process to determine which process limits the throughput. The concept

does not limit this process examination to merely the operational processes. For example, returning again to Figure 10.2, suppose the sales department was only selling the product output at the rate of 3 per hour. In that case, the sales department would be considered the constraint and not process 3. It must be kept in mind that a constraint limits throughput with respect to overall business sales, not merely inventory production.

2. ***Exploit the constraint.*** Find methods to maximize the utilization of the constraint toward productive throughput. For example, in many operations all processes are shut down during lunchtime or during breaks. If a process is a constraint, the operation should consider rotating lunch periods so that the constraint is never allowed to be idle. Suppose, for example, an operation has a certain process that represents a clear and large constraint. Suppose also that they currently have 7 productive hours for an 8-hour shift (30 minutes for lunch and two 15-minute breaks). Assuming they have multiple workers that can operate the process (or can train more), they could stagger lunch times and break times for just that one process, allowing it to operate the full 8 hours. In such a case the business would add an entire productive hour of output per shift with the addition of no more resources of any kind.

3. ***Subordinate everything to the constraint.*** Effective utilization of the constraint is the most important issue. Everything else is secondary.

4. ***Elevate the constraint.*** Essentially this means to find ways to increase the available hours of the constraint, including adding more of it.

5. ***Once the constraint is a constraint no longer, find the new one and repeat the steps.*** As the constraint effective utilization increases, it may cease to be a constraint as another process becomes one. In that case the emphasis shifts to the new process constraint. It is also possible (even likely in many businesses) that a sales-related change in the product mix will cause a different process to become the constraint.

Notes on the five steps:

1. The first two steps are really a method to loosely link measures (including throughput and utilization) to the logistics of the system.

2. The third step, as we will discover in the section on scheduling with TOC, is really accomplished by
   - Releasing material at the gateway (first processing) center at a rate that will keep the constraint busy.
   - Prioritization of nonconstraint tasks based almost exclusively on constraint needs.

3. The concept of *exploit* really implies getting the most from existing constraint resources. TOC suggests that exploiting should be maximized prior to spending additional money to acquire more of the constraint resource.

4. The fifth step is really a warning to continually check to ensure the constraint has not shifted. Effective exploitation of existing constraints and a shift in product mix are examples of events that can cause the constraint to shift.

After understanding these five steps, it may be helpful to consider that not all facilities operating in all types of business environments may find the approach to TOC easy to implement. For example, if an operation has a highly volatile product mix due to constantly shifting customer orders for a large variety of products, they may discover that the constraint will also be volatile. At one time the mix of process requirements may point to one constraint, while at another time the mix may create an entirely different constraint. If the constraint shifting occurs frequently, then there could be far too little opportunity to apply the TOC approaches on one constraint before it shifts to another point in the process.

10.4   IMPACT ON OPERATION STRATEGY

Knowledge of the Theory of Constraints can impact the operations strategy of the business in several ways. Some of the impacts on strategy can include:

- For a given type and mix of products, management can elect to consciously decide where the constraint should be located and then proceed to develop the operational strategy around that selected constraint.
- Marketing and Sales can be tightly tied to the constraint. Specifically, an analysis can be made to determine the mix of products to sell to maximize profits, and also it is possible to sell more of products that do not use the constraint (implying that excess capacity is available to make more of those products).
- Engineering and other process improvement activities can and should be focused on making the constraint process more efficient and effective.
- The company should consider if and how the nonconstraint processes may be used to supplement or be used to make the constraint resources more effective.
- If the company has a choice as to where the constraint is located in the process, they may elect to have the constraint early in the process. In that way the size of the required buffer needed to guard the constraint against "starvation" of material will be minimized. This will become clearer when the method for determining buffer size is explained later in the chapter.
- If, on the other hand, there are processes early in the overall process that have poor quality yield, the constraint should be placed later in the overall process. Some processes, especially certain chemical processes, have poor yield by their very nature. The idea is to have those processes placed prior

to the constraint. If they were placed after the constraint, then the implication is that some product that has already been through the constraint will not be scrapped or need rework using the constraint. Since the idea behind TOC is to have all items going through the constraint be turned into sales, clearly it is not a good idea to have constraint time being wasted by being used for a product that will later be rejected.

- There are other considerations that may also impact the strategic issue. They include the response time needed for customers and the amount of capital investment necessary for various combinations of resources.

10.5 GENERAL TYPES OF CONSTRAINT CAUSES

The sources of constraints can be classified in several ways. The most common ways are policy constraints, capacity constraints, and marketing constraints:

POLICY:

- Pricing policies that may affect demand.
- Incorrect focus on sales commissions (selling the wrong product).
- Production measures inhibiting good production performance.
- Personnel policies that promote conflict between people or production areas.

CAPACITY:

- Investment policies, including methods of justification, planning horizon, and fund availability.
- Human resource policies.
- Governmental regulations.
- Traditional measurement systems.
- Product development process.

MARKETING CONSTRAINTS:

- Product "niche" policies.
- Distribution systems.
- Perceived capacity versus demand.

10.6 LOGISTICS AND THE THEORY OF CONSTRAINTS

Logistics, of course, deals with the physical movement of material through the production process. The Theory of Constraints has specific issues dealing with logistics, as well as some methods to deal with making logistical movement effective. In general, TOC highlights two essential characteristics of any logistics system:

- Most systems are made up of a series of dependent events, or a series of specific steps that must be followed in a correct order to complete a job. This implies that any lateness at an early station in the process will potentially impact negatively later stations in the process.

- Most activities have statistical fluctuations inherent in their operation. This implies that activity times are not deterministic and deviations about the mean will exist. The TOC approach suggests that it is these statistical fluctuations that make traditional assembly line balancing approaches impractical.

There are often three reasons given for a loss of throughput, and again these reasons are focused on the constraint in the system. The three reasons are given here, together with the typical approach suggested for minimizing or eliminating the potential loss of throughput:

1. *The constraint is "broken."* There are many reasons a constraint could be nonoperational. The reason is not as important as the fact that when the constraint is down it cannot be used to produce. Since no excess capacity exists on a constraint, the loss of capacity will directly result in a loss of throughput for the entire business. One major solution to this potential problem is a good program of preventive maintenance. Such a program needs to be scheduled and managed carefully, for even preventive maintenance represents a use of capacity for the constraint. In general, this situation is compatible with a basic principle of maintenance—the higher the cost of an unscheduled breakdown of a process, the more critical the following of a well-designed preventive maintenance program. This is the same basic issue we found with a lean production system. Without much inventory in the system, processes tend to be tightly linked, and the loss of any operation will quickly bring the entire system down. Maintenance becomes important for TOC for roughly the same reason as for lean production systems—the potential high cost of a drop in throughput for the entire system.

2. *The constraint is starved.* In this condition, there is no inventory from the preceding processes available for work by the constraint. The constraint is capable of production, but cannot produce without material to work on. The solution to this problem is using a buffer in front of the constraint. The buffer is inventory released early into the system, but is really a "time" buffer, for reasons explained in the scheduling section below.

3. *The constraint is blocked.* In this condition, the constraint is available and there is material available on which to work, but there is no physical space in which to place the completed units. The solution to this potential problem is to have a space buffer available after the constraint in the process in which to place production completed by the constraint operation.

10.7   SCHEDULING AND THE THEORY OF CONSTRAINTS

The scheduling system developed for the Theory of Constraints has its own specific approach, although fairly closely related to a pull system inherent with lean production. It is often described as *drum–buffer–rope:*

- *Drum.*   The drum of the system refers to the "drumbeat" or pace of production. Essentially, it represents the master schedule for the operation, which is focused around the pace of throughput *as defined by the constraint.* Put in other terms, the drum can simply be considered as the work schedule of the organization's constraint. In order for the organization to take full advantage of this knowledge, it must be assumed that all nonconstraint functions understand this "drumbeat" schedule and provide total support.
- *Buffer.*   Since it is so important that the constraint never be "starved" for needed inventory, a "time" buffer is often established in front of the constraint. It is called a time buffer because it represents the amount of time that material is released into the system prior to the minimal normal throughput time to reach the constraint. The idea is to protect the system from normal variations and thereby protect the constraint from disruptions or material starvation. Even though the buffer manifests itself as inventory released into the system ahead of the minimal processing time, the product mix of this material can be very different based on the schedule. Since it is not based on specific inventory of specific products or components, it is generally called a time buffer. This is a key difference in the conceptual use of a time buffer instead of an inventory buffer—the time buffers tend to be largely immune to variations in product mix. As an example, suppose variations in processing and the probability of some disruptions in operations upstream from the constraint could mean that material could be "held up" for as much as 4 hours. The implication, then, would be that based on the processing schedule at the constraint the material for constraint processing would be released into the first operation 4 hours earlier than the normal expected throughput to the constraint would dictate.
- *Rope.*   The analogy is that the rope "pulls" production to the constraint for necessary processing. While this may imply a Kanban-type pull system, it can be done by a well-coordinated release of material into the system at the right time.

As can be seen, even the scheduling system has its primary focus on effective management of the organization's constraint to throughput and sales.

10.8   MULTIPLE TIME BUFFERS

Time buffers are used to make sure the constraint is not "starved," but other time buffers are also necessary. An example may help to illustrate:

Suppose you have a product made from three components. Component 1 is processed from raw material and then assembled with component 2 after it is processed from raw material. The subassembly is then assembled with component 3 after it is processed from raw material. The final product is then shipped to the customer. The constraint in the system is located in the middle of the processing for component 1. Figure 10.3 illustrates this.

Once component 1 has been processed on the constraint, its value to the system has risen significantly because constraint time has been invested. Nothing should, therefore, impede the progress of component 1. The problem could arise, however, that component 1 will arrive at the Assembly 1 area before component 2 because of some problem with component 2. Since we would never want constraint-invested material to wait for nonconstrained material, we should stage a time buffer of material for component 2 before the Assembly 1 area. This is done by releasing it earlier—the amount earlier depending on the time buffer based on the time estimate needed to overcome any unanticipated shock in the system. In this case the time buffer is called an **assembly time buffer,** as opposed to the time buffer before the constraint, which is usually called a **constraint time buffer.**

The same argument applies to the Assembly 2 area. The subassembly from components 1 and 2 have constraint time invested, so we would not want them waiting for component 3. This calls for another assembly time buffer to be generated at the Assembly 2 area.

Unfortunately, the need for buffers has not been fulfilled. It is possible that the final product with its constraint-invested material could be held up at shipping, since the processes that take place between assembly and shipping have not been part of the protection. This implies an additional time buffer before the shipping area, referred to as a *shipping time buffer.*

In general, then, these buffers have a major purpose in protecting the system. They help ensure good throughput and also help maintain good due date

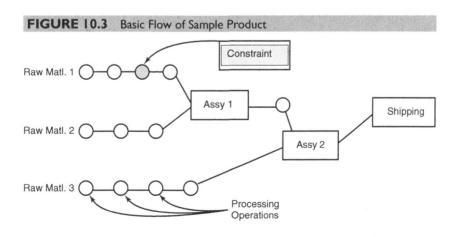

FIGURE 10.3   Basic Flow of Sample Product

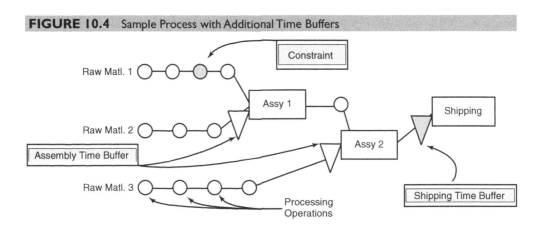

FIGURE 10.4 Sample Process with Additional Time Buffers

performance. In addition, however, they also can be the source of information for continuous improvement approaches undertaken by the operation. This information can help establish a prioritization for processes being targeted for Total Quality Management process improvement and for lean production approaches. In general, one should always be asking the question, "Where should we target which production technique in order to maximize the overall profitability of the company?"

10.9   CONTROL POINTS AND BATCHES

All this discussion regarding buffers and scheduling may start one to think that the scheduling using TOC approaches are more difficult and complex than standard approaches. That does not need to be the case. Based on the flow of material and the type of operation, there are specifically defined types of control points that may be important for TOC scheduling, measurement and control. A control point is a point in the process where measures are taken and decisions made based on those measures. Typical control points for TOC include:

- *The constraint*—this is clearly the most critical control point, and needs to be scheduled carefully based on sales.
- *The first operation (or the gateway)*—it is quite important to release the right material at the right time into the system so it will reach the constraint. This is, in effect, the "rope" of the drum–buffer–rope system.
- *Diverging points*—these points are where a common part can be processed into one of several different options. They must be managed to ensure that material, especially constraint material, is used in the correct manner for the correct assembly.
- *Converging points*—these are really assembly operations where material from nonconstraint operations is combined with constraint material to produce an assembly or subassembly. It is important to manage these

points to make sure constraint material is not held up from being processed.

- *The buffers*—these include constraint buffers, assembly buffers, and shipping buffers as described earlier.

TOC also recognizes there can be fundamental differences between **process batches** (the amount of material produced at an operation for a given setup) and **transfer batches** (the amount of material moved from one operation to the next operation). In general, process batches should be fairly large for constraint operations in order to minimize the time lost for setups. Process batches for nonconstraints are largely irrelevant (to a point) since those operations will have excess capacity. Transfer batches, on the other hand, should be fairly small to minimize work-in-process inventory levels.

10.10 MAJOR STEPS IN USING THE DRUM–BUFFER–ROPE METHOD

The following steps are generally given as a summary of how to use the drum–buffer–rope method to plan and control an operation under TOC principles:

1. Identify the constraint in the operation.
2. Examine options and select the preferable method to exploit the constraint.
3. Develop a Gantt schedule (see the section on Gantt chart scheduling in Chapter 8) for the constraint operation.
4. Calculate the appropriate size for the buffers (shipping, assembly, and constraint) based on the time it takes to move material through the operation to those buffer areas.
5. Develop a raw material release schedule to support the constraint schedule and also to support the assembly of other nonconstraint parts, especially with the constraint parts.
6. Determine product ship date. For products not using the constraint, often the ship dates can be based purely on customer request. The major issue here is to not load the nonconstraint areas to the point where they can become a temporary constraint.
7. For work centers that have not been identified as a control point, work can be done as it becomes available.

KEY TERMS

Constraint	Drum–Buffer–Rope	Time Buffers
Process Batch	Transfer Batch	

SUMMARY

The Theory of Constraints (TOC) brings a different perspective to visualizing an operation, and therefore brings potentially different approaches to planning and control for that operation. TOC forces a linked system view of the organization, allowing the identification of the total system constraint. Once identified, there are systematic approaches suggested to increase the capacity and output of the constraint, thereby increasing the throughput of the organization as a whole. As this can and should be done while still minimizing the amount of excess inventory and capacity in the system.

REFERENCES

Goldratt, E. M., *It's Not Luck.* Croton-on-Hudson, NY: North River Press, 1994.

Goldratt, E. M., and J. Cox, *The Goal.* Croton-on-Hudson, NY: North River Press, 1994.

Goldratt, E. M., and R. E. Fox, *The Race.* Croton-on-Hudson, NY: North River Press, 1986.

DISCUSSION QUESTIONS

1. Describe the possible special challenges to implementing TOC in a make-to-order environment.
2. Describe the possible implications of a major change in product mix or a major change in design to a TOC-run operation. How would you approach dealing with those implications?
3. Compare and contrast the design of the drum–buffer–rope system and the pull system described in Chapter 9. What are the similarities and differences, and why do they exist?
4. Comment (with supporting reasons) on the following overheard statement, stated by an operations manager: "We don't have any constraints in our company. Our capacity plans show we have plenty of capacity to produce the master schedule for some time to come."
5. Discuss the implication that TOC can bring to a company when they develop their business strategy. How will it possibly impact the approach taken to the sales and operations planning process?
6. Do you believe that TOC will have any impact on other functions in the organization? If so, what might they be? In specific, comment on the possible implications to:
   - Engineering
   - Human Resources
   - Accounting
   - Information Technology
   - Marketing
   - Sales

Lean synchronization

Key questions

➤ What is lean synchronization?

➤ How does lean synchronization eliminate waste?

➤ How does lean synchronization apply throughout the supply network?

Introduction

This chapter examines an approach that we call 'lean synchronization' or just 'lean'. It was originally called 'just-in-time' (JIT) when it started to be adopted outside its birthplace, Japan. It is both a philosophy and a method of operations planning and control. Lean synchronization aims to meet demand instantaneously, with perfect quality and no waste. This involves supplying services and products in perfect synchronization with the demand for them. These principles were once a radical departure from traditional operations practice, but have now become orthodox in promoting the synchronization of flow through processes, operations and supply networks. Although we will focus on planning and control issues, in practice the 'lean' concept has much wider implications for improving operations performance. Figure 11.1 shows where this chapter fits into the overall operations model.

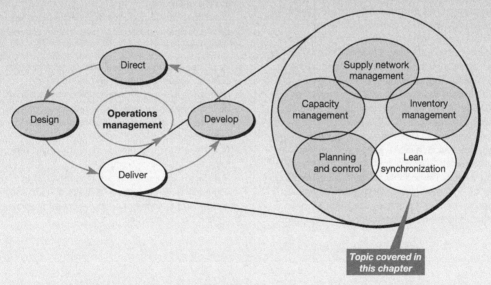

Figure 11.1 This chapter examines lean synchronization

 Check and improve your understanding of this chapter using self-assessment questions and a personalized study plan, audio and video downloads, and an eBook – all at www.myomlab.com.

Operations in practice Toyota

Seen as the leading practitioner and the main originator of the lean approach, the Toyota Motor Company has progressively synchronized all its processes simultaneously to give high-quality, fast throughput and exceptional productivity. It has done this by developing a set of practices that has largely shaped what we now call 'lean' or 'just-in-time' but which Toyota calls the Toyota Production System (TPS). The TPS has two themes, 'just-in-time' and 'jidoka'. Just-in-time is defined as the rapid and coordinated movement of parts throughout the production system and supply network to meet customer demand. It is operationalized by means of *heijunka* (levelling and smoothing the flow of items), *kanban* (signalling to the preceding process that more parts are needed) and *nagare* (laying out processes to achieve smoother flow of parts throughout the production process). *Jidoka* is described as 'humanizing the interface between operator and machine'. Toyota's philosophy is that the machine is there to serve the operator's purpose. The operator should be left free to exercise his or her judgement. Jidoka is operationalized by means of fail-safeing (or machine jidoka), line-stop authority (or human jidoka) and visual control (at-a-glance status of production processes and visibility of process standards).

Toyota believes that both just-in-time and jidoka should be applied ruthlessly to the elimination of waste, where waste is defined as 'anything other than the minimum amount of equipment, items, parts and workers that are absolutely essential to production'. Fujio Cho of Toyota identified seven types of waste that must be eliminated from all operations processes. They are: waste from over-production, waste from waiting time, transportation waste, inventory waste, processing waste, waste of motion and waste from product defects. Beyond this, authorities on Toyota claim that its strength lies in understanding the differences between the tools and practices used with Toyota operations and the overall philosophy of their approach

Source: Corbis/Denis Ballhouse

to lean synchronization. This is what some have called the apparent paradox of the Toyota production system: 'namely, that activities, connections and production flows in a Toyota factory are rigidly scripted, yet at the same time Toyota's operations are enormously flexible and adaptable. Activities and processes are constantly being challenged and pushed to a higher level of performance, enabling the company to continually innovate and improve.'

One influential study of Toyota identified four rules that guide the design, delivery, and development activities within the company.[1]

● *Rule one* – all work shall be highly specified as to content, sequence, timing, and outcome.
● *Rule two* – every customer–supplier connection must be direct and there must be an unambiguous yes or no method of sending requests and receiving responses.
● *Rule three* – the route for every product and service must be simple and direct.
● *Rule four* – any improvement must be made in accordance with the scientific method, under the guidance of a teacher, and at the lowest possible level in the organization.

What is lean synchronization?

Synchronization

Synchronization means that the flow of products and services always delivers exactly what customers want (perfect quality), in exact quantities (neither too much nor too little), exactly when needed (not too early or too late), and exactly where required (not to the wrong location). *Lean* synchronization is to do all this at the lowest possible cost. It results in items flowing rapidly and smoothly through processes, operations and supply networks.

The benefits of synchronized flow

Lean

Just-in-time

When first introduced, the lean synchronization (or 'lean' or 'just-in-time') approach was relatively radical, even for large and sophisticated companies. Now the lean, just-in-time approach is being adopted outside its traditional automotive, high-volume and manufacturing roots. But wherever it is applied, the principles remain the same. The best way to understand how lean synchronization differs from more traditional approaches to managing flow is to contrast the two simple processes in Figure 11.2. The traditional approach assumes that each stage in the process will place its output in an inventory that 'buffers' that stage from the next one downstream in the process. The next stage down will then take outputs from the inventory, process them, and pass them through to the next buffer inventory. These buffers are there to insulate each stage from its neighbours, making each stage relatively independent so that if, for example, stage A stops operating for some reason, stage B can continue, at least for a time. The larger the buffer inventory, the greater the degree of insulation between the stages. This insulation has to be paid for in terms of inventory and slow throughput times because items will spend time waiting in the buffer inventories.

But, the main argument against this traditional approach lies in the very conditions it seeks to promote, namely the insulation of the stages from one another. When a problem occurs at one stage, the problem will not immediately be apparent elsewhere in the system. The responsibility for solving the problem will be centred largely on the people within that stage, and the consequences of the problem will be prevented from spreading to the whole system. However, contrast this with the pure lean synchronized process illustrated in Figure 11.2b.

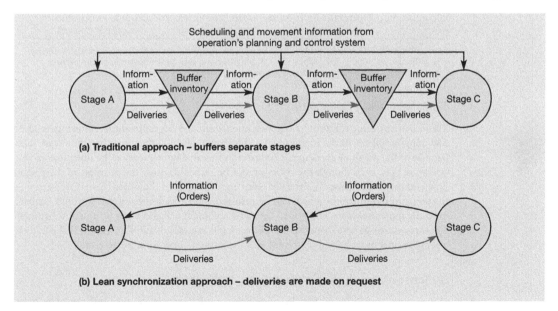

Figure 11.2 (a) Traditional and (b) lean synchronized flow between stages

Here items are processed and then passed directly to the next stage 'just-in-time' for them to be processed further. Problems at any stage have a very different effect in such a system. Now if stage A stops processing, stage B will notice immediately and stage C very soon after. Stage A's problem is now quickly exposed to the whole process, which is immediately affected by the problem. This means that the responsibility for solving the problem is no longer confined to the staff at stage A. It is now shared by everyone, considerably improving the chances of the problem being solved, if only because it is now too important to be ignored. In other words, by preventing items accumulating between stages, the operation has increased the chances of the intrinsic efficiency of the plant being improved.

Non-synchronized approaches seek to encourage efficiency by protecting each part of the process from disruption. The lean synchronized approach takes the opposite view. Exposure of the system to problems can both make them more evident and change the 'motivation structure' of the whole system towards solving the problems. Lean synchronization sees accumulations of inventory as a 'blanket of obscurity' that lies over the system and prevents problems being noticed. This same argument can be applied when, instead of queues of material, or information, an operation has to deal with queues of customers. Table 11.1 shows how certain aspects of inventory are analogous to certain aspects of queues.

Table 11.1 Inventories of materials, information or customers have similar characteristics

	Inventory		
	Of material (queue of material)	Of information (queue of information)	Of customers (queue of people)
Cost	Ties up working capital	Less current information and so worth less	Wastes customers' time
Space	Needs storage space	Needs memory capacity	Needs waiting area
Quality	Defects hidden, possible damage	Defects hidden, possible data corruption	Gives negative perception
De-coupling	Makes stages independent	Makes stages independent	Promotes job specialization/ fragmentation
Utilization	Stages kept busy by work-in-progress	Stages kept busy by work in data queues	Servers kept busy by waiting customers
Coordination	Avoids need for synchronization	Avoids need for straight-through processing	Avoids having to match supply and demand

Source: Adapted from Fitzsimmons, J.A. (1990) Making continual improvement: a competitive strategy for service firms, in Bowen, D.E., Chase, R.B., Cummings, T.G. and Associates (eds) *Service Management Effectiveness*, Copyright © 1990 Jossey-Bass. Reproduced with permission of John Wiley & Sons Inc.

The river and rocks analogy

The idea of obscuring effects of inventory is often illustrated diagrammatically, as in Figure 11.3. The many problems of the operation are shown as rocks in a river bed that cannot be seen because of the depth of the water. The water in this analogy represents the inventory in the operation. Yet, even though the rocks cannot be seen, they slow the progress of the river's flow and cause turbulence. Gradually reducing the depth of the water (inventory) exposes the worst of the problems which can be resolved, after which the water is lowered further, exposing more problems, and so on. The same argument will also apply for the flow between whole processes, or whole operations. For example, stages A, B and C in Figure 11.2 could be a supplier operation, a focal operation and a customer's operation, respectively.

Synchronization, 'lean' and 'just-in-time'

Different terms are used to describe what here we call 'lean synchronization'. Our definition – *'lean synchronization aims to meet demand instantaneously, with perfect quality and no*

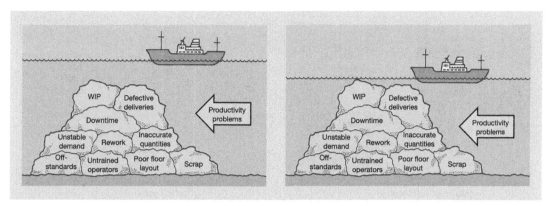

Figure 11.3 Reducing the level of inventory (water) allows operations management (the ship) to see the problems in the operation (the rocks) and work to reduce them

waste' – could also be used to describe the general concept of 'lean', or 'just-in-time' (JIT). The concept of 'lean' stresses the elimination of waste, while 'just-in-time' emphasizes the idea of producing items only when they are needed. But all three concepts overlap to a large degree, and no definition fully conveys the full implications for operations practice. Here we use the term 'lean synchronization' because it best describes the impact of these ideas on flow and delivery.

Lean synchronization and capacity utilization

Lean synchronization has many benefits but these come at the cost of capacity utilization. Return to the process shown in Figure 11.2. When stoppages occur in the traditional system, the buffers allow each stage to continue working and thus achieve high-capacity utilization. The high utilization does not necessarily make the process as a whole produce more. Often extra 'production' goes into buffer inventories. In a lean process, any stoppage will affect the whole process. This will necessarily lead to lower-capacity utilization, at least in the short term. However, there is no point in producing output just for its own sake. Unless the output is useful and allows the operation as a whole to produce saleable products or to process customers satisfactorily, there is no point in doing it anyway. In fact, working just to keep utilization high is not only pointless, it is counter-productive, because the extra inventory produced (or queues created in the case of customer-processing operations) merely serves to make improvements less likely. Figure 11.4 illustrates the two approaches to capacity utilization.

The lean philosophy

Lean synchronization can be viewed in different ways: as a broad philosophy of operations management, as a set of useful prescriptions of how to manage day-to-day operations, or a collection of tools and techniques for improving operations performance. Some of these tools and techniques are well known outside the lean sphere and relate to activities covered in other chapters of this book. As a philosophy, lean synchronization is founded on smoothing flow through processes by doing all the simple things well, on gradually doing them better and (above all) on squeezing out waste every step of the way. Three key issues define the lean philosophy: the involvement of staff in the operation, the drive for continuous improvement, and the elimination of waste. We will look at the first two issues briefly, but devote a whole section to the central idea of the elimination of waste.

The involvement of everyone

Lean philosophy is often put forward as a 'total' system. Its aim is to provide guidelines which embrace everyone and every process in the organization. An organization's culture is seen

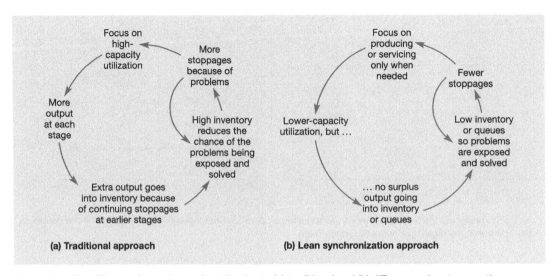

(a) Traditional approach

(b) Lean synchronization approach

Figure 11.4 The different views of capacity utilization in (a) traditional and (b) JIT approaches to operations

Respect for humans

as being important in supporting these objectives through an emphasis on involving all of the organization's staff. This culture is sometimes seen as synonymous with 'total quality' and is discussed in detail in Chapter 12. The lean approach to people management has also been called the **respect-for-humans** system. It encourages (and often requires) team-based problem-solving, job enrichment (by including maintenance and set-up tasks in operators' jobs), job rotation and multi-skilling. The intention is to encourage a high degree of personal responsibility, engagement and 'ownership' of the job.

Critical commentary

Not all commentators see JIT-influenced people-management practices as entirely positive. The JIT approach to people management can be viewed as patronizing. It may be, to some extent, less autocratic than some Japanese management practice dating from earlier times. However, it is certainly not in line with some of the job design philosophies which place a high emphasis on contribution and commitment. Even in Japan the approach of JIT is not without its critics. Kamata wrote an autobiographical description of life as an employee at a Toyota plant called *Japan in the Passing Lane*.[2] His account speaks of 'the inhumanity and the unquestioning adherence' of working under such a system. Similar criticisms have been voiced by some trade union representatives.

Continuous improvement

Kaizen

Lean objectives are often expressed as ideals, such as our definition: 'to meet demand instantaneously with perfect quality and no waste'. While any operation's current performance may be far removed from such ideals, a fundamental lean belief is that it is possible to get closer to them over time. Without such beliefs to drive progress, lean proponents claim improvement is more likely to be transitory than continuous. This is why the concept of continuous improvement is such an important part of the lean philosophy. If its aims are set in terms of ideals which individual organizations may never fully achieve, then the emphasis must be on the way in which an organization moves closer to the ideal state. The Japanese word for continuous improvement is **kaizen**, and it is a key part of the lean philosophy. It is explained fully in Chapter 13.

The elimination of waste

The elimination of waste is central to lean approaches

Arguably the most significant part of the lean philosophy is its focus on the **elimination of all forms of waste**. Waste can be defined as any activity that does not add value. For example, studies often show that as little as 5 per cent of total throughput time is actually spent directly adding value. This means that for 95 per cent of its time, an operation is adding cost to the service or product, but not adding value. Such calculations can alert even relatively efficient operations to the enormous waste which is dormant within their processes and supply networks. This same phenomenon applies as much to service processes as it does to manufacturing ones. Relatively simple requests, such as applying for a driving licence, may only take a few minutes to actually process, yet take days or weeks to be returned.

The seven types of waste

The seven types of waste Identifying waste is the first step towards eliminating it. Toyota have identified **seven types of waste**, which have been found to apply in many different types of operations – both service and production – and which form the core of lean philosophy:

1 *Over-production.* Producing more than is immediately needed by the next process in the operation is the greatest source of waste according to Toyota.
2 *Waiting time.* Equipment efficiency and labour efficiency are two popular measures which are widely used to measure equipment and labour waiting time, respectively. Less obvious is the amount of waiting time of items, disguised by operators who are kept busy doing things that are not needed at the time.
3 *Transport.* Moving items or customers around the operation often does not add value. Layout changes which bring processes closer together, improvements in transport methods and workplace organization can all reduce waste.
4 *Process.* The process itself may be a source of waste. Some operations may only exist because of poor product or service design, or poor maintenance, and so could be eliminated.
5 *Inventory.* All inventory should become a target for elimination. However, it is only by tackling the causes of inventory that it can be reduced.
6 *Motion.* An operator may look busy but sometimes no value is being added by the work. Simplification of work is a rich source of reduction in the waste of motion.
7 *Defectives.* Quality waste is often very significant in operations. Total costs of quality are much greater than has traditionally been considered, and it is therefore more important to attack the causes of such costs. This is discussed further in Chapter 12.

Between them, these seven types of waste contribute to four barriers to any operation achieving lean synchronization. They are: waste from irregular (non-streamlined) flow, waste from inexact supply, waste from inflexible response, and waste from variability. We will examine each of these barriers to achieving lean synchronization.

Eliminate waste through streamlined flow

The smooth flow of materials, information and people in the operation is a central idea of lean synchronization. Long process routes provide opportunities for delay and inventory build-up, add no value, and slow down throughput time. So, the first contribution any operation can make to streamlining flow is to reconsider the basic layout of its processes. Primarily, reconfiguring the layout of a process to aid lean synchronization involves moving it down the 'natural diagonal' of process design that was discussed in Chapter 5. Broadly speaking, this means moving from functional layouts towards cell-based layouts, or from cell-based layouts towards line layouts. Either way, it is necessary to move towards a layout that brings more systematization and control to the process flow. At a more detailed level, typical layout techniques include: placing workstations close together so that inventory of materials or customers just cannot build up because there is no space for it to do so, and arranging workstations in such a way that all those who contribute to a common activity are in sight of each other and can provide mutual help, for example by facilitating movement between workstations to balance capacity.

Examine all elements of throughput time

Throughput time is often taken as a surrogate measure for waste in a process. The longer that items being processed are held in inventory, moved, checked, or subject to anything else that does not add value, the longer they take to progress through the process. So, looking at exactly what happens to items within a process is an excellent method of identifying sources of waste.

Value stream mapping

Value stream mapping (also known as 'end-to-end' system mapping) is a simple but effective approach to understanding the flow of material, customers and information as value is added as it progresses through a process, operation, or supply network. It visually maps a product or services path from start to finish. In doing so it records, not only the direct activities of creating products and services, but also the 'indirect' information systems that support the direct process. It is called 'value stream' mapping because it focuses on value-adding activities and distinguishes between value-adding and non-value-adding activities. It is similar to process mapping (see Chapter 5) but different in four ways:

- It uses a broader range of information than most process maps.
- It is usually at a higher level (5–10 activities) than most process maps.
- It often has a wider scope, frequently spanning the whole supply network.
- It can be used to identify where to focus future improvement activities.

A value stream perspective involves working on and improving the 'big picture', rather than just optimizing individual processes. Value stream mapping is seen by many practitioners as a starting point to help recognize waste and identify its causes. It is a four-step technique that identifies waste and suggests ways in which activities can be streamlined. Firstly, it involves identifying the value stream (the process, operation or supply chain) to map. Secondly, it involves physically mapping a process, then above it mapping the information flow that enables the process to occur. This is the so-called 'current state' map. Thirdly, problems are diagnosed and changes suggested, making a future state map that represents the improved process, operation or supply chain. Finally, the changes are implemented. Figure 11.5 shows a value stream map for an air conditioning installation service. The service process itself is broken down into five relatively large stages and various items of data for each stage are marked on the chart. The type of data collected here does vary, but all types of value stream map compare the total throughput time with the amount of value-added time within the larger process. In this case, only 8 of the 258 hours of the process is value-adding.

Worked example[3]

An ordinary flight, just a trip to Amsterdam for two or three days. Breakfast was a little rushed but left the house at 6.15. Had to return a few minutes later, forgot my passport. Managed to find it and leave (again) by 6.30. Arrived at the airport 7.00, dropped Angela off with bags at terminal and went to the long-term car park. Eventually found a parking space after 10 minutes. Waited 8 minutes for the courtesy bus. Six minute journey back to the terminal, we start queuing at the check-in counters by 7.24. Twenty minute wait. Eventually get to check-in and find that we have been allocated seats at different ends of the plane. Staff helpful but takes 8 minutes to sort it out. Wait in queue for security checks for 10 minutes. Security decide I look suspicious and search bags for 3 minutes. Waiting in lounge by 8.05. Spend 1 hour and 5 minutes in lounge reading computer magazine and looking at small plastic souvenirs. Hurrah, flight is called 9.10, takes 2 minutes to rush to the gate and queue for further 5 minutes at gate. Through the gate and on to air bridge

→

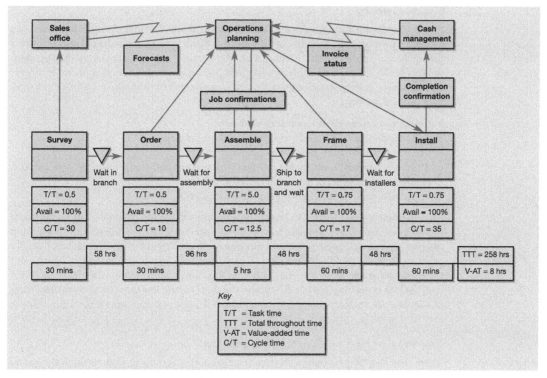

Figure 11.5 Value stream map for an industrial air conditioning installation service

which is continuous queue going onto plane, takes 4 minutes but finally in seats by 9.21. Wait for plane to fill up with other passengers for 14 minutes. Plane starts to taxi to runway at 9.35. Plane queues to take-off for 10 minutes. Plan takes off 9.45. Smooth flight to Amsterdam, 55 minutes. Stacked in queue of planes waiting to land for 10 minutes. Touch down at Schipol Airport 10.50. Taxi to terminal and wait 15 minutes to disembark. Disembark at 11.05 and walk to luggage collection (calling at lavatory on way), arrive luggage collection 11.15. Wait for luggage 8 minutes. Through customs (not searched by Netherlands security who decide I look trustworthy) and to taxi rank by 11.26. Wait for taxi 4 minutes. In to taxi by 11.30, 30 minutes ride into Amsterdam. Arrive hotel 12.00.

Analysis

How much of all this time was value-added? The total elapsed time, or throughput time, for the whole process was between 6.15 and 12.00, i.e. 5 hours 45 minutes. A detailed analysis of what was happening to the items being processed (Angela and me) indicates the following breakdown.

Time waiting in queue for check-in, luggage, etc. = 59 minutes
Time being 'served' at end of queue = 11 minutes
Waiting in lounge/plane etc. = 1 hour 55 minutes
Generally non-value-added moving about in airports, car parks etc. = 31 minutes
Quality error because I forgot my passport = 15 minutes
Value-added travelling time in car + plane + taxi = 1 hour 55 minutes.

So, only 1 hour 55 minutes of a total throughput time of 5 hours 45 minutes was spent in value-added activity. That is, 33.3 per cent value-added. Note, this was a smooth flight with no appreciable problems or delays.

195

Ensure visibility

Visibiity

Appropriate layout also includes the extent to which all movement is transparent to everyone within the process. High **visibility** of flow makes it easier to recognize potential improvements to flow. It also promotes quality within a process because the more transparent the operation or process, the easier it is for all staff to share in its management and improvement. Problems are more easily detectable and information becomes simple, fast and visual. Visibility measures include the following.

- Clearly indicated process routes using signage.
- Performance measures clearly displayed in the workplace.
- Coloured lights used to indicate stoppages.
- An area is devoted to displaying samples of one's own and competitors' process outputs, together with samples of good and defective output.
- Visual control systems (e.g. kanbans, discussed later).

An important technique used to ensure flow visibility is the use of simple, but highly visual signals to indicate that a problem has occurred, together with operational authority to stop the process. For example, on an assembly line, if an employee detects some kind of quality problem, he or she could activate a signal that illuminates a light (called an 'andon' light) above the workstation and stops the line. Although this may seem to reduce the efficiency of the line, the idea is that this loss of efficiency in the short term is less than the accumulated losses of allowing defects to continue on in the process. Unless problems are tackled immediately, they may never be corrected.

Use small-scale simple process technology

Several small units instead of one large unit

There may also be possibilities to encourage smooth streamlined flow through the use of small-scale technologies. That is, using several small units of process technology rather than one large unit. Small machines have several advantages over large ones. First, they can process different products and services simultaneously. For example, in Figure 11.6 one large machine produces a batch of A, followed by a batch of B, and followed by a batch of C. However, if three smaller machines are used they can each produce A, B or C simultaneously. The system is also more robust. If one large machine breaks down, the whole system ceases to operate. If one of the three smaller machines breaks down, it is still operating at two-thirds effectiveness. Small machines are also easily moved, so that layout flexibility is enhanced, and the risks of making errors in investment decisions are reduced. However, investment in capacity may increase in total because parallel facilities are needed, so utilization may be lower.

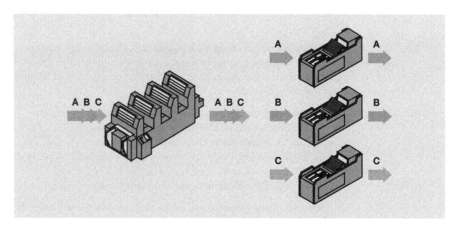

Figure 11.6 Using several small machines rather than one large one, allows simultaneous processing, is more robust, and is more flexible

Short case
Lean hospitals[4]

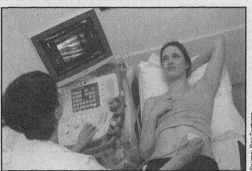

Source: Rex Features

One of the increasing number of health-care services to adopt lean principles, the Bolton Hospitals National Health Service Trust in the north of England, has reduced its hospitals' mortality rate in one injury by more than a third. David Fillingham, chief executive of Bolton Hospitals NHS Trust said, '*We had far more people dying from fractured hips than should have been dying.*' Then the trust greatly reduced its mortality rate for fractured neck of femur by redesigning the patient's stay in hospital to reduce or remove the waits between 'useful activity'. The mortality rate fell from 22.9% to 14.6%, which is the equivalent of 14 more patients surviving every six months. At the same time, average length of stay fell by a third from 34.6 days to 23.5 days. The trust held five 'rapid improvement events', involving employees from across the organization who spent several days examining processes and identifying alternative ways to improve them. Some management consultants were also used but strictly in an advisory role. In addition third-party experts were brought in. These included staff from the Royal Air Force, who had been applying lean principles to running aircraft carriers. The value of these outsiders was not only their expertise, '*They asked all sorts of innocent, naïve questions*', said Mr Fillingham, '*to which, often, no member of staff has an answer.*' Other lean-based improvement initiatives included examining the patient's whole experience from start to finish so that delays (some of which could prove fatal) could be removed on their journey to the operating theatre, speeding up the radiology process and eliminating unnecessary paperwork. Cutting the length of stay and reducing process complications should also start to reduce costs, although Mr Fillingham says that it could take several years for the savings to become substantial. Not only that, but staff are also said to be helped by the changes because they can spend more time helping patients rather than doing non-value-added activities.

Meanwhile at Salisbury district hospital in the south of the UK, lean principles have reduced delays in waiting for the results of tests from the ultrasound department. Waiting lists have been reduced from 12 weeks to between 2 weeks and zero after an investigation showed that 67% of demand was coming from just 5% of possible ultrasound tests: abdominal, gynaecological and urological. So all work was streamed into routine 'green' streams and complex 'red' ones. This is like having different traffic lanes on a motorway dedicated to different types of traffic with fast cars in one lane and slow trucks in another. Mixing both types of work is like mixing fast cars and slow-moving trucks in all lanes. The department then concentrated on doing the routine 'green' work more efficiently. For example, the initial date scan used to check the age of a foetus took only two minutes, so a series of five-minute slots were allocated just for these. '*The secret is to get the steady stream of high-volume, low-variety chugging down the ultrasound motorway*', says Kate Hobson, who runs the department. Streaming routine work in this way has left more time to deal with the more complex jobs, yet staff are not overloaded. They are more likely to leave work on time and also believe that the department is doing a better job, all of which has improved morale, says Kate Hobson, '*I think people feel their day is more structured now. It's not that madness, opening the doors and people coming at you.*' Nor has this more disciplined approach impaired the department's ability to treat really urgent jobs. In fact it has stopped leaving space in its schedule for emergencies – the, now standard, short waiting time is usually sufficient for urgent jobs.

Eliminate waste through matching supply and demand exactly

The value of the supply of services or products is always time-dependent. Something that is delivered early or late often has less value than something delivered exactly when it is needed. We can see many everyday examples of this. For example, parcel delivery companies charge more for guaranteed faster delivery. This is because our real need for the delivery is often for it to be as fast as possible. The closer to instantaneous delivery we can get the more value the delivery has for us and the more we are willing to pay for it. In fact delivery of information earlier than it is required can be even more harmful than late delivery because it results in information inventories that serve to confuse flow through the process. For example, an Australian tax office used to receive applications by mail, open the mail and send it through to the relevant department which, after processing it, sent it to the next department. This led to piles of unprocessed applications building up within its processes, causing problems in tracing applications, and losing them, sorting through and prioritizing applications, and worst of all, long throughput times. Now they only open mail when the stages in front can process it. Each department requests more work only when they have processed previous work.

Pull control

The exact matching of supply and demand is often best served by using 'pull control' wherever possible (discussed in Chapter 10). At its simplest, consider how some fast-food restaurants cook and assemble food and place it in the warm area only when the customer-facing server has sold an item. Production is being triggered only by real customer demand. Similarly supermarkets usually replenish their shelves only when customers have taken sufficient products off the shelf. The movement of goods from the 'back-office' store to the shelf is triggered only by the 'empty-shelf' demand signal. Some construction companies make it a rule to call for material deliveries to their sites, only the day before those items are actually needed. This not only reduces clutter and the chances of theft, it speeds up throughput time and reduces confusion and inventories. The essence of pull control is to let the downstream stage in a process, operation, or supply network, pull items through the system rather than have them 'pushed' to them by the supplying stage. As Richard Hall, an authority on lean operations put it, *'Don't send nothing nowhere, make 'em come and get it.'*[5]

Kanbans

The use of kanbans is one method of operationalizing pull control. **Kanban** is the Japanese for card or signal. It is sometimes called the 'invisible conveyor' that controls the transfer of items between the stages of an operation. In its simplest form, it is a card used by a customer stage to instruct its supplier stage to send more items. Kanbans can also take other forms. In some Japanese companies, they are solid plastic markers or even coloured ping-pong balls. Whichever kind of kanban is being used, the principle is always the same: the receipt of a kanban triggers the movement, production or supply of one unit. If two kanbans are received, this triggers the movement, production or supply of two units and so on. Kanbans are the only means by which movement, production or supply can be authorized. Some companies use 'kanban squares'. These are marked spaces on the shop floor or bench that are drawn to fit one or more work pieces or containers. Only the existence of an empty square triggers production at the stage that supplies the square. As one would expect, at Toyota the key control tool is its kanban system. The kanban is seen as serving three purposes:

- It is an instruction for the preceding process to send more work.
- It is a visual control tool to show up areas of over-production and lack of synchronization.
- It is a tool for kaizen (continuous improvement). Toyota's rules state that 'the number of kanbans should be reduced over time'.

Critical commentary

Just-in-time principles can be taken to an extreme. When lean ideas first started to have an impact on operations practice in the West, some authorities advocated the reduction of between-process inventories to zero. While in the long term this provides the ultimate in motivation for operations managers to ensure the efficiency and reliability of each process stage, it does not admit the possibility of some processes always being intrinsically less than totally reliable. An alternative view is to allow inventories (albeit small ones) around process stages with higher than average uncertainty. This at least allows some protection for the rest of the system. The same ideas apply to just-in-time delivery between factories. The Toyota Motor Corp., often seen as the epitome of lean, has suffered from its low inter-plant inventory policies. Both the Kobe earthquake and fires in supplier plants have caused production at Toyota's main factories to close down for several days because of a shortage of key parts. Even in the best-regulated networks, one cannot always account for such events.

Eliminate waste through flexible processes

Responding exactly and instantaneously to customer demand implies that operations resources need to be sufficiently flexible to change both what they do and how much they do of it without incurring high cost or long delays. In fact, flexible processes (often with flexible technologies) can significantly enhance smooth and synchronized flow. For example, new publishing technologies allow professors to assemble printed and e-learning course material customized to the needs of individual courses or even individual students. In this case flexibility is allowing customized, small batches to be delivered 'to order'. In another example, a firm of lawyers used to take ten days to prepare its bills for customers. This meant that customers were not asked to pay until ten days after the work had been done. Now they use a system that, every day, updates each customer's account. So, when a bill is sent it includes all work up to the day before the billing date. The principle here is that process inflexibility also delays cash flow.

Reduce set-up times

Set-up time reduction

For many technologies, increasing process flexibility, means reducing set-up times; defined as the time taken to change over the process from one activity to the next. Compare the time it takes you to change the tyre on your car with the time taken by a Formula 1 team. **Set-up reduction** can be achieved by a variety of methods such as cutting out time taken to search for tools and equipment, the pre-preparation of tasks which delay changeovers, and the constant practice of set-up routines. The other common approach to set-up time reduction is to convert work which was previously performed while the machine was stopped (called internal work) to work that is performed while the machine is running (called external work). There are three major methods of achieving the transfer of internal set-up work to external work:[6]

- Pre-prepare equipment instead of having to do it while the process is stopped. Preferably, all adjustment should be carried out externally.
- Make equipment capable of performing all required tasks so that changeovers become a simple adjustment.
- Facilitate the change of equipment, for example by using simple devices such as roller conveyors.

Fast changeovers are particularly important for airlines because they can't make money from aircraft that are sitting idle on the ground. It is called 'running the aircraft hot' in the industry. For many smaller airlines, the biggest barrier to running hot is that their markets are not large enough to justify passenger flights during the day and night. So, in order to avoid aircraft being idle over night, they must be used in some other way. That was the motive behind Boeing's 737 'Quick Change' (QC) aircraft. With it, airlines have the flexibility to use it for passenger flights during the day and, with less than a one-hour changeover (set-up) time, use it as a cargo aircraft throughout the night. Boeing engineers designed frames that hold entire rows of seats that could smoothly glide on and off the aircraft, allowing twelve seats to be rolled into place at once. When used for cargo, the seats are simply rolled out and replaced by special cargo containers designed to fit the curve of the fuselage and prevent damage to the interior. Before reinstalling the seats the sidewalls are thoroughly cleaned so that, once the seats are in place, passengers cannot tell the difference between a QC aircraft and a normal 737. Some airlines particularly value the aircraft's flexibility. It allows them to provide frequent reliable services in both passenger and cargo markets.

Eliminate waste through minimizing variability

One of the biggest causes of the variability that will disrupt flow and prevent lean synchronization is variation in the quality of items. This is why a discussion of lean synchronization should always include an evaluation of how quality conformance is ensured within processes. In particular, the principles of statistical process control (SPC) can be used to understand quality variability. Chapter 12 examines this subject, so in this section we shall focus on other causes of variability. The first of these is variability in the mix of products and services moving through processes, operations, or supply networks.

Level schedules as much as possible

Heijunka

Levelled scheduling (or **heijunka**) means keeping the mix and volume of flow between stages even over time. For example, instead of producing 500 parts in one batch, which would cover the needs for the next three months, levelled scheduling would require the process to make only one piece per hour regularly. Thus, the principle of levelled scheduling is very straightforward. However, the requirements to put it into practice are quite severe. The move from conventional to levelled scheduling is illustrated in Figure 11.7. Conventionally, if a mix of products were required in a time period (usually a month), a batch size would be calculated for each product and the batches produced in some sequence. Figure 11.7(a) shows three products that are produced in a 20-day time period in a production unit.

Quantity of product A required = 3,000
Quantity of product B required = 1,000
Quantity of product C required = 1,000

Batch size of product A = 600
Batch size of product B = 200
Batch size of product C = 200

Starting at day 1, the unit commences producing product A. During day 3, the batch of 600 As is finished and dispatched to the next stage. The batch of Bs is started but is not finished until day 4. The remainder of day 4 is spent making the batch of Cs and both batches are dispatched at the end of that day. The cycle then repeats itself. The consequence of using large batches is, first, that relatively large amounts of inventory accumulate within and between the units, and second, that most days are different from one another in terms of what they are expected to produce (in more complex circumstances, no two days would be the same).

Now suppose that the flexibility of the unit could be increased to the point where the batch sizes for the products were reduced to a quarter of their previous levels without loss of capacity (see Fig. 11.7(b)):

Batch size of product A = 150
Batch size of product B = 50
Batch size of product C = 50

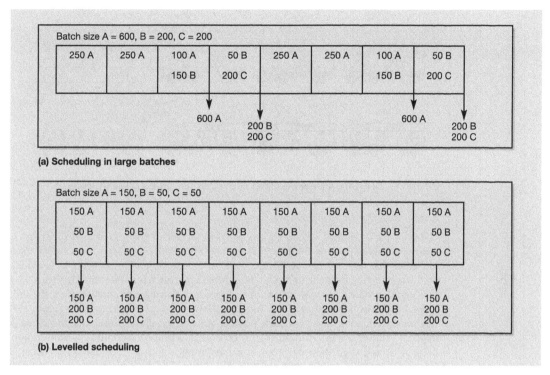

Figure 11.7 Levelled scheduling equalizes the mix of products made each day

A batch of each product can now be completed in a single day, at the end of which the three batches are dispatched to their next stage. Smaller batches of inventory are moving between each stage, which will reduce the overall level of work-in-progress in the operation. Just as significant, however, is the effect on the regularity and rhythm of production at the unit. Now every day in the month is the same in terms of what needs to be produced. This makes planning and control of each stage in the operation much easier. For example, if on day 1 of the month the daily batch of As was finished by 11.00 am, and all the batches were successfully completed in the day, then the following day the unit will know that, if it again completes all the As by 11.00 am, it is on schedule. When every day is different, the simple question 'Are we on schedule to complete our production today?' requires some investigation before it can be answered. However, when every day is the same, everyone in the unit can tell whether production is on target by looking at the clock. Control becomes visible and transparent to all, and the advantages of regular, daily schedules can be passed to upstream suppliers.

Level delivery schedules

A similar concept to levelled scheduling can be applied to many transportation processes. For example, a chain of convenience stores may need to make deliveries of all the different types of products it sells every week. Traditionally it may have dispatched a truck loaded with one particular product around all its stores so that each store received the appropriate amount of the product that would last them for one week. This is equivalent to the large batches discussed in the previous example. An alternative would be to dispatch smaller quantities of all products in a single truck more frequently. Then, each store would receive smaller deliveries more frequently, inventory levels would be lower and the system could respond to trends in demand more readily because more deliveries means more opportunity to change the quantity delivered to a store. This is illustrated in Figure 11.8.

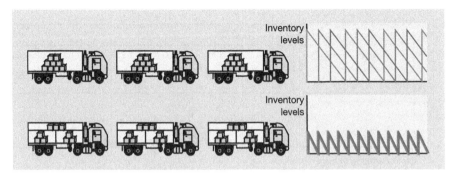

Figure 11.8 Delivering smaller quantities more often can reduce inventory levels

Adopt mixed modelling where possible

The principle of levelled scheduling can be taken further to give mixed modelling; that is, a repeated mix of outputs. Suppose that the machines in the production unit can be made so flexible that they achieve the JIT ideal of a batch size of one. The sequence of individual products emerging from the unit could be reduced progressively as illustrated in Figure 11.9. This would produce a steady stream of each product flowing continuously from the unit. However, the sequence of products does not always fall as conveniently as in Figure 11.9. The unit production times for each product are not usually identical and the ratios of required volumes are less convenient. For example, if a process is required to produce products A, B and C in the ratio 8:5:4, it could produce 800 of A, followed by 500 of B, followed by 400 of A, or 80A, 50B, and 40C. But ideally, sequencing the products as smoothly as possible, it would produce in the order . . . BACABACABACABACAB . . . repeated . . . repeated . . . etc. Doing this achieves relatively smooth flow (but does rely on significant process flexibility).

Keep things simple – the 5 Ss

The 5-S terminology came originally from Japan, and although the translation into English is approximate, they are generally taken to represent the following.

1 **Sort** (*Seiri*) – eliminate what is not needed and keep what is needed.
2 **Straighten** (*Seiton*) – position things in such a way that they can be easily reached whenever they are needed.

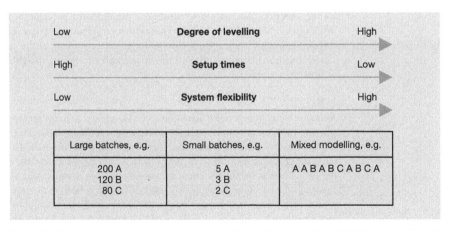

Large batches, e.g.	Small batches, e.g.	Mixed modelling, e.g.
200 A 120 B 80 C	5 A 3 B 2 C	A A B A B C A B C A

Figure 11.9 Levelled scheduling and mixed modelling: mixed modelling becomes possible as the batch size approaches one

202

3 **Shine** (*Seiso*) – keep things clean and tidy; no refuse or dirt in the work area.
4 **Standardize** (*Seiketsu*) – maintain cleanliness and order – perpetual neatness.
5 **Sustain** (*Shitsuke*) – develop a commitment and pride in keeping to standards.

The 5 Ss can be thought of as a simple housekeeping methodology to organize work areas that focuses on visual order, organization, cleanliness and standardization. It helps to eliminate all types of waste relating to uncertainty, waiting, searching for relevant information, creating variation, and so on. By eliminating what is unnecessary, and making everything clear and predictable, clutter is reduced, needed items are always in the same place and work is made easier and faster.

Lean synchronization applied throughout the supply network

Lean supply networks

Although most of the concepts and techniques discussed in this chapter are devoted to the management of stages *within* processes and processes *within* an operation, the same principles can apply to the whole supply network. In this context, the stages in a process are the whole businesses, operations or processes between which services and products flow. And as any business starts to approach lean synchronization it will eventually come up against the constraints imposed by the lack of lean synchronization of the other operations in its supply network. So, achieving further gains must involve trying to spread lean synchronization practice outward to its partners in the network; a far more demanding task than doing the same within a single process. And it becomes more complex as more of the supply network embraces the lean philosophy. The nature of the interaction between whole operations is far more complex than between individual stages within a process. To make a **supply network lean** means more than making each operation lean. A collection of localized lean operations rarely leads to an overall lean network. Rather one needs to apply the lean synchronization philosophy to the supply network as a whole. And essentially the principles of lean synchronization are the same for a supply network as they are for a process. Fast throughput throughout the whole supply network is still valuable and will save cost. Lower levels of inventory will still make it easier to achieve lean synchronization. Waste is just as evident (and even larger) at the level of the supply network and reducing waste is still a worthwhile task. Streamline flow, exact matching of supply and demand, enhanced flexibility, and minimizing variability are all still tasks that will benefit the whole network. The principles of pull control can work between whole operations in the same way as they can between stages within a single process. In fact, the principles and the techniques of lean synchronization are essentially the same no matter what level of analysis is being used.

Lean supply networks are like air traffic control systems[7]

The concept of the lean supply network has been likened to an air traffic control system, in that it attempts to provide continuous, 'real-time visibility and control' to all elements in the network. This is the secret of how the world's busiest airports handle thousands of departures and arrivals daily. All aircraft are given an identification number that shows up on a radar map. Aircraft approaching an airport are detected by the radar and contacted using radio. The control tower precisely positions the aircraft in an approach pattern which it coordinates. The radar detects any small adjustments that are necessary, which are communicated to the aircraft. This real-time visibility and control can optimize airport throughput while maintaining extremely high safety and reliability.

Contrast this to how most supply networks are coordinated. Information is captured only periodically, probably once a day, and any adjustments to logistics, output levels at the various operations in the supply network are adjusted, and plans rearranged. But imagine what would happen if this was how the airport operated, with only a 'radar snapshot' once a day. Coordinating aircraft with sufficient tolerance to arrange take-offs and landings every two minutes would be out of the question. Aircraft would be jeopardized, or alternatively, if aircraft were spaced further apart to maintain safety, throughput would be drastically reduced. Yet this is how most supply networks have traditionally operated. They use a daily 'snapshot' from their ERP systems (see Chapter 10 for an explanation of ERP). This limited visibility means operations must either space their work out to avoid 'collisions' (i.e. missed customer orders) thereby reducing output, or they must 'fly blind' thereby jeopardizing reliability.

Lean service

Any attempt to consider how lean ideas apply throughout a whole supply network must also confront the fact that these networks include service operations. So how can lean principles be applied in these parts of the network? The idea of lean factory operations is relatively easy to understand. Waste is evident in over-stocked inventories, excess scrap, badly sited machines and so on. In services it is less obvious, inefficiencies are more difficult to see. Yet most of the principles and techniques of lean synchronization, although often described in the context of manufacturing operations, are also applicable to service settings. In fact, some of the philosophical underpinning to lean synchronization can also be seen as having its equivalent in the service sector. Take, for example, the role of inventory. The comparison between manufacturing systems that hold large stocks of inventory between stages and those that did not centred on the effect which inventory had on improvement and problem-solving. Exactly the same argument can be applied when, instead of queues of material (inventory), an operation has to deal with queues of information or customers. With its customer focus, standardization, continuous quality improvement, smooth flow and efficiency, lean thinking has direct application in all operations, manufacturing or service. Bradley Staats and David Upton of Harvard Business School[8] have studied how lean ideas can be applied in service operations. They make three main points:

1 In terms of operations and improvements, the service industries in general are a long way behind manufacturing.
2 Not all lean manufacturing ideas translate from factory floor to office cubicle. For example, tools such as empowering manufacturing workers to 'stop the line' when they encounter a problem is not directly replicable when there is no line to stop.
3 Adopting lean operations principles alters the way a company learns through changes in problem solving, coordination through connections, and pathways and standardization.

Examples of lean service

Many of the examples of lean philosophy and lean techniques in service industries are directly analogous to those found in manufacturing industries because physical items are being moved or processed in some way. Consider the following examples.

- Supermarkets usually replenish their shelves only when customers have taken sufficient products off the shelf. The movement of goods from the 'back-office' store to the shelf is triggered only by the 'empty-shelf' demand signal. *Principle: pull control.*
- An Australian tax office used to receive applications by mail, open the mail and send it through to the relevant department which, after processing it, sent it to the next department. Now they only open mail when the stages in front can process it. Each department requests more work only when they have processed previous work. *Principle: don't let inventories build up, use pull control.*
- One construction company makes a rule of only calling for material deliveries to its sites the day before materials are needed. This reduces clutter and the chances of theft. *Principle: pull control reduces confusion.*

- Many fast-food restaurants cook and assemble food and place it in the warm area only when the customer-facing server has sold an item. *Principle: pull control reduces throughput time.*

Other examples of lean concepts and methods apply even when most of the service elements are intangible.

- Some web sites allow customers to register for a reminder service that automatically e-mails reminders for action to be taken, for example, the day before a partner's birthday, in time to prepare for a meeting, etc. *Principle: the value of delivered information, like delivered items, can be time-dependent; too early and it deteriorates (you forget it), too late and it's useless (because it's too late).*
- A firm of lawyers used to take ten days to prepare its bills for customers. This meant that customers were not asked to pay until ten days after the work had been done. Now they use a system that, every day, updates each customer's account. So, when a bill is sent it includes all work up to the day before the billing date. *Principle: process delays also delay cash flow, fast throughput improves cash flow.*
- New publishing technologies allow professors to assemble printed and e-learning course material customized to the needs of individual courses or even individual students. *Principle: flexibility allows customization and small batch sizes delivered 'to order'.*

Summary answers to key questions

Check and improve your understanding of this chapter using self-assessment questions and a personalized study plan, audio and video downloads, and an eBook – all at www.myomlab.com.

➤ What is lean synchronization?

- Lean synchronization is an approach to operations which tries to meet demand instantaneously with perfect quality and no waste. It is an approach which differs from traditional operations practices insomuch as it stresses waste elimination and fast throughput, both of which contribute to low inventories.
- The ability to deliver just-in-time not only saves working capital (through reducing inventory levels) but also has a significant impact on the ability of an operation to improve its intrinsic efficiency.
- The lean synchronization philosophy can be summarized as concerning three overlapping elements, (a) the elimination of waste in all its forms, (b) the inclusion of all staff of the operation in its improvement, and (c) the idea that all improvement should be on a continuous basis.

➤ How does lean synchronization eliminate waste?

- The most significant part of the lean philosophy is its focus on the elimination of all forms of waste, defined as any activity that does not add value.
- Lean synchronization identifies seven types of waste that, together, form four barriers to achieving lean synchronization. They are: waste from irregular (non-streamlined) flow, waste from inexact supply, waste from inflexible response, and waste from variability.

> ➤ **How does lean synchronization apply throughout the supply network?**

■ Most of the concepts and techniques of lean synchronization, although usually described as applying to individual processes and operations, also apply to the whole supply networks.

■ The concept of the lean supply network has been likened to an air traffic control system, in that it attempts to provide continuous, 'real-time visibility and control' to all elements in the network.

■ Most of the ideas of lean synchronization are directly applicable to all the service operations in the supply network.

Learning exercises

These problems and applications will help to improve your analysis of operations. You can find more practice problems as well as worked examples and guided solutions on MyOMLab at www.myomlab.com.

1 Revisit the worked example earlier in the chapter that analysed a journey in terms of value-added time (actually going somewhere) and non-value-added time (the time spent queuing etc.). Calculate the value-added time for a recent journey that you have taken.

2 A production process is required to produce 1,400 of product X, 840 of product Y and 420 of product Z in a 4-week period. If the process works 7 hours per day and 5 days per week, devise a mixed model schedule in terms of the number of each products required to be produced every hour, that would satisfy demand.

3 Revisit the 'Operations in action' at the beginning of this chapter, and (a) list all the different techniques and practices which Toyota adopts. (b) How are operations objectives (quality, speed, dependability, flexibility, cost) influenced by the practices which Toyota adopts?

4 Consider how set-up reduction principles can be used on the following:

(a) changing a tyre at the side of the road (following a puncture);

(b) cleaning out an aircraft and preparing it for the next flight between an aircraft on its inbound flight landing and disembarking its passengers, and the same aircraft being ready to take-off on its outbound flight;

(c) the time between the finish of one surgical procedure in a hospital's operating theatre, and the start of the next one;

(d) the 'pitstop' activities during a Formula One race (how does this compare to (a) above?).

Want to know more?

Ahlstrom, P. (2004) Lean service operations: translating lean production principles to service operations, *International Journal of Services, Technology and Management*, vol. 5, nos 5/6. Explains how lean can be used in services.

Bicheno, J. and Holweg, M. (2009) *The Lean Toolbox: The Essential Guide to Lean Transformation*, 4th edn, Piscie Press, Buckingham. A manual of lean techniques, very much a 'how to do it' book, and none the worse for it.

Holweg, M. (2007) The genealogy of lean production, *Journal of Operations Management*, vol. 25, 420–37. An excellent overview of how lean ideas developed.

Spear, S. and Bowen, H.K. (1999) Decoding the DNA of the Toyota Production System, *Harvard Business Review*, September–October. Revisits the leading company as regards JIT practice and re-evaluates the underlying philosophy behind the way it manages its operations. Recommended.

Womack, J.P. and Jones, D.T. (1996) *Lean Thinking: Banish Waste and Create Wealth in Your Corporation*, Simon and Schuster, New York. Some of the lessons from *The Machine that Changed the World* but applied in a broader context.

Womack, J.P., Jones, D.T. and Roos, D. (1990) *The Machine that Changed the World*, Rawson Associates, New York. Arguably the most influential book on operations management practice of the last fifty years. Firmly rooted in the automotive sector but did much to establish lean.

Useful websites

www.lean.org/ Site of the lean enterprise unit, set up by one of the founders of the lean thinking movement.

www.theiet.org/index.cfm The site of the Institution Electrical Engineers (which includes manufacturing engineers surprisingly) has material on this and related topics as well as other issues covered in this book.

www.mfgeng.com The manufacturing engineering site.

www.opsman.org Lots of useful stuff.

 *Now that you have finished reading this chapter, why not visit MyOMLab at www.myomlab.com where you'll find more learning resources to help you make the most of your studies and get a better grade.*

Operations improvement

Key questions

➤ Why is improvement so important in operations management?

➤ What are the key elements of operations improvement?

➤ What are the broad approaches to managing improvement?

➤ What techniques can be used for improvement?

Introduction

Even when an operation is designed and its activities planned and controlled, the operations manager's task is not finished. All operations, no matter how well managed, are capable of improvement. In fact, in recent years the emphasis has shifted markedly towards making improvement one of the main responsibilities of operations managers. We treat improvement activities in three stages. This chapter looks at the elements commonly found in various improvement approaches, examines four of the more widely used approaches, then illustrates some of the techniques which can be adopted to improve the operation. Chapter 19 looks at improvement from another perspective, that is, how operations can improve by managing risks. Finally, Chapter 20, looks at how improvement activities can be organized, supported and implemented. These three stages are interrelated as shown in Figure 18.1.

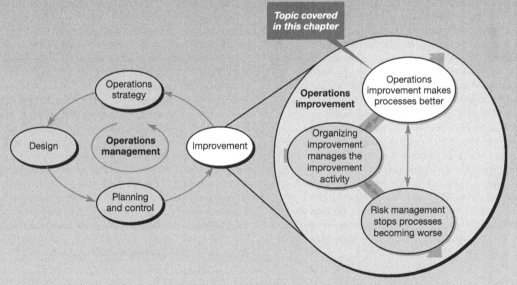

Figure 18.1 This chapter covers operations improvement

Check and improve your understanding of this chapter using self assessment questions and a personalised study plan, audio and video downloads, and an eBook – all at www.myomlab.com.

Operations in practice Improvement at Heineken[1]

Heineken International brews beer that is sold around the world. Operating in over 170 countries, it has succeeded in growing sales, especially in its Heineken and Amstel brands. However, sales growth can put pressure on any company's operations. For example, Heineken's Zoeterwoude facility, a packaging plant that fills bottles and cans in The Netherlands has had to increase its volume by between 8 and 10 per cent per year on a regular basis. In a competitive market, the company faced two challenges. First, it needed to improve its operations processes to reduce its costs. Second, because it would have taken a year to build a new packaging line, it needed to improve the efficiency of its existing lines in order to increase its capacity. Improving line efficiency therefore was vital if the plant was to cut its costs and create the extra capacity it needed to delay investment in a new packaging line.

The objective of the improvement project was to improve the plant's operating equipment efficiency (OEE) (see Chapter 11 for a discussion of OEE) by 20 per cent. Setting a target of 20 per cent was seen as important because it was challenging yet achievable as well as meeting the cost and capacity objectives of the project. It was also decided to focus the improvement project around two themes: (a) obtaining accurate operational data that could be converted into useful business information on which improvement decisions could be based, and (b) changing the culture of the operation to promote fast and effective decision-making. This would help people at all levels in the plant to have access to accurate and up-to-date information as well as encouraging staff to focus on the improvement of how they do their job rather than just 'doing the job'. Before the improvement, project staff at the Zoeterwoude plant had approached problem-solving as an *ad hoc* activity, only to be done when circumstances made it unavoidable. By contrast, the improvement initiative taught the staff on each packaging line to use various problem-solving techniques such as cause–effect and Pareto diagrams (discussed later in this chapter). Other techniques included the analysis of improved equipment maintenance and failure mode and effective analysis (FMEA) (both discussed in Chapter 19).

Source: Getty Images

'*Until we started using these techniques*', says Wilbert Raaijmakers, Heineken Netherlands Brewery Director, '*there was little consent regarding what was causing any problems. There was poor communication between the various departments and job grades. For example, maintenance staff believed that production stops were caused by operating errors, while operators were of the opinion that poor maintenance was the cause.*' The use of better information, analysis and improvement techniques helped the staff to identify and treat the root causes of problems. With many potential improvements to make, staff teams were encouraged to set priorities that would reflect the overall improvement target. There was also widespread use of benchmarking performance against targets periodically so that progress could be reviewed.

At the end of twelve months the improvement project had achieved its objectives of a 20 per cent improvement in OEE, not just for one packaging line but for all nine. This allowed the plant to increase the volume of its exports and cut its costs significantly. Not only that, but other aspects of the plant's performance improved. Up to that point, the plant had gained a reputation for poor delivery dependability. After the project it was seen by the other operations in its supply chain as a much more reliable partner. Yet Wilbert Raaijmakers still sees room for improvement, '*The optimization of an organization is a never-ending process. If you sit back and do the same thing tomorrow as you did today, you'll never make it. We must remain alert to the latest developments and stress the resulting information to its full potential.*'

Why improvement is so important

Operations management involves four areas of activity, as we explained in Chapter 1. These are: devising a strategy for the operations function, designing operations processes and the products and services they produce, planning and controlling; that is, running operations over time, and improving operations processes. At one time the focus of most operations management was seen as the planning and control activity. Operations managers were expected to get on with running the operation on a day-by-day and month-by-month basis (but rarely thinking in the longer term). Design activities such as process design, layout, etc. were often the domain of specialists, and changes in process design would happen relatively infrequently. Similarly, improvement was organized separately from mainstream operations management and again was often the province of specialists. Operations strategy was rarely considered at all. This has changed radically. Two things have happened. First, all four activities (strategy, design, planning and control, and improvement) are seen as interrelated and interdependent. Second, the locus of the operations management job has moved from planning and control (important though this still is) to improvement. Operations managers are judged not only on how they meet their ongoing responsibilities of producing products and services to acceptable levels of quality, speed, dependability, flexibility and cost, but also on how they improve the performance of the operations function overall.

The Red Queen effect

The scientist Leigh Van Valen was looking to describe a discovery that he had made while studying marine fossils. He had established that, no matter how long a family of animals had already existed, the probability that the family will become extinct is unaffected. In other words, the struggle for survival never gets easier. However well a species fits with its environment it can never relax. The analogy that Van Valen drew came from *Alice's Adventures through the Looking Glass*, by Lewis Carroll. In the book, Alice had encountered living chess pieces and, in particular, the Red Queen.

> 'Well, in our country', said Alice, still panting a little, 'you'd generally get to somewhere else – if you ran very fast for a long time, as we've been doing.' 'A slow sort of country!' said the Queen. 'Now, here, you see, it takes all the running you can do, to keep in the same place. If you want to get somewhere else, you must run at least twice as fast as that!'[2]

In many respects this is like business. Improvements and innovations may be imitated or countered by competitors. For example, in the automotive sector, the quality of most firms' products is very significantly better than it was two decades ago. This reflects the improvement in those firms' operations processes. Yet their relative competitive position has in many cases not changed. Those firms that have improved their competitive position have improved their operations performance *more than* competitors. Where improvement has simply matched competitors, survival has been the main benefit. The implications for operations improvement are clear. It is even more important, especially when competitors are actively improving their operations.

Elements of improvement

There are many approaches to improvement. Some have been used for over a century (for example some work study techniques come from the 'scientific management' movement of the early 20th century, see Chapter 9), others are relatively recent (for example, Six Sigma, explained later). But do not think that these approaches to improvement are different in all respects. There are many elements that are common to several approaches. Think of these 'elements' as the building blocks of the various improvement approaches. Furthermore, as these approaches develop over time, they may acquire elements from elsewhere. So the Six Sigma approach has developed beyond its process control roots to encompass many other elements. This section explains some of these elements. The following section (Improvement approaches) will then show how these elements are combined to form different improvement approaches.

Radical or breakthrough change

Radical **breakthrough improvement** (or 'innovation'-based improvement as it is sometimes called) is a philosophy that assumes that the main vehicle of improvement is major and dramatic change in the way the operation works. The introduction of a new, more efficient machine in a factory, the total redesign of a computer-based hotel reservation system, and the introduction of an improved degree programme at a university are all examples of breakthrough improvement. The impact of these improvements is relatively sudden and represents a step change in practice (and hopefully performance). Such improvements are rarely inexpensive, usually calling for high investment of capital, often disrupting the ongoing workings of the operation, and frequently involving changes in the product/service or process technology. The bold line in Figure 18.2(a) illustrates the pattern of performance with several breakthrough improvements. The improvement pattern illustrated by the dashed line in Figure 18.2(a) is regarded by some as being more representative of what really occurs when operations rely on pure breakthrough improvement. Breakthrough improvement places a high value on creative solutions. It encourages free thinking and individualism. It is a radical philosophy insomuch as it fosters an approach to improvement which does not accept many constraints on what is possible. 'Starting with a clean sheet of paper', 'going back to first principles' and 'completely rethinking the system' are all typical breakthrough improvement principles.

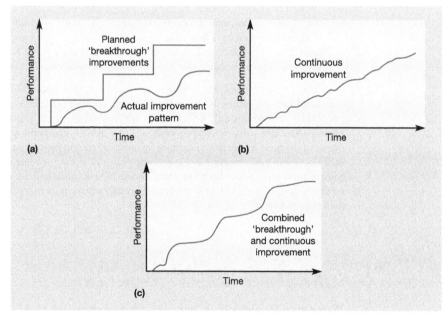

Figure 18.2 (a) 'Breakthrough' improvement, (b) 'continuous' improvement and (c) combined improvement patterns

Continuous improvement

Continuous improvement

Continuous improvement, as the name implies, adopts an approach to improving performance which assumes many small incremental improvement steps. For example, modifying the way a product is fixed to a machine to reduce changeover time, simplifying the question sequence when taking a hotel reservation, and rescheduling the assignment completion dates on a university course so as to smooth the students' workload are all examples of incremental improvements. While there is no guarantee that such small steps towards better performance will be followed by other steps, the whole philosophy of continuous improvement attempts to ensure that they will be. Continuous improvement is not concerned with promoting small improvements *per se*. It does see small improvements, however, as having one significant advantage over large ones – they can be followed relatively painlessly by other

Kaizen

small improvements (*see* Fig. 18.2(b)). Continuous improvement is also known as **kaizen**. Kaizen is a Japanese word, the definition of which is given by Masaaki Imai[3] (who has been one of the main proponents of continuous improvement) as follows. '*Kaizen means improvement. Moreover, it means improvement in personal life, home life, social life and work life. When applied to the workplace, kaizen means continuing improvement involving everyone – managers and workers alike.*'

In continuous improvement it is not the *rate* of improvement which is important; it is the *momentum* of improvement. It does not matter if successive improvements are small; what does matter is that every month (or week, or quarter, or whatever period is appropriate) some kind of improvement has actually taken place.

Improvement cycles

An important element within some improvement approaches is the use of a literally never-ending process of repeatedly questioning and re-questioning the detailed working of a process or activity. This repeated and cyclical questioning is usually summarized by the idea

Improvement cycle

of the **improvement cycle**, of which there are many, but two are widely used models – the PDCA cycle (sometimes called the Deming cycle, named after the famous quality 'guru', W.E. Deming) and the DMAIC (pronounced de-make) cycle, made popular by the Six Sigma

PDCA cycle

approach (see later). The **PDCA cycle** model is shown in Figure 18.3(a). It starts with the P (for plan) stage, which involves an examination of the current method or the problem area being studied. This involves collecting and analysing data so as to formulate a plan of action which is intended to improve performance. Once a plan for improvement has been agreed, the next step is the D (for do) stage. This is the implementation stage during which the plan is tried out in the operation. This stage may itself involve a mini-PDCA cycle as the problems of implementation are resolved. Next comes the C (for check) stage where the new implemented

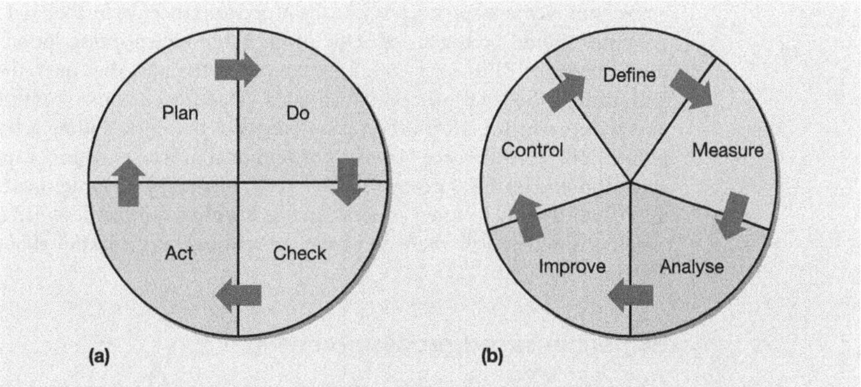

Figure 18.3 (a) The plan–do–check–act, or Deming improvement cycle, and (b) the define–measure–analyse–improve–control, or DMAIC Six Sigma improvement cycle

solution is evaluated to see whether it has resulted in the expected performance improvement. Finally, at least for this cycle, comes the A (for act) stage. During this stage the change is consolidated or standardized if it has been successful. Alternatively, if the change has not been successful, the lessons learned from the 'trial' are formalized before the cycle starts again.

DMAIC cycle

The DMAIC cycle is in some ways more intuitively obvious than the PDCA cycle insomuch as it follows a more 'experimental' approach. The **DMAIC cycle** starts with defining the problem or problems, partly to understand the scope of what needs to be done and partly to define exactly the requirements of the process improvement. Often at this stage a formal goal or target for the improvement is set. After definition comes the measurement stage. This stage involves validating the problem to make sure that it really is a problem worth solving, using data to refine the problem and measuring exactly what is happening. Once these measurements have been established, they can be analysed. The analysis stage is sometimes seen as an opportunity to develop hypotheses as to what the root causes of the problem really are. Such hypotheses are validated (or not) by the analysis and the main root causes of the problem identified. Once the causes of the problem are identified, work can begin on improving the process. Ideas are developed to remove the root causes of problems, solutions are tested and those solutions that seem to work are implemented and formalized and results measured. The improved process needs then to be continually monitored and controlled to check that the improved level of performance is sustaining. After this point the cycle starts again and defines the problems which are preventing further improvement. Remember though, it is the last point about both cycles that is the most important – the cycle starts again. It is only by accepting that in a continuous improvement philosophy these cycles quite literally never stop that improvement becomes part of every person's job.

A process perspective

Even if some improvement approaches do not explicitly or formally include the idea that taking a process perspective should be central to operations improvement, almost all do so implicitly. This has two major advantages. First, it means that improvement can be focused on what actually happens rather than on which part of the organization has responsibility for what happens. In other words, if improvement is not reflected in the process of creating products and services, then it is not really improvement as such. Second, as we have mentioned before, all parts of the business manage processes. This is what we call operations as activity rather than operations as a function. So, if improvement is described in terms of how processes can be made more effective, those messages will have relevance for all the other functions of the business in addition to the operations function.

End-to-end processes

Some improvement approaches take the process perspective further and prescribe exactly how processes should be organized. One of the more radical prescriptions of business process re-engineering (BPR, see later), for example, is the idea that operations should be organized around the total process which adds value for customers, rather than the functions or activities which perform the various stages of the value-adding activity. We have already pointed out the difference between conventional processes within a specialist function, and an end-to-end business process in Chapter 1. Identified customer needs are entirely fulfilled by an 'end-to-end' business process. In fact the processes are designed specifically to do this, which is why they will often cut across conventional organizational boundaries. Figure 18.4 illustrates this idea.

Evidence-based problem-solving

In recent years there has been a resurgence of the use of quantitative techniques in improvement approaches. Six Sigma (see later) in particular promotes systematic use of (preferably quantitative) evidence. Yet Six Sigma is not the first of the improvement approaches to

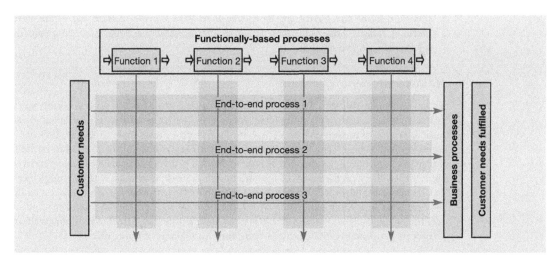

Figure 18.4 BPR advocates reorganizing (re-engineering) micro-operations to reflect the natural customer-focused business processes

use quantitative methods (some of the TQM gurus promoted statistical process control for example) although it has done a lot to emphasize the use of quantitative evidence. In fact, much of the considerable training required by Six Sigma consultants is devoted to mastering quantitative analytical techniques. However, the statistical methods used in improvement activities do not always reflect conventional academic statistical knowledge as such. They emphasize observational methods of collecting data and the use of experimentation to examine hypotheses. Techniques include graphical methods, analysis of variance, and two-level factorial experiment design. Underlying the use of these techniques is an emphasis on the scientific method, responding only to hard evidence, and using statistical software to facilitate analysis.

Customer-centricity

There is little point in improvement unless it meets the requirements of the customers. However, in most improvement approaches, meeting the expectations of customers means more than this. It involves the whole organization in understanding the central importance of customers to its success and even to its survival. Customers are seen not as being external to the organization but as the most important part of it. However, the idea of being customer-centric does not mean that customers must be provided with everything that they want. Although 'What's good for customers' may frequently be the same as 'What's good for the business', it is not always. Operations managers are always having to strike a balance between what customers would like and what the operation can afford (or wants) to do.

Systems and procedures

Improvement is not something that happens simply by getting everyone to 'think improve-ment'. Some type of system that supports the improvement effort may be needed. An improvement system (sometimes called a 'quality system') is defined as:

'*the organizational structure, responsibilities, procedures, processes and resources for imple-menting quality management*'.[4]

It should

'*define and cover all facets of an organization's operation, from identifying and meeting the needs and requirements of customers, design, planning, purchasing, manufacturing, packaging,*

215

storage, delivery and service, together with all relevant activities carried out within these functions. It deals with organization, responsibilities, procedures and processes. Put simply [it] is good management practice.'[5]

Reduce process variation

Processes change over time, as does their performance. Some aspect of process performance (usually an important one) is measured periodically (either as a single measurement or as a small sample of measurements). These are then plotted on a simple timescale. This has a number of advantages. The first is to check that the performance of the process is, in itself, acceptable (capable). They can also be used to check if process performance is changing over time, and to check on the extent of the variation in process performance. In the supplement to Chapter 17 we illustrated how random variation in the performance of any process could obscure what was really happening within the process. So a potentially useful method of identifying improvement opportunities is to try and identify the sources of random variation in process performance. Statistical process control is one way of doing this.

Synchronized flow

This is another idea that we have seen before – in Chapter 15, as part of the lean philosophy. Synchronized flow means that items in a process, operation or supply network flow smoothly and with even velocity from start to finish. This is a function of how inventory accumulates within the operation. Whether inventory is accumulated in order to smooth differences between demand and supply, or as a contingency against unexpected delays, or simply to batch for purposes of processing or movement, it all means that flow becomes asynchronous. It waits as inventory rather than progressing smoothly on. Once this state of perfect synchronization of flow has been achieved, it becomes easier to expose any irregularities of flow which may be the symptoms of more deep-rooted underlying problems.

Emphasize education and training

Several improvement approaches stress the idea that structured training and organization of improvement should be central to improvement. Not only should the techniques of improvement be fully understood by everyone engaged in the improvement process, the business and organizational context of improvement should also be understood. After all, how can one improve without knowing what kind of improvement would best benefit the organization and its customers? Furthermore, education and training have an important part to play in motivating all staff towards seeing improvement as a worthwhile activity. Some improvement approaches in particular place great emphasis on formal education. Six Sigma for example (see later) and its proponents often mandate a minimum level of training (measured in hours) that they deem necessary before improvement projects should be undertaken.

Perfection is the goal

Almost all organization-wide improvement programmes will have some kind of goal or target that the improvement effort should achieve. And while targets can be set in many different ways, some improvement authorities hold that measuring process performance against some kind of absolute target does most for encouraging improvement. By an 'absolute target' one literally means the theoretical level of perfection, for example, zero errors, instant delivery, delivery absolutely when promised, infinite flexibility, zero waste, etc. Of course, in reality such perfection may never be achievable. That is not the point. What is important is that current performance can be calibrated against this target of perfection in order to indicate how much more improvement is possible. Improving (for example) delivery accuracy by five per cent may seem good until it is realized that only an improvement of thirty per cent would eliminate all late deliveries.

Waste identification

All improvement approaches aspire to eliminate waste. In fact, any improvement implies that some waste has been eliminated, where waste is any activity that does not add value. But the identification and elimination of waste is sometimes a central feature. For example, as we discussed in Chapter 15, it is arguably the most significant part of the lean philosophy.

Include everybody

Harnessing the skills and enthusiasm of every person and all parts of the organization seems an obvious principle of improvement. The phrase 'quality at source' is sometimes used, stressing the impact that each individual has on improvement. The contribution of all individuals in the organization may go beyond understanding their contribution to 'not make mistakes'. Individuals are expected to bring something positive to improving the way they perform their jobs. The principles of 'empowerment' are frequently cited as supporting this aspect of improvement. When Japanese improvement practices first began to migrate in the late 1970s, this idea seemed even more radical. Yet now it is generally accepted that individual creativity and effort from all staff represents a valuable source of development. However, not all improvement approaches have adopted this idea. Some authorities believe that a small number of internal improvement consultants or specialists offer a better method of organizing improvement. However, these two ideas are not incompatible. Even with improvement specialists used to lead improvement efforts, the staff who actually operate the process can still be used as a valuable source of information and improvement ideas.

Develop internal customer–supplier relationships

One of the best ways to ensure that external customers are satisfied is to establish the idea that every part of the organization contributes to external customer satisfaction by satisfying its own internal customers. This idea was introduced in Chapter 17, as was the related concept of service-level agreements (SLAs). It means stressing that each process in an operation has a responsibility to manage these internal customer–supplier relationships. They do this primarily by defining as clearly as possible what their own and their customers' *requirements* are. In effect this means defining what constitutes 'error-free' service – the quality, speed, dependability and flexibility required by internal customers.

Short case
Erdington embraces the spirit of improvement[6]

The Erdington Group is a major private group in the Scotch whisky industry with a number of specialist operations covering every facet of Scotch whisky distilling, blending and bottling. With a history that goes back to the 1850s, the Group is owned by The Robertson Trust, which gives more than £7m of dividend income to charitable causes in Scotland each year, and its employees, more than 90% of whom are shareholders. Erdington's brands are well known: The Famous Grouse,

Source: Rex Features

Cutty Sark, and a malt, The Macallan, which is matured in selected ex-sherry oak casks. Another, Highland Park, was recently named 'best spirit in the world' by *The Spirit Journal*, USA. The Group's Glasgow site has been commended in a 'Best Factory' award scheme for its use of improvement approaches in achieving excellence in quality, productivity and flexibility. This is a real achievement given the constraints of whisky production, bottling and distribution. Some whisky can take 30 years to mature and with malts, there is a limited number of available ex-sherry casks. Production planning must look forward to what may be needed in 10, 18 or even 30 years' time, and having the right malts in stock is crucial. After the whisky has been blended in vats, it is decanted into casks again for the 'marrying' process. The whisky stays in these casks for three months. After

this, it is ready for bottling. The main bottling line runs at 600 bottles per minute, which is fast, so dealing with problems in the plant is important. Production must be efficient and reliable, with changeovers as fast as possible.

This is where the company's improvement efforts have paid dividends. It has used several improvement approaches to help it maintain its operations performance. *'We did TQM, then CIP and six sigma (there are 10 black belts on site and 30 green belts) and now lean, which is an evolution for us'* explains Stan Marshall, director of operational excellence. *'Lean has helped the line and has helped us'*, says Roseann McAlindon, a line operator on line 8, the lean pilot line, who has worked in the site for 17 years. *'On changeovers, parts were reviewed for ease of fitment, made lighter and easier to handle, and procedures written down.'*

Approaches to improvement

Many of the elements described above are present in one or more of the commonly used approaches to improvement. Some of these approaches have already been described. For example, both lean (Chapter 15) and TQM (Chapter 17) have been discussed in some detail. In this section we will briefly re-examine TQM and lean, specifically from an improvement perspective and also add two further approaches – business process re-engineering (BPR) and Six Sigma.

Total quality management as an improvement approach

Total quality management was one of the earliest management 'fashions'. Its peak of popularity was in the late 1980s and early 1990s. As such it has suffered from something of a backlash in recent years. Yet the general precepts and principles that constitute TQM are still hugely influential. Few, if any, managers have not heard of TQM and its impact on improvement. Indeed, TQM has come to be seen as an approach to the way operations and processes should be managed and improved, generally. It is best thought of as a philosophy of how to approach improvement. This philosophy, above everything, stresses the 'total' of TQM. It is an approach that puts quality (and indeed improvement generally) at the heart of everything that is done by an operation. As a reminder, this totality can be summarized by the way TQM lays particular stress on the following elements (see Chapter 17):

- Meeting the needs and expectations of customers;
- Improvement covers all parts of the organization (and should be group-based);
- Improvement includes every person in the organization (and success is recognized);
- Including all costs of quality;
- Getting things 'right first time', i.e. designing-in quality rather than inspecting it in;
- Developing the systems and procedures which support improvement.

Even if TQM is not the label given to an improvement initiative, many of its elements will almost certainly have become routine. The fundamentals of TQM have entered the vernacular of operations improvement. Elements such as the internal customer concept, the idea of internal and external failure-related costs, and many aspects of individual staff empowerment, have all become widespread.

Lean as an improvement approach

The idea of lean (also known as just-in-time, lean synchronization, continuous flow operations, and so on) spread beyond its Japanese roots and became fashionable in the West at about the same time as TQM. And although its popularity has not declined to the same extent as TQM's, over 25 years of experience (at least in manufacturing), have diminished the excitement once associated with the approach. But, unlike TQM, it was seen initially as an approach to be used exclusively in manufacturing. Now, lean has become newly fashionable as an approach that can be applied in service operations. As a reminder (see Chapter 15) the lean approach aims to meet demand instantaneously, with perfect quality and no waste. Put another way, it means that the flow of products and services always delivers exactly what customers want (perfect quality), in exact quantities (neither too much nor too little), exactly when needed (not too early or too late), exactly where required (not to the wrong location), and at the lowest possible cost. It results in items flowing rapidly and smoothly through processes, operations and supply networks. The key elements of the lean when used as an improvement approach are as follows.

- Customer-centricity
- Internal customer–supplier relationships
- Perfection is the goal
- Synchronized flow
- Reduce variation
- Include all people
- Waste elimination.

Some organizations, especially now that lean is being applied more widely in service operations, view waste elimination as the most important of all the elements of the lean approach. In fact, they sometimes see the lean approach as consisting almost exclusively of waste elimination. What they fail to realize is that effective waste elimination is best achieved through changes in behaviour. It is the behavioural change brought about through synchronized flow and customer triggering that provides the window onto exposing and eliminating waste.

It is easy to forget just how radical, and more importantly, counter-intuitive lean once seemed. Although ideas of continuous improvement were starting to be accepted, the idea that inventories were generally a bad thing, and that throughput time was more important than capacity utilization seemed to border on the insane to the more traditionally minded. So, as lean ideas have been gradually accepted, we have likewise come to be far more tolerant of ideas that are radical and/or counter-intuitive. This is an important legacy because it opened up the debate on operations practice and broadened the scope of what are regarded as acceptable approaches. It is also worth remembering that when Taiichi Ohno wrote his seminal book[7] on lean (after retiring from Toyota in 1978) he was able to portray Toyota's manufacturing plants as embodying a coherent production approach. However, this encouraged observers to focus in on the specific techniques of lean production and de-emphasized the importance of 30 years of 'trial and error'. Maybe the real achievement of Toyota was not so much what they did but how long they stuck at it.

Business process re-engineering (BPR)

The idea of business process re-engineering originated in the early 1990s when Michael Hammer proposed that rather than using technology to automate work, it would be better applied to doing away with the need for the work in the first place ('don't automate, obliterate'). In doing this he was warning against establishing non-value-added work within an information technology system where it would be even more difficult to identify and eliminate. All work, he said, should be examined for whether it adds value for the customer and if not processes should be redesigned to eliminate it. In doing this BPR was echoing similar objectives in both scientific management and more recently lean approaches. But BPR, unlike those two earlier approaches, advocated radical changes rather than incremental changes to processes. Shortly after Hammer's article, other authors developed the ideas, again the majority of them stressing the importance of a radical approach to elimination of non-value-added work. This radicalism was summarized by Davenport who, when discussing the difference between BPR and continuous improvement, held that 'Today's firms must seek not fractional, but multiplicative levels of improvement – ten times rather than ten per cent'.

BPR has been defined[8] as

> 'the fundamental rethinking and radical redesign of business processes to achieve dramatic improvements in critical, contemporary measures of performance, such as cost, quality, service and speed'.

But there is far more to it than that. In fact, BPR was a blend of a number of ideas which had been current in operations management for some time. Lean concepts, process flow charting, critical examination in method study, operations network management and customer-focused operations all contribute to the BPR concept. It was the potential of information technologies to enable the fundamental redesign of processes, however, which acted as the catalyst in bringing these ideas together. It was the information technology that allowed radical process redesign even if many of the methods used to achieve the redesign had been explored before. For example, 'Business Process Reengineering, although a close relative, seeks radical rather than merely continuous improvement. It escalates the effort of . . . [lean] . . . and TQM to make process orientation a strategic tool and a core competence of the organization. BPR concentrates on core business processes, and uses the specific techniques within the . . . [lean] . . . and TQM tool boxes as enablers, while broadening the process vision.'[9]

The main principles of BPR can be summarized in the following points.

- Rethink business processes in a cross-functional manner which organizes work around the natural flow of information (or materials or customers).
- Strive for dramatic improvements in performance by radically rethinking and redesigning the process.
- Have those who use the output from a process, perform the process. Check to see if all internal customers can be their own supplier rather than depending on another function in the business to supply them (which takes longer and separates out the stages in the process).
- Put decision points where the work is performed. Do not separate those who do the work from those who control and manage the work.

Example[10]

We can illustrate this idea of reorganizing (or re-engineering) around business processes through the following simple example. Figure 18.5(a) shows the traditional organization of a trading company which purchases consumer goods from several suppliers, stores them, and sells them on to retail outlets. At the heart of the operation is the warehouse which receives the goods, stores them, and packs and dispatches them when they are required by customers. Orders for more stock are placed by Purchasing which also takes charge of materials planning and stock control. Purchasing buys the goods based on a forecast which is prepared by Marketing, which takes advice from the Sales department which is processing customers' orders. When a customer does place an order, it is the Sales department's job to instruct the warehouse to pack and dispatch the order and tell the Finance department to invoice the customer for the goods. So, traditionally, five departments (each a micro-operation) have between them organized the flow of materials and information within the total operation. But at each interface between the departments there is the possibility of errors and miscommunication arising. Furthermore, *who is responsible for looking after the customer's needs?* Currently, three separate departments all have dealings with the customer. Similarly, *who is responsible for liaising with suppliers?* This time two departments have contact with suppliers.

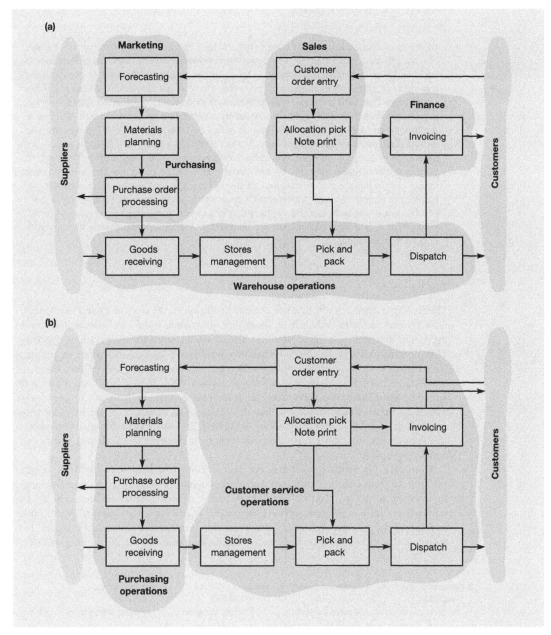

Figure 18.5 (a) Before and (b) after re-engineering a consumer goods trading company

Eventually the company reorganized around two essential business processes. The first process (called purchasing operations) dealt with everything concerning relationships with suppliers. It was this process's focused and unambiguous responsibility to develop good working relationships with suppliers. The other business process (called customer service operations) had total responsibility for satisfying customers' needs. This included speaking 'with one voice' to the customer.

BPR has aroused considerable controversy, mainly because BPR sometimes looks only at work activities rather than at the people who perform the work. Because of this, people become 'cogs in a machine'. Many of these critics equate BPR with the much earlier principles of scientific management, pejoratively known as 'Taylorism'. Generally these critics mean that BPR is overly harsh in the way it views human resources. Certainly there is evidence that BPR is often accompanied by a significant reduction in staff. Studies at the time when BPR was at its peak often revealed that the majority of BPR projects could reduce staff levels by over 20 per cent.[11] Often BPR was viewed as merely an excuse for getting rid of staff. Companies that wished to 'downsize' were using BPR as the pretext, putting the short-term interests of the shareholders of the company above either their longer-term interests or the interests of the company's employees. Moreover, a combination of radical redesign together with downsizing could mean that the essential core of experience was lost from the operation. This leaves it vulnerable to any marked turbulence since it no longer possessed the knowledge and experience of how to cope with unexpected changes.

Six Sigma

The Six Sigma approach was first popularized by Motorola, the electronics and communications systems company. When it set its quality objective as 'total customer satisfaction' in the 1980s, it started to explore what the slogan would mean to its operations processes. They decided that true customer satisfaction would only be achieved when its products were delivered when promised, with no defects, with no early-life failures and when the product did not fail excessively in service. To achieve this, Motorola initially focused on removing manufacturing defects. However, it soon came to realize that many problems were caused by latent defects, hidden within the design of its products. These may not show initially but eventually could cause failure in the field. The only way to eliminate these defects was to make sure that design specifications were tight (i.e. narrow tolerances) and its processes very capable.

Motorola's Six Sigma quality concept was so named because it required the natural variation of processes ($\pm$ 3 standard deviations) should be half their specification range. In other words, the specification range of any part of a product or service should be $\pm$ 6 the standard deviation of the process (see Chapter 17). The Greek letter sigma (σ) is often used to indicate the standard deviation of a process, hence the Six Sigma label. Figure 18.6 illustrates the effect of progressively narrowing process variation on the number of defects

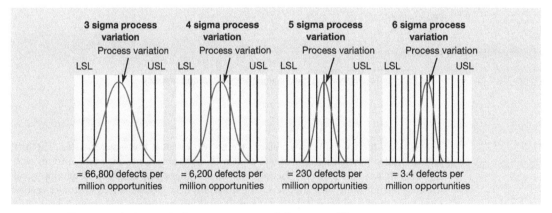

Figure 18.6 Process variation and its impact on process defects per million

produced by the process, in terms of **defects per million**. The defects per million measure is used within the Six Sigma approach to emphasize the drive towards a virtually **zero defect** objective. Now the definition of Six Sigma has widened to well beyond this rather narrow statistical perspective. General Electric (GE), who were probably the best known of the early adopters of Six Sigma, defined it as, 'A disciplined methodology of defining, measuring, analysing, improving, and controlling the quality in every one of the company's products, processes, and transactions – with the ultimate goal of virtually eliminating all defects'. So, now Six Sigma should be seen as a broad improvement concept rather than a simple examination of process variation, even though this is still an important part of process control, learning and improvement.

Measuring performance

The Six Sigma approach uses a number of related measures to assess the performance of operations processes.

- A *defect* is a failure to meet customer-required performance (defining performance measures from a customer's perspective is an important part of the Six Sigma approach).
- A *defect unit or item* is any unit of output that contains a defect (i.e. only units of output with no defects are not defective, defective units will have one or more than one defect).
- A *defect opportunity* is the number of different ways a unit of output can fail to meet customer requirements (simple products or services will have few defect opportunities, but very complex products or services may have hundreds of different ways of being defective).
- *Proportion defective* is the percentage or fraction of units that have one or more defect.
- *Process yield* is the percentage or fraction of total units produced by a process that are defect-free (i.e. 1 – proportion defective).
- *Defect per unit (DPU)* is the average number of defects on a unit of output (the number of defects divided by the number of items produced).
- *Defects per opportunity* is the proportion or percentage of defects divided by the total number of defect opportunities (the number of defects divided by (the number items produced × the number of opportunities per item)).
- *Defects per million opportunities (DPMO)* is exactly what it says, the number of defects which the process will produce if there were one million opportunities to do so.
- *The Sigma measurement* is derived from the DPMO and is the number of standard deviations of the process variability that will fit within the customer specification limits.

Worked example

An insurance process checks details of insurance claims and arranges for customers to be paid. It samples 300 claims at random at the end of the process. They find that 51 claims had one or more defects and there were 74 defects in total. Four types of error were observed, coding errors, policy conditions errors, liability errors and notification errors.

$$\text{Proportion defective} = \frac{\text{Number of defects}}{\text{Number of units processed}}$$

$$= \frac{51}{300} = 0.17 \ (17\% \text{ defective})$$

$$\text{Yield} = 1 - \text{Proportion of defectives}$$

$$= 1 - 0.17 = 0.83 \text{ or } (83\% \text{ yield})$$

$$\text{Defects per unit} = \frac{\text{Number of defects}}{\text{Number of units processed}}$$

$$= \frac{74}{300} = 0.247 \text{ (or 24.7) DPU}$$

$$\text{Defects per opportunity} = \frac{\text{Number of defects}}{\text{Number of units produced} \times \text{Number of opportunities}}$$

$$= \frac{74}{300 \times 4} = 0.062 \text{ DPO}$$

$$\text{Defects per million opportunities} = \text{DPO} \times 10^6$$

$$= 62{,}000 \text{ DPMO}$$

Although the scope of Six Sigma is disputed, among elements frequently associated with Six Sigma include the following:

- *Customer-driven objectives* – Six Sigma is sometimes defined as 'the process of comparing process outputs against customer requirements'. It uses a number of measures to assess the performance of operations processes. In particular it expresses performance in terms of defects per million opportunities (DPMO). This is exactly what it says, the number of defects which the process will produce if there were one million opportunities to do so. This is then related to the 'Sigma measurement' of a process and is the number of standard deviations of the process variability that will fit within the customer specification limits.
- *Use of evidence* – Although Six Sigma is not the first of the new approaches to operations to use statistical methods it has done a lot to emphasize the use of quantitative evidence. In fact much of the considerable training required by Six Sigma consultants is devoted to mastering quantitative analytical techniques.
- *Structured improvement cycle* – The structured improvement cycle used in Six Sigma is the DMAIC cycle.
- *Process capability and control* – Not surprisingly, given its origins, process capability and control is important within the Six Sigma approach.
- *Process design* – Latterly Six Sigma proponents also include process design into the collection of elements that define the Six Sigma approach.
- *Structured training and organization of improvement* – The Six Sigma approach holds that improvement initiatives can only be successful if significant resources and training are devoted to their management. It recommends a specially trained cadre of practitioners and internal consultants named after 'martial arts' grades, see below.

The 'martial arts' analogy

The terms that have become associated with Six Sigma experts (and denote their level of expertise) are, Master Black Belt, Black Belt and Green Belt. Master Black Belts are experts in the use of Six Sigma tools and techniques as well as how such techniques can be used and implemented. Primarily Master Black Belts are seen as teachers who can not only guide improvement projects, but also coach and mentor Black Belts and Green Belts who are closer to the day-to-day improvement activity. They are expected to have the quantitative analytical skills to help with Six Sigma techniques and also the organizational and interpersonal skills to teach and mentor. Given their responsibilities, it is expected that Master Black Belts are employed full-time on their improvement activities. Black Belts can take a direct hand in organizing improvement teams. Like Master Black Belts, Black Belts are expected to develop their quantitative analytical skills and also act as coaches for Green Belt. Black Belts are dedicated full-time to improvement, and although opinions vary on how many Black Belts should be employed in an operation, some organizations recommend one Black Belt for every hundred employees. Green Belts work within improvement teams, possibly as team leaders. They have significant amounts of training, although less than Black Belts. Green Belts are not full-time positions; they have normal day-to-day process responsibilities but are expected to spend at least twenty per cent of their time on improvement projects.

Source: Rex Features

'I think Six Sigma is powerful because of its definition; it is the process of comparing process outputs against customer requirements. Processes operating at less than 3.4 defects per million opportunities means that you must strive to get closer to perfection and it is the customer that defines the goal. Measuring defects per opportunity means that you can actually compare the process of, say, a human resources process with a billing and collection process.' Paul Ruggier head of Process at Xchanging is a powerful advocate of Six Sigma, and credits the success of the company, at least partly, to the approach.

Xchanging, created in 1998, is one of a new breed of companies, operating as an outsourcing business for 'back-office' functions for a range of companies, such as Lloyds of London, the insurance centre. Xchanging's business proposition is for the client company to transfer the running of the whole or part of their back office to Xchanging, either for a fixed price or one determined by cost savings achieved. The challenge Xchanging faces is to run that back office in a more effective and efficient manner than the client company had managed in the past. So, the more effective Xchanging is at running the processes, the greater its profit. To achieve these efficiencies Xchanging offers larger scale, a higher level of process expertise, focus and investment in technology. But above all, they offer, a Six Sigma approach. *'Everything we do can be broken down into a process'*, says Paul Ruggier. *'It may be more straightforward in a manufacturing business, frankly they've been using a lot of Six Sigma tools and techniques for decades. But the concept of process improvement is relatively new in many service companies. Yet the concept is powerful. Through the implementation of this approach we have achieved 30% productivity improvements in 6 months.'*

The company also adopts the Six Sigma terminology for its improvement practitioners – Master Black Belts, Black Belts and Green Belts. Attaining the status of Black Belt is very much sought after as well as being fulfilling, says Rebecca Whittaker who is a Master Black Belt at Xchanging. *'At the end of a project it is about having a process which is redesigned to such an extent, that is simplified and consolidated and people come back and say, "It's so much better than it used to be". It makes their lives better and it makes the business results better and those are the things that make being a Black Belt worthwhile.'*

Rebecca was recruited by Xchanging along with a number of other Master Black Belts as part of a strategic decision to kick-start Six Sigma in the company. It is seen as a particularly responsible position by the company and Master Black Belts are expected to be well versed in the Six Sigma techniques and be able to provide the training and knowhow to develop other staff within the company. In Rebecca's case she has been working as a Six Sigma facilitator for five years, initially as a Green Belt, then as a Black Belt.

Typically a person identified as having the right analytical and interpersonal skills will be taken off their job for at least a year, training and immersed in the concepts of improvement and then sent to work with line staff as project manager/facilitator. Their role as Black Belt will be to guide the line staff to make improvements in the way they do the job. One of the new Black Belts at Xchanging, Sarah Frost, is keen to stress the responsibility she owes to the people who will have to work in the improvement process. *'Being a Black Belt is about being a project manager. It is about working with the staff and combining our skills in facilitation and our knowledge of the Six Sigma process with their knowledge of the business. You always have to remember that you will go onto another project but they [process staff] will have to live with the new process. It is about building solutions that they can believe in.'*

One common criticism of Six Sigma is that it does not offer anything that was not available before. Its emphasis on improvement cycles comes from TQM, its emphasis on reducing variability comes from statistical process control, its use of experimentation and data analysis is simply good quantitative analysis. The only contribution that Six Sigma has made, argue its critics, is using the rather gimmicky martial arts analogy of Black Belt etc. to indicate a level of expertise in Six Sigma methods. All Six Sigma has done is package pre-existing elements together in order for consultants to be able to sell them to gullible chief executives. In fact it's difficult to deny some of these points. Maybe the real issue is whether it is really a criticism. If bringing these elements together really does form an effective problem-solving approach, why is this is a problem? Six Sigma is also accused of being too hierarchical in the way it structures its various levels of involvement in the improvement activity (as well as the dubious use of martial-arts-derived names such as Black Belt). It is also expensive. Devoting such large amount of training and time to improvement is a significant investment, especially for small companies. Nevertheless, Six Sigma proponents argue that the improvement activity is generally neglected in most operations and if it is to be taken seriously, it deserves the significant investment implied by the Six Sigma approach. Furthermore, they argue, if operated well, Six Sigma improvement projects run by experienced practitioners can save far more than their cost. There are also technical criticisms of Six Sigma. Most notably that in purely statistical terms the normal distribution which is used extensively in Six Sigma analysis does not actually represent most process behaviour. Other technical criticisms (that are not really the subject of this book) imply that aiming for the very low levels of defects per million opportunities, as recommended by Six Sigma proponents, is far too onerous.

Differences and similarities

In this chapter we have chosen to very briefly explain four improvement approaches. It could have been more. Enterprise resource planning (ERP, see Chapter 14), total preventive maintenance (TPM, see Chapter 19), lean Sigma (a combination of lean and Six Sigma), and others could have been added. But these four constitute a representative sample of the most commonly used approaches. Nor do we have the space to describe them fully. Each of the approaches is the subject of several books that describe them in great detail. There is no shortage of advice from consultants and academics as to how they should be used. And there are clearly some common elements between some of these approaches that we have described. Yet there are also differences between them in that each approach includes a different set of elements and therefore a different emphasis and these differences need to be understood. For example, one important difference relates to whether the approaches emphasize a gradual, continuous approach to change, or whether they recommend a more radical 'breakthrough' change. Another difference concerns the aim of the approach. What is the balance between whether the approach emphasizes *what* changes should be made or *how* changes should be made? Some approaches have a firm view of what is the best way to organize the operation's processes and resources. Other approaches hold no particular view on what an operation should do but rather concentrate on how the management of an operation should decide what to do. Indeed we can position each of the elements and the approaches that include them. This is illustrated in Figure 18.7. The approaches differ in the extent that they prescribe appropriate operations practice. BPR for example is very clear in what it is recommending. Namely, that all processes should be organized on an end-to-end basis. Its focus is *what* should happen rather than *how* it should happen. To a slightly lesser extent lean is the same. It has a definite list of things that processes should or should not be – waste should be eliminated, inventory should be reduced, technology should be flexible, and so on. Contrast this with both Six Sigma and TQM which focus to a far greater extent

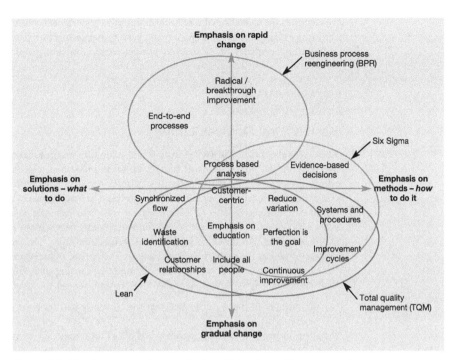

Figure 18.7 The four approaches on the two dimensions of improvement

on *how* operations should be improved. Six Sigma in particular has relatively little to say about what is good or bad in the way operations resources are organized (with the possible exception of its emphasizing the negative effects of process variation). Its concern is largely the way improvements should be made: using evidence, using quantitative analysis, using the DMAIC cycle, and so on. They also differ in terms of whether they emphasize gradual or rapid change. BPR is explicit in its radical nature. By contrast TQM and lean both incorporate ideas of continuous improvement. Six Sigma is relatively neutral on this issue and can be used for small or very large changes.

Improvement techniques

All the techniques described in this book and its supplements can be regarded as 'improvement' techniques. However, some techniques are particularly useful for improving operations and processes generally. Here we select some techniques which either have not been described elsewhere or need to be reintroduced in their role of helping operations improvement particularly.

Scatter diagrams

Scatter diagrams

Scatter diagrams provide a quick and simple method of identifying whether there is evidence of a connection between two sets of data: for example, the time at which you set off for work every morning and how long the journey to work takes. Plotting each journey on a graph which has departure time on one axis and journey time on the other could give an indication of whether departure time and journey time are related, and if so, how. Scatter diagrams can be treated in a far more sophisticated manner by quantifying how strong is the relationship between the sets of data. But, however sophisticated the approach, this type of graph only identifies the existence of a relationship, not necessarily the existence of a cause–effect relationship. If the scatter diagram shows a very strong connection between the sets of data, it is important evidence of a cause–effect relationship, but not proof positive. It could be coincidence!

Kaston Pyral Services Ltd (A)

Kaston Pyral Services Ltd (KPS) installs and maintains environmental control, heating and air conditioning systems. It has set up an improvement team to suggest ways in which it might improve its levels of customer service. The improvement team has completed its first customer satisfaction survey. The survey asked customers to score the service they received from KPS in several ways. For example, it asked customers to score services on a scale of one to ten on promptness, friendliness, level of advice, etc. Scores were then summed to give a 'total satisfaction score' for each customer – the higher the score, the greater the satisfaction. The spread of satisfaction scores puzzled the team and they considered what factors might be causing such differences in the way their customers viewed them. Two factors were put forward to explain the differences.

(a) the number of times in the past year the customer had received a preventive maintenance visit;
(b) the number of times the customer had called for emergency service.

All these data were collected and plotted on scatter diagrams as shown in Figure 18.8(a). It shows that there seems to be a clear relationship between a customer's satisfaction score and the number of times the customer was visited for regular servicing. The scatter diagram in Figure 18.8(b) is less clear. Although all customers who had very high satisfaction scores had made very few emergency calls, so had some customers with low satisfaction scores. As a result of this analysis, the team decided to survey customers' views on its emergency service.

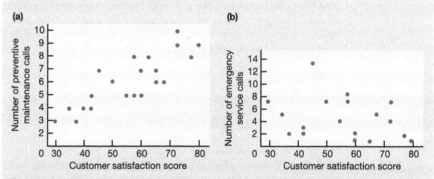

Figure 18.8 Scatter diagrams for customer satisfaction versus (a) number of preventive maintenance calls and (b) number of emergency service calls

Process maps (flow charts)

Process maps

Process maps (sometimes called 'flow charts' in this context) can be used to give a detailed understanding prior to improvement. They were described in Chapter 4 and are widely used in improvement activities. The act of recording each stage in the process quickly shows up poorly organized flows. Process maps can also clarify improvement opportunities and shed further light on the internal mechanics or workings of an operation. Finally, and probably most importantly, they highlight problem areas where no procedure exists to cope with a particular set of circumstances.

Kaston Pyral Services Ltd (B)

As part of its improvement programme the team at KPS is concerned that customers are not being served well when they phone in with minor queries over the operation of their heating systems. These queries are not usually concerned with serious problems, but often concern minor irritations which can be equally damaging to the customers' perception of KPS's service. Figure 18.9 shows the process map for this type of customer query. The team found the map illuminating. The procedure had never been formally laid out in this way before, and it showed up three areas where information was not being recorded. These are the three points marked with question marks on the process map in Figure 18.9. As a result of this investigation, it was decided to log all customer queries so that analysis could reveal further information on the nature of customer problems.

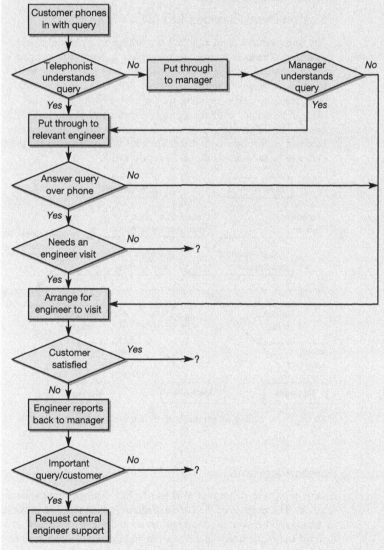

Figure 18.9 Process map for customer query

Cause–effect diagrams

Cause–effect diagrams **Cause–effect diagrams** are a particularly effective method of helping to search for the root causes of problems. They do this by asking what, when, where, how and why questions, but also add some possible 'answers' in an explicit way. They can also be used to identify areas where further data are needed. Cause–effect diagrams (which are also known as 'Ishikawa diagrams') have become extensively used in improvement programmes. This is because they provide a way of structuring group brainstorming sessions. Often the structure involves identifying possible causes under the (rather old-fashioned) headings of: machinery, manpower, materials, methods and money. Yet in practice, any categorization that comprehensively covers all relevant possible causes could be used.

Worked example

Kaston Pyral Services Ltd (C)

The improvement team at KPS was working on a particular area which was proving a problem. Whenever service engineers were called out to perform emergency servicing for a customer, they took with them the spares and equipment which they thought would be necessary to repair the system. Although engineers could never be sure exactly what materials and equipment they would need for a job, they could guess what was likely to be needed and take a range of spares and equipment which would cover most eventualities. Too often, however, the engineers would find that they needed a spare that they had not brought with them. The cause–effect diagram for this particular problem, as drawn by the team, is shown in Figure 18.10.

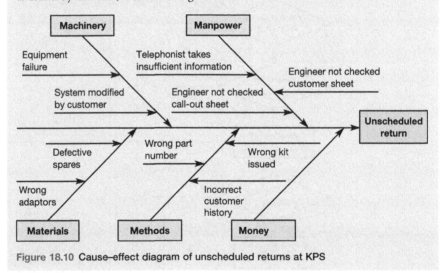

Figure 18.10 Cause–effect diagram of unscheduled returns at KPS

Pareto diagrams

In any improvement process, it is worthwhile distinguishing what is important and what is less so. The purpose of the Pareto diagram (which was first introduced in Chapter 12) is to distinguish between the 'vital few' issues and the 'trivial many'. It is a relatively straight-forward technique which involves arranging items of information on the types of problem or causes of problem into their order of importance (usually measured by 'frequency of occurrence'). This can be used to highlight areas where further decision-making will be useful. **Pareto analysis** is based on the phenomenon of relatively few causes explaining the majority of effects. For example, most revenue for any company is likely to come from relatively few of the company's customers. Similarly, relatively few of a doctor's patients will probably occupy most of his or her time.

Worked example

Kaston Pyral Services Ltd (D)

The KPS improvement team which was investigating unscheduled returns from emergency servicing (the issue which was described in the cause–effect diagram in Fig. 18.11) examined all occasions over the previous 12 months on which an unscheduled return had been made. They categorized the reasons for unscheduled returns as follows:

1 The wrong part had been taken to a job because, although the information which the engineer received was sound, he or she had incorrectly predicted the nature of the fault.
2 The wrong part had been taken to the job because there was insufficient information given when the call was taken.
3 The wrong part had been taken to the job because the system had been modified in some way not recorded on KPS's records.
4 The wrong part had been taken to the job because the part had been incorrectly issued to the engineer by stores.
5 No part had been taken because the relevant part was out of stock.
6 The wrong equipment had been taken for whatever reason.
7 Any other reason.

The relative frequency of occurrence of these causes is shown in Figure 18.11. About a third of all unscheduled returns were due to the first category, and more than half the returns were accounted for by the first and second categories together. It was decided that the problem could best be tackled by concentrating on how to get more information to the engineers which would enable them to predict the causes of failure accurately.

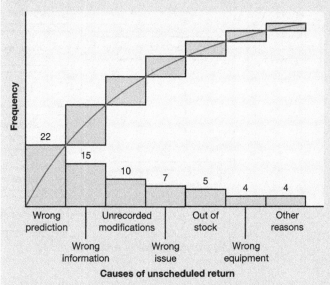

Figure 18.11 Pareto diagram for causes of unscheduled returns

231

Why–why analysis

Why–why analysis

Why–why analysis starts by stating the problem and asking *why* that problem has occurred. Once the reasons for the problem occurring have been identified, each of the reasons is taken in turn and again the question is asked *why* those reasons have occurred, and so on. This procedure is continued until either a cause seems sufficiently self-contained to be addressed by itself or no more answers to the question 'Why?' can be generated.

Worked example

Kaston Pyral Services Ltd (E)

The major cause of unscheduled returns at KPS was the incorrect prediction of reasons for the customer's system failure. This is stated as the 'problem' in the why–why analysis in Figure 18.12. The question is then asked, why was the failure wrongly predicted? Three answers are proposed: first, that the engineers were not trained correctly; second, that they had insufficient knowledge of the particular product installed in the customer's location; and third, that they had insufficient knowledge of the customer's particular system with its modifications. Each of these three reasons is taken in turn, and the questions are asked, why is there a lack of training, why is there a lack of product knowledge, and why is there a lack of customer knowledge? And so on.

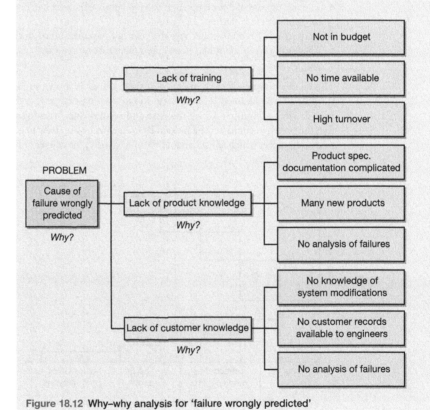

Figure 18.12 Why–why analysis for 'failure wrongly predicted'

Check and improve your understanding of this chapter using self assessment questions and a personalised study plan, audio and video downloads, and an eBook – all at www.myomlab.com.

➤ Why is improvement so important in operations management?

■ Improvement is now seen as the prime responsibility of operations management. Of the four areas of operations management activity (operations strategy, design, planning and control, and improvement) the focus of most operations managers has shifted from planning and control to improvement. Furthermore all operations management activities are really concerned with improvement in the long term. And all four activities are really interrelated and interdependent. Also, companies in many industries are having to improve simply to retain their position relative to their competitors. This is sometimes called the 'Red Queen' effect.

➤ What are the key elements of operations improvement?

■ There are many 'elements' that are the building blocks of improvement approaches. The ones described in this chapter are:
  - Radical or breakthrough improvement
  - Continuous improvement
  - Improvement cycles
  - A process perspective
  - End-to-end processes
  - Radical change
  - Evidence-based problem-solving
  - Customer-centricity
  - Systems and procedures
  - Reduce process variation
  - Synchronized flow
  - Emphasize education and training
  - Perfection is the goal
  - Waste identification
  - Include everybody
  - Develop internal customer–supplier relationships.

➤ What are the broad approaches to managing improvement?

■ What we have called 'the broad approaches to improvement' are relatively coherent collections of some of the 'elements' of improvement. The four most common are total quality management (TQM), lean, business process re-engineering (BPR) and Six Sigma.

■ BPR is a typical example of the radical approach to improvement. It attempts to redesign operations along customer-focused processes rather than on the traditional functional basis. The main criticisms are that it pays little attention to the rights of staff who are the victims of the 'downsizing' which often accompanies BPR, and that the radical nature of the changes can strip out valuable experience from the operation.

■ Total quality management was one of the earliest management 'fashions' and has suffered from a backlash, but the general precepts and principles of TQM are still influential. It is an approach that puts quality (and indeed improvement generally) at the heart of everything that is done by an operation.

- Lean was seen initially as an approach to be used exclusively in manufacturing, but has become seen as an approach that can be applied in service operations. Also lean, when first introduced was radical, and counter-intuitive. The idea that inventories had a negative effect, and that throughput time was more important than capacity utilization was difficult to accept by the more traditionally minded. So, as lean ideas have been gradually accepted, we have likewise come to be far more tolerant of ideas that are radical and/or counter-intuitive.

- Six Sigma is 'A disciplined methodology of defining, measuring, analysing, improving, and controlling the quality in every one of the company's products, processes, and transactions – with the ultimate goal of virtually eliminating all defects'. First popularized by Motorola, it was so named because it required that natural variation of processes ($\pm$ 3 standard deviations) should be half their specification range. In other words, the specification range of any part of a product or service should be $\pm$ 6 times the standard deviation of the process. Now the definition of Six Sigma has widened beyond its statistical origins. It should be seen as a broad improvement concept rather than a simple examination of process variation, even though this is still an important part of process control, learning and improvement.

- There are differences between these improvement approaches. Each includes a different set of elements and therefore a different emphasis. They can be positioned on two dimensions. The first is whether the approaches emphasize a gradual, continuous approach to change or a more radical 'breakthrough' change. The second is whether the approach emphasizes *what* changes should be made or *how* changes should be made.

> ## ➤ What techniques can be used for improvement?

- Many of the techniques described throughout this book could be considered improvement techniques, for example statistical process control (SPC).

- Techniques often seen as 'improvement techniques' are:
  - scatter diagrams, which attempt to identify relationships and influences within processes;
  - flow charts, which attempt to describe the nature of information flow and decision-making within operations;
  - cause–effect diagrams, which structure the brainstorming that can help to reveal the root causes of problems;
  - Pareto diagrams, which attempt to sort out the 'important few' causes from the 'trivial many' causes;
  - Why–why analysis that pursues a formal questioning to find root causes of problems.

Case study
Geneva Construction and Risk

'This is not going to be like last time. Then, we were adopting an improvement programme because we were told to. This time it's our idea and, if it's successful, it will be us that are telling the rest of the group how to do it.' (Tyko Mattson, Six Sigma Champion, GCR)

Tyko Mattson was speaking as the newly appointed 'Champion' at Geneva Construction and Risk Insurance, which had been charged with 'steering the Six Sigma programme until it is firmly established as part of our ongoing practice'. The previous improvement initiative that he was referring to dated back many years to when GCR's parent company, Wichita Mutual Insurance, had insisted on the adoption of total quality management (TQM) in all its businesses. The TQM initiative had never been pronounced a failure and had managed to make some improvements, especially in customers' perception of the company's levels of service. However, the initiative had 'faded out' during the 1990s and, even though all departments still had to formally report on their improvement projects, their number and impact was now relatively minor.

History

The Geneva Construction Insurance Company was founded in 1922 to provide insurance for building contractors and construction companies, initially in German-speaking Europe and then, because of the emigration of some family members to the USA, in North America. The company had remained relatively small and had specialized in housing construction projects until the early 1950s when it had started to grow, partly because of geographical expansion and partly because it has moved into larger (sometimes very large) construction insurance in the industrial, oil, petrochemical, and power plant construction areas. In 1983 it had been bought by the Wichita Mutual Group and had absorbed the group's existing construction insurance businesses.

By 2000 it had established itself as one of the leading providers of insurance for construction projects, especially complex, high-risk projects, where contractual and other legal issues, physical exposures and design uncertainty needed 'customized' insurance responses. Providing such insurance needed particular knowledge and skills from specialists including construction underwriters, loss adjusters, engineers, international lawyers and specialist risk consultants. Typically, the company would insure losses resulting from contractor failure, related public liability issues, delays in project completion, associated litigation, other litigation (such as ongoing asbestos risks), and negligence issues.

The company's headquarters were in Geneva and housed all major departments, including sales and marketing, underwriting, risk analysis, claims and settlement, financial control, general admin, specialist and general legal advice, and business research. There were also 37 local offices around the world, organized into four regional areas: North America, South America, Europe Middle East and Africa, and Asia. These regional offices provided localized help and advice directly to clients and also to the 890 agents that GCR used worldwide.

The previous improvement initiative

When Wichita Mutual had insisted that CGR adopt a TQM initiative, it had gone as far as to specify exactly how it should do it and which consultants should be used to help establish the programme. Tyko Mattson shakes his head as he describes it. *'I was not with the company at that time but, looking back; it's amazing that it ever managed to do any good. You can't impose the structure of an improvement initiative from the top. It has to, at least partially, be shaped by the people who are going to be involved in it. But everything had to be done according to the handbook. The cost of quality was measured for different departments according to the handbook. Everyone had to learn the improvement techniques that were described in the handbook. Everyone had to be part of a quality circle that was organized according to the handbook. We even had to have annual award ceremonies where we gave out special "certificates of merit" to those quality circles that had achieved the type of improvement that the handbook said they should.'* The TQM initiative had been run by the 'Quality Committee', a group of eight people with representatives from all the major departments at head office. Initially, it had spent much of its time setting up the improvement groups and organizing training in quality techniques. However, soon it had become swamped by the work needed to evaluate which improvement suggestions should be implemented. Soon the work load associated with assessing improvement ideas had become so great that the company decided to allocate small improvement budgets to each department on a quarterly basis that they could spend without reference to the Quality Committee. Projects requiring larger investment or that had a significant impact on other parts of the business still needed to be approved by the committee before they were implemented.

Department improvement budgets were still used within the business and improvement plans were still required from each department on an annual basis. However, the quality committee had stopped meeting by 1994 and the annual award ceremony had become a general communications meeting for all staff at the headquarters. *'Looking back'*, said Tyko, *'the TQM initiative faded away for three reasons. First, people just got tired of it. It was always seen as something extra rather than part of normal business life, so it was always seen as taking time away from doing your normal job. Second, many of the supervisory and middle management levels never really bought into it, I guess because they felt threatened. Third, only a very few of the local offices around the world ever adopted the TQM philosophy. Sometimes this was because they did not want the extra effort. Sometimes, however, they would argue that improvement initiatives of this type may be OK for head office processes, but not for the more dynamic world of supporting clients in the field.'*

The Six Sigma initiative

Early in 2005 Tyko Mattson, who for the last two years had been overseeing the outsourcing of some of GCR's claims processing to India, had attended a conference on 'Operations Excellence in Financial Services', and had heard several speakers detail the success they had achieved through using a Six Sigma approach to operations improvement. He had persuaded his immediate boss, Marie-Dominique Tomas, the head of claims for the company, to allow him to investigate its applicability to GCR. He had interviewed a number of other financial services that had implemented Six Sigma as well as a number of consultants and in September 2005 had submitted a report entitled *'What is Six Sigma and how might it be applied in GRC?'* Extracts from this are included in Appendix 1. Marie-Dominique Tomas was particularly concerned that they should avoid the mistakes of the TQM initiative.

'Looking back, it is almost embarrassing to see how naïve we were. We really did think that it would change the whole way that we did business. And although it did produce some benefits, it absorbed a large amount of time at all levels in the organization. This time we want something that will deliver results without costing too much or distracting us from focusing on business performance. That is why I like Six Sigma. It starts with clarifying business objectives and works from there.'

By late 2005 Tyko's report had been approved both by GCR and by Wichita Mutual's main board. Tyko had been given the challenge of carrying out the recommendations in his report, reporting directly to GCR's executive board. Marie-Dominique Tomas, was cautiously optimistic, *'It is quite a challenge for Tyko. Most of us on the executive board remember the TQM initiative and some are still sceptical concerning the value of such initiatives. However, Tyko's gradualist approach and his emphasis on the "three pronged" attack on revenue, costs, and risk, impressed the board. We now have to see whether he can make it work.'*

Appendix
Extract from *'What is Six Sigma and how might it be applied in GCR?'*

Six Sigma – pitfalls and benefits

Some pitfalls of Six Sigma

It is not simple to implement, and is resource hungry. The focus on measurement implies that the process data is available and reasonably robust. If this is not the case it is possible to waste a lot of effort in obtaining process performance data. It may also over-complicate things if advanced techniques are used on simple problems.

It is easier to apply Six Sigma to repetitive processes – characterized by high volume, low variety and low visibility to customers. It is more difficult to apply Six Sigma to low volume, higher variety and high visibility processes where standardization is harder to achieve and the focus is on managing the variety.

Six Sigma is not a 'quick fix'. Companies that have implemented Six Sigma effectively have not treated it as just another new initiative but as an approach that requires the long term systematic reduction of waste. Equally, it is not a panacea and should not be implemented as one.

Some benefits of Six Sigma

Companies have achieved significant benefits in reducing cost and improving customer service through implementing Six Sigma.

Six Sigma can reduce process variation, which will have a significant impact on operational risk. It is a tried and tested methodology, which combines the strongest parts of existing improvement methodologies. It lends itself to being customized to fit individual companies' circumstances. For example, Mestech Assurance has extended their Six Sigma initiative to examine operational risk processes.

Six Sigma could leverage a number of current initiatives. The risk self assessment methodology, Sarbanes Oxley, the process library, and our performance metrics work are all laying the foundations for better knowledge and measurement of process data.

Six Sigma – key conclusions for GCR

Six Sigma is a powerful improvement methodology. It is not all new but what it does do successfully is to combine some of the best parts of existing improvement methodologies, tools and techniques. Six Sigma has helped many companies achieve significant benefits.

Six Sigma could help GCR significantly improve risk management because it focuses on driving errors and exceptions out of processes.

Six Sigma has significant advantages over other process improvement methodologies.

→

- It engages senior management actively by establishing process ownership and linkage to strategic objectives. This is seen as integral to successful implementation in the literature and by all companies interviewed who had implemented it.
- It forces a rigorous approach to driving out variance in processes by analyzing the root cause of defects and errors and measuring improvement.
- It is an 'umbrella' approach, combining all the best parts of other improvement approaches.

Implementing Six Sigma across GCR is not the right approach

Companies who are widely quoted as having achieved the most significant headline benefits from Six Sigma were already relatively mature in terms of process management. Those companies, who understood their process capability, typically had achieved a degree of process standardization and had an established process improvement culture.

Six Sigma requires significant investment in performance metrics and process knowledge. GCR is probably not yet sufficiently advanced. However, we are working towards a position where key process data are measured and known and this will provide a foundation for Six Sigma.

A targeted implementation is recommended because:

Full implementation is resource hungry. Dedicated resource and budget for implementation of improvements is required. Even if the approach is modified, resource and budget will still be needed, just to a lesser extent. However, the evidence is that the investment is well worth it and pays back relatively quickly.

There was strong evidence from companies interviewed that the best implementation approach was to pilot Six Sigma, and select failing processes for the pilot. In addition, previous internal piloting of implementations has been successful in GCR – we know this approach works within our culture.

Six Sigma would provide a platform for GSR to build on and evolve over time. It is a way of leveraging the on-going work on processes, and the risk methodology (being developed by the Operational Risk Group). This diagnostic tool could be blended into Six Sigma, giving GCR a powerful model to drive reduction in process variation and improved operational risk management.

Recommendations

It is recommended that GCR management implement a Six Sigma pilot. The characteristics of the pilot would be as follows:

- A tailored approach to Six Sigma that would fit GCR's objectives and operating environment. Implementing Six Sigma in its entirety would not be appropriate.
- The use of an external partner: GCR does not have sufficient internal Six Sigma, and external experience will be critical to tailoring the approach, and providing training.
- Establishing where GCR's sigma performance is now. Different tools and approaches will be required to advance from 2 to 3 Sigma than those required to move from 3 to 4 Sigma.
- Quantifying the potential benefits. Is the investment worth making? What would a 1 Sigma increase in performance vs. risk be worth to us?
- Keeping the methods simple, if simple will achieve our objectives. As a minimum for us that means Team Based Problem Solving and basic statistical techniques.

Next steps

1 Decide priority and confirm budget and resourcing for initial analysis to develop a Six Sigma risk improvement programme in 2006.
2 Select external partner experienced in improvement and Six Sigma methodologies.
3 Assess GCR current state to confirm where to start in implementing Six Sigma.
4 Establish how much GCR is prepared to invest in Six Sigma and quantify the potential benefits.
5 Tailor Six Sigma to focus on risk management.
6 Identify potential pilot area (s) and criteria for assessing its suitability.
7 Develop a Six Sigma pilot plan.
8 Conduct and review the pilot programme.

Questions

1 How does the Six Sigma approach seem to differ from the TQM approach adopted by the company almost twenty years ago?

2 Is Six Sigma a better approach for this type of company?

3 Do you think Tyko can avoid the Six Sigma initiative suffering the same fate as the TQM initiative?

Problems and applications

1 Sophie was sick of her daily commute. 'Why', she thought 'should I have to spend so much time in a morning stuck in traffic listening to some babbling half-wit on the radio? We can work flexi-time after all. Perhaps I should leave the apartment at some other time? So resolved, Sophie deliberately varied her time of departure from her usual 8.30. Also, being an organized soul, she recorded her time of departure each day and her journey time. Her records are shown in Table 18.1.

(a) Draw a scatter diagram that will help Sophie decide on the best time to leave her apartment.

(b) How much time per (5-day) week should she expect to be saved from having to listen to a babbling half-wit?

Table 18.1 Sophie's journey times (in minutes)

Day	Leaving time	Journey time	Day	Leaving time	Journey time	Day	Leaving time	Journey time
1	7.15	19	6	8.45	40	11	8.35	46
2	8.15	40	7	8.55	32	12	8.40	45
3	7.30	25	8	7.55	31	13	8.20	47
4	7.20	19	9	7.40	22	14	8.00	34
5	8.40	46	10	8.30	49	15	7.45	27

2 The Printospeed Laser printer company was proud of its reputation for high-quality products and services. Because of this it was especially concerned with the problems that it was having with its customers returning defective toner cartridges. About 2,000 of these were being returned every month. Its European service team suspected that not all the returns were actually the result of a faulty product, which is why the team decided to investigate the problem. Three major problems were identified. First, some users were not as familiar as they should have been with the correct method of loading the cartridge into the printer, or in being able to solve their own minor printing problems. Second, some of the dealers were also unaware of how to sort out minor problems. Third, there was clearly some abuse of Hewlett-Packard's 'no-questions-asked' returns policy. Empty toner cartridges were being sent to unauthorized refilling companies who would sell the refilled cartridges at reduced prices. Some cartridges were being refilled up to five times and were understandably wearing out. Furthermore, the toner in the refilled cartridges was often not up to Printospeed's high quality standards.

(a) Draw a cause–effect diagram that includes both the possible causes mentioned, and any other possible causes that you think worth investigating.

(b) What is your opinion of the alleged abuse of the 'no-questions-asked' returns policy adopted by Printospeed?

3 Think back to the last product or service failure that caused you some degree of inconvenience. Draw a cause–effect diagram that identifies all the main causes of why the failure could have occurred. Try and identify the frequency with which such causes happen. This could be done by talking with the staff of the operation that provided the service. Draw a Pareto diagram that indicates the relatively frequency of each cause of failure. Suggest ways in which the operation could reduce the chances of failure.

Selected further reading

Goldratt, E.M. and Cox, J. (2004) *The Goal: A Process of Ongoing Improvement*, Gower, Aldershot. Updated version of a classic.

Hendry, L. and Nonthaleerak, P. (2004) Six sigma: Literature review and key future research areas, Lancaster University Management School, Working Paper, 2005/044 www.lums.lancs.ac.uk/publications/. Good overview of the literature on Six Sigma.

Hindo, B., At 3M, a struggle between efficiency and creativity: how CEO George Buckley is managing the yin and yang of discipline and imagination, *Business Week*, 11 June 2007. Readable article from the popular business press.

Pande, P.S., Neuman, R.P. and Cavanagh, R. (2002) *Six Sigma Way Team Field Book: An Implementation Guide for Project Improvement teams*, McGraw-Hill, New York. Obviously based on the Six Sigma principle and related to the book by the same author team recommended in Chapter 17, this is an unashamedly practical guide to the Six Sigma approach.

Paper, D.J., Rodger, J.A. and Pendharkar, P.C. (2001) A BPR case study at Honeywell, *Business Process Management Journal*, vol. 7, no. 2, 85–99. Interesting, if somewhat academic, case study.

Xingxing Zu, Fredendall L.D. and Douglas, T.J. (2008) the evolving theory of quality management: the role of Six Sigma, *Journal of Operations Management*, vol. 26, 630–50. As it says . . .

Useful web sites

www.processimprovement.com/ Commercial site but some content that could be useful.

www.kaizen-institute.com/ Professional institute for kaizen. Gives some insight into practitioner views.

www.imeche.org.uk/mx/index.asp The Manufacturing Excellence Awards site. Dedicated to rewarding excellence and best practice in UK manufacturing. Obviously manufacturing biased, but some good examples.

www.ebenchmarking.com Benchmarking information.

www.quality.nist.gov/ American Quality Assurance Institute. Well-established institution for all types of business quality assurance.

www.balancedscorecard.org/ Site of an American organization with plenty of useful links.

www.opsman.org Lots of useful stuff.

Now that you have finished reading this chapter, why not visit MyOMLab at www.myomlab.com where you'll find more learning resources to help you make the most of your studies and get a better grade?

Organizing for improvement

Key questions

➤ Why does improvement need organizing?

➤ How should the improvement effort be linked to strategy?

➤ What information is needed for improvement?

➤ What should be improvement priorities?

➤ How can organizational culture affect improvement?

➤ What are the key implementation issues?

Introduction

This is the third, and final, chapter devoted to operations improvement. It examines some of the managerial issues associated with improvement can be organized. There are no techniques as such in this chapter. Nor are all the issues dealt with easily defined. Rather it covers the 'soft' side of improvement. But do not dismiss this as in any way less important. In practice it is often the 'soft' stuff that determines the success or failure of improvement efforts. Moreover, the 'soft' stuff can be more difficult to get right than the 'hard', more technique-based, aspects of improvement. The 'hard' stuff is hard, but the 'soft' stuff is harder!

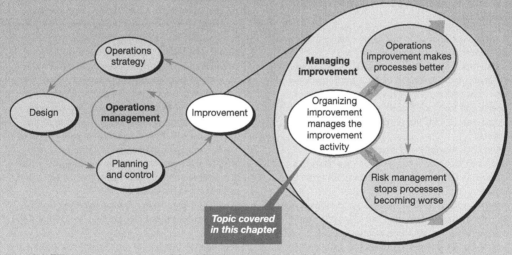

Figure 20.1 This chapter covers organizing of improvement

Check and improve your understanding of this chapter using self assessment questions and a personalised study plan, audio and video downloads, and an eBook – all at www.myomlab.com.

Operations effectiveness is just as important an issue in public-sector operations as it is for commercial companies. People have the right to expect that their taxes are not wasted on inefficient or inappropriate public processes. This is especially true of the tax collecting system itself. It is never a popular organization in any country, and taxpayers can be especially critical when the tax collection process is not well managed. This was very much on the minds of the Aarhus Region Customs and Tax unit (Aarhus CT) when they developed their award-winning quality initiative. The Aarhus Region is the largest of Denmark's twenty-nine local customs and tax offices. It acts as an agent for central government in collecting taxes in a professional and efficient manner while being able to respond to taxpayers' queries. Aarhus CT must, *'keep the user (customer) in focus'*, they say, *'Users must pay what is due – no more, no less and on time. But users are entitled to fair control and collection, fast and efficient case work, service and guidance, flexible employees, polite behaviour and a professional telephone service.'* The Aarhus CT approach to managing its quality initiative was built around a number of key points.

Source: Rex Features

- A recognition that poor-quality processes cause waste both internally and externally.
- A determination to adopt a practice of regularly surveying the satisfaction of its users. Employees were also surveyed, both to understand their views on quality and to check that their working environment would help to instil the principles of high-quality service.
- Although a not-for-profit organization, quality measures included measuring the organization's adherence to financial targets as well as error reporting.
- Internal processes were redefined and redesigned to emphasize customer needs and internal staff requirements. For example, Aarhus CT was the only tax region in Denmark to develop an independent information process that was used to analyse customers' needs and 'prevent misunderstanding in users' perception of legislation'.

- Internal processes were designed to allow staff the time and opportunity to develop their own skills, exchange ideas with colleagues and take on greater responsibility for management of their own work processes.
- The organization set up what it called its 'Quality Organization' (QO) structure which spanned all divisions and processes. The idea of the QO was to foster staff commitment to continuous improvement and to encourage the development of ideas for improving process performance. Within the QO was the Quality Group (QG). This consisted of four managers and four process staff, and reported directly to senior management. It also set up a number of improvement groups and suggestion groups consisting of managers as well as process staff. The role of the suggestion groups was to collect and process ideas for improvement which the improvement groups would then analyse and if appropriate implement.
- Aarhus CT was keen to stress that their Quality Groups would eventually become redundant if they were to be successful. In the short term they would maintain a stream of improvement ideas, but in the long term they should have fully integrated the idea of quality improvement into the day-to-day activities of all staff.

Why the improvement effort needs organizing

Improvement does not just happen. It needs organizing and it needs implementing. It also needs a purpose that is well thought through and clearly articulated. Although much operations improvement will take place at an operational level, and especially if one is following a continuous improvement philosophy (see previous chapter), it will be small-scale and incremental. Nevertheless, it must be placed in some kind of context. That is, it should be clear *why* improvement is happening as well as what it consists of. This means linking the improvement to the overall strategic objectives of the organization. This is why we start this chapter by thinking about improvement in a strategic context. Improvement must also be based on sound information. If the performance of operations and the processes within them are to be improved, one must first be able to define and measure exactly what we mean by 'performance'. Furthermore, benchmarking one's own activities and performance against other organizations' activities and performance can lead to valuable insights and help to quantify progress. It also helps to answer some basic improvement questions such as who should be in charge of it, when should it take place, and how one should go about ensuring that improvement really does impact the performance of the organization. This is why in this chapter we will deal with such issues as measuring performance, benchmarking, prioritization, learning and culture, and the role of systems of procedures in the implementation process.

Remember also that the issue of how improvement should be organized is not a new concern. It has been a concern of management writers for decades. For example, W.E. **Deming** (considered in Japan to be the father of quality control) asserted that quality starts with top management and is a strategic activity.[2] It is claimed that much of the success in terms of quality in Japanese industry was the result of his lectures to Japanese companies in the 1950s.[3] Deming's basic philosophy is that quality and productivity increase as 'process variability' (the unpredictability of the process) decreases. In his *14 points for quality improvement*, he emphasizes the need for statistical control methods, participation, education, openness and purposeful improvement:

1 Create constancy of purpose.
2 Adopt new philosophy.
3 Cease dependence on inspection.
4 End awarding business on price.
5 Improve constantly the system of production and service.
6 Institute training on the job.
7 Institute leadership.
8 Drive out fear.
9 Break down barriers between departments.
10 Eliminate slogans and exhortations.
11 Eliminate quotas or work standards.
12 Give people pride in their job.
13 Institute education and a self-improvement programme.
14 Put everyone to work to accomplish it.

Linking improvement to strategy

At one level, the objective of any improvement is obvious – it tries to make things better! But, does this mean better in every way or better in some specific manner? And how much better does better mean? This is why we need some more general framework to put any

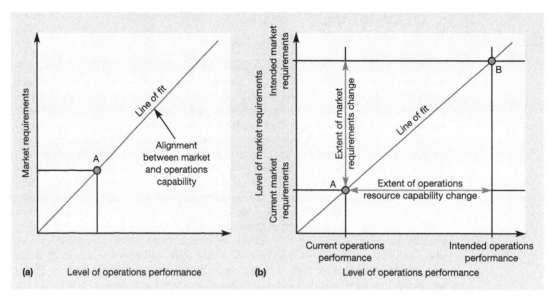

Figure 20.2 In operations improvement should achieve 'fit' between market requirements and operations performance

organization's improvement efforts into a broader context, preferably one that brings together an overall operation's performance with its market objectives. After all, at a strategic level, the whole purpose of operations improvement is to make operations performance better serve its markets. Figure 20.2(a) illustrates this idea by showing diagrammatically the approximate alignment or 'fit' between an operation's performance and the requirements of its markets.

The vertical dimension represents the level of market requirements either because they reflect the intrinsic needs of customers or because their expectations have been shaped by the firm's marketing activity. This includes such factors as the strength of brand and reputation, the degree of market differentiation and the extent of plausible market promises. Moving along this dimension indicates a broadly enhanced level of market performance. The horizontal scale represents the level of the organization's operations performance. This includes such things as its ability to achieve its competitive objectives and the efficiency with which it uses its resources. Again, moving along the dimension indicates a broadly enhanced level of operations performance and therefore operations capabilities. Be careful, however, in using this diagrammatic representation. It is a conceptual model rather than a practical tool. We have deliberately been vague in calibrating or even defining precisely the two axes in the figure. The model is intended merely to illustrate some ideas around the concept of strategic improvement.

In terms of the framework illustrated in Figure 20.2(a), improvement means three things.

1 *Achieving 'alignment'* – This means achieving an approximate balance between 'required market performance' and 'actual operations performance'. So when alignment is achieved a firm's customers do not need, or expect, levels of operations performance which it is unable to supply. Nor does the firm have operations strengths which are either in-appropriate for market needs or remain unexploited in the market. The diagonal line in Figure 20.2(a) therefore represents a '**line of fit**' with market and operations in balance.

Line of fit

2 *Achieving 'sustainable' alignment* – It is not enough to achieve some degree of alignment to a single point in time. It also has to be sustained over time. So, asking the question 'how good are our operations at delivering the performance which our market requires?' is necessary but not sufficient over the long term. Equally important questions are 'how

244

could the market change and make current performance inadequate?' and 'how can we develop our operations processes so that they could adapt to the new market conditions?'

3 *Improving overall performance* – If the requirements placed on the organization by its markets are relatively undemanding, then the corresponding level of operations performance will not need to be particularly high. While the more demanding the level of market requirements, the greater will have to be the level of operations performance. But most firms would see their overall strategic objectives as achieving alignment at a level that implies some degree of long-term competitive success. In Figure 20.2(b) point A represents alignment at a low level, while point B represents alignment at a higher level. The assumption in most firms' operations strategies is that point B is a more desirable position than point A because it is more likely to represent a financially successful position. High levels of market performance, achieved as a result of high levels of operations performance being generally more difficult for competitors to match.

Deviating from the line of fit

During the improvement path from A to B in Figure 20.2 it may not be possible to maintain the balance between market requirements and operations performance. Sometimes the market may expect something that the operation cannot (temporarily) deliver. Sometimes operations may have capabilities that cannot be exploited in the market. At a strategic level, there are risks deriving from any deviation from the 'line of fit'. For example, delays in the improvement to a new web site could mean that customers do not receive the level of service they were promised. This is shown as position X in Figure 20.3. Under these circumstances, the risk to the organization is that its reputation (or brand) will suffer because market expectations exceed the operation's capability to perform at the appropriate level. At other times, the operation may make improvements before they could be fully exploited in the market. For example, the same online retailer may have improved its web site so that it can offer extra services, such as the ability to customize products, before those products have been stocked in its distribution centre. This means that, although an improvement to its ordering processes has been made, problems elsewhere in the company prevent the improvement from giving value to the company. This is represented by point Y on Figure 20.3. In both instances, improvement activity needs to move the operation back to the line of fit.

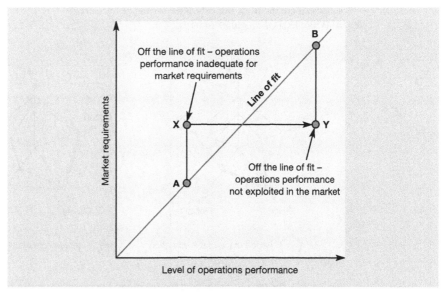

Figure 20.3 Deviation from the 'line of fit' between market requirements and operations performance can expose the operation to risk

Before operations managers can devise their approach to the improvement of their operations, they need to know how good they are already. The urgency, direction and priorities of improvement will be determined partly by whether the current performance of an operation is judged to be good, bad or indifferent. Therefore all operations need some kind of **performance measurement** as a prerequisite for improvement.

Performance measurement

Performance measurement

Performance measurement is the process of *quantifying action*, where measurement means the process of quantification and the performance of the operation is assumed to derive from actions taken by its management.[4] Performance here is defined as the degree to which an operation fulfils the five performance objectives at any point in time, in order to satisfy its customers. Some kind of *performance measurement* is a prerequisite for judging whether an operation is good, bad or indifferent. Without performance measurement, it would be impossible to exert any control over an operation on an ongoing basis. A performance measurement system that gives no help to ongoing improvement is only partially effective. The **polar diagrams** (which we introduced in Chapter 2) in Figure 20.4 illustrate this concept. The five performance objectives which we have used throughout this book can be regarded as the dimensions of overall performance that satisfy customers. The market's needs and expectations of each performance objective will vary. The extent to which an operation meets market requirements will also vary. In addition, market requirements and the operation's performance could change over time. In Figure 20.4 the operation is originally almost meeting the requirements of the market as far as quality and flexibility are concerned, but is under-performing on its speed, dependability and cost. Sometime later the operation has improved its speed and cost to match market requirements but its flexibility no longer matches market requirements, not because it has deteriorated in an absolute sense but because the requirements of the market have changed.

Polar diagram

Performance measurement, as we are treating it here, concerns three generic issues.

- What factors to include as performance measures?
- Which are the most important performance measures?
- What detailed measures to use?

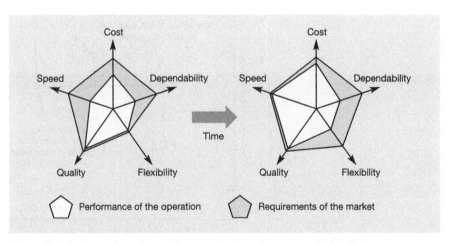

Figure 20.4 Customers' needs and the operation's performance might both change over time

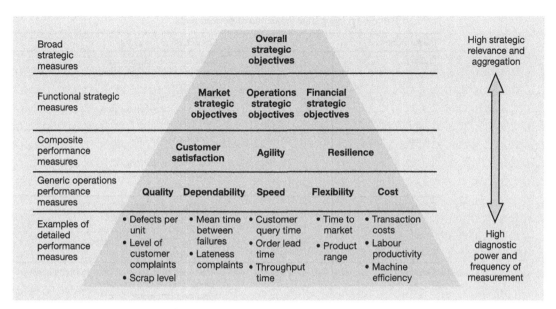

Figure 20.5 Performance measures can involve different levels of aggregation

What factors to include as performance measures?

The five generic performance objectives, quality, speed, dependability, flexibility and cost, can be broken down into more detailed measures, or they can be aggregated into 'composite' measures, such as 'customer satisfaction', 'overall service level', or 'operations agility'. These composite measures may be further aggregated by using measures such as 'achieve market objectives', 'achieve financial objectives', 'achieve operations objectives' or even 'achieve overall strategic objectives'. The more aggregated performance measures have greater strategic relevance insomuch as they help to draw a picture of the overall performance of the business, although by doing so they necessarily include many influences outside those that operations performance improvement would normally address. The more detailed performance measures are usually monitored more closely and more often, and although they provide a limited view of an operation's performance, they do provide a more descriptive and complete picture of what should be and what is happening within the operation. In practice, most organizations will choose to use performance targets from throughout the range. This idea is illustrated in Figure 20.5.

Choosing the important performance measures

One of the problems of devising a useful performance measurement system is trying to achieve some balance between having a few key measures on one hand (straightforward and simple, but may not reflect the full range of organizational objectives), and, on the other hand, having many detailed measures (complex and difficult to manage, but capable of conveying many nuances of performance). Broadly, a compromise is reached by making sure that there is a clear link between the operation's overall strategy, the most important (or 'key') **performance indicators** (KPIs) that reflect strategic objectives, and the bundle of detailed measures that are used to 'flesh out' each key performance indicator. Obviously, unless strategy is well defined then it is difficult to 'target' a narrow range of key performance indicators.

Key performance indicators

What detailed measures to use?

The five performance objectives – quality, speed, dependability, flexibility and cost – are really composites of many smaller measures. For example, an operation's cost is derived from many factors which could include the purchasing efficiency of the operation, the efficiency

247

Table 20.1 Some typical partial measures of performance

Performance objective	Some typical measures
Quality	Number of defects per unit Level of customer complaints Scrap level Warranty claims Mean time between failures Customer satisfaction score
Speed	Customer query time Order lead time Frequency of delivery Actual *versus* theoretical throughput time Cycle time
Dependability	Percentage of orders delivered late Average lateness of orders Proportion of products in stock Mean deviation from promised arrival Schedule adherence
Flexibility	Time needed to develop new products/services Range of products/services Machine changeover time Average batch size Time to increase activity rate Average capacity/maximum capacity Time to change schedules
Cost	Minimum delivery time/average delivery time Variance against budget Utilization of resources Labour productivity Added value Efficiency Cost per operation hour

with which it converts materials, the productivity of its staff, the ratio of direct to indirect staff, and so on. All of these measures individually give a partial view of the operation's cost performance, and many of them overlap in terms of the information they include. However, each of them does give a perspective on the cost performance of an operation that could be useful either to identify areas for improvement or to monitor the extent of improvement. If an organization regards its 'cost' performance as unsatisfactory, disaggregating it into 'purchasing efficiency', 'operations efficiency', 'staff productivity', etc. might explain the root cause of the poor performance. Table 20.1 shows some of the partial measures which can be used to judge an operation's performance.

The balanced scorecard approach

Generally operations performance measures have been broadening in their scope. It is now generally accepted that the scope of measurement should, at some level, include external as well as internal, long-term as well as short-term, and 'soft' as well as 'hard' measures. The best-known manifestation of this trend is the '**balanced scorecard**' approach taken by Kaplan and Norton.

The balanced scorecard approach brings together the elements that reflect a business's strategic position

> 'The balanced scorecard retains traditional financial measures. But financial measures tell the story of past events, an adequate story for industrial age companies for which investments in long-term capabilities are customer relationships were not critical for success. These financial measures are inadequate, however, for guiding and evaluating the journey that information age companies must make to create future value through investment in customers, suppliers, employees, processes, technology, and innovation.'[5]

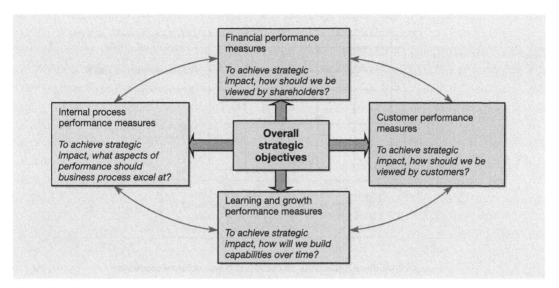

Figure 20.6 The measures used in the balanced scorecard

As well as including financial measures of performance, in the same way as traditional performance measurement systems, the balanced scorecard approach, also attempts to provide the important information that is required to allow the overall strategy of an organization to be reflected adequately in specific performance measures. In addition to financial measures of performance, it also includes more operational measures of customer satisfaction, internal processes, innovation and other improvement activities. In doing so it measures the factors behind financial performance which are seen as the key drivers of future financial success. In particular, it is argued that a balanced range of measures enables managers to address the following questions (see Figure 20.6).

- How do we look to our shareholders (financial perspective)?
- What must we excel at (internal process perspective)?
- How do our customers see us (the customer perspective)?
- How can we continue to improve and build capabilities (the learning and growth perspective)?

The balanced scorecard attempts to bring together the elements that reflect a business's strategic position, including product or service quality measures, product and service development times, customer complaints, labour productivity, and so on. At the same time it attempts to avoid performance reporting becoming unwieldy by restricting the number of measures and focusing especially on those seen to be essential. The advantages of the approach are that it presents an overall picture of the organization's performance in a single report, and by being comprehensive in the measures of performance it uses, encourages companies to take decisions in the interests of the whole organization rather than sub-optimizing around narrow measures. Developing a balanced scorecard is a complex process and is now the subject of considerable debate. One of the key questions that have to be considered is how specific measures of performance should be designed. Inadequately designed performance measures can result in dysfunctional behaviour, so teams of managers are often used to develop a scorecard which reflects their organization's specific needs.

Setting target performance

A performance measure means relatively little until it is compared against some kind of target. Knowing that only one document in five hundred is sent out to customers containing an error, tells us relatively little unless we know whether this is better or worse than we were

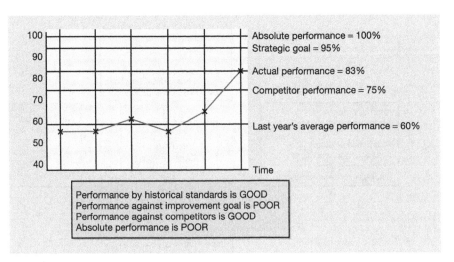

Figure 20.7 Different standards of comparison give different messages

achieving previously, and whether it is better or worse than other similar operations (especially competitors) are achieving. Setting performance targets transforms performance measures into performance 'judgements'. Several approaches to setting targets can be used, including the following.

- *Historically based targets* – targets that compare current against previous performance.
- *Strategic targets* – targets set to reflect the level of performance that is regarded as appropriate to achieve strategic objectives.
- *External performance-based targets* – targets set to reflect the performance that is achieved by similar, or competitor, external operations.
- *Absolute performance targets* – targets based on the theoretical upper limit of performance.

One of the problems in setting targets is that different targets can give very different messages regarding the improvement being achieved. So, for example, in Figure 20.7, one of an operation's performance measures is 'delivery' (in this case defined as the proportion of orders delivered on-time). The performance for one month has been measured at 83 per cent, but any judgement regarding performance will be dependent on the performance targets. Using a *historical* target, when compared to last year's performance of 60 per cent, this month's performance of 83 per cent is good. But, if the operation's *strategy* calls for a 95 per cent delivery performance, the actual performance of 83 per cent looks decidedly poor. The company may also be concerned with how they perform against *competitors'* performance. If competitors are currently averaging delivery performances of around 80 per cent the company's performance looks rather good. Finally, the more ambitious managers within the company may wish to at least try and seek perfection. Why not, they argue, use an *absolute* performance standard of 100 per cent delivery on time? Against this standard the company's actual 83 per cent again looks disappointing.

Performance measurement and performance management

It is worth noting the difference between performance *measurement*, which we describe here, and performance *management*. They are closely related (and sometimes are confused with each other). Performance management is broader than performance measurement. It is the 'process of assessing progress toward achieving predetermined goals. It involves building on that process, adding the relevant communication and action on the progress achieved against these predetermined goals. It helps organizations achieve their strategic goals'.[6] The objectives of performance management are to ensure coordination and coherence between individual, process or team objectives and overall strategic and organizational objectives. But more than that, performance management attempts to influence decisions, behaviours and skills development so that individuals and processes are better equipped to meet strategic objectives.

Benchmarking

Benchmarking, is 'the process of learning from others' and involves comparing one's own performance or methods against other comparable operations. It is a broader issue than setting performance targets, and includes investigating other organizations' operations practice in order to derive ideas that could contribute to performance improvement. Its rationale is based on the idea that (a) problems in managing processes are almost certainly shared by processes elsewhere, and (b) that there is probably another operation somewhere that has developed a better way of doing things. For example, a bank might learn some things from a supermarket about how it could cope with demand fluctuations during the day. **Benchmarking** is essentially about stimulating creativity in improvement practice.

Benchmarking is the process of learning from others

Types of benchmarking

There are many different types of benchmarking (which are not necessarily mutually exclusive), some of which are listed below:

- *Internal benchmarking* is a comparison between operations or parts of operations which are within the same total organization. For example, a large motor vehicle manufacturer with several factories might choose to benchmark each factory against the others.
- *External benchmarking* is a comparison between an operation and other operations which are part of a different organization.
- *Non-competitive benchmarking* is benchmarking against external organizations which do not compete directly in the same markets.
- *Competitive benchmarking* is a comparison directly between competitors in the same, or similar, markets.
- *Performance benchmarking* is a comparison between the levels of achieved performance in different operations. For example, an operation might compare its own performance in terms of some or all of our performance objectives – quality, speed, dependability, flexibility and cost – against other organizations' performance in the same dimensions.
- *Practice benchmarking* is a comparison between an organization's operations practices, or way of doing things, and those adopted by another operation. For example, a large retail store might compare its systems and procedures for controlling stock levels with those used by another department store.

Benchmarking as an improvement tool

Although benchmarking has become popular, some businesses have failed to derive maximum benefit from it. Partly this may be because there are some misunderstandings as to what benchmarking actually entails. First, it is not a 'one-off' project. It is best practised as a continuous process of comparison. Second, it does not provide 'solutions'. Rather, it provides ideas and information that can lead to solutions. Third, it does not involve simply copying or imitating other operations. It is a process of learning and adapting in a pragmatic manner. Fourth, it means devoting resources to the activity. Benchmarking cannot be done without some investment, but this does not necessarily mean allocating exclusive responsibility to a set of highly paid managers. In fact, there can be advantages in organizing staff at all levels to investigate and collate information from benchmarking targets.

It can be argued that there is a fundamental flaw in the whole concept of benchmarking. Operations that rely on others to stimulate their creativity, especially those that are in search of 'best practice', are always limiting themselves to currently accepted methods of operating or currently accepted limits to performance. In other words, benchmarking leads companies only as far as others have gone. 'Best practice' is not 'best' in the sense that it cannot be bettered, it is only 'best' in the sense that it is the best one can currently find. Indeed accepting what is currently defined as 'best' may prevent operations from ever making the radical breakthrough or improvement that takes the concept of 'best' to a new and fundamentally improved level. This argument is closely related to the concept of breakthrough improvement discussed later in this chapter. Furthermore, methods or performance levels that are appropriate in one operation may not be in another. Because one operation has a set of successful practices in the way it manages its process does not mean that adopting those same practices in another context will prove equally successful. It is possible that subtle differences in the resources within a process (such as staff skills or technical capabilities) or the strategic context of an operation (for example, the relative priorities of performance objectives) will be sufficiently different to make the adoption of seemingly successful practices inappropriate.

Improvement priorities – what to start on?[7]

Improvement priorities

In Chapter 3, when discussing the 'market requirements' perspective, we identified two major influences on the way in which operations decide on their **improvement priorities**:

- the needs and preferences of customers;
- the performance and activities of competitors.

The consideration of customers' needs has particular significance in shaping the objectives of all operations. The fundamental purpose of operations is to create goods and services in such a way as to meet the needs of their customers. What customers find important, therefore, the operation should also regard as important. If customers for a particular product or service prefer low prices to wide range, then the operation should devote more energy to reducing its costs than to increasing the flexibility which enables it to provide a range of products or services. The needs and preferences of customers shape the *importance* of operations objectives within the operation.

The role of competitors is different from that of customers. Competitors are the points of comparison against which the operation can judge its performance. From a competitive viewpoint, as operations improve their performance, the improvement which matters most is that which takes the operation past the performance levels achieved by its competitors. The role of competitors then is in determining achieved *performance*.

Both importance and performance have to be brought together before any judgement can be made as to the relative priorities for improvement. Just because something is particularly important to its customers does not mean that an operation should necessarily give it immediate priority for improvement. It may be that the operation is already considerably better than its competitors at serving customers in this respect. Similarly, just because an operation is not very good at something when compared with its competitors' performance, it does not necessarily mean that it should be immediately improved. Customers may not particularly value this aspect of performance. Both importance and performance need to be viewed together to judge the prioritization of objectives.

(a) Importance scale for competitive factors		(b) Performance scale for competitive factors	
Rating	**Description**	**Rating**	**Description**
1	Provides a crucial advantage	1	Considerably better than competitors
2	Provides an important advantage	2	Clearly better than competitors
3	Provides a useful advantage	3	Marginally better than competitors
4	Needs to be up to good industry standards	4	Sometimes marginally better than competitors
5	Needs to be up to median industry standards	5	About the same as most competitors
6	Needs to be within close range of rest of industry	6	Slightly worse than the average of most competitors
7	Not usually important but could become so	7	Usually marginally worse than most competitors
8	Very rarely considered by customers	8	Generally worse than most competitors
9	Never considered by customers	9	Consistently worse than competitors

Figure 20.8 Nine-point scales for judging importance and performance

Judging importance to customers

Order winners
Qualifiers
Less important

In Chapter 3 we introduced the idea of **order-winning, qualifying** and **less important** competitive factors. *Order-winning competitive factors* are those which directly win business for the operation. *Qualifying competitive factors* are those which may not win extra business if the operation improves its performance, but can certainly lose business if performance falls below a particular point, known as the qualifying level. *Less important competitive factors*, as their name implies, are those which are relatively unimportant compared with the others. In fact, to judge the relative importance of its competitive factors, an operation will usually need to use a slightly more discriminating scale. One way to do this is to take our three broad categories of competitive factors – order-winning, qualifying and less important – and to divide each category into three further points representing strong, medium and weak positions. Figure 20.8(a) illustrates such a scale.

Judging performance against competitors

At its simplest, a competitive performance standard would consist merely of judging whether the achieved performance of an operation is better than, the same, or worse than that of its competitors. However, in much the same way as the nine-point importance scale was derived, we can derive a more discriminating nine-point performance scale, as shown in Figure 20.8(b).

The importance–performance matrix

Importance–performance
matrix

The priority for improvement which each competitive factor should be given can be assessed from a comparison of their importance and performance. This can be shown on an **importance–performance matrix** which, as its name implies, positions each competitive

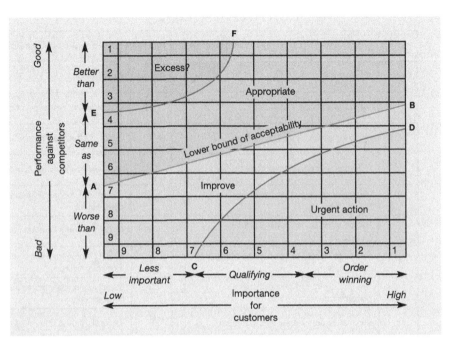

Figure 20.9 Priority zones in the importance–performance matrix

factor according to its scores or ratings on these criteria. Figure 20.9 shows an importance–performance matrix divided into zones of improvement priority. The first zone boundary is the 'lower bound of acceptability' shown as line AB in Figure 20.9. This is the boundary between acceptable and unacceptable performance. When a competitive factor is rated as relatively unimportant (8 or 9 on the importance scale), this boundary will in practice be low. Most operations are prepared to tolerate performance levels which are 'in the same ballpark' as their competitors (even at the bottom end of the rating) for unimportant competitive factors. They only become concerned when performance levels are clearly below those of their competitors. Conversely, when judging competitive factors which are rated highly (1 or 2 on the importance scale) they will be markedly less sanguine at poor or mediocre levels of performance. Minimum levels of acceptability for these competitive factors will usually be at the lower end of the 'better than competitors' class. Below this minimum bound of acceptability (AB) there is clearly a need for improvement; above this line there is no immediate urgency for any improvement. However, not all competitive factors falling below the minimum line will be seen as having the same degree of improvement priority. A boundary approximately represented by line CD represents a distinction between an urgent priority zone and a less urgent improvement zone. Similarly, above the line AB, not all competitive factors are regarded as having the same priority. The line EF can be seen as the approximate boundary between performance levels which are regarded as 'good' or 'appropriate' on one hand and those regarded as 'too good' or 'excess' on the other. Segregating the matrix in this way results in four zones which imply very different priorities:

● *The 'appropriate' zone* – competitive factors in this area lie above the lower bound of acceptability and so should be considered satisfactory.
● *The 'improve' zone* – lying below the lower bound of acceptability, any factors in this zone must be candidates for improvement.
● *The 'urgent-action' zone* – these factors are important to customers but performance is below that of competitors. They must be considered as candidates for immediate improvement.

- *The 'excess?' zone* – factors in this area are 'high-performing', but not important to customers. The question must be asked, therefore, whether the resources devoted to achieving such a performance could be used better elsewhere.

EXL Laboratories is a subsidiary of an electronics company. It carries out research and development as well as technical problem-solving work for a wide range of companies, including companies in its own group. It is particularly keen to improve the level of service which it gives to its customers. However, it needs to decide which aspect of its performance to improve first. It has devised a list of the most important aspects of its service:

- *The quality of its technical solutions* – the perceived appropriateness by customers.
- *The quality of its communications with customers* – the frequency and usefulness of information.
- *The quality of post-project documentation* – the usefulness of the documentation which goes with the final report.
- *Delivery speed* – the time between customer request and the delivery of the final report.
- *Delivery dependability* – the ability to deliver on the promised date.
- *Delivery flexibility* – the ability to deliver the report on a revised date.
- *Specification flexibility* – the ability to change the nature of the investigation.
- *Price* – the total charge to the customer.

EXL assigns a score to each of these factors using the 1–9 scale described in Figure 20.8. After this, EXL turned their attention to judging the laboratory's performance against competitor organizations. Although they have benchmarked information for some aspects of performance, they have to make estimates for the others. Both these scores are shown in Figure 20.10.

EXL Laboratories plotted the importance and performance ratings it had given to each of its competitive factors on an importance–performance matrix. This is shown in Figure 20.11. It shows that the most important aspect of competitiveness – the ability to deliver sound technical solutions to its customers – falls comfortably within the appropriate zone. Specification flexibility and delivery flexibility are also in the appropriate zone, although only just. Both delivery speed and delivery dependability seem to be in

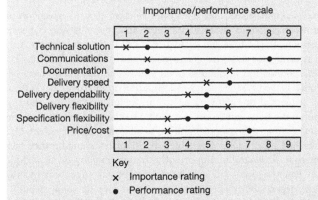

Figure 20.10 Rating 'importance to customers' and 'performance against competitors' on the nine-point scales for EXL Laboratories

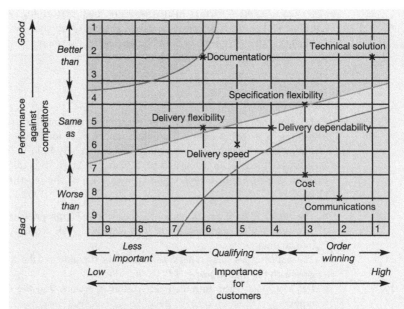

Figure 20.11 The importance–performance matrix for EXL Laboratories

need of improvement as each is below the minimum level of acceptability for their respective importance positions. However, two competitive factors, communications and cost/price, are clearly in need of immediate improvement. These two factors should therefore be assigned the most urgent priority for improvement. The matrix also indicates that the company's documentation could almost be regarded as 'too good'.

The matrix may not reveal any total surprises. The competitive factors in the 'urgent-action' zone may be known to be in need of improvement already. However, the exercise is useful for two reasons:

- It helps to discriminate between many factors which may be in need of improvement.
- The exercise gives purpose and structure to the debate on improvement priorities.

The sandcone theory

As well as approaches that base improvement priority given on an operation's specific circumstances, some authorities believe that there is also a generic 'best' sequence of improvement. The best-known theory is called *the sandcone theory*,[8] so called because the sand is analogous to management effort and resources. Building a stable **sandcone** needs a stable foundation of quality, upon which one can build layers of dependability, speed, flexibility and cost, see Figure 20.12. Building up improvement is thus a cumulative process, not a sequential one. Moving on to the second priority for improvement does not mean dropping the first, and so on. According to the sandcone theory: the first priority should be *quality*, since this is a precondition to all lasting improvement. Only when the operation has reached a minimally acceptable level in quality should it then tackle the next issue, that of internal *dependability*. Importantly though, moving on to include dependability in the improvement process will actually require further improvement in quality. Once a critical level of dependability is reached, enough to provide some stability to the operation, the next stage is to improve the *speed* of internal throughput. But again only while continuing to improve quality and dependability further. Soon it will become evident that the most effective way to improve speed is through improvements in response *flexibility*, that is,

The sandcone theory holds that objectives should be prioritized in a particular order

256

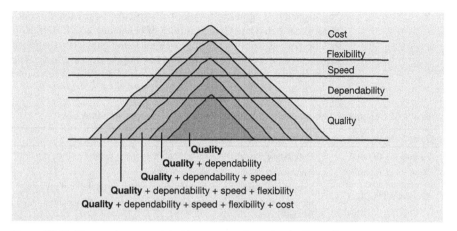

Figure 20.12 The sandcone model of improvement: cost reduction relies on a cumulative foundation of improvement in the other performance objectives

changing things within the operation faster. Again, including flexibility in the improvement process should not divert attention from continuing to work further on quality, dependability and speed. Only now, according to the sandcone theory, should *cost* be tackled head-on.

Improvement culture

Culture is the pattern of shared assumption

It is generally held by most organizational theorists that an organization's ability to improve its operations performance depends to a large extent on its '**culture**'. By 'organizational culture' we here mean '*the pattern of shared basic assumptions ... that have worked well enough to be considered valid*',[9] or as some put it, '*the way we do things around here*'. Professor Gerry Johnson[10] is more specific, describing the elements of organizational culture as follows.

- The organization's mission and values
- Its control systems
- Its organizational structures, hierarchies, and processes
- Its power structures
- Its symbols, logos and designs including its symbols of power
- Its rituals, meetings and routines
- Its stories and myths that develop about people and events.

So, organizational culture and improvement are clearly related. A receptive organizational culture that encourages a constant search for improved ways to do things nurtures improvement. At the same time the organization's view of improvement is an important indication of its culture. But what is meant by 'an improvement culture'? Here we look at two aspects, first are the various elements that make up an improvement culture, second is the recurring theme of 'learning' as a key element of improvement culture.

Building an improvement capability

The ability to improve, especially on a continuous basis, is not something which always comes naturally to operations managers and staff. There are specific abilities, behaviours and actions which need to be consciously developed if improvement is to be sustained over the long term. Bessant and Caffyn[11] distinguish between what they call 'organizational abilities' (the capacity or aptitude to adopt a particular approach to continuous improvement), 'constituent behaviours' (the routines of behaviour which staff adopt and which reinforce the approach to continuous improvement) and 'enablers' (the procedural devices or techniques used to progress the continuous improvement effort). They identify six generic organizational abilities, each with its own set of constituent behaviours. These are identified

Table 20.2 Continuous improvement (CI) abilities and some associated behaviours

Organizational ability	Constituent behaviours
Getting the CI habit Developing the ability to generate sustained involvement in CI	People use formal problem-finding and solving cycle
	People use simple tools and techniques
	People use simple measurement to shape the improvement process
	Individuals and/or groups initiate and carry through CI activities – they participate in the process
	Ideas are responded to in a timely fashion – either implemented or otherwise dealt with
	Managers support the CI process through allocation of resources
	Managers recognize in formal ways the contribution of employees to CI
	Managers lead by example, becoming actively involved in design and implementation of CI
	Managers support experiment by not punishing mistakes, but instead encouraging learning from them
Focusing on CI Generating and sustaining the ability to link CI activities to the strategic goals of the company	Individuals and groups use the organization's strategic objectives to prioritize improvements
	Everyone is able to explain what the operation's strategy and objectives are
	Individuals and groups assess their proposed changes against the operation's objectives
	Individuals and groups monitor/measure the results of their improvement activity CI activities are an integral part of the individual's or group's work, not a parallel activity
Spreading the word Generating the ability to move CI activity across organizational boundaries	People cooperate in cross-functional groups
	People understand and share a holistic view (process understanding and ownership)
	People are oriented towards internal and external customers in their CI activity
	Specific CI projects with outside agencies (customers, suppliers, etc.) take place
	Relevant CI activities involve representatives from different organizational levels
CI on the CI system Generating the ability to manage strategically the development of CI	The CI system is continually monitored and developed
	There is a cyclical planning process whereby the CI system is regularly reviewed and amended
	There is periodic review of the CI system in relation to the organization as a whole
	Senior management make available sufficient resources (time, money, personnel) to support the continuing development of the CI system
	The CI system itself is designed to fit within the current structure and infrastructure
	When a major organizational change is planned, its potential impact on the CI system is assessed
Walking the talk Generating the ability to articulate and demonstrate CI's values	The 'management style' reflects commitment to CI values
	When something goes wrong, people at all levels look for reasons why, rather than blame individuals
	People at all levels demonstrate a shared belief in the value of small steps and that everyone can contribute, by themselves being actively involved in making and recognizing incremental improvements
Building the learning organization Generating the ability to learn through CI activity	Everyone learns from their experiences, both good and bad
	Individuals seeks out opportunities for learning/personal development
	Individuals and groups at all levels share their learning
	The organization captures and shares the learning of individuals and groups
	Managers accept and act on all the learning that takes place
	Organizational mechanisms are used to deploy what has been learned across the organization

in Table 20.2. Examples of enablers are the improvement techniques that were described in Chapter 18.

Improvement as learning

Note that many of the abilities and behaviours describes in Table 20.2 are directly or indirectly related to learning in some way. This is not surprising given that operations improvement implies some kind of intervention or change to the operation, and change will be evaluated in terms of whatever improvement occurs. This evaluation adds to our knowledge of how the operation really works, which in turn increases the chances that future interventions will also result in improvement. This idea of an improvement cycle was discussed in Chapter 18. What is important is to realize that it is a learning process, and it is crucial that improvement is organized so that it encourages, facilitates and exploits the learning that occurs during improvement. This requires us to recognize that there is a distinction between single- and double-loop learning.[12]

Single- and double-loop learning

Single-loop learning

Single-loop learning occurs when there is a repetitive and predictable link between cause and effect. Statistical process control (see Chapter 17), for example, measures output characteristics from a process, such as product weight, telephone response time, etc. These can then be used to alter input conditions, such as supplier quality, manufacturing consistency, staff training, with the intention of 'improving' the output. Every time an operational error or problem is detected, it is corrected or solved, and more is learned about the process. However, this happens without questioning or altering the underlying values and objectives of the process, which may, over time, create an unquestioning inertia that prevents it adapting to a changing

Double-loop learning

environment. **Double-loop learning**, by contrast, questions the fundamental objectives or service or even the underlying culture of the operation. This kind of learning implies an ability to challenge existing operating assumptions in a fundamental way. It seeks to re-frame competitive assumptions and remain open to any changes in the competitive environment. But being receptive to new opportunities sometimes requires abandoning existing operating routines which may be difficult to achieve in practice, especially as many operations reward experience and past achievement (rather than potential) at both an individual and a group level. Figure 20.13 illustrates single and double-loop learning.

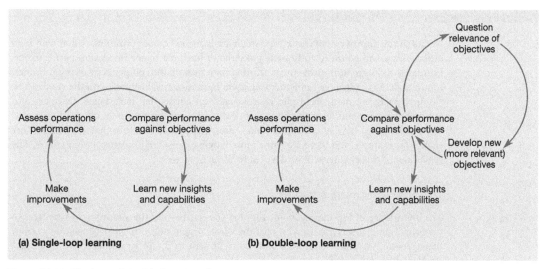

Figure 20.13 Single- and double-loop learning

Improvement at Heineken – Part II[13]

The improvement approach of Heineken's Zoeterwoude facility was described in Chapter 18. Although this description emphasized issues such as target setting and the use of techniques, of equal or more importance in making a success of the initiative was the way improvement teams were empowered, organized and motivated. In fact, before this improvement initiative, the company had started a 'cultural change' programme. *'Its aim'*, according to Wilbert Raaijmakers, the Brewery Director, *'was to move away from a command-and-control situation and evolve towards a more team-oriented organization.'* Fundamental to this was a programme to improve the skills and knowledge of individual operators through special training programmes. Nevertheless, the improvement initiative exposed a number of challenges. For example, the improvement team discovered that it was easier to motivate people to work on improvements when the demand on the plant clearly exceeded its capacity. What was more difficult was to keep them focused when the pressures of keeping up production levels were lower, such as during the winter season. In an attempt to overcome this, communication was improved so that staff were kept fully informed of future production levels and the upcoming schedule of training and maintenance activities that were planned during

slumps in demand. The lesson that the improvement team learnt was that it is difficult to convince people of the necessity for change if they are not aware of the underlying reason for it. Notwithstanding these efforts it soon became evident that some groups were more ready to make changes than others. Some staff much preferred to stick with their traditional methods rather than explore how these could be improved. Similarly, some team leaders were more skilled at encouraging change than others. Many staff needed coaching and reassurance as well as more formal training on how to take ownership of problems and focus on achieving results in line with targets. Also, it was found that setting improvement targets in a step-by-step series of milestones could help to maintain the momentum of motivation.

During the improvement initiative, Heineken staff worked closely with a group of consultants (Celerant Consulting). Towards the end of the initiative, as is common in such improvement projects, the consultants gradually reduced their involvement to allow Heineken staff to take over control of the initiative. At this point there was a dip in the momentum of the improvement project. It needed the appointment of a special coordinator within the company to 'monitor, secure and audit' the various activities included in the project before it regained its momentum. Yet it did regain its momentum and, looking back over the experience, Heineken see one of the most significant outcomes from the initiative as its success in bringing home to every person in the company the realization that improvement is an ongoing process.

Implementing improvement

Not all of the improvement initiatives which are launched by organizations, often with high expectations, will go on to fulfil their potential of having a major impact on performance. Estimates of failure in improvement efforts range from half to 80 per cent of programmes, resulting in the companies implementing them becoming disillusioned with the results. Yet, although there are many examples of improvement efforts that have failed, there are also examples of successful implementations. So why do some improvement efforts disappoint? Some reasons we have already identified – an organizational culture that discourages any change for example. But there are some more tangible causes of implementation failure. The remainder of this chapter will be devoted to some of these.

Top-management support

Top-management support

The importance of **top-management support** goes far beyond the allocation of resources to the programme; it sets the priorities for the whole organization. If the organization's senior managers do not understand and show commitment to the programme, it is only understandable that others will ask why they should do so. Usually this is taken to mean that top management must:

- understand and believe in the benefits of the improvement approach
- communicate the principles and techniques of improvement
- participate in the improvement process
- formulate and maintain a clear 'improvement strategy'.

This last point is particularly important. Without thinking through the overall purpose and long-term goals of improvement it is difficult for any organization to know where it is going. An improvement strategy is necessary to provide the goals and guidelines which help to keep improvement efforts in line with strategic aims. Specifically, the improvement strategy should have something to say about the competitive priorities of the organization, the roles and improvement responsibilities of all parts of the organization, the resources available for improvement, and its overall improvement philosophy.

Senior managers may not fully understand the improvement approach

In Chapter 18, we described how there were several (related) improvement approaches. Each of these approaches is the subject of several books that describe them in great detail. There is no shortage of advice from consultants and academics as to how they should be used. Yet it is not difficult to find examples of where senior management have used one or more of these approaches without fully understanding them. The details of Six Sigma or lean, for example, are not simply technical matters. They are fundamental to how appropriate the approach could be in different contexts. Not every approach fits every set of circumstances. So understanding in detail what each approach means must be the first step in deciding whether it is appropriate.

Avoid excessive 'hype'

Operations improvement has, to some extent, become a fashion industry with new ideas and concepts continually being introduced as offering a novel way to improve business performance. There is nothing intrinsically wrong with this. Fashion stimulates and refreshes, through introducing novel ideas. Without it, things would stagnate. The problem lies not with new improvement ideas, but rather with some managers becoming victims of the process, where some new idea will entirely displace whatever went before. Most new ideas have something to say, but jumping from one fad to another will not only generate a backlash against any new idea, but also destroy the ability to accumulate the experience that comes from experimenting with each one. Avoiding becoming an improvement fashion victim is not easy. It requires that those directing the strategy process take responsibility for a number of issues.

(a) They must take responsibility for improvement as an ongoing activity, rather than becoming champions for only one specific improvement initiative.
(b) They must take responsibility for understanding the underlying ideas behind each new concept. Improvement is not 'following a recipe' or 'painting by numbers'. Unless one understands *why* improvement ideas are supposed to work, it is difficult to understand *how* they can be made to work properly.
(c) They must take responsibility for understanding the antecedents to a 'new' improvement idea, because it helps to understand it better and to judge how appropriate it may be for one's own operation.
(d) They must be prepared to adapt new ideas so that they make sense within the context of their own operation. 'One size' rarely fits all.
(e) They must take responsibility for the (often significant) education and learning effort that will be needed if new ideas are to be intelligently exploited.
(f) Above all they must avoid the over-exaggeration and hype that many new ideas attract. Although it is sometimes tempting to exploit the motivational 'pull' of new ideas

through slogans, posters and exhortations, carefully thought-out plans will always be superior in the long run, and will help avoid the inevitable backlash that follows 'over-selling' a single approach.

Short case
Work-Out at GE[14]

The idea of including all staff in the process of improvement has formed the core of many improvement approaches. One of the best-known ways of this is the 'Work-Out' approach that originated in the US conglomerate GE. Jack Welch, the then boss of GE, reputedly developed the approach to recognize that employees were an important source of brainpower for new and creative ideas, and as a mechanism for *'creating an environment that pushes towards a relentless, endless companywide search for a better way to do everything we do'*. The Work-Out programme was seen as a way to reduce the bureaucracy often associated with improvement and *'giving every employee, from managers to factory workers, an opportunity to influence and improve GE's day-to-day operations'*. According to Welch, Work-Out was meant to help people stop *'wrestling with the boundaries, the absurdities that grow in large organizations. We're all familiar with those absurdities: too many approvals, duplication, pomposity, waste. Work-Out in essence turned the company upside down, so that the workers told the bosses what to do. That forever changed the way people behaved at the company. Work-Out is also designed to reduce, and ultimately eliminate all of the waste hours and energy that organizations like GE typically expend in performing day-to-day operations.'* GE also used what it called 'town meetings' of employees. And although proponents of Work-Out emphasize the need to modify the specifics of the approach to fit the context in which it is applied, there is a broad sequence of activities implied within the approach:

- Staff, other key stakeholders and their manager hold a meeting away from the operation (a so-called 'off-siter').
- At this meeting the manager gives the group the responsibility to solve a problem or set of problems shared by the group but which are ultimately the manager's responsibility.
- The manager then leaves and the group spend time (maybe two or three days) working on developing

solutions to the problems, sometimes using outside facilitators.

- At the end of the meeting, the responsible manager (and sometimes the manager's boss) rejoins the group to be presented with its recommendations.
- The manager can respond in three ways to each recommendation; 'yes', 'no' or 'I have to consider it more'. If it is the last response the manager must clarify what further issues must be considered and how and when the decision will be made.

Work-Out programmes are expensive; outside facilitators, off-site facilities and the payroll costs of a sizeable group of people meeting away from work can be substantial, even without considering the potential disruption to everyday activities. But arguably the most important implications of adopting Work-Out are cultural. In its purest form Work-Out reinforces an underlying culture of fast (and some would claim, superficial) problem-solving. It also relies on full and near universal employee involvement and empowerment together with direct dialogue between managers and their subordinates. What distinguishes the Work-Out approach from the many other types of group-based problem-solving is fast decision-making and the idea that managers must respond immediately and decisively to team suggestions. But some claim that it is intolerant of staff and managers who are not committed to its values. In fact, it is acknowledged in GE that resistance to the process or outcome is not tolerated and that obstructing the efforts of the Work-Out process is 'a career-limiting move'.

Improvement or quality awards

Deming Prize
Malcolm Baldrige
National Quality Award
European Quality Award

Various bodies have sought to stimulate improvement through establishing improvement (sometimes called 'quality') awards. The three best-known awards are the **Deming Prize**, the **Malcolm Baldrige National Quality Award** and the **European Quality Award**.

The Deming Prize

The Deming Prize was instituted by the Union of Japanese Scientists and Engineers in 1951 and is awarded to those companies, initially in Japan, but more recently opened to overseas companies, which have successfully applied 'company-wide quality control' based upon statistical quality control. There are 10 major assessment categories: policy and objectives, organization and its operation, education and its extension, assembling and disseminating of information, analysis, standardization, control, quality assurance, effects and future plans. The applicants are required to submit a detailed description of quality practices. This is a significant activity in itself and some companies claim a great deal of benefit from having done so.

The Malcolm Baldrige National Quality Award

In the early 1980s the American Productivity and Quality Center recommended that an annual prize, similar to the Deming Prize, should be awarded in America. The purpose of the awards was to stimulate American companies to improve quality and productivity, to recognize achievements, to establish criteria for a wider quality effort and to provide guidance on quality improvement. The main examination categories are: leadership, information and analysis, strategic quality planning, human resource utilization, quality assurance of products and services, quality results and customer satisfaction. The process, like that of the Deming Prize, includes a detailed application and site visits.

The EFQM Excellence Model

The EFQM Excellence Model, or Business Excellence Model

In 1988, 14 leading Western European companies formed the European Foundation for Quality Management (EFQM). An important objective of the EFQM is to recognize quality achievement. Because of this, it launched the European Quality Award (EQA), awarded to the most successful exponent of total quality management in Europe each year. To receive a prize, companies must demonstrate that their approach to total quality management has contributed significantly to satisfying the expectations of customers, employees and others with an interest in the company for the past few years. In 1999, the model on which the European Quality Award was based was modified and renamed **The EFQM Excellence Model or Business Excellence Model**. The changes made were not fundamental but did attempt to reflect some new areas of management and quality thinking (for example, partnerships and innovation) and placed more emphasis on customer and market focus. It is based on the idea that the outcomes of quality management in terms of what it calls 'people results', 'customer results', 'society results' and 'key performance results' are achieved through a number of 'enablers'. These enablers are leadership and constancy of purpose, policy and strategy, how the organization develops its people, partnerships and resources, and the way it organizes its processes. These ideas are incorporated in the EFQM Excellence Model as shown in Figure 20.14. The five enablers are concerned with how results are being achieved, while the four 'results' are concerned with what the company has achieved and is achieving.

Self-assessment

Self-assessment

The European Foundation for Quality Management (EFQM) defines **self-assessment** as *'a comprehensive, systematic, and regular review of an organization's activities and results referenced against a model of business excellence'*, in its case the model shown in Figure 20.14. The main advantage of using such models for self-assessment seems to be that companies find it easier to understand some of the more philosophical concepts of TQM when they are translated into specific areas, questions and percentages. Self-assessment also allows organizations to measure their progress in changing their organization and in achieving the benefits of TQM. An important aspect of self-assessment is an organization's ability to judge the relative importance of the assessment categories to its own circumstances. The EFQM Excellence Model originally placed emphasis on a generic set of weighting for each of its nine categories. With the increasing importance of self-assessment, the EFQM moved to encourage organizations using its model to allocate their own weightings in a rational and systematic manner.

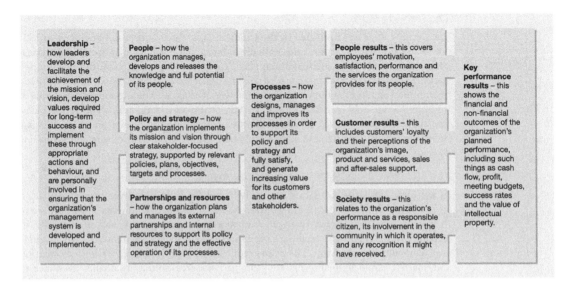

Figure 20.14 The EFQM Excellence Model

Summary answers to key questions

Check and improve your understanding of this chapter using self assessment questions and a personalised study plan, audio and video downloads, and an eBook – all at www.myomlab.com.

➤ Why does improvement need organizing?

▪ Improvement does not just happen by itself. It needs organizing, information must be gathered so that improvement is treating the most appropriate issues, responsibility for looking after the improvement effort must be allocated, and resources must be allocated. It must also be linked to the organization's overall strategy. Without these decisions, it is unlikely that real improvement will take place.

➤ How should the improvement effort be linked to strategy?

▪ At a strategic level, the whole purpose of operations improvement is to make operations performance better serve its markets. Therefore there should be approximate alignment or 'fit' between an operation's performance and the requirements of its markets. In fact, improvement should do three things to achieve this:

1 It should achieve an approximate balance between 'required market performance' and 'actual operations performance'.

2 It should make this alignment 'sustainable' over time.

3 It should 'move up' the line of fit, the assumption being that high levels of market performance, achieved as a result of high levels of operations performance are difficult for competitors to match.

➤ What information is needed for improvement?

- It is unlikely that for any operation a single measure of performance will adequately reflect the whole of a performance objective. Usually operations have to collect a whole bundle of partial measures of performance.
- Each partial measure then has to be compared against some performance standard. There are four types of performance standard commonly used:
  - historical standards, which compare performance now against performance sometime in the past;
  - target performance standards, which compare current performance against some desired level of performance;
  - competitor performance standards, which compare current performance against competitors' performance;
  - absolute performance standards, which compare current performance against its theoretically perfect state.
- The process of benchmarking is often used as a means of obtaining competitor performance standards.

➤ What should be improvement priorities?

- Improvement priorities can be determined by bringing together the relative importance of each performance objective or competitive factor as judged by customers, with the performance which the operation achieves as compared with its competition. This idea can be consolidated on an 'importance–performance matrix'.
- The 'sandcone model' provides an alternative approach to prioritization. It recommends that improvement should cumulatively emphasize quality, dependability, speed, flexibility, and then cost.

➤ How can organizational culture affect improvement?

- An organization's ability to improve its operations performance depends to a large extent on its 'culture', that is *the pattern of shared basic assumptions . . . that have worked well enough to be considered valid*. A receptive organizational culture that encourages a constant search for improved ways to do things can encourage improvement.
- According to Bessant and Caffyn there are specific abilities, behaviours and actions which need to be consciously developed if improvement is to sustain over the long term.
- Many of the abilities and behaviours related to an improvement culture relate to learning in some way. The learning process is important because it encourages, facilitates and exploits the learning that occurs during improvement. This involves two types of learning, single- and double-loop learning.
  - Single-loop learning occurs when there is repetitive and predictable link between cause and effect.
  - Double-loop learning questions the fundamental objectives, service or even the underlying culture of the operation.

- Improvement efforts often fail (estimates range from half to 80 per cent of programmes failing). Included in the reasons for this are the following.
  - Top-management support may be lacking
  - Senior managers may not fully understand the improvement approach
  - The improvement may be 'hyped up' excessively, leading to unrealistic (and therefore unrealized) expectations
  - Implementation problems may not be anticipated.
- ISO 9000 and its associated family of standards may be used to provide a structure around improvement implementation. They are concerned with the processes and procedures that support quality.
- So-called 'quality awards' and models may contribute towards implementation of improvement by providing a focused structure for organizations to assess their improvement efforts. The best known of these is probably the EFQM (Business Excellence Model). This is based on a nine-point model which distinguishes between the 'enablers' of quality and the 'results' of quality. It is often now used as a self-certification model.

Case study
Re-inventing Singapore's libraries[15]

By Professors Robert Johnston, Warwick Business School, Chai Kah Hin and Jochen Wirtz, National University of Singapore, and Christopher Lovelock, Yale University.

The National Library Board (NLB) in Singapore oversees the management of the national, reference, regional, community and children's libraries, as well as over 30 libraries belonging to government agencies, schools and private institutions. Over the last 15 years the NLB has completely changed the nature of libraries in Singapore and its work has been used as a blueprint for many other libraries across the world. Yet it was not always like this. In 1995 libraries in Singapore were traditional, quiet places full of old books where you went to study or borrow books if you could not afford to buy them. There were long queues to have books stamped or returned and the staff seemed unhelpful and unfriendly. But today, things are very different. There are cafés in libraries to encourage people to come in, browse and sit down with a book, and libraries in community centres (putting libraries where the people are). The NLB has developed specialist libraries aimed at children, libraries in shopping malls aimed at attracting busy 18–35-year-olds into the library while they are shopping. There are libraries dedicated to teenagers, one of the most difficult groups to entice into the library. These have

Source: National Library Board Singapore

even been designed by the teenagers themselves so they include drinks machines, cushions and music systems. The library also hosts a wide range of events from mother and baby reading sessions to rock concerts to encourage a wide range of people into the library.

'We started this journey back in 1995 when Dr Christopher Chia was appointed as Chief Executive. Looking back, we were a very traditional public service. Our customers used words like "cold" and "unfriendly", though, in fairness, our staff were working under great pressure to deal with the long queues for books and to answer enquiries on library materials posed by our customers. Christopher Chia and his team made a study of the problems, undertook surveys and ran focus groups. They then began to address the challenges with vision and imagination through the application of the project management methodology and the innovative use of technology. Staff involvement and contribution was key to the success of the transformation. We knew where we wanted to go, and were committed to the cause.' (Ms Ngian Lek Choh, the Deputy Chief Executive and Director of the National Library)

Underpinning many of the changes was the NLB's innovative use of technology. It was the first public library in the world to prototype radio-frequency identification (RFID) to create its Electronic Library Management System (ELiMS). RFID is an electronic system for automatically identifying items. It uses RFID tags, or transponders, which are contained in smart labels consisting of a silicon chip and coiled antenna. They receive and respond to radio-frequency queries from an RFID transceiver, which enables the remote and automatic retrieval, storing and sharing of information (see Chapter 8). RFID tags are installed in its 10 million books making it one of the largest users of the technology in the world. Customers spend very little time queuing, with book issuing and returns automated. Indeed books can be returned to any of the NLB's 24-hour book drops (which look a bit like ATM machines) where RFID enables not only fast and easy returns but also fast and easy sorting. The NLB has also launched a mobile service via SMS (text messaging). This allows users to manage their library accounts anytime and anywhere through their mobile phones. They can check their loan records, renew their books, pay library payments, and get reminder alerts to return library items before the due-date.

Improving its services meant fully understanding the Library's customers. Customers were studied using surveys and focus groups to understand how the library added value for customers, how customers could be segmented, the main learning and reading motivators, and people's general reading habits. And feedback from customers, both formal and informal, is an important source of design innovation – as are ideas from staff. Everyone in NLB, from the chief executive to the library assistant is expected to contribute to work improvement and innovations. So much so that innovation has become an integral part of NLB's culture, leading to a steady stream of both large and small innovations. In order to facilitate this, the chief executive holds 'express-o' sessions discussions with staff. He also has a strategy called 'ask stupid questions' (ASQ) which encourages staff to challenge what is normally accepted. Dr Varaprasad, the chief executive commented, 'In my view there are no stupid questions there are only stupid answers! What we try to do is engage the staff by letting them feel they can ask stupid questions and that they are entitled to an answer.'

The NLB also makes use of small improvement teams to brainstorm ideas and test them out with colleagues from other libraries across the island. Good ideas attract financial rewards from S$5 to $1,000. One such idea was using a simple system of coloured bands on the spines of books (representing the identification number of each book) which make it much easier to shelve the books in the right places and also spot books that have been misplaced by customers. Staff are also encouraged to travel overseas to visit other libraries to learn about how they use their space, their programmes and collections, attend and speak at conventions and also visit very different organizations to get new ideas. The automatic book return for example was an idea borrowed and modified from the Mass Rapid Transport stations in Hong Kong where, with the flash of a card, the user is identified and given access across the system. NLB applied a similar line of thought for seamless check-in and check-out of books and a return anywhere concept. NLB harvests ideas from many different industries including logistics, manufacturing, IT and supermarkets. However, some elements of NLB's improvement process have changed. In the early days their approach to implementing ideas was informal and intuitive. It is now much more structured. Now, each good idea that comes forward is managed as a project, starting with a 'proof of concept' stage which involves selling the idea to management and checking with a range of people that the idea seems feasible. Then the services or processes are re-engineered, often involving customers or users. The new concepts are then prototyped and piloted allowing managers to gather customer feedback to enable them to assess, refine and, if appropriate, develop them for other sites.

Questions

1 How would the culture of NLB have changed in order for it to make such improvements?

2 Where did the ideas for improvement originate? And how did NLB encourage improvement ideas?

3 Why, do you think, has the improvement process become more systematic over the years?

4 What could be the biggest challenges to NLB's improvement activities in the future?

Problems and applications

1 Reread the 'Operations in action' piece at the beginning of the chapter on 'Taxing quality' which describes the improvement initiative carried out by the Aarhus region customs and tax unit.

   (a) How does the idea of a customer-focused approach to improvement need to be adapted for a customs and tax unit.

   (b) Generally, how might the ideas of improvement organization outlined in this chapter need to be adapted for public-sector operations such as this one?

2 What are the differences and similarities between the approach taken by the Aarhus customs and tax unit and the example described in the short case on 'Improvement at Heineken'?

3 Compare and contrast the approaches taken by GE in their Work-Out approach described in a short case and that taken by Heineken, also described in a short case.

4 Ruggo Carpets encourages continuous improvement based around the 'drive for customer focus'. The company's total quality process has graduated from 'total customer satisfaction' to 'total customer delight', to its present form – 'bridging the gap', which is effectively a 'where we are' and 'where we should be' yardstick for the company. Developments in the warehouse are typical. The supervisor has been replaced by a group leader who acts as a 'facilitator', working within the team. They are also trained to carry out their own job plus five others. Fixed hours are a thing of the past, as is overtime. At peak times the team works the required hours to dispatch orders, and at off-peak times, when work is completed the team can leave. Dispatch labels and address labels are computer-generated and the carpets are bar-coded to reduce human error. Each process within the warehouse has been analysed and re-engineered.

   (a) What is implied by the progression of the company's three initiatives from 'total customer satisfaction' to 'total customer delight' to 'bridging the gap'?

   (b) Evaluate this example against the criteria included in the Business Excellence Model.

5 Look through the financial or business pages of a (serious) newspaper and find examples of businesses that have 'deviated from the line of fit', as described in the early part of this chapter.

6 Devise a performance measurement scheme for the performance of the course you are following.

Selected further reading

Deming, W.E. (1986) *Out of the Crisis*, MIT Press, Cambridge, Mass. One of the gurus. It had a huge impact in its day. Read it if you want to know what all the fuss was about.

George, M.L., Rowlands, D. and Kastle, B. (2003) *What Is Lean Six Sigma?* McGraw-Hill Publishing Co. Very much a quick introduction on what Lean Six Sigma is and how to use it.

Kaplan, R.S. and Norton, D.P. (2001) *The Strategy Focused Organisation*, Harvard Business School Press, Boston, MA.

Neely, A.D. and Adams, C. (2001) The performance prism perspective, *Journal of Cost Management*, vol. 25, no. 1, 7–15.

Schein, E.H. (2004) *Organizational Culture and Leadership*, 3rd edn, Jossey-Bass. A classic.

Index